ROTH FAMILY FOUNDATION

Music in America Imprint

Michael P. Roth

and Sukey Garcetti

have endowed this

imprint to honor the

memory of their parents,

Julia and Harry Roth,

whose deep love of music

they wish to share

with others.

The publisher gratefully acknowledges the generous support of the Music in America Endowment Fund of the University of California Press Foundation, which was established by a major gift from Sukey and Gil Garcetti, Michael P. Roth, and the Roth Family Foundation.

BETTER GIT IT IN YOUR SOUL

Better Git It in Your Soul

An Interpretive Biography of Charles Mingus

KRIN GABBARD

UNIVERSITY OF CALIFORNIA PRESS

University of California Press, one of the most distinguished university presses in the United States, enriches lives around the world by advancing scholarship in the humanities, social sciences, and natural sciences. Its activities are supported by the UC Press Foundation and by philanthropic contributions from individuals and institutions. For more information, visit www.ucpress.edu.

University of California Press
Oakland, California

Library of Congress Cataloging-in-Publication Data

Gabbard, Krin, author.
    Better git it in your soul : an interpretive biography of Charles Mingus / Krin Gabbard.
        pages   cm
    Includes bibliographical references and index.
    ISBN 978-0-520-26037-5 (cloth : alk. paper)
    ISBN 978-0-520-96374-0 (ebook)
    1. Mingus, Charles, 1922–1979.   2. Jazz musicians—United States—Biography.   3. Double bassists—United States—Biography.
I. Title.
    ML418.M45G33   2016
    781.65092—dc23
    [B]

                                           2015031907

Manufactured in the United States of America

24   23   22   21   20   19   18   17   16
10   9   8   7   6   5   4   3   2   1

In keeping with a commitment to support environmentally responsible and sustainable printing practices, UC Press has printed this book on Natures Natural, a fiber that contains 30% post-consumer waste and meets the minimum requirements of ANSI/NISO Z39.48-1992 (R 1997) (*Permanence of Paper*).

For more Mingus Mondays

And as always, for Paula, who may even love this music as much as I do

Contents

Introduction

Charles Mingus Changed My Life

It was 1963 and I was fifteen, growing up in Charleston, Illinois, a town with a population of ten thousand located two hundred miles south of Chicago. I may have been especially prone to a transformation at that moment because of my devotion to *Mad* magazine. In the late 1950s and early 1960s, long before it was a child's comic book featuring "Spy vs. Spy," *Mad* approached American culture with irreverent satire, much of which I understood, and with New York Jewish humor, much of which I did not. Nevertheless, had it not been for *Mad*, I might have grown up believing that tail fins on cars were not stupid.

Mad essentially confirmed what I was already learning from my non-conformist parents: that much of what seems healthy and normal must be approached with scrupulous skepticism. Like my slightly bohemian father, a professor of theater arts at Eastern Illinois University in Charleston, the writers at *Mad* were much more critical of "The Day People," who carried briefcases and wore generic fedoras with small brims, than of "The Night People," who lived mostly in New York and stayed up all night, without watching television.

In *Mad*, jazz artists were definitely among The Night People, but that did not prevent them from being frequent targets for ridicule. Of course, with their berets, cigarette holders, goatees, and bopspeak, they were asking for it: they relished bourgeois contempt, even going so far as to embrace the claim that they and their music were insane. With the kind of irony I was just beginning to appreciate, they made "crazy" a synonym for excellent.

I had become unironically devoted to jazz as a high school sophomore, largely because of Alan Coutant, a senior who played alto saxophone in the school band and the university jazz ensemble with the liquid, lickety-split facility of Lee Konitz. His ability with the saxophone was especially astounding in contrast to my clunky cornet, an instrument that did not allow for the speed with which Alan could play his saxophone. Just warming up before high school band practice, Alan would play mysterious but logical patterns, always with startling velocity. He buried his head in his music stand as he played, so I assumed he was playing something written down. I was amazed the first time I walked around behind him and discovered there was nothing but an unopened folder on his stand. He was improvising!

Even though I certainly could not play improvised jazz myself, I knew this was *my* music. Soon I was buying jazz LPs at a record store in nearby Mattoon, Illinois. The jazz aficionado who owned the store sold me LPs by Stan Kenton, Shelley Manne, Stan Getz, and André Previn.[1] I also began listening to a disc jockey named Pete George who played jazz for two hours every Sunday afternoon on a Mattoon radio station. Pete's tastes ran to Dixieland and the white swing bands, but he did introduce me to Duke Ellington. I have maintained a lifelong devotion to Ellington, ever since Pete insisted that I start listing seriously to Duke after I called to tell him I preferred Count Basie. To this day, I feel a bit smug when someone tells me they prefer Basie to Ellington.

I was still fifteen when I acquired a copy of the Schwann Catalog, a monthly periodical that listed every record in print. Although I would never hear many of the jazz musicians listed in that issue of the Schwann, including a group with the intriguing name Firehouse Five Plus Two, I knew all their names from my careful and repeated perusings of the catalog's jazz section. The pages were eventually dog-eared down to the print.

One night I was listening to the little cracker-box AM radio my grandmother had recently given me. It was eleven o'clock, and I was supposed to be asleep. My parents may have been unusual, but they did try to enforce bedtime rules, except on Sunday nights when I was allowed to stay up to watch *Alfred Hitchcock Presents*. But listening to the radio after ten was not even in the gray zone, so I had to be careful.

Usually I listened to WLS, a station out of Chicago that played the pop music so essential to the lives of me and my high school friends. One night, while trying to tune in WLS at 890 on the AM dial, I discovered a station out of Dallas/Ft. Worth, probably at 870. They were playing jazz, and it was *modern*. No Dixieland or Tommy Dorsey. I had never heard such enchanting music on the radio. The DJ, I learned, was Dick Harp, and he had a regular Tuesday-Thursday show, beginning at 11:00 P.M. From then on, unless I was totally exhausted, I would tune in. Many years later, at a jazz studies conference in Dallas, I asked some colleagues who were roughly my age what they knew about Dick Harp. One remembered him and his program and told me that Dick also played polite piano jazz in Dallas night clubs.

Like most jazz DJs in those days, Dick Harp played the LPs the record companies sent to his radio station. These included the conscientiously marketed, strikingly designed LPs on the impulse! label. In the 1960s, impulse! released some of the best jazz records ever, among them Benny Carter's *Further Definitions,* Oliver Nelson's *Blues and the Abstract Truth,* Max Roach's *Percussion, Bitter Sweet,* Gil Evans's *Out of the Cool,* and several LPs by John Coltrane that represent his most distinguished work at the end of his life. The producers Creed Taylor and Bob Thiele made sure that most of the music they released was recorded at the state-of-the-art studio of Rudy van Gelder, without question the most important recording engineer since the 1950s.

And impulse! LPs were visually beautiful. The exclamation mark at the end of the label's name was a perfect inversion of the letter *i* at the beginning. The LPs always opened in a gatefold, unlike the envelope-like covers of other labels. Most strikingly, the spines of impulse! LPs were orange on top and black on the bottom, one notable exception being Coltrane's *A Love Supreme,* among the best-selling albums in jazz history. The cover of that one was black and white, as specifically requested by Coltrane. As Tony Whyton has pointed out, thus did Coltrane try and succeed in making *A Love Supreme* unique.[2]

Because of their design, impulse! LPs were perfect fetish objects for collectors, to whom their physical presence was at least as important as the music they contained. Many collectors—including me—are more devoted to that physicality than they would care to admit. A friend from my graduate school days did not file his impulse! LPs with his other records alphabetically by artist as I did; instead he put them all together, filed by catalogue number, right there on the desk where he wrote his term papers. With those thick spines, the albums constituted a solid block of orange on black. It was an impressive sight.

To add to their cachet, impulse! LPs cost a dollar more than the records released on other jazz labels such as Prestige, Blue Note, and Verve.

Charles Mingus made some of his best LPs with impulse!, *Mingus Mingus Mingus Mingus Mingus* and *Mingus Plays Piano* among them. But first came his ballet suite, *The Black Saint and the Sinner Lady,* released in the fall of 1963. Dick Harp played it on his radio show late one Tuesday night. Although he surely knew that anything on impulse! was worth hearing, I wonder if he really knew what to expect when he opened that record. His taste, after all, ran to more sedate music.

Not mine, apparently.

This was my road to Damascus moment. When I heard Mingus's *The Black Saint and the Sinner Lady* that autumn night in 1963, I could not believe my ears. I had no idea that such textures and harmonies were even possible. As Mingus magisterially drove the band with his bass, saxophones howled in the upper register while rumbling brass instruments growled at the lower end. No sooner had I decided that the music was full of menace than peaceful, lyrical harmonies seamlessly emerged from the mix. The tempo would speed up, then slow down, giving the music an exhilarating, nervous edge, as if it were searching for a direction. Scott Saul would later write that Mingus was "a pioneer of inner expression in jazz, a composer who developed a nuanced musical language for emotions that ran the gamut from extremes of tenderness to extremes of rage."[3]

I was hardly literate in Mingus's "language for emotions," but that did not stop me from deciding then and there that I did not belong in Charleston, Illinois. There was another world out there, and I wanted to be in it. No one else in my little town knew about this music, I told myself, let alone possessed the same capacity to find it as exhilarating as I did. Although I was surely wrong about a town that included a university with an active music school and jazz ensemble, this did not prevent me from deciding that I wanted to be in New York. I did not even know that Mingus was then living in New York or that he associated with Allen Ginsberg and other Beat artists, but I did know that my sympathies were for the New York Night People and not the repressed, bourgeois Day People that *Mad* magazine so appealingly skewered.

It's not easy for a fifteen-year-old to act on his dreams, however, and various circumstances kept me in the Midwest for several more years. And so it was in 1975 that I heard and finally *saw* Mingus with his last great quintet, not in New York, but in Bloomington, Indiana. You can hear this band on two CDs, *Changes One* and *Changes Two*: George Adams (tenor saxophone), Jack Walrath (trumpet), Don Pullen (piano), Dannie Richmond (drums), and Mingus on bass.[4] Again, I simply could not believe what I was hearing. A deeply lush ballad would suddenly give way to cacophonic free-blowing and then just as suddenly become tender and delicate. Mingus kept the tempo solid as a rock until he would glance at Dannie Richmond and then, as one, the ensemble would speed up or slow down in perfect synchrony. To this day, I have never heard a jazz ensemble do this so consistently and so effortlessly. Don Pullen used every square inch of his hands to create startling effects on the piano, whether he was in a deep romantic groove or pounding out "energy music" à la Cecil Taylor. When George

Adams put down his sax to sing "Devil Blues," avant-garde jazz invaded the blues.

Mingus only played two nights in Bloomington, a brief stop between a gig in Chicago and a return to New York, but I was there both nights. On the second night, he invited to the bandstand a young alto saxophone player who had been recommended by local aficionados as an up-and-comer. When the young man made the mistake of playing too long, Mingus unceremoniously stopped the band and ordered him to stop doing what way too many other alto saxophonists do—try to play like Charlie Parker. As he was leaving the bandstand, the young man forgot to pick up his saxophone stand. More than a little terrified of Mingus, he never went back for it.

Indeed, Mingus could have that effect on people. By 1975 he weighed at least three hundred pounds and wore a no-nonsense expression that told fools he was in no mood to suffer them. Jack Walrath later told me that the pressure Mingus put on members of the band did not necessarily make them play better. "How well are you going to play when you know that at any minute you're about to be hit over the head with a string bass?"[5] But when I saw Mingus on stage in 1975, I regarded him as a force of nature, a law unto himself.

I finally got to New York for more than a few days in 1979. Within weeks I had heard Art Blakey, Jackie McLean, Johnny Griffin, Annie Ross, Barry Harris, Betty Carter, Frank Foster, and Chico Hamilton. But I never saw Mingus in New York. He died on January 5, 1979, just a few months before I moved into an apartment in Morningside Heights.

Better Git It in Your Soul grows out of those first experiences of what many now call "Mingus Music" and the several decades of listening that came later. This book begins with a chronological biography of Mingus (part I)—though I frequently pause to focus more deeply on aspects of Mingus's career that deserve special attention, such as his childhood proximity to the Watts Towers of Sam Rodia and his brief encounter with novelist and critic Ralph Ellison.

The rest of the book (parts II, III, and IV) explores aspects of Mingus's career that I believe are essential to understanding his achievements as an artist. I have deliberately begun this second half of the book with a section on Mingus the writer of prose and poetry (part II) in order to establish the breadth of his accomplishments in this arena. He was a world-class bassist and one of the most distinctive composers in the history of American music, but he was also the author of some beautiful poetry and a vivid and candid autobiography, *Beneath the Underdog: His World According to Mingus.*[6]

Part III is a musical biography. Avoiding repetition unless absolutely necessary, I retell Mingus's story in terms of the musicians with whom he performed and the stylistic movements in which he played a role. This segment of the book culminates with an account of his participation in the Third Stream Music of the 1950s. Third Stream attempted to fuse jazz with classical music, evoking an ambivalent but fascinating response from Mingus.

In part IV I explore Mingus's interactions with Dannie Richmond, Eric Dolphy, and Jimmy Knepper, three key musicians with whom he worked closely. In each case, the collaborations yielded extraordinary music; indeed, what the sidemen created with Mingus was like nothing else they ever did. That said, each dealt with Mingus at his most difficult. The interactions with Knepper were, in a word, tragic.

The epilogue looks at several films that feature Mingus or his music. I close with a few words about the film *Stations of the Elevated*, directed by Manfred Kirchheimer. This forty-five–minute poem in moving images, shot in 1977, uses bits and pieces of Mingus Music as it explores the work of young renegade artists who painted subway trains in New York City, often creating images of beauty and power. Released in 1980, shortly after Mingus's death, the film is an especially appropriate elegy.

Even though I have relied on the two preexisting, well-researched biographies by Brian Priestley (1982) and Gene Santoro (2000), this book is a new biography of Mingus.[7] Priestley and Santoro consulted all the resources available at the time, and Santoro in particular seems to have interviewed just about everyone who ever knew Mingus. I have also benefited from the double memoir *Mingus/Mingus* by Janet Coleman and Al Young (1989).[8] But a great deal of new material has appeared since the publication of these books, most notably Sue Graham Mingus's account of her life with Charles after the two met in 1965.[9] She became his fourth wife when they married in 1975 and his widow when he died four years later. Several other memoirs have been published in the meantime, most helpfully those of Buddy Collette, George Wein, and Clark Terry, as well as John F. Goodman's *Mingus Speaks*.[10] I have also been fortunate to have at my fingertips the recent work of some excellent jazz scholars who have taken a special interest in Mingus—Eric Porter, Scott Saul, John Gennari, Nichole Rustin, and Jennifer Griffith.[11]

I spent several days with an early, unedited draft of Mingus's autobiography in the Charles Mingus Collection at the Library of Congress in Washington, D.C. Also at the Library of Congress I listened to the many reel-to-reel tapes that Mingus left behind and that Sue Mingus had recently donated to the collection. I know I was the first to listen to many of these tapes because they were being digitized on a daily basis as I worked my way through them. I may also be the first scholar to have examined the Mingus correspondence in the Alfred A. Knopf Archive at the Harry Ransom Center in Austin, Texas. There I found numerous letters and memos documenting the complex process by which Mingus's draft autobiography became *Beneath the Underdog: His World According to Mingus*.

An important addition to Mingus studies is a series of interviews with his two older sisters, Vivian and Grace. In 2001, when both were in their eighties, Shelby Johnson spoke with them extensively, ultimately compiling more than four hours' worth of conversation about their lives collected on four CDs under the title *The Mingus Sisters Speak*.[12] The sisters provided an intimate account of their childhood years, and since a great deal of what Charles wrote in *Beneath the Underdog* may seem exaggerated or even fabricated, I was surprised that the sisters validated much of what Mingus wrote. I was also surprised by their response when Johnson asked if they ever saw Charles in one of his legendary fits of anger. They both matter-of-factly said no. There was no defensiveness; they simply denied ever seeing that side of their brother. Vivian did, however, recall a scene late in his life when she and her daughter visited Charles in New York: when Vivian's daughter lit up a joint, Charles was furious and told her to get rid of it. Grace also remarked that Charles's friend Buddy Collette once told her that if one of Mingus's musicians "hit a wrong note," he would get "yelled at." Otherwise, though, they remembered their younger brother as cheerful, funny, and loving. Grace's fondest memories were of the times when her brother visited her house at Christmas: "He brought a lot of joy to the house." At the end of the long interview, both sisters expressed complete and uncritical love for Charles.

The Mingus sisters' memories of their brother as benevolent and joyful contrast sharply with the many stories of Mingus abusing people who displeased him in some way or another. Two of his musicians—one black, one white—have said that he struck their faces with enough force to knock out a tooth. Had he not been so difficult to work with, he might have had a very different career, perhaps one like the composer/musician/leader he most admired, Duke Ellington. But Mingus could be tender and thoughtful, just as he could be angry and destructive. He could also be a faithful friend. When the white saxophonist Pepper Adams, who regularly played in Mingus's groups, told Charles that he had to go into the hospital, Mingus offered to pay his medical expenses.

Willie Ruff, who played jazz on both the French horn and the string bass, tells how Mingus could forge a profound human connection. Mingus was one of several jazz artists invited to a 1972 event at Yale University to honor Duke Ellington. The event was organized by Ruff, then a Yale faculty member. After the concerts and ceremonies, Mingus embraced Ruff, pulling him into his three hundred pounds of girth. He said, "You gave me the greatest gift of my life just by making it possible for me to see Duke and all these great artists get the honor they deserve." These words and the warmth with which Mingus uttered them brought Ruff to the verge of tears. When Mingus saw the beginning of a tear, he spoke with sudden forcefulness: "Oh, no. Naw, man. Hold that tear! Call it back. Don't let that one fall. Call that one back. I mean it. Call it *back!*" Although he had heard stories about Mingus's violent nature, Ruff said that he heard no menace in Mingus's voice. Charles continued, "Keep that tear. Save it for another time on down the road. You need to keep that one—it's special. Hold it in reserve!" Although Ruff did not think it physiologically possible, he did indeed call back the tear. Years later, Ruff made this encounter the culminating event in his own autobiography.[13]

But Mingus was not always so focused and forceful. He would be hospitalized for depression more than once. Before he met Susan Graham at age forty-two, Mingus had intense romantic involvements with at least seven women, but he never sustained a relationship for more than a few years, sometimes not even a few months.[14] Mingus was fascinated by religion and read widely about meditation, spirituality, and reincarnation. But Nat Hentoff, one of his closest friends, told me that he saw no evidence that Mingus was particularly religious.[15]

Anyone hoping to read the biography of a man with a single, unified identity should read no further. Mingus himself, after all, opened his autobiography with the phrase, "In other words, I am three."[16] There is no question, however, that Mingus's paradoxical, tempestuous, loving, angry, spiritual, defiant, and questing self was always nurturing his extraordinary music. And when it came to music, he was entirely consistent. He always insisted that "all music is one" and that the only way to play it well is to know as much of it as possible. Throughout his career, Mingus had no patience with musicians who seized on an advanced style without being able to play what had come before.

Can a biography have a thesis? If it can, then this book argues that Mingus was exceptional. No other jazz artist has written an autobiography as complex and compelling as *Beneath the Underdog*. With the possible exception of Ellington, no other jazz composer was as bold, as diverse, and as innovative as Mingus. No one else wrote jazz tunes so profoundly beautiful and emotionally rich. And no one played jazz bass as brilliantly. Like very few of his peers, Mingus took an active role in recording and distributing his own music as well as the music of artists he admired. For these distinctions alone, Mingus stands out.

But Mingus is also exceptional for his association with practically every stylistic movement in jazz history. Other jazz artists whose achievements we most often celebrate are associated primarily with a single moment. Jelly Roll Morton, Louis Armstrong, Charlie Parker, Art Tatum, Thelonious Monk, and a handful of others who rank with Mingus basically played the same music—however brilliantly—throughout their entire careers.

A useful point of comparison is Miles Davis. He definitely changed music several times, but Mingus was as innovative, if not as influential. Mingus was playing bebop, cool, hard bop, modal jazz, soul jazz, and combinations of these all at the same time as Davis, and sometimes even earlier. Miles, however, was better at promoting himself and creating his own myth, while Mingus was more interested in making music and insisting that people listen to it. If he did engage in self-mythology, Mingus did not do so as purposefully or as successfully as Davis. Whereas Miles carefully established himself as the epitome of cool, Mingus, largely in spite of himself, was "jazz's angry man." He was never able to project an image that placed him in a coherent category like the one Davis so comfortably occupied.

And Davis could be accessible in ways that Mingus was not. Mingus wrote music of breathtaking beauty and depth, and even though his music always rewards those who commit to it, not everyone has been prepared to make that commitment. While I was writing this book, many people who do not know jazz asked me what I was working on. They typically knew the name Mingus but little else. Even when I mentioned Joni Mitchell's 1979 LP *Mingus,* only her most committed fans knew what I was talking about.

I present this book in hopes that it will bring Mingus more of the esteem he deserves.

PART I

A Circus in a Bathtub

> You had to see how difficult it was to cram himself into the
> confines of black *or* white American society. It was like putting
> a circus into a bathtub.
>
> **Janet Coleman, Mingus/Mingus**

MODERNISM YEAR ONE

Charles Mingus was born in 1922, the same year that James Joyce's *Ulysses*
and T. S. Eliot's "The Wasteland" appeared in print. On the basis of those two
literary behemoths alone, Kevin Jackson has written an entire book about
1922, which he calls "Modernism Year One."[1] Joyce and Eliot displayed so
much erudition that even serious graduate students in English departments
have failed to master their works. But without question, Joyce transformed
the novel just as Eliot remade lyric poetry. In the same year, another modernist icon, Franz Kafka, published "The Hunger Artist," the allegorical tale
of a circus performer whose death-defying art audiences ignore. Mingus's
seminal recording from 1957, "The Clown," carries a similar message. Also
in 1922, Marcel Proust published a section of *Remembrances of Things Past*,
yet another novel that transformed the genre. Mingus, the shape-shifter, the
genre-buster, and author of the most captivating autobiography by a major
jazz artist, was born just as a new day was dawning in Western literature.

Mingus was also born in the same year that the tomb of King
Tutankhamen was opened in Egypt's Valley of the Kings. It was the year
Benito Mussolini seized power in Italy and Joseph Stalin was appointed
general secretary of the Communist Party of the Soviet Union. The
Ottoman Empire was abolished in 1922, and construction began on Yankee
stadium. The presidency of Warren G. Harding was upended by the Teapot
Dome scandal, and Christian K. Nelson patented the Eskimo Pie. At the
movie houses, Americans could see the first important documentary film,
Robert J. Flaherty's *Nanook of the North,* a view of the primitive life of an
Inuit tribe. With life in the "civilized" world suddenly becoming faster,
louder, and more mechanized, the world of Nanook must have offered
pleasures both reassuring and nostalgic.

More significantly for the career of Charles Mingus, 1922 was the year that Bert Williams, possibly the most popular black entertainer of his day, who performed in a tattered tuxedo with black shoe polish on his face, passed away. Also that year, a new era in African American art began when Louis Armstrong left New Orleans for Chicago, where he joined the Creole Jazz Band and his idol, King Oliver. Less than a year later, Armstrong and Oliver went into a recording studio for the first time, and Jelly Roll Morton and his orchestra also made their first recordings. Many consider the music that these artists committed to vinyl in 1923 to be the first "real" jazz records.

But even without these epochal recordings, Mingus was born into the "Jazz Age," a term introduced by F. Scott Fitzgerald.[2] Like *Ulysses* and "The Wasteland," Fitzgerald's *Tales of the Jazz Age*, was also published in 1922. Of course, Fitzgerald's "jazz" was about fast dancing, nightlife, and speak-easies, with music performed by the likes of Paul Whiteman, Sophie Tucker, and Al Jolson. Many black musicians in the early 1920s still called their music "ragtime." But by the time Mingus was coming of age as a musician in the late 1930s, even white people were learning what jazz was really about.

Mingus was much younger than Jelly Roll Morton (born 1885), Louis Armstrong (1901), and Duke Ellington (1899). He played very briefly with Armstrong and just as briefly with Ellington, and he always expressed great admiration for Morton, who died in 1941. Had Jelly Roll Morton lived longer, Mingus might have played with him as well. Mingus was a few years younger than two other giants with whom he later shared a stage, Charlie Parker (1920) and Dizzy Gillespie (1917). He was born before Bud Powell (1924), John Coltrane and Miles Davis (both 1926), and Ornette Coleman (1930), whose "free" jazz he anticipated by several years.

My mother, Lucina Paquet Gabbard, an actress, university professor, and the author of books about Harold Pinter and Tom Stoppard, was born in 1922. So was Jack Kerouac, who may have been as famous as Mingus but whose exclusive association with the Beat Generation reminds us that Mingus is not so easily connected with a single moment in American cultural history. Helen Gurley Brown, Judy Garland, Kurt Vonnegut, and Ava Gardner were also born in 1922, as were the film director Arthur Penn (*Bonnie and Clyde*), the avant-garde composer Iannis Xenakis, and Stan Lee, co-creator of the comic book superheroes Spider-Man, the Hulk, Thor, Dr. Strange, and the Fantastic Four. These innovators may not have transformed their genres as dramatically as Joyce and Eliot transformed literature, but like Mingus, each took what was familiar and made it new.

Several black entertainers were born in the same year as Mingus. As a teenager, Redd Foxx (born September 9, 1922) played the washboard in a swing band in the 1930s, but he honed his craft as a comedian listening to the same radio programs that Mingus grew up with: Amos and Andy flourished in the late 1920s, and Jack Benny made Eddie "Rochester" Anderson part of his program in the early 1930s. Foxx took the humor and the colorful argot of these characters to a new level. Ralph Ellison said of Foxx, "When he, a black comedian, makes remarks about ugly white women which once were reserved only for black women, he allows us to bring attitudes and emotions that were once tabooed into the realm of the rational, where, protected by the comic mode, we may confront our guilt and prejudices and perhaps resolve them."[3] Although Ellison and Mingus would have agreed on some important issues, Mingus was not so interested in resolving anything in a comic mode. For him, resolution had to be out front and up close. He was, however, more than happy to violate taboos. Foxx would strike it rich with the television comedy *Sanford and Son* (1972–77), in which he played an ignorant, cantankerous junk dealer possessed by get-rich schemes that inevitably failed. The sitcom was set in Watts, Los Angeles, where Mingus grew up.

Dorothy Dandridge (born November 9, 1922) won an Academy Award nomination in 1954 for her dazzling performance in *Carmen Jones*. Yet despite her sensuous beauty, Dandridge was unable to find regular work as a performer primarily because of her color. She died of barbiturate poisoning in 1965.

Juanita Moore (October 19, 1922) co-starred with Lana Turner in *Imitation of Life* (1959), playing the Turner character's loyal maid and the mother of a tragic mulatto (Susan Kohner) who pays a high price when she tries to pass for white. Unlike Dandridge, Moore worked regularly in film and television but almost always as a servant, a maid, or a mammy.

Mingus was one of the first black artists to build an important career even as he consistently and aggressively asserted himself as an African American. Although the jazz life took its toll on Mingus, the entertainment business did not destroy him as it did Dandridge, nor did it force him to live with racist representations as it did Moore.

FROM NOGALES TO WATTS

Charles Mingus Sr. was a noncommissioned army officer stationed in Nogales, Arizona, a small village on the Mexican border. His daughters, Grace and Vivian, were born in 1919 and 1920; Charles Jr. was born on the

numerologically auspicious date of April 22, 1922. He would later tell
Whitney Balliett, "My birth date is four, two two, two two. The astrologists
have never been able to get over that."[4] The proximity of Nogales, Arizona,
to Mexico was also auspicious in that Mingus would eventually die in that
country.

Another connection to Mexico appears early in Mingus's published
autobiography, *Beneath the Underdog*. Before he begins unspooling his life
story, Charles claims to have had sex with twenty-three women in a Tijuana
brothel, all on the same night.[5] Claims such as this have led many to read
Beneath the Underdog as autofiction rather than autobiography. But as I
hope to demonstrate in part II of this book, artists can tell their stories in
many ways, and much can be learned if readers allow for a bit of hyperbole—even self-mythologizing—in the telling.

Regardless of what actually happened that night at the brothel, only a
few days would go by before Mingus recorded an extraordinary LP, *Tijuana
Moods*.[6] Tijuana, of course, is near the western coast of Mexico in the Baja
region, not at all close to the Norteña town also known as Nogales, across
the border from Arizona. For that matter, "Tijuana Moods" does not specifically suggest the music of Tijuana. It's Mingus Music.

The elder Charles Mingus left home at fourteen to join the army. At
least according to a passage in *Beneath the Underdog*, Mingus Sr. was the
son of a Swedish woman and a former slave. Because of his light skin, his
mother's family assumed that he was the son of her white husband. When
they learned the identity of his real father, Mingus Sr. effectively had to
run for his life.[7] He became a "Buffalo Soldier," one of the many blacks in
an American army that was segregated for more than a hundred years after
the Civil War. Congress officially formed regiments of black soldiers in
1866 to fight Native Americans, who may have coined the term "Buffalo
Soldier" because the men's hair resembled the coat of a buffalo. The Indians
also admired the tenacity and bravery of the black soldiers and compared
them to an animal that was an essential part of their culture.[8]

Mingus Senior was assigned to a black regiment stationed at Camp Little
near the Mexican border to stop people from crossing the border "illegally."
Then as now, if not for the soldiers and their guns, the border at Nogales
would provide a pleasant pathway into the US not at all like the many miles
of forbidding desert west and east of the town. Today, an enormous, ugly
iron fence separates the two Nogaleses and stretches as far as the eye can
see in either direction (figure 1).[9]

With blue eyes and pale skin, Charles Mingus Sr. could pass for white.
Mingus's mother, Harriet, had a black mother and a Chinese father who

Figure 1. The fence separating Nogales, Arizona, from Nogales, Mexico, in 2013. Photograph by the author.

was born in Hong Kong. But for most white people in the 1920s and 1930s, Charles Mingus Jr. was African American. He spoke the argot of the black culture and eventually self-identified as black. But the vaguely yellow hue of Mingus's skin marked him as different among the black people with whom he grew up. Charles said that he did not dare use the world *black*, even calling the blackboard a chalkboard in order to prevent certain aggressive young black men from punishing him for using a word he was not fully entitled to deploy.[10] From birth Mingus was a true American creole with a small *c*, every bit as small-c creole as the music then coming of age in New Orleans, Chicago, New York, and Los Angeles—a music that combined elements from the Pentecostal church, country blues, Italian opera, military marches, South of the Border musics with their "Latin tinge," and the polite dance music of the late nineteenth century.

When Camp Little closed and Charles Sr. left the army, Harriet, the mother of baby Charles, was in good health. But when the family began its journey to California, she became ill and died shortly after, less than six months after the birth of Charles Jr. At first the family lived with Harriet's mother while Charles Sr. went to work at the post office. There was talk of breaking up the motherless family and leaving the children with their grandmother. Primarily in order to keep his family together, Charles Sr. married Mamie Newton Carson, a woman he met in church only a few months after Harriet's death. In 1923, the newly reconstituted family moved to Watts, a neighborhood in Los Angeles made up of African Americans, Mexicans, Irish, Italians, and even a few Asian families. In the 1920s, Watts was not exclusively a ghetto for blacks. Not until the 1930s did more and more black people move in while everyone else moved out. In the 1920s, except for a handful of middle-class blacks, the one thing the residents of Watts had in common was poverty. Mingus's family was somewhat more affluent than most residents of Watts, but when Charles Sr. married a woman who was clearly not white, he had very few other options about where he could live.

In 2001, when Vivian and Grace Mingus were interviewed extensively, they described a childhood with very little love.[11] Charles Sr. was a withholding father who was not reluctant to beat his children, even with his fist. Grace said she could not remember him ever kissing her or holding her on his lap. Mamie, their stepmother, was "old-fashioned" and willing to accept the role of subservient wife. She had been married once before and had a son, Odell, who was about twelve years older than Vivian and Grace. Charles Jr. speaks affectionately of Odell in *Beneath the Underdog*,[12] but the sisters recalled with bitterness Odell and his acts of sexual molestation.

At dinner Mamie served rice, beans, coleslaw, and whatever was growing in her backyard garden. As children, the sisters never saw steak or even pork chops. Daddy, however, ate much better. He was receiving a pension after twenty-seven years in the army, and he was making a good salary as a supervisor in the local post office. Grace said that she reproached her father years later for withholding love and enforcing penurious conditions on the family. She said that he began crying and insisted that in those days he did not know any better.

Charles Jr. was not exempt from beatings and harsh discipline. When he brought a note home from school accusing him of looking up a girl's skirt, his father shaved all the hair off his head. "That's the way they do convicts," he said. But in general, Charles Jr. received much better treatment than his sisters. As Vivian Mingus phrased it, "He was it." The father took much more interest in his son and would later tell him that he was "twenty years ahead of his time."

When the sisters tell the story of baby Charles falling and cutting the flesh above his eye, they include a significant detail that Charles omits in his own account of the incident.[13] When Charles Sr. took his son to the hospital, it was the only time anyone in the family had ever seen a doctor. Grace broke her arm at about this same time, and Mamie wrapped it in brown paper soaked in vinegar: that was the extent of her treatment. Grace lived with a partially disabled, often painful arm for the rest of her life.

Charles Jr. was unquestionably the favorite of his father, and his stepmother pampered him. And yet his older sisters expressed no jealousy or anger.

This did not mean, however, that Charles and his father had a positive relationship. Several pages in *Beneath the Underdog* are devoted to the abuse that young Charles received for urinating in his bed. In fact, Charles Jr. had a kidney disorder, but Charles Sr. punished the boy with a belt strap rather than stopping to wonder if there was a medical reason for the bed-wetting. Later Charles Sr. abandoned his children and their stepmother and moved in with Pearl Garrett, a woman he met in church. In one of the more affecting chapters in *Beneath the Underdog*, a twenty-one-year-old Charles goes to visit his father at Pearl's house, and the two men make awkward gestures toward reconciliation.[14]

IN THE SHADOW OF THE TOWERS

The Mingus family lived close by the Watts Towers (figure 2), a stunning example of outsider art constructed by an illiterate Italian immigrant named Sabato Rodia, usually known as Simon or Sam Rodia. Begun in 1920 and abandoned in 1954, the towers were added to the National Register of Historic Places in 1990. The tallest of the several structures in the triangular lot where Rodia also built his house is nearly one hundred feet tall. Smaller structures in the lot resemble a giant wedding cake, an oven, and a birdbath, all of them extravagantly decorated with seashells, broken tiles, and glass bottles. For the cage of each tower, Rodia wrapped wire around steel rods and then covered it all with concrete. The decorative items set in elaborate patterns were mostly junk that Rodia found in his neighborhood. He nearly exhausted the supply of seashells on the shore a few miles from his house. Because he would give a penny to any child who brought him items he could use, and because a candy store was just around the corner, the neighborhood children called him "the Candy Man."

The towers are often compared to the cathedral spires of the Spanish architect Antoni Gaudí, but Rodia knew nothing of his work. In the 1960s, long after he had abandoned his towers and was invited to lecture at Berkeley, a student showed him some photos of Gaudí's work. Rodia replied, "Did this man have helpers? I had no helpers."[15] His place in the history of art was not as important as the stature and dignity he could claim as sole creator of the towers.

The towers play an important role in Mingus's autobiography just as it reaches its first climactic moment. Nine-year-old Charles has become completely smitten with a young girl named Lee-Marie who, like Charles, plays cello in the Los Angeles Junior Philharmonic. Much of *Beneath the Underdog*

Figure 2. The Watts Towers as seen from the Charles
Mingus Youth Arts Center in Watts, Los Angeles, 2012.
Photograph by the author.

will be devoted to this woman, whom he calls at the outset "a princess—a
movie star!"[16] Charles even says that he practiced more assiduously so that
he could sit closer to her at the front of the cello section. Was his attraction
for this little girl the beginning of a serious devotion to music? Although we
may never know if the real-life Mary Ellen Kelly (the name was changed to
Lee-Marie Spendell in the published version of Mingus's autobiography) felt
as much preadolescent passion for Charles as he did for her, the Lee-Marie of
the autobiography is clearly enchanted by the young cellist. The children
have several intense encounters just looking at each other—but always
under the watchful eyes of their parents, especially Lee-Marie's father, a
burly police officer with a revolver on his belt.

When summer vacation begins, Charles knows that Lee-Marie will be returning to Southgate, a neighborhood a few miles from Watts, and despairs of ever seeing her again. He is therefore overjoyed to learn that she and her family will be coming to his neighborhood to see the towers. Mingus meets Lee-Marie at the streetcar stop on San Pedro Boulevard, just a few blocks from his house. She is accompanied by several younger children but not by her meddling parents. The adult in charge is her aunt Ridey, who gives the two young people space, being either too busy caring for the other children or too amused by her niece's fascination with the polite young man who meets them at the streetcar. Charles and Lee-Marie whisper intimately while he gives her a private tour of the towers. The two will not meet again for several years, but in *Beneath the Underdog* Mingus fondly recalls those few enchanted moments exploring Rodia's work with Lee-Marie.

Sam Rodia was born in a small town near Naples, Italy, in 1879. Perhaps because his family wished to protect him from the crime and corruption of Naples, perhaps because they simply hoped to give him a better life, he was sent to the United States when he was fourteen. Eventually settling in Watts, Rodia built his towers on the east corner of his lot at 1765 East 107th Street. Mingus grew up at 1621 East 108th Street, literally in the shadow of the towers. Rodia began work on the towers less than three years before the Mingus family arrived in Watts.

In *Beneath the Underdog* Mingus calls the plan of the towers boatlike, revealing that he understood exactly what Rodia was trying to accomplish. Rodia himself was evasive about assigning them any special meaning. "They mean lots of things, son," he told an interviewer.[17] To some, they looked like oil wells. During World War II, others suspected that Rodia had built radio towers to send secret messages, presumably to support the Axis powers, which then included Italy as well as Germany and Japan.[18]

Although we may never know exactly what was going through his mind in 1920, Rodia was looking for a triangular-shaped piece of land pointing east where he could build his house and, as he would say in his broken English, "make something they never got 'em in the world."[19] He found one such plot in Beverly Hills, but of course he got a much better deal on a similar plot in Watts. Rodia was not merely illiterate; he could not even do simple arithmetic. When the towers became so prominent that city officials could no longer ignore them, Rodia was told that he could build nothing higher than one hundred feet. At Rodia's request, a neighbor cut a piece of rope so that it measured 99 ½ feet. By unraveling the rope from the highest point on his towers, Rodia knew where to stop.[20]

Rodia may have known little about English letters and Arabic numbers, but he did know some basic facts about steel and concrete from a long career working for building contractors. Although in the end Rodia's towers were strong enough to survive several earthquakes and a failed attempt by the city to tear them down in 1957, Mingus says that he often saw him undo one day what he had built the day before: "pinnacles tall as a two-story building would rise up, disappear and rise again."[21] The towers were always a work-in-progress. Rodia may never have been entirely satisfied with what he had, and he certainly did not stick around to admire what he had achieved. In 1954, after he suffered a stroke and decided that he was no longer fit to continue his high-wire construction acts, he gave ownership of his land and everything on it to a neighbor. Then he walked away.

Even though Rodia never publicly said what the towers were supposed to represent, Mingus figured it out. He knew that the towers were intended to resemble the masts of a ship and that the eastern point on Rodia's lot where the two walls come together suggested the prow of a boat, one that might cut through land and then an ocean as it headed back to the Old Country. As if to confirm the nautical design, Rodia placed a large steering wheel on the west side of one of the towers (figure 3). Along with all the marvelous aspects of Rodia's achievement, pathos hangs over a ship that can never leave its harbor. As Thomas Harrison points out, Rodia's boat was what James Joyce called "a disappointed bridge," like the pier that juts out into the water knowing that it will never reach the opposite shore.[22]

As a child, Rodia would have witnessed the Gigli Festival in Nola, Italy, not far from where he grew up. Each year at the festival, men from various craft guilds carried a series of tall, pointed towers into the village on their shoulders. The towers consisted of wooden rings covered with paper— lightweight, portable versions of what Rodia would later build. The festival began in the Middle Ages to celebrate the return to the village of a beloved bishop who had sold himself into slavery in order to save Nola citizens from the same fate. Because he returned to Nola by sea, the men at the festival also carried a stylized boat.[23]

Although Rodia was no doubt influenced by the childhood memory of the festival, the idea of building a concrete boat that pointed east toward a land a continent and an ocean away was unique to his project. This fantastic monument to the dream of going home likely appealed to the African American residents of Watts, including Mingus. Difficult, even impossible journeys have been an essential part of African American tradition since the days of slavery. John Szwed elegantly describes this tradition in his biography of Sun Ra, the jazz musician and bandleader who repeatedly

Figure 3. Watts Towers, detail (steering wheel). Photograph by the author.

claimed that he came to earth from another planet and that someday he would return. Unlike most jazz writers, Szwed does not completely dismiss Sun Ra's claims. Instead he compares them to the extraterrestrial travel described in the "Afro-Baptist" conversion narratives of Nat Turner, Father Divine, and Elijah Muhammad and to stories of people who could fly back to Africa or "take chariots and trains to heaven, the Underground Railroad, Marcus Garvey's steamship line, Rosa Parks on the Mobile bus, freedom riders."[24]

Don DeLillo unites Rodia and his African American neighbors even more strikingly in his novel *Underworld,* when he refers to the towers as "a kind of swirling free-souled noise, a jazz cathedral."[25] Mingus, the nascent jazz musician, was especially intrigued by Rodia's constant revision of his sculptures. Like Rodia's thirty-four-year work-in-progress, Mingus's Jazz Workshop always presented music in a state of becoming. Audiences were often, shall we say, nonplussed when Mingus would stop the band in the middle of a performance to upbraid or reinstruct a musician, much as he did the hapless alto sax player years later in Indiana. He would even stop the band to insist that the audience themselves listen more carefully to the music. Just as Rodia would tear down a structure and rebuild it the next day with some variation, either slight or major, Mingus too was always revising work he had written earlier. "Duke's Choice" would become "Open Letter to Duke" and then "I X Love." "Weird Nightmare" would become "Smooch" and then "Vassarlean."

Rodia is one of the most prominent outsider artists in American history. He knew virtually nothing about the history and the art of sculpture, but there is no denying the beauty and majesty of what he created. Mingus, in contrast, knew the history and art of music—classical, jazz, and much more—but he too was something of an outsider artist. He surely knew that he could have widened his audience and his reputation by associating himself with a single style of music. He could have become the Charlie Parker of the bass, the Duke Ellington of the small orchestra, or the *éminence grise* of the avant-garde. Instead, he was all of these and none of these.

He would even say that his entire life was essentially a work-in-progress. Like Sam Rodia's masterpiece—built, rebuilt, and then mysteriously abandoned—Mingus never saw himself as a complete, finished individual.

WEDNESDAY NIGHT PRAYER MEETING

Another essential element in Mingus's music that can be traced back to his childhood is black religious practice, some of which matched up with Sam Rodia's dreams of traveling to a better place. Mingus would cry, "Talking 'bout Jesus!" in the middle of a performance, and he would often recreate the ecstatic sounds of communal worship by directing several members of his ensemble to engage in intense, simultaneous improvisation.

Charles's father attended the African Methodist Episcopal Church in Watts, where middle-class blacks gathered for mostly staid worship. His stepmother, Mamie, was certainly a middle-class woman—with enough respect for classical music to encourage her stepdaughters to take up piano and violin—but as Brian Priestley observed in his biography of Mingus, Mamie was "only able to abandon her strict deportment in a religious context."[26] She occasionally attended the Holiness Church, a place of much more vigorous worship; Grace Mingus called it "that dark church where everyone was screaming."[27] Mamie would often bring Charles Jr. along with her. Later, Mingus attended the same church with the family of Britt Woodman, the distinguished jazz trombonist who was an early participant in Mingus's musical life. Mingus paid a tribute to these middle-of-the-week worship services in 1959 when he recorded the rousing, gospel-tinged "Wednesday Night Prayer Meeting," complete with his own soulful shouts.[28]

Mingus was a generation younger than Louis Armstrong, but Armstrong's religious upbringing in New Orleans is relevant to Mingus's experience. As Armstrong once wrote, "It all came from the Old Sanctified Churches."[29] Much of what we think of as unique to jazz—syncopated rhythms, call and response, speaking-in-tongues improvisation—was already present in what preachers and congregations were doing at the turn of the century. But what Armstrong meant by "Old Sanctified Churches" must be distinguished from virtually all other churches in the United States, even in the South.

In the late nineteenth century, Baptist missionaries had successfully reached out to a large group of freed slaves and their families. Inspired by these missionaries' emotional power, many blacks formed their own Baptist churches, employing preachers with no seminary training but with the ability to rouse parishioners to energetic worship. Many black Baptists believed that ecstatic singing and dancing was the only proper way to praise God and celebrate the Good News.

As Thomas Brothers points out in his book *Louis Armstrong's New Orleans*, in the early years of the twentieth century a new wave of missionaries from the North came to preach the rewards of respectable behavior and assimilation.[30] By the 1910s, many congregations had given up group singing. Instead, like the African Methodist Episcopal church that Mingus's father attended, they sat sedately and listened to a choir and soloists perform carefully rehearsed songs. But unassimilated, impoverished blacks rejected the new Baptist rituals and preserved ecstatic, in-the-moment worship by forming the Sanctified Churches. The church of the young Louis Armstrong and many poor blacks was held in contempt by middle-class African Americans. Nevertheless, Armstrong acquired his first musical experiences there.

The same was true for jazz vibraphonist Milt Jackson, born in Detroit, Michigan, just a few months after Mingus. When asked about "soul in jazz," Jackson replied, "It's what comes from within: it's what happens when the inner part of you comes out. It's the part of playing you can't get out of the books and studies. In my case, I believe that what I heard and felt in the music of my church was the most powerful influence on my musical career. Everyone wants to know where I got that funky style. Well, it came from the church. The music I heard there was open, relaxed, impromptu—soul music."[31] By the 1920s, many southern blacks had migrated to places like Detroit and Los Angeles where they started up their own Sanctified Churches in neighborhoods like the ones where Mingus and Jackson grew up.

Born just a few months before Mingus, Ioannis Alexandres Veliotes was a Greek American growing up in Berkeley, California. He first began popping into black churches because they provided free chocolate milk and graham crackers, but he kept coming back because he was so affected by the ecstatic music.[32] Johnny Otis, as he eventually called himself, soon decided that he was a black man. He regularly refers to "we black people" in his autobiographical writings. Otis spent the rest of his life living in an African American community, married to a black woman, and always playing with black musicians. His most successful recording was "Willie and the Hand Jive." The young Charles Mingus was moved by the same ecstatic, communal music that changed Otis's sense of who he was. Although Mingus, like Armstrong, eventually turned his back on the rituals of the church, he never took the church out of his music.

In grade school, Mingus had a brief flirtation with the trombone. He may have been trying to make the music of the Holiness Church come out of an instrument that is often associated with the folk preacher. In fact, Mingus wrote that he took up the instrument because a local choirmaster played one that "glittered and glistened" when he conducted the largest African American choir in Watts.[33] When he wrote "God's Trombones" in 1927, James Weldon Johnson understood that the trumpet may be associated with the angels but that the more earthy trombone can be made to preach.[34]

MINGUS'S DAMASCUS MOMENT

Then he heard Duke Ellington. Charles Sr. had a crystal set, a simple device that could be cheaply purchased in pieces; once assembled, it picked up local radio stations, but it required a set of headphones because it had no speakers. Mingus was twelve and playing with the gadget (though his father had told him not to touch it) when he heard Ellington's band playing what was then its theme song, "East St. Louis Toodle-oo."

Ellington always said that the song was inspired by the sight of a hunched-over old man walking down a city street, but it was much more than that for Mingus. In a 1960 interview with Ira Gitler, Mingus compared what Duke was playing to what he had heard in church.[35] He definitely preferred Ellington's music, but it is significant that he connected it with the only other music that had really moved him.

When Britt Woodman took the young Charles to hear Ellington when his orchestra was in Los Angeles, Mingus was even more astounded. As he later told Nat Hentoff, "When I first heard Duke Ellington in person, I almost jumped out of the balcony. One piece excited me so much that I screamed."[36] Nichole T. Rustin regards Mingus's reaction as crucial to what she calls "the creative madness" of his music. "Experiencing the music as a member of the audience was like experiencing something more than freedom, the experience was potentially dangerous, it was extrasensory, it was passionate."[37] Mingus would be under Ellington's spell for the rest of his life. As he later wrote in the song "Duke Ellington's Sound of Love," Duke "taught me to hear music out of love."[38] Ellington showed Mingus that music was the language of emotions.

The music of Ellington also made Mingus think of himself as a black man, even if his father had taught his children to feel superior to the African American men and women of Watts. Grace and Vivian recall their father strictly forbidding any interaction with the neighborhood children he called "black niggers." Because their neighborhood was almost completely African American, Charles and his sisters grew up without playmates, save the three of them. In his autobiography, Charles says that he was eight before someone called him "nigger." He was shocked. Referring to himself in the third person, as he often does in *Beneath the Underdog*, Mingus wrote, "For the first time it came to him that whatever shade he was, he was going to be nothing but a nigger to some people."[39]

Part of the father's regimen of racial denial was to keep classical music constantly on the radio and the Mingus girls playing the piano and violin for an hour each day. When Britt Woodman found out about this, he convinced Mingus to switch from trombone to cello. As with the trombone, Mingus was mostly self-taught, using his ear to figure out how to make the best sounds. By the time he was playing in his school orchestra and the Los Angeles Junior Philharmonic—and falling in love with Mary Ellen—he had become a serious musician.

One image of the ten-year-old Mingus powerfully demonstrates how serious he was about music. Imagine the young Mingus carrying his bulky cello case through the streets of Watts in spite of the constant hazing and even beatings by the Irish, Mexican, and black kids he encountered along the way. Mingus had been brought up to believe that he was special, but it surely took a great deal of courage and devotion to run the gauntlet day after day in the quixotic pursuit of a career as a classical musician in Watts.

This is not to say that the young Mingus was always a victim. In *Beneath the Underdog*, he speaks warmly of a Japanese American family named

Oke who protected him during this period, when his perilous journey to and from school took him past their grocery store in Watts. The store was also a hangout for some of the same young people who taunted the boy. One day one of the Oke sons, seeing what he was up against, invited a terrified but determined Mingus into their home and offered to teach him judo. Mingus called him "a young Nijinsky" as he demonstrated the ancient art of self-defense. Charles apparently learned quickly, and it was not long before he was surprising even the bigger boys who had harassed him. Mrs. Oke, apparently taken by Charles, served him Japanese food. For Mingus the assiduous gourmet and ravenous gourmand, the exotic food may have been as life-changing as the judo.

By the time he was thirteen, Mingus had become an instantly recognizable figure in his neighborhood. Not only was he the fearless cello-playing judo expert, but he was physically singular as well. Always bow-legged and a bit tubby, he had begun wearing his hair in a style he learned from the Mexicans in the neighborhood. As Gene Santoro writes in his biography of Mingus, "He looked like an amalgam of leftover parts—the baby-fat body pitched on bowlegs and pigeon-toes, the hot-combed-and-greased Spanish hair, the saffron-meets-taffy complexion."[40]

Buddy Collette, therefore, had no difficulty locating the remarkable young man when he was looking for a bass player for his band. One year older than Charles, Collette eventually formed a lifelong friendship with Mingus. He also established himself as a distinguished multi-reed man, recording on clarinet, flute, and various saxophones and regularly working as a studio musician in and around Hollywood. In his memoir, *Jazz Generations*, Collette says that he was only thirteen when he decided to start up his own jazz band. A year later he sought out Mingus, then a minor celebrity in Watts. Collette knew that Charles played cello, but he also knew that a musician from Watts with Mingus's racial background was not likely to break into the highly segregated world of classical music: "You gotta learn to slap that bass, Charlie," he'd coach him.[41] When Collette walked up to Mingus on the street and said, "You must be Mingus," Charles was taken aback, but he was immediately receptive to the idea of switching to the bass and playing in a jazz band. He ran home that day and told his father that he wanted to play the bass.

THE CLASSICAL CELLIST BECOMES THE JAZZ BASSIST

Collette may have caught Mingus just as he was losing his passion for classical music. In interviews, Mingus always expressed great admiration for

Debussy and Ravel. Like most young people discovering European art music, he was partial to the cello suites of Bach and the string quartets of Beethoven. But he was also fascinated by less well known works, such as Richard Strauss's *Death and Transfiguration*. For the most part, however, by playing in a classical music trio with Grace and Vivian, Mingus was following his father's wishes. In switching to bass, the thirteen-year-old Mingus claimed some independence—and of course, he also hoped to make some money.

Mingus also liked the idea of playing the kind of music that had so moved him when he first heard Duke Ellington. He somehow convinced his father to accompany him to a music store to trade in his cello for a string bass. Charles Sr. even put down an additional $130 for the new instrument. In their interviews, the Mingus sisters have cataloged the many ways their father inflicted poverty on them while insisting that they maintain their superiority over the neighborhood blacks by playing classical music every day. The father's willingness to finance his son's move away from the classical is yet more evidence of how much pride he took in his son.

As proud as he may have been of his son, and as much as he may have indulged him, Charles Sr. was not an attentive father. Buddy Collette's father, however, took a genuine interest in his son's friend Charles. In an early section of *Beneath the Underdog*, for example, Mingus describes Pop Collette instructing him on the techniques of pleasing a woman in order to extract money from her.[42] The elder Collette salaciously tells Mingus how to tease a woman and withhold full penetration until she begs for it: "Then—*when you make up your mind to*—let her have it again hard, fast and deep. Hit it and hold it in there and rock from side to side, kiss her and hold her in your steady rock. Then ease it back and pretend you're gonna quit. Take it out. And if she don't grab you and plead and beg to please fuck her *your* way then you can have one of them Cadillacs sitting out there!"[43] This early reference to sex and extracting payment from a woman anticipates what Mingus was trying to accomplish in *Beneath the Underdog*. Throughout the book, especially in the earlier, longer draft that is now at the Library of Congress, jazz artists are regularly compared to prostitutes who can only take control of their lives by becoming pimps.

Buddy Collette also introduced Mingus to Lloyd Reese, one of the most prominent music teachers in the Los Angeles black community. An elegant gentleman with manners as impeccable as his tastes in music, he was often compared to Duke Ellington. Many of the best jazz artists on the West Coast, including Dexter Gordon and Eric Dolphy, passed through the salon/conservatory in his elegant house on Central Avenue. Jazz veterans such as

Rex Stewart and Ben Webster would stop by to talk music and to get help with whatever problems they may have had with their playing.

In the liner notes to his 1971 LP *Let My Children Hear Music*, Mingus recalls Reese putting on a record and asking "What is this?" Mingus never says what music it was, only that he was completely baffled. Reese than sat down at the piano and began dissecting the piece and explaining how it all came together. This may have been the moment when Mingus became a composer. After his lessons with Reese, which also included instruction on the piano, he too began sitting at the keyboard and figuring out what made a piece of music work.[44] He was still in high school when he wrote "What Love" and "Half-Mast Inhibitions." Although he did not record either piece until many years later, and surely rewrote them to a small or large extent, both pieces exhibit the complex but compelling blend of jazz and classical that is Mingus Music.[45]

Just as important as his introduction to Reese was Collette's suggestion that Mingus study with Red Callender. Barely out of high school, Callender was on his way to becoming an eminent jazz bassist. He would eventually record with Lester Young, Nat King Cole, Erroll Garner, Charlie Parker, Wardell Gray, and Dexter Gordon. When Gene Santoro interviewed Callender in the 1990s, he said that Mingus appeared alone at his door one morning and asked for lessons. Callender knew that he himself was still in need of instruction, but Mingus was persistent, and they began working together regularly.[46]

With the exception of Reese and Callender, Mingus's musical instructors up until this point had run the gamut from adequate to larcenous. In his autobiography, Mingus mentions a certain "Mr. Arson" who went door-to-door in black neighborhoods asking for small change in return for music lessons.[47] Arson, who was white, was surely not a qualified teacher, but, like Harold Hill in the Broadway musical *The Music Man*, he was able to help children sound as if they knew what they were doing. However, since most of Mr. Arson's teachings involved playing by ear, he was, whether he knew it or not, the ideal teacher for a child on his way to the jazz life.

Even after he moved on from Mr. Arson, Mingus mostly relied on his perfect pitch and as much technique as he could acquire with long hours of practice. Callender taught Mingus a great deal about bowing and finger position, and it was probably from Callender that Mingus learned the big, dominating sound that jumps out at you even on his first recordings. You can hear Callender himself reaching for that sound on his early recordings with Young and Cole.[48]

Knowing that he had an exceptional pupil, Callender eventually introduced Mingus to his own teacher, Herman Reinshagen. Mingus could not have found a better teacher anywhere in the world. Reinshagen had played in the New York Philharmonic as principal bassist before retiring in 1934. He then moved west to teach at the University of Southern California. His pupils went on to become principal players throughout the world. At one point, all of the bassists in the Los Angeles Philharmonic were taking lessons with Reinshagen.

In the 1940s, many black jazz artists would not study with white teachers for fear that they would lose their edge and begin sounding "white." As Mingus's teacher, Herman Reinshagen was probably concerned simply with teaching him acceptable orchestral technique and helping him to improve his skills. Reinshagen definitely contributed to Mingus's huge sound by suggesting that he spend as much time as possible squeezing hard rubber balls in order to build up the strength in his hands. Nel King, who worked closely with Mingus when she edited *Beneath the Underdog*, has said that he took only a few lessons with Reinshagen, leaving after he became convinced that Reinshagen was a "racist."[49] Nevertheless, an enthusiastic pupil can learn a great deal even from only a few meetings with so distinguished a teacher.

Jimmy Knepper was still in Los Angeles playing in a bebop band with Dean Benedetti when Charles Mingus was invited to substitute for the group's regular bassist. "Mingus came in and about fifteen or twenty years later he told me that it was the first white band he'd ever worked with. But I remember he didn't say a word all night long; he didn't make any comments. This was about 1945 I guess."[50] Mingus had been playing professionally in various groups at least since he was sixteen. If he was in fact twenty-three when he first played with whites, his lessons with Reinshagen were all the more unusual. How many black pupils in the early 1940s studied with a teacher as eminent as Reinshagen? Reinshagen's willingness to give instruction to Callender and Mingus was part of a sea change in race relations in the United States in the early 1940s, to a large extent because of the willingness of so many black Americans to participate in the war effort.

Indeed, young black men who had grown up during the Harlem Renaissance were asserting themselves in various new ways, and not only by signing up to fight fascism in World War II. Music was one such mode of self-assertion. Black GIs and black musicians were being admitted into a less rigidly segregated culture, and white people were taking notice. Some whites even began believing for the first time that blacks were human beings. The changing tide allowed Mingus, like a handful of others, to succeed in ways that were not available to black artists even a few years older.

Mingus would consistently condemn whites in general for their racism, but he also formed lasting bonds with many white people. In an interview with Gary Carner, Pepper Adams reported an especially revealing anecdote about Mingus's ability to hate white racism but not individual white people. Sometime in the early 1960s, Adams arrived at Mingus's studio to give him some music and heard Mingus inside yelling into the telephone at someone in the musicians' union. He was shouting phrases like, "You white mother-fuckers. I'm gonna bring a shotgun down there! I'm gonna blast all you whities away!" When he saw Adams walk in, Mingus said into the phone, "Wait a minute." He then turned to Adams and said, "Cold beer in the fridge, Pepper." Then back to the phone, "And another thing, you mother!"[51]

Chico Hamilton was another Young Turk from Los Angeles who was becoming known in the late 1930s as a jazz drummer. Like Collette, he was one year older than Mingus. All three boys were still in high school when they began playing in a territory band led by Floyd Ray that mostly played along the rail lines between Los Angeles and San Francisco. Although he was still taking classes at Jordan High School, Mingus did not always come home after a gig. It was probably at this time that he became something of a sexual adventurer, putting Pop Collette's advice into practice. But he was still smitten with Mary Ellen, the Lee-Marie of *Beneath the Underdog*. According to Buddy Collette, Mary Ellen's father insisted, as Mingus confirms in his autobiography, that Charles stay away from his daughter. Mingus was devastated.[52]

He was seventeen and between gigs in San Francisco when he ventured into the studio of Farwell Taylor, a painter of murals and a bohemian social-ite who welcomed all sorts of artistic types into his life. Taylor, who was white, was intrigued by the intense young Mingus and took him under his wing. As with Reinshagen, a white person was connecting with a young black man at a time when many whites would not even dream of letting an African American man into their homes.

Taylor was in fact ahead of his time. He taught Mingus about Vedanta Hinduism and Karma Yoga with their claims to a path toward the meaning of reality. In 1960, in an interview with Ira Gitler, Mingus talked about his experiences with Taylor: "I learned through meditation the will to control and actually feel calmness. I found a thing that made me think I could die if I wanted to. And I used to work at it. Not death and destruction but just to will yourself to death."[53] How many seventeen-year-olds have ever talked this way? Or for that matter, how many thirty-nine-year-olds have ever spoken so frankly about their adolescent obsessions?

Mingus read the Vedanta teachers, but he also picked up books by Freud, H.G. Wells, Dostoevsky, and many others that were scattered around Taylor's apartment. He practiced yoga and meditation. The friendship with

Taylor lasted for many years and allowed Mingus to interact with the white artists and rebels who would eventually create the Beat—as in beatitude—culture of the postwar years. In 1959 Mingus recorded "Far Wells, Mill Valley" as a tribute to his friend.[54]

BEBOP BEGINS

In July 1941, Duke Ellington's *Jump for Joy* opened at the flamboyantly decorated Mayan Theater in downtown Los Angeles. The theater, which seated 1,600, regularly featured premier black performers. Mingus went to see the show with Buddy Collette.[55] Although *Jump for Joy* was basically a series of sketches in the old traditions of vaudeville, it marked a watershed in the history of the representation of blacks on the American stage. The show was written primarily by Paul Francis Webster and Sid Kuller with contributions by a handful of others, the most eminent being Langston Hughes. Dorothy Dandridge and Herb Jeffries were among the stars, and Ellington himself conducted his orchestra in the pit. Duke contributed no less than eleven songs, including "I Got It Bad and That Ain't Good." The subject of the skits was mostly the situation of blacks in America, and the tone was consistently witty and urbane without being abrasive. At least, that was the intention.

One of the numbers in *Jump for Joy*, a wry attempt at discarding the old minstrel stereotypes, was called "Uncle Tom's Cabin Is a Drive-In Now." In his autobiography, Ellington wrote that the original script showed Uncle Tom about to expire with "a Hollywood producer on one side of the bed and a Broadway producer on the other side, and both were trying to keep him alive by injecting adrenalin into his arms!"[56] Mingus was as impressed by the show's racial politics—and by the male performer's hip clothing—as he was by Duke's music.[57]

Jump for Joy closed after only three months and never arrived on Broadway. Some felt that the show failed because its ironic approach to black stereotypes was too subtle for large audiences. The show also had the bad luck to play opposite several highly successful shows at the nearby Biltmore Theater, including a production of *Cabin in the Sky* starring Ethel Waters with an all-black cast.[58]

The Ellington band's bassist at that time was Jimmie Blanton. Although only twenty-two during the show's run, Blanton had already become one of the most important bass players in jazz history. When he joined the band in 1939, he immediately began transforming the bass into a solo instrument. Ellington gave him solo choruses on "Jack the Bear" and "Jumpin'

Punkins," both recorded by the full orchestra. But in 1939 and 1940, Duke took the highly unusual step of recording a series of duets with Blanton, just piano and bass.[59] Mingus had all of these recordings and listened to them repeatedly.[60]

During the run of *Jump for Joy,* Blanton was living in Watts in an apartment with Billy Strayhorn, Ellington's writing and arranging partner. After hours, Blanton would drop in to jam at various venues, including the Capri Club, where Mingus had started playing regularly with Lee Young's house band some months before. The club was run by Billy Berg, who in 1945 would open a club bearing his name. Mingus got to know Blanton before Jimmie went back on the road with Duke. Less than a year later, Blanton died from tuberculosis at the age of twenty-three.

Mingus wrote that he avoided military service in 1942 by putting powdered sugar under his fingernails so that he would test as diabetic and win a 4-F deferment.[61] His sisters, however, insist that he drank lye soap in order to fail the physical exam.[62] Later, Charles tried to enlist in hopes of sitting out the war in a Navy band. Buddy Collette wrote that he took a bus with Mingus and the drummer Bill Douglass to San Francisco to try out, but Mingus did not do well because he was not yet skilled in reading music.[63]

Without military obligations, Mingus began moving out of obscurity in 1942. Before the war, Mingus had mostly played with leaders who were willing to hire musicians of high school age or with other young artists like Collette, Chico Hamilton, Dexter Gordon, and Art Pepper, none of whom had yet achieved a reputation. But clarinetist and saxophonist Barney Bigard, a featured star with the Duke Ellington Orchestra since 1928, was hardly obscure. Bigard was impressed by Mingus when he heard him at the Capri Club and hired him to play in a band that briefly included Kid Ory, the Creole trombonist who had actually hired the young Louis Armstrong in 1919. When Armstrong himself passed through Los Angeles and went to hear Bigard's band perform, he too was impressed by Mingus.

Thus it was that by 1943, at age twenty, Mingus was playing in a band led by the great Armstrong. Alas, a recording ban and a musicians strike that lasted all of that year leave us with no recordings of their music together. Nevertheless, this was a turning point. With this gig, Mingus began a string of jobs as both a sideman and a leader that took him through almost every stylistic moment in the history of jazz. Many jazz musicians with long careers have played with a variety of artists and in diverse contexts. But no other artist cut as wide a swath through jazz history as Charles Mingus.

In *Beneath the Underdog,* he writes about his attempts to unite with "Lee-Marie" and the punishment he received at the hands of her father. In his version, Lee-Marie and Charles elope to Mexico, prompting the father eventually to shoot Mingus in the shoulder, annul the marriage, and arrange for Lee-Marie to have a tubal ligation. Despite these traumatic events, Mingus the storyteller ends a chapter with Charles and Lee-Marie happily married in Mexico.[64]

The full details of this awful story are revealed only incrementally in subsequent chapters of the autobiography. None of my research, however, has turned up evidence that Mingus was actually shot by a girlfriend's father, even though in general I've found that much of *Beneath the Underdog* is rooted in some degree of truth. As for the storytelling talent that led Mingus to deftly parcel out the full story of his affair with Lee-Marie, see part II.

In 1960, Mingus told Ira Gitler that in the mid-1940s, perhaps because of his crises with Mary Ellen Kelly, he was afraid to continue writing music and had decided to "lay down to die." We do know that Mingus married Canilla Jeanne Gross, the "Barbara" of *Beneath the Underdog*, in January 1944. They met at the playground where Mingus and his friends lifted weights and exercised and where her father was the playground director. Later that year she became the mother of Charles Mingus III. In the interview with Gitler, Mingus suggests that Jeanne helped him recover from his fear and begin writing music again.[65]

In *Beneath the Underdog*, Mingus portrays Barbara as a sympathetic woman who took a real interest in him. "Come on, Barbara," he writes, "I like you 'cause you listened to my funny talk."[66] Although Mingus would rather have been with Lee-Marie, in the autobiography the patient, thoughtful Barbara, who knew all about Lee-Marie, seemed like the right person for him. Nevertheless, the marriage of Charles and Jeanne was troubled almost from the beginning, especially when there was a child in the house who distracted Mingus from his music.

Collette, who joined the navy on the day they all took the bus to San Francisco, returned to Los Angeles in 1946 to visit Mingus and his new wife. Here is his report: "Jean [*sic*] told me that Charles would get up around 8 a.m. and go straight to the bass in his pajamas. He'd play until noon, when he'd get a bowl of cereal and toast—something simple not to waste any time—and then continue playing until about 6 p.m. Then he'd switch to the piano, take a dinner break at nine o'clock, and return to the piano until two o'clock in the morning. That was his daily routine and Jean was ready to go out of her mind."[67] Grace Mingus recalls a moment when Jeanne became so angry at her inattentive husband that she threw a telephone at him and chipped his tooth. Both sisters agree that Charles could not really love a woman because he never had love from his parents and did not know how to practice it.[68]

Were the sisters right that Mingus was avoiding Jeanne because he did not know how to love her? Or was he simply too devoted to his music to have time for her? Or was it both? In *Beneath the Underdog,* Mingus later walks away from a ménage à trois with Lee-Marie, the love of his life, and a beautiful white woman named Donna because they were keeping him from his music. Even though Mingus insists in his autobiography that his life was all about the music, the book is mostly about his sex life. But as Eric Porter points out, music and sex are connected in *Beneath the Underdog.* Much of the sexism, homophobia, and masculinist rhetoric in the book circulates around Mingus's need to express himself in his music. "Women and family responsibilities," Porter notes, "present a threat to black male creativity, and musicians are in danger of being emasculated when they are victimized by the corruption permeating society."[69]

Mingus did not remain faithful to Jeanne, as he makes abundantly clear in *Beneath the Underdog.* When the book was being edited at Knopf in 1970, the editors Nel King and Regina Ryan agreed that the failure of the marriage should have a good reason, one that did not portray Charles as the villain. They suggested that Barbara should complain of pain during intercourse, even though Jeanne had never said any such thing. Mingus went along with the change. The editors then contacted Jeanne, who by this time had remarried and become Jeanne Page; she signed an agreement allowing Mingus to portray her any way he wished so long as her name and the names of her parents were changed.[70]

One of the women Mingus was seeing during his marriage to Jeanne was probably the Nesa of chapter 19 of *Beneath the Underdog.* She was married to the man who ran a club in Venice, California, where Charles was working with a band called Strings and Keys. This was the first of many white women with whom he became involved, still another way that Mingus confounded the racial proscriptions of his day.

By 1944 Mingus was sufficiently well known that Norman Granz began inviting him to play at the Jazz at the Philharmonic Hall gigs, including one with Billie Holiday. Mingus apparently hit it off with Holiday, and had she not run into trouble with police and drugs, she might have recorded "Eclipse," a tune he wrote especially for her. The tune, a somber hymn to interracial romance, was eventually recorded in 1953 with a vocal by Janet Thurlow.[71] Holiday may also have given Mingus the idea to write an autobiography. When her auto-narrative *Lady Sings the Blues* made a splash in 1956, Mingus began contemplating the book that became *Beneath the Underdog.* At first he called it *Memoirs of a Half Yellow, Schitt-Colored Nigger,* but he probably did not begin seriously writing it until 1963.

Mingus recorded with Coleman Hawkins at a Jazz at the Philharmonic event in 1945, and thanks to the boom in independent labels immediately after World War II, he began showing up in the discographies of several important players, including Howard McGhee. Hawkins, who was already an elder statesman in 1945, was intrigued by bebop and hired many of the first innovators. The somewhat younger McGhee had played in swing bands, but adopted many of the protocols of bebop at about this same time. Just as Mingus had been present at the reemergence of Kid Ory and the roots of the New Orleans revival, he was also a player in the beginnings of bebop. Surprisingly, he was not impressed by the early work of Charlie Parker, Dizzy Gillespie, and the other bop pioneers. He would, however, record memorably and historically with Parker and Gillespie (and Bud Powell and Max Roach) at Massey Hall in Toronto in 1953, and he would eventually place Parker in his personal pantheon alongside Duke Ellington. But in 1945 he was too devoted to the coloristic delights of Ellington's compositions to embrace Parker's solo music.

Also in 1945, Lloyd Reese helped Mingus land a job with the eminent film composer Dmitri Tiomkin. During his long career Tiomkin worked on more than 140 films, including *It's a Wonderful Life* (1946), *Red River* (1948), *The Thing from Another World* (1951), and *The Guns of Navarone* (1961). Mingus was one of numerous Hollywood journeymen who helped composers by arranging and filling out parts. He worked on and off with Tiomkin for a year and surely learned a great deal about orchestration and the possibilities open to composers. Gene Santoro speculates that Mingus's work with Tiomkin prompted his lifelong practice of asking musicians to expand on music that he merely sketched out for them.[72]

He also played a few gigs with Lucky Thompson, a master of the soprano saxophone. Thanks to Thompson, Mingus was hired to do some arranging for Dinah Washington. And as always, he was a completely reliable virtuoso for anyone who needed a bass player. While he was playing with increasingly visible jazz musicians, he was also composing music and writing arrangements that were especially ambitious for the late 1940s. He was on his way.

BARON MINGUS

Mingus made his first records under his own name in the fall of 1945. The variety of material he took into the studios displays both the breadth of his aesthetic and his desire for success. He recorded a straight-ahead blues ("Lonesome Woman Blues"), a sing-songy jump tune ("Texas Hop"), and a well-crafted romantic ballad ("Baby Take a Chance with Me") with a fairly conventional vocal by Everett Pettis.[73] The arrangements are workmanlike, but nothing stands out except the striking, Blantonesque solos by Mingus.

In 1946, at the second recording session under his name, Mingus recorded "Weird Nightmare" with a vocal by Claude Trenier. Like Pettis from the earlier session, Trenier had an overripe masculine presentation typical of many African American vocalists in the wake of Billy Eckstine. But "Weird Nightmare" was one of Mingus's most mature compositions, at least among those he took into recording studios. He would rework the tune several times, most memorably as "Smooch," recorded elegantly in 1953 with Mingus himself on piano, Percy Heath on bass, and Max Roach on drums. Miles Davis, with whom he had worked in a rehearsal band in 1946 when Davis was briefly in Los Angeles, was the trumpeter at the 1953 session.[74]

Also in 1946, he made several recordings as "Baron" Mingus, an unapologetic ploy to join the jazz royalty of Count Basie, Nat King Cole, and of course, Duke Ellington. "Make Believe," recorded with five horns and a rhythm section, reveals just how closely he had been listening to Ellington. As Andrew Homzy points out, the tune has a great deal in common with Duke's "Everything but You," which the Ellington band recorded for RCA Victor in May 1945.[75] At the same session as "Make Believe," Mingus channels Duke again, but without quoting so directly from a specific composition. "This Subdues My Passion" recalls the kind of intense ballad writing that Ellington was able to accomplish with the help of Billy Strayhorn. The piece becomes especially Ellingtonian when Buddy Collette's alto recalls Johnny Hodges and Britt Woodman takes a trombone solo in the bel canto style of Lawrence Brown.

Late in 1946 Mingus fell into one of his several periods of depression after his marriage to Jeanne began to fall apart. She moved in with her parents, taking with her their sons, Charles III and Eugene (born September 1946). Mingus went to San Francisco looking for work and also to reconnect with his spiritual mentor, Falwell Taylor. As he would do more than once, Taylor took the young man under his wing, making sure that he ate right and that he continued to explore his spirituality. Taylor also hooked Mingus up with some musicians, but the job did not last because the segregated union would not allow him to play with whites on a regular basis. Desperate for money, Mingus reluctantly followed the example of his father and took a job at the post office.

When he came back to Los Angeles early in 1947, he began one of his first efforts as a civil rights activist, attempting to unite the two musicians' unions in Los Angeles. Members of the whites-only union were earning substantially more than the members of the black performers' union, and Mingus participated in "early conversations about amalgamation."[76] In addition, Buddy Collette and Mingus were part of a team that formed the Community Symphony Orchestra, designed to bring white and black musicians together. A good number of white and black artists did in fact join the CSO, and they gained some media attention as an interracial band playing classical music in schools and parks.[77]

HOT MALLETS TIMES TWO

Even as he was promoting the merging of musicians' unions (the black and white unions would finally merge in 1953), Mingus was working at the post office. But as always, he was constantly writing music and practicing bass and piano. He knew that he was a musician and that his future must be with music. So when Lionel Hampton brought his big band to Los Angeles in August 1947 and offered Mingus a job, he took it. Almost as soon as Mingus joined, vibraphonist Hampton recorded his composition "Mingus Fingers," a unique combination of bebop and modernist classical music. It was nothing like Hampton had ever recorded, and he played the tune regularly while Mingus was in the band.

For a few months in 1948, the trumpeter Fats Navarro played in the Hampton band along with Mingus. Navarro was a year younger than Mingus, but he was already on his way to becoming one of the most esteemed innovators in the history of the jazz trumpet. He had clearly listened to Gillespie and Parker, but he was finding ways of phrasing and structuring an improvisation that were his alone. He and Mingus immediately hit it off, and the two remained friends after they left Hampton.

In some of the best writing in *Beneath the Underdog,* Mingus recreates conversations he had with Navarro just before his death in 1950 from tuberculosis exacerbated by drug abuse. Few of the many early deaths among jazz artists were as tragic, if only because of the poignant conversations recorded by Mingus. In Mingus's account of their dialogues, they talk primarily about religion and racial politics. Although Mingus could be a firebrand when it came to race, in his autobiography he takes an understated position, questioning Navarro as the trumpeter rages on about racists and racism. But there was a genuine connection between the two musicians. In a letter he wrote to Sonny Rollins in 1961, Mingus said that he loved Fats more than he loved himself.[78] In the book's last lines, Charles and Fats say goodbye to each other in matter-of-fact terms. The understated pathos is a moving finale to an extraordinary autobiography.

Jimi Hendrix, Brian Jones, Jim Morrison, Janis Joplin, Alan Wilson, Amy Winehouse, and Kurt Cobain all died when they were twenty-seven years old. So did the African American painter Jean-Michel Basquiat and the legendary bluesman Robert Johnson. Bix Beiderbecke lived just a few months past his twenty-seventh year. In every one of these cases, the artists destroyed themselves or put themselves in danger by overindulging in drugs or alcohol. Navarro was a few months shy of his twenty-seventh birthday when he died in July 1950. Mingus had just turned twenty-eight. It was a difficult time for him, but he made it through, despite periods of depression. At least at this moment, he was a survivor.

While he was touring with Hampton, Mingus met a white woman named Lucille Gemanis, or Celia. She would eventually become Mingus's second wife. Mingus predicted as much, even though she was already engaged to her childhood sweetheart, a trumpet player named Jim Nielsen. Mingus even told Celia that her first child would be his, which turned out to be the case. By now, Mingus had given up on a rapprochement with Jeanne and was living with a black vocalist named Shirley Holiday. (When they performed together, Mingus made sure that the singer's last name was much larger than her first name when it appeared on the sandwich board outside the club.)[79] Holiday would bear Mingus's third child, Yanine, in October 1949. Nevertheless, Charles began pursuing Celia, looking for any opportunity to be with her while he was touring.

When in New York with Hampton, Mingus met Allen Ginsberg, who took to him much as that other bohemian artist, Farwell Taylor, had. Mingus read Ginsberg's "Howl" and Kerouac's *On the Road*, both of which were essential influences when he began writing *Beneath the Underdog*. Also in 1949, Mingus played in a rehearsal band where he met Jimmy Knepper and Eric Dolphy. Along with drummer Dannie Richmond, those two would eventually number among the most important sidepeople in Mingus's career (see part IV).

Lionel Hampton taught Mingus how to engage with an audience and keep everyone interested. In a 1962 interview with Nesuhi Ertegun of Atlantic records, Mingus expressed admiration for Hampton, saying that he was not just a "showman"; rather, when he played, "he put his whole heart into it."[80] After several months on the road, however, Hampton's crowd-pleasing routines were starting to grate on Mingus. He was especially upset when Hampton insisted on playing the strings of Mingus's bass with his vibraphone mallets. At one point, Mingus yanked his bass away from Hampton's mallets and held it above his head during a performance. Soon he was out of a job and scrambling again.

Figure 4. The Embers, 1951: Tal Farlow (guitar), Charles Mingus (bass), Red Norvo (vibes). Photograph © Charles Peterson, used with permission.

As always, there were intriguing new recordings by Mingus, especially a session with a large orchestra called "Charles 'Baron' Mingus Presents His Symphonic Airs." In 1949 he enrolled twenty people for the ensemble and recorded his own composition, "Story of Love." Largely inspired by Ellington, the piece had the intense romantic dissonance that would soon become the dominant sound of a Mingus band. Brian Priestley speculates that the tune was inspired by his "honeymoon" in Mexico with Mary Ellen.[81] Later in 1949 Mingus recorded "Boppin' in Boston" with a wordless vocal reminiscent of Dizzy Gillespie's playful singing on up-tempo tunes in the late 1940s.[82] But the money was not coming in, and Mingus once again began delivering mail for the post office. He even considered giving up on the music business entirely.

Just as Hampton had come through town and given Mingus desperately needed steady work in 1948, in 1950 another vibraphonist, Red Norvo, was in Los Angeles and in need of a bassist. Mingus spent nearly a year in the Red Norvo Trio (figure 4) along with guitarist Tal Farlow. The music they made was "cool" but much more complex than most of the West Coast jazz that was also connected to the adjective. Norvo's trio toured and recorded frequently from early 1950 until early 1951. Unfortunately, as the trio grew in popularity and as the venues became more upscale, a mixed-race group became a problem. Lionel Hampton and Teddy Wilson had performed with Benny Goodman in the 1930s, but that was different: neither black artist ever played with the all-white big band. Instead, Hampton and Wilson played off to one side with Goodman and his drummer Gene Krupa. The black musicians were, in a sense, part of a novelty act set off from the band's "real" business.

Much the same could be said of Roy Eldridge's tenure with the big bands of Gene Krupa and Artie Shaw and of Charlie Shavers's years with Tommy Dorsey in the 1940s. In both cases, a black trumpeter stood out in a sea of white faces. While the hipper whites in the audience realized that Eldridge and Shavers were first-rate musicians playing great jazz, the rest of the whites saw them as something more like mascots.

Mingus was hardly an ornament in the Norvo Trio. He was playing with ferocious technique, providing a powerful beat that eliminated the need for a drummer while inspiring Norvo and Farlow with his emotional immediacy. But racism eventually reared its ugly head. While the Norvo Trio was playing regularly in New York at a club called the Embers, they were also contracted to appear on a series of television broadcasts with singer Mel Tormé. It was one thing for Mingus to appear with Farlow and Norvo at the Embers. It was another for him to be broadcast into the homes of white people who might be unnerved at the sight of a black man playing side by side with whites.

Because Mingus was not a member of the local musicians' union, Norvo may have had to replace him for reasons that were not strictly racist. The New York union was not segregated, but the officers often excluded out-of-towners like Mingus. A news story in *Down Beat* reported, "Because Charles Mingus is not a member of Local 802, he was nixed out of the show at the last minute and Red used Clyde Lombardi instead."[83] Would an exception have been made for a visitor from California if he were the right color? Probably yes.

A few months earlier, when he was in Buffalo with Norvo, Charles had convinced Celia to join him on the tour. In Toronto he proposed marriage. By the end of 1951 they were settled in New York, where Mingus would reside for the rest of his life. Just a few days after he left Norvo, he appeared with no less than Miles Davis at that most prestigious of jazz establishments, Birdland.

SCENES IN THE CITY

Today, a club called Birdland is a great place to hear jazz in New York City. It is a large space with three tiers of tables, all of them reasonably far apart, so you never sit at one long table with your knees touching the stranger next to you, as is often the case at New York jazz venues. And no matter where you sit, you can hear and see the musicians clearly. This is not, however, the Birdland where Mingus went to work with Miles Davis, effectively beginning his career as a jazz musician in New York City. The current Birdland opened on West 44th Street in 1996, on the heels of another club called Birdland that occupied a space on Broadway and 105th from 1988 until 1996. But the *original* Birdland was located on Broadway just south of 53rd, a spur at the end of "The Street," as the several-block scatter of jazz clubs dotting West 52nd Street was known. The Three Deuces, the Spotlite Club, Onyx, Jimmy Ryan's, and several others came and went on 52nd Street throughout the 1930s, '40s, and '50s as the center of jazz activity moved from Harlem to midtown.

The first Birdland was named after Charlie Parker. The club opened for business on December 15, 1949, at what may have been the apex of bebop's appeal to jazz critics and musicians. Parker himself was too unreliable to work regularly at Birdland, but he did take the stage on a few occasions, right up until his death in 1955, the same year that Count Basie's band recorded George Shearing's composition "Lullaby of Birdland." The club was established primarily by Morris Levy and Morris Primack and managed by Oscar Goodstein. Morris's brother Irving Levy tended bar. When Irving—whom Mingus recalls calling musicians "nigger" while throwing them down the stairs—was shot in the club in 1959, the press called it a "bebop murder." Morris Levy was known to have mob connections and, according to an article in Wikipedia, may have been the model for Hesh, the Jewish gangster on the television series *The Sopranos.*[84] He eventually died in jail in 1989 after being convicted of extorting a music wholesaler.

Birdland was one of the few clubs in 1950s New York to regularly feature the most progressive jazz, and it became a stylish place to be seen (and to buy drugs). Almost from the beginning, the disc jockey "Symphony Sid" Torin was broadcasting live performances from Birdland over the high-power AM station WJZ (later WABC). The diminutive Pee Wee Marquette, who began life as a woman, announced the acts from the bandstand in his distinctive staccato soprano. Offstage, Pee Wee demanded that musicians pay if they wanted their names pronounced correctly.

Birdland closed in 1965, but the original layout remained unchanged in 2008 when I made a pilgrimage to the hallowed space where so many great jazz artists had performed. By then it had become a "gentleman's club" called Flashdancers, but the old bandstand was still there, affording plenty of space for women who took turns doing inept pole dances. As I walked down the same stairs that had supported the jazz elite of mid-twentieth-century America, I was surprised by the size of the club, with clusters of tables stretching deep into the building.

When I took a seat far from the bandstand, I was approached by a series of women, virtually all of them from Jamaica or Eastern Europe. Each of them asked if I wanted a "dance," which meant that they would take off everything except their panties and gyrate just a few inches from my knees. The price was thirty dollars plus tip, and no touching was allowed. The beer that I had to drink out of the bottle cost twelve dollars. The old Birdland had its unsavory aspects—in a 1971 interview at WKCR, the radio station of Columbia University, Mingus called it "Pee Wee's Slave Kitchen"[85]—but it was nothing like Flashdancers.

THE JAZZ CORNER OF THE WORLD
AND THE BIRTH OF DEBUT

By 1951 Mingus had known Miles Davis for several years, ever since Miles had come to Los Angeles in 1946 as a member of Benny Carter's big band. Davis eventually found himself penniless with no way to get back to New York. Fortunately, there was an opening in Billy Eckstine's band when it was in LA at that moment, so Miles joined as they were about to head back to New York. In LA, Miles stayed for several days in the apartment of saxophonist Lucky Thompson, who is probably the one who first told him about Mingus. Davis may even have sat in with Mingus's rehearsal band on a few occasions. This was back in the days when Miles was, by all accounts, an agreeable young man. By the time Mingus began playing with him at Birdland, however, Miles had begun abusing drugs and was developing a mean streak. Mingus, however, at age twenty-nine was not intimidated by Davis or by any aspect of his new life in New York with a white wife.

Because Red Norvo did not give sufficient notice when he booted him from the trio, Mingus filed a grievance with the musician's union and was granted $500. With this money, and with a few hundred more that Celia was able to raise, he started a record company. Debut Records made its first recordings just days before Mingus turned thirty. He had long complained about the mistreatment of black musicians by the white businessmen who ran the major labels. It is a constant theme in his autobiography. His plan to control all aspects of at least a corner of the music business had as much to do with civil rights as with entrepreneurship.

Unlike many African Americans in the early 1950s, Charles vociferously pointed out that the country was built upon a profoundly racist foundation, the powerlessness of minorities being essential to its economy. As always, Mingus was ahead of his time. It took the lynching of Emmett Till in August 1955 and the arrest of Rosa Parks for refusing to move to the back of a bus in Birmingham to inspire large groups of African Americans to openly and assertively seek integration and equality.

Charles and Celia soon brought in drummer Max Roach as a partner in their Debut venture. Born in North Carolina and raised in Brooklyn, Max Roach was eighteen in 1942 when he began playing with Charlie Parker, eventually becoming the saxophonist's regular drummer from mid-1947 until mid-1949. During this period he established himself as the definitive bebop drummer. From 1954 until 1956, Roach made some of his greatest recordings as the co-leader of a group with Clifford Brown, a brilliant trumpeter who died tragically in 1956. Unlike Mingus's beloved friend Fats Navarro, Brown was not at all self-destructive. In college he majored in mathematics. He was an excellent chess player and by all accounts a lovely person. When Brown died at age twenty-five in an automobile accident, Roach said that he took two bottles of Cognac to his hotel room and remained there for several days.[86]

Roach was one of the few jazz artists who shared Mingus's intense convictions about racial injustice. And like Mingus, he brought those feelings into his music. In 1960, the same year that Mingus recorded the unexpurgated "Fables of Faubus," Roach recorded the LP *We Insist! Freedom Now Suite,* which traced African American oppression from the beginnings of slavery to the present. On a track called "Driva' Man," Roach's partner, the distinguished actor and singer Abbey Lincoln, put aside her usual musicianship and screamed the rage of a slave.

Unlike Charles and Celia, Roach could spare a few dollars to keep Debut in business. Santoro suggests that Roach's money came from his girlfriend of the moment, who worked as a hooker.[87] Unfortunately, Mingus and Roach were not good business partners. There were disputes about money from the beginning, and even after Debut was shut down in 1957, they continued to argue about who owed what to whom.

There are several revealing letters from Mingus in the Max Roach archives at the Library of Congress. In the first, dated February 17, 1961, Mingus rambles on for four pages about spirituality and the meaning of life. He is clearly reaching out to Roach for friendship. In the second letter, written just five days later, he angrily demands money.[88]

A third letter from Mingus to Roach begins with a brief parody of the pretentious prose we all know from those businesslike letters telling us that we owe money to some organization. Instead of money, the issue in Mingus's message is letters that have not been answered. The body of the letter is a series of lines, empty except for a few clusters of random symbols that traditionally stand in for swear words. In his own unique fashion— simultaneously facetious and aggressive—Mingus is providing a template for the multiple letters he apparently assumes he will write and that Roach will ignore.[89] The two would play together memorably on several occasions, but when they did reconcile it was never for long.

Shortly after the gig at Birdland with Davis, Billy Taylor invited Mingus to travel with him to Boston to play at the Storyville Club. "Doctor Billy Taylor" would eventually become one of America's most respected jazz educators. In 1951, he was a promising bebop pianist who, like Mingus but very few other members of the bop fraternity, still had great admiration for Duke Ellington.

During his two weeks in Boston with Taylor, Mingus met two individuals who would loom large in the story of his life. Nat Hentoff, a jazz disc jockey who had taken courses in the American Studies graduate program at Harvard, was on his way to becoming a prolific writer of political commentary and jazz criticism as well as several novels. He would eventually become one of Mingus's best friends and, in a long series of liner notes and journalism, one of his most perceptive chroniclers. Hentoff would also rescue Mingus from the Bellevue psychiatric hospital, where Charles committed himself only to discover that he could not walk out as easily as he could walk in.

The other important connection Mingus made in Boston was George Wein, who would eventually run the Newport Jazz Festival and employ Mingus more than once. In 1951, he was the owner of Boston's Storyville Club as well as a more than adequate jazz pianist. One night during Mingus's stint with Taylor at Storyville, Mingus asked if he could sit in with Wein. Wein, impressed by Mingus's talent, asked his own bass player to step aside, leaving Mingus on stage with Wein and the drummer Jo Jones. Jones had played in the great Count Basie bands of the 1930s and 1940s and can be credited with some of the best big-band and swing drumming. But this did not stop Mingus from telling Jones that he was not playing fast enough. While Wein was soloing on "I've Found a New Baby," Mingus and Jones began a race to see who could play the fastest. They challenged and chased each other until they were playing with such velocity and aggression that Wein could not keep up. In his memoirs, Wein wrote, "What was I doing on the stand with these maniacs?"[90]

At first Mingus and Celia were living in the less-than-glamorous Maryland Hotel, but as soon as Mingus managed to get a few decent-paying gigs and Celia was making a good salary as a secretary, they moved to 1594 Third Avenue near 89th Street on the East Side of Manhattan. But even though he was landing a few jobs with the best young musicians in New York, Mingus was still underemployed. With time on their hands, Mingus and Celia would go to the movies, where Mingus, the American romantic experimental artist, was especially intrigued by the films of Jean Cocteau, the French romantic experimental artist.[91]

The money did not come in fast enough to pay all their bills, however, and by Christmas 1952 Mingus was back at the post office and making reasonably good money. He says that he would have stayed there had not Charlie Parker talked him into becoming a regular member of his band. But with his complete devotion to music, Mingus might have left his job at the post office even if a less august musician had offered him a steady gig and a decent salary.

In 1951, he was still devoted to Ellington, and as many of the early Debut recordings indicate, he favored a music that was more inflected with classical influences. But Celia would "bombard" him with Parker recordings and lecture him about Bird's ability.[92] Finally he came around to acknowledging Parker's startling originality and technique. The actual gig with Parker, however, was brief, and although Bird had promised to pay Mingus more than he was earning at the post office, in the end he received substantially less.

MEET JUAN TIZOL

The prospect of playing regularly with Parker would have been a career pinnacle for many jazz artists. But after seeing how unreliable Parker could be, especially with money, Mingus seized the opportunity of a lifetime and joined the orchestra of his idol and inspiration, Duke Ellington. He would be subbing for the band's regular bassist, Wendell Marshall, who had a special relationship with Ellington if only because he was the cousin of Jimmie Blanton. But Mingus knew that subbing might lead to a regular place in the band. In the end, however, his association with Ellington was almost as brief as his tenure with Parker. The reason: an altercation with valve-trombonist Juan Tizol in early 1953.

Tizol was from Puerto Rico, an island known for its thriving culture of brass players. Moving to the United States to seek work as a trombonist, in 1920 he took a job playing in a pit orchestra for a show in Washington, D.C., where he met the young Ellington, a DC native. Several years later, in 1929, Ellington decided that his band ought to have a valve-trombonist, and he hired Tizol. Although Tizol was not much of an improviser, Duke liked his mellow sound and polished technique. Tizol soon became one of the mainstays of the orchestra, even contributing several compositions to the band's book— "Caravan," "Perdido," "Conga Brava," and "Moonlight Fiesta." Like many of the musicians who worked with Ellington, however, he grew tired of the constant touring and left in 1944. A few months later he took a position in Harry James's orchestra.

Tizol and his wife remained friends with Duke, however, and Ellington has especially fond words for the trombonist in his autobiography, *Music Is My Mistress*. In 1951, when Ellington was at an especially difficult time in his career, he paid the Tizols a visit in search of advice or just some solace. Johnny Hodges, Lawrence Brown, and Sonny Greer, all essential players for many years, had just left the band. Greer had grown up in Washington with Ellington and had been the band's drummer since the beginning. Hodges, who joined the band in 1928, played lead alto saxophone and supplied the band with solos so romantic that Duke described them as "excruciating ecstasy." Trombonist Brown had joined in 1932 and contributed a mellow, singing sound that contrasted with the growling, wa-wa trombone of another of the band's mainstays, "Tricky Sam" Nanton.

Ellington wrote that during his visit with Juan and his wife, Tizol said, "Say the word and take Louis Bellson, Willie Smith, and me, and we'll leave Harry James and come with you."[93] Bellson was a younger and more facile drummer than Greer, and alto saxophonist Smith was an accomplished section leader, though not as charismatic a soloist as Hodges. With Tizol also offering to return, the loss of the three veterans was not fatal. Harry James did not seem to take the loss to his band personally. At least, he had a sense of humor about it; when James heard that the three were leaving to join Ellington, he asked, "Can I come too?"[94]

Still, it was not the best time for Ellington and his band. In 1953, they recorded "Satin Doll," Ellington's last hit record. It was not until the band played the Newport Jazz Festival in 1956 and the crowd went crazy that Duke was reborn. But even during the lean years when Mingus passed through, the band had Cat Anderson, Clark Terry, and Ray Nance in the trumpet section, Quentin Jackson and Mingus's old friend Britt Woodman on trombones, and Paul Gonsalves, Harry Carney, and Jimmy Hamilton on saxes. Mingus was in good company, if only for a few days.

Tizol himself remained with Duke for only two years after what the jazz press called the "Great James Raid," but he was there long enough to tangle with Mingus. As was the case throughout most of his life, Mingus did not take well to insults, real or perceived. According to most commentators, the trouble began when Tizol asked Mingus to play the bass part for music he wanted the band to consider playing. In *Beneath the Underdog*, Mingus writes that he found the bass part pitched too low, so he played it an octave higher. Tizol then remarked that Mingus, like "the rest of the niggers in the band," could not read music.[95]

Tizol's racial slur led to an argument in which the trombonist eventually pulled a knife. It also led to one of the most memorable passages in *Beneath the Underdog*. Mingus is quoting Ellington himself after the incident:

> "Now, Charles," he says, looking amused, putting Cartier links into the cuffs of his beautiful hand-made shirt, "you could have forewarned me—you left me out of the act entirely! At least you could have let me cue in a few chords as you ran through that Nijinksy routine. I congratulate you on your performance, but why didn't you and Juan inform me about the adagio you planned so that we could score it? I must say I never saw a large man so agile—I never saw anybody make such tremendous leaps! The gambado over the piano carrying your bass was colossal."

Ellington then said that everyone knew Tizol carried a knife but that it was not really a problem. "But you seem to have a whole bag of new tricks," he tells Mingus. Although Ellington almost never fired a musician in a face-to-face encounter, he seems to have made an exception with Mingus. The chapter ends: "The charming way he says it, you feel like he's paying you a compliment. Feeling honored, you shake hands and resign."[96]

Tizol's version of the story is equally self-serving but very different— and not nearly as amusing. Tizol claimed that he *used* to carry a knife, but that he had stopped doing so by 1953. When Mingus looked at the piece of music he had brought in (Tizol said that it wasn't even something he had written), and when Mingus played it an octave higher, Tizol said, "If I wanted to write for a cello, I would have wrote for a cello." After trading insults, Tizol retired to his dressing room. When he came back, Mingus apparently thought that Tizol had a knife and grabbed a piece of iron attached to the curtains. A stage hand restrained him from attacking Tizol with it. After the show that night, Tizol said he was so upset that he broke down and cried in his dressing room. Mingus appeared at the door, still angry and still arguing. His manner was so menacing that he had to be restrained again. Not long afterward, Ellington told his road manager to give Mingus two weeks' notice. Tizol also insisted that he never used the word *nigger*.[97]

Another version of the encounter appears in the autobiography of Clark Terry, who had been in the Ellington trumpet section for two years when the altercation took place. Terry writes that he was in the room with the two men when the Tizol asked Mingus to play the music. When the trombonist claimed that Mingus had hit a wrong note, Mingus insisted that he had not. The argument escalated until Mingus pulled a fire ax off the wall. Terry agrees with Mingus that Tizol did indeed have a knife. It was a switchblade, or as Terry calls it, a "Cuban frog sticker." When Tizol pushed the button to release the blade, Terry jumped into action. In his youth he had trained as a boxer, and he had the skill and the confidence to grab them both until they cooled down. At least according to Terry, that was the end of it. Moments later, they all went on stage and played the gig. Terry says that Mingus was subsequently dismissed because it was not the first time he had been in "a scrap."[98]

There is even more to the story of Mingus's dismissal. Gene Santoro suggests that Charles wanted to show off his chops and play bebop while Duke wanted him to play like Jimmie Blanton. And even though Duke expressed interest in Charles's "Mingus Fingers," he had no regrets about letting him go once Tizol told him that he would quit if Mingus did not.[99]

Duke has a few nice words for Mingus in *Music Is My Mistress*, but he does not express the kind of affection that he does for Tizol.[100] Regardless of whether there is any truth in Mingus's account of how Ellington fired him, it is surely one of the funniest and most convincing accounts of how Ellington behaved backstage with his musicians. Mingus and Ellington would meet again on several occasions, most memorably when they joined Max Roach in the studio for the *Money Jungle* session. Tizol seems to have scrupulously avoided Mingus after 1953.

BACK TO BIRDLAND

After his much too brief stint with Duke Ellington, Mingus was once again a hired hand on the New York music scene. He almost immediately landed a job with Bud Powell at Birdland. Oscar Goodstein was not only taking care of business at Birdland at this time; he was also the manager—and caretaker—for the severely troubled Powell. Goodstein had infuriated many musicians by withholding payment and even banning some from returning. When Thelonious Monk first appeared at Birdland in 1949, Goodstein told him not to leave his glass on the piano. Not only did Monk not move his glass off the bare wood of the piano; he then lit a cigarette and left it burning on the wood. Goodstein shouted at him furiously even while he was playing. He then banned him from the club—which was fine with Monk.[101] But when Goodstein heard Bud Powell perform in 1950, he was so moved that he put off a trip to Florida and declared himself Powell's manager.[102]

We do not know much about Mingus's interactions with Powell when he became part of his trio in March 1953. Powell's poor health and regular institutionalizations may have been due to a head injury he received in a racially charged incident with a policeman in 1945, though that account has been disputed. Powell's biographers have confirmed that he was committed to Bellevue in 1947 and that he spent almost the entire year of 1948 in Creedmoor State Hospital in Queens, New York, where he was given electroconvulsive therapy.[103] Although he made his greatest recordings between 1949 and 1953, his condition was always precarious. After an arrest for the possession of marijuana led to another term at Creedmoor, he was eventually handed over to Goodstein as his official guardian. Powell's complex composition "The Glass Enclosure" is named for the time when he was essentially a prisoner in Goodstein's apartment.[104]

When Mingus became Powell's regular bassist, the pianist had already developed the habit of sitting at his piano bench between sets or during sidemen's solos and staring unsettlingly at members of the audience.[105] After Mingus left the trio, he was replaced by George Duvivier, who worked with Powell off and on until 1957. When asked what Powell was like, Duvivier would say that he didn't really know; if they spoke at all, it was a brief conversation about baseball.[106] Duvivier suspected that Goodstein had actually hired him to "babysit" the pianist.[107]

When Debut Records got going in 1951, Mingus recorded an intriguing group of musicians. While various peers in the jazz world were destroying themselves with drugs, Mingus had lived past the dangerous age of twenty-seven and become an entrepreneur. But as Eric Porter points out, he could not have kept Debut going without the consistent and conscientious contributions of his second wife, Celia.[108]

Many of the Debut recordings featured players who were less committed to bebop than was the fashion or who were engaged in composing unusual music. In spite of Mingus's commitment to freeing black artists from servitude to record companies, many of the artists he recorded were white, including Paul Bley, Teo Macero, Jimmy Knepper, Lee Konitz, and the singer

Jackie Paris.[109] After all, Mingus did compose a piece called "Meditations on Integration."

During the Debut years, Mingus regularly sat in with musicians who were recording as leaders. He went out on a limb to record bebop bassist Oscar Pettiford with the French hornist Julius Watkins. He also experimented with a group that included four trombonists. J.J. Johnson and Kai Winding had already made a few recordings together as sidemen, so Mingus invited them to join trombonists Willie Dennis and Benny Green for a Debut LP. This may have been the beginning of a partnership for Johnson and Winding as leaders. "Jay and Kai" had substantial success after they recorded with Savoy Records. And they were wise enough to hire Mingus to play bass on their first sessions as co-leaders.[110]

"THE GREATEST JAZZ CONCERT EVER"

Charlie Parker's reputation for being unreliable was making it difficult for him to find work, so he briefly gave music lessons at the Hartnett Music Studios on Broadway. In January 1953, four young jazz enthusiasts from the New Jazz Society of Toronto found him there and offered him $200 plus a percentage of the profits to play at what they were calling the First Annual Festival of Creative Jazz in Toronto. Parker signed a contract on the spot.[111] The young Canadians also wanted Max Roach, Dizzy Gillespie, and Bud Powell, all of whom would sign on eventually.

They wanted to hire Oscar Pettiford as well, but Max Roach has written that Pettiford was not able to join the group at that time because he had just broken his arm playing softball in Central Park. Several other commentators have repeated this as Roach's reason for recommending Mingus instead.[112] But Brian Priestley writes that Pettiford broke his arm in 1949, not 1953, and that Roach suggested Mingus because they were, at least at the time, on good terms.[113] Mingus was in the early days of his short stint with Ellington, so he could not have been aware of the plans for a concert in Toronto. This did not stop him, however, years later from telling a reporter that "the gig was mine."[114] To this day it is often claimed that Mingus organized the concert at Toronto's Massey Hall, perhaps because he took sole possession of the recordings made at the concert.

The members of the New Jazz Society of Toronto surely had no idea what they were getting into with this collection of, shall we say, temperamental musicians. But the event went off surprisingly well. Gillespie and Roach, scrupulously dependable, arrived on time. Bud Powell was released from Creedmoor just two days beforehand. Although Oscar Goodstein made sure that he was on the plane and at the hall, Powell briefly gave him the slip and ended up in a bar, where the concert organizers eventually found him. Mingus came with Celia, and suspecting that the concert might someday be of consequence, he brought along several reels of new, high-end Scotch-brand recording tape that was not yet available in Toronto. One of the organizers borrowed a state-of-the-art Ampex tape deck for the occasion.[115]

Parker arrived on time and in a good mood, carrying the white plastic alto saxophone he often used when his regular alto was in hock. Upon arriving at the hall, he approached Dick Wattam, the president of the jazz society with whom he had signed the contract. Bird said, "Dick, one thing. Before I go on I have to have a drink." Hoping for the best, Wattam accompanied Parker across the street to a bar called the Silver Rail. Parker ordered a triple Scotch and, according to Wattam, drank it "practically in one gulp." He then said, "Dick, I'm ready."[116]

The band did not rehearse. As Guy Ramsey has pointed out, "By this time it was clear that the original beboppers were now such an eclectic bunch, with so many different personalities, financial demands, professional goals and profiles, and personal challenges, that it would be difficult to sustain these connections, and to hear them all play together often."[117] At Massey Hall, the quintet would play standards and canonical bop tunes, but there was no way around the fact that it had been eight years since Parker and Gillespie were in the same room playing "Salt Peanuts," a Gillespie composition and a popular bop anthem. But they were all pros, and they rose to the occasion, to say the least.

On May 15, 1953, in Massey Hall in Toronto, Canada, a group of studio musicians led by trumpeter Graham Topping took the stage first and, after a rendition of "God Save the Queen," played a set of swing tunes. Topping's group was there to provide "Canadian content" and to satisfy union regulations. They were followed by the all-star quintet—the last recorded documentation of Parker and Gillespie playing together. It was a momentous occasion, even though the hall was half empty (the crowd likely depleted because a match between two well-known boxers, Jersey Joe Walcott and Rocky Marciano, was being broadcast live on Canadian television that same evening).

Despite a few glitches and various backstage arguments, the musicians played brilliantly. Parker and Gillespie created several solos of power, fluidity, and grace, and Mingus and Roach provided a foundation that flattered the soloists. But Powell was the most inspired musician that evening. In two sets with the quintet and one with just Mingus and Roach, he played poignant and moving melodies even while improvising at lightning speed.

After the concert, when Mingus asked if he could hear the tape record-ings, Dick Wattam took him to a nearby radio station for a listen. Mingus was upset to discover that his bass was practically inaudible, probably because the acoustics in the hall did not favor the lower registers. Nevertheless, he took possession of the tapes before the night was over. When one of the young Canadians asked about their whereabouts, Mingus looked at him and said, "These are mine, white boy."[118]

Mingus had in fact purchased the Scotch recording tape himself, and by claiming the recordings after the concert, he was continuing the project he had begun with Debut Records that included paying musicians a larger share of the profits than they would have received from white-owned record companies. But it was not just the young Canadians who were upset when Mingus walked away with the tapes. In 1979, Dizzy Gillespie wrote, "I ain't seen no royalties until recently."[119]

Alan Scharf, a member of the New Jazz Society, knew that Mingus was unhappy with the quality of the recordings and even feared that he would erase the tapes. Scharf sent a telegram to Barry Ulanov, an established jazz critic in New York, urging him to prevent Mingus from doing so.[120] Scharf may have known that Mingus had reached out to Ulanov the year before to publicize his new venture with Debut, perhaps on the recommen-dation of Fats Navarro, who said that Ulanov "understood musicians."[121] Nevertheless, a few years later, in the unedited typescript of his autobiog-raphy (now in the Library of Congress), Mingus listed Ulanov, together with several other jazz critics—Gene Lees, Leonard Feather, and Ralph Gleason—as "enemies."[122] To impress on Ulanov the urgency of the situa-tion, Scharf added a statement to his telegram declaring Mingus to be "unbalanced."

The concert, by the way, did not make any money for anyone. The mem-bers of the quintet had been promised a percentage of the profits, but because of the low turnout, there were none. Mingus did not erase the tapes. Instead, he went about the elaborate work of overdubbing them with new bass parts. He did this in Hackensack, New Jersey, at Rudy van Gelder's studio, which at this point was in the living room of his parents' house. In 1959, he would build a studio in Englewood Cliffs that resembled nothing so much as a cathedral. A vast number of the most honored jazz recordings were made there. More than anyone in jazz history, van Gelder is respon-sible for what most people regard as the true sound of jazz. After listening to the elegantly crafted recordings that van Gelder engineered for Blue Note, Prestige, impulse!, and many other labels, people listening to live jazz in a nightclub may hear a chaotic, unbalanced music with the drummer making too much noise. Mingus's 1953 overdubbing session with van Gelder anticipated the elaborate layering of tracks he would undertake on the impulse! recordings they made in the early 1960s.

At first, Mingus released the music from Massey Hall on three ten-inch Debut LPs. Because Parker was under contract to Norman Granz at the time, he was listed on the cover as "Charlie Chan," punning both on the 1930s movie detective and on the name of Parker's common-law wife, Chan Richardson. Bearing the title "Jazz at Massey Hall," the LPs sold well. In the 1970s, after Fantasy Records acquired the Debut catalog, the music was repackaged as a two-LP set on the Prestige label and titled "The Greatest Jazz Concert Ever." It was only a slight exaggeration.

BECOMING ESTABLISHED, BECOMING CHARLES

The year 1953 continued to be an eventful one for Mingus. Shortly after he and Celia returned from Toronto, he worked again with Parker, this time in a studio where Parker played in front of a small ensemble and a group of singers that included Dave Lambert and Annie Ross. A few years later, the two singers joined Jon Hendricks to form Lambert, Hendricks, and Ross, surely the most important jazz vocal group since the Boswell Sisters. The 1953 date with Parker was arranged and conducted by Gil Evans, who was working with a wide range of talents at this time.[123] Before teaming up with Miles Davis for the ground-breaking "Miles + 19" session in 1957, he provided arrangements for Tony Bennett, Johnny Mathis, Helen Merrill, and the bop vibraphonist Teddy Charles. Together with Ellington and very few others, Gil Evans and Charles Mingus were among the most distinctive composers in jazz. It's a pity they never worked together again. Evans would, however, hire former Mingus saxophonist George Adams and record several of Mingus's compositions in the 1970s and 1980s.

Mingus continued working with Powell at Birdland in 1953, where Parker and Gillespie—always separately—would occasionally sit in. One day he heard from Max Roach that Miles Davis was bored to death staying on his wealthy father's farm near East St. Louis, Illinois. Having realized that drugs were ruining his life, Davis had called his father and asked for a ticket home where he could kick the habit. Roach and Mingus were already planning to drive to California in August 1953 in a new car donated for the cause by Roach's girlfriend. Davis invited them to stay with him and his father before they continued on to California.

After spending a night sampling the wide open spaces and luxurious dwellings on Davis Sr.'s farm, Mingus and Max drove off with young Miles, who had decided that he was ready to move on. Since Mingus was the lightest skinned of the three, the two others insisted that he be the one to buy food in stores and restaurants. Mingus balked at the idea of playing games with the racism of middle America, and he had to be talked out of blowing up a restaurant in Oklahoma that refused to serve him.[124] In Los Angeles, Miles decided to stay on, where he was soon back to his old habits and using his father's money to buy drugs.

Shortly after Mingus and Roach returned to New York, Charles discovered that he had won the "New Star" award in the annual *Down Beat* poll. It seems to have been around this time that he ceased referring to himself as Charlie Mingus. In August 1954, he took Thad Jones, who had recently made an auspicious debut in Count Basie's trumpet section, into the studio to record an LP for Debut called *The Fabulous Thad Jones* (not to be confused with a Blue Note release two years later, *The Magnificent Thad Jones*). On the liner notes for the Debut LP, the bass player is listed as Charles Mingus.[125] He would later tell an interviewer, "Don't call me Charlie, that's not a man's name, that's a name for a horse."[126]

In 1954, Art Tatum invited Mingus to join his trio, an offer Charles could not refuse. He had actually sat in with Tatum years earlier when he was still freelancing in LA. Tatum put tremendous demands on sidepeople, who could barely keep up when Tatum began improvising in hyper-drive. (When an interviewer remarked to Tiny Grimes, who played guitar in Tatum's trio in the 1940s, that he had had the "honor and pleasure" of playing with the pianist, Grimes replied, "It was my honor, but it was not my pleasure.") Tatum must have known that Mingus could keep up and hired him for a four-week gig at a club in Miami.

On his return to New York, in March 1955, Mingus played one last gig with Charlie Parker and Bud Powell. Both men were deteriorating rapidly and blaming each other for their troubles, even taunting each other on the bandstand. At this last gig, Mingus dissociated himself, announcing over the microphone, "These are sick people." Thelonious Monk, who was backstage that night, told Powell and Parker, "I told you guys to act crazy. But I didn't tell you to fall in love with your act. You're really crazy now."[127] A week later, Parker was dead.

In a radio interview from 1974, Mingus reminisced about Parker. He said he heard a thunder clap on a cloudless day the moment that Parker died in the apartment of his benefactor the Baroness Pannonica de Koenigswarter. "A piece of me died, man," he told the interviewer. Mingus called Parker a "very learned man." One night when they were playing together at a club, Mingus and Parker were talking about Buddhism, a subject Parker knew well. Mingus says that Parker picked up his horn and said, "Let's finish this discussion on the bandstand."[128]

By early 1955, Mingus had become serious about forming a regular group of musicians with whom he could develop his music. Before leaving for Florida and his month with Tatum, Mingus had been invited to join the newly established Jazz Composers Workshop. According to John LaPorta, the critic Bill Coss asked him to put together a group of composers/performers to present original music.[129] The first group to be invited to rehearse at Carnegie Recital Hall included Mingus, Teddy Charles (vibraphone), Teo Macero (saxophone), Ed Shaughnessy (drums), and Wally Cirillo (piano). The group would later expand with the addition of more brass players.

In his memoir, LaPorta expressed ambivalence about Mingus's participation at the rehearsals. "His first three compositions were written long before we formed the Jazz Composers Workshop, yet Mingus insisted upon dominating our rehearsal time with them. After he was finished working on his numbers, we had hardly any time left to rehearse anyone else's music."[130] Things went more smoothly after Mingus left to play with Tatum. But it was clear that Mingus was beginning his tumultuous career as a leader.

The Jazz Composers Workshop never recorded, but an LP made under Mingus's name late in 1954 provides some idea of what they might have sounded like.[131] Recording with the Savoy label, the most established company with which Mingus had yet recorded, the band included Macero, LaPorta, George Barrow (baritone sax), Mal Waldron (piano), and Kenny Clarke (drums). The music is ingenious, intellectual, playful, and mostly low-key. It includes contrapuntal lines for horns and several moments of group improvisation. The remnants of the JCW continued to work with Mingus if only because he was able to book them into concert halls and clubs.

By the fall of 1955, Mingus was calling his group the Jazz Workshop. The band's first regular engagement was at the Café Bohemia, newly opened on Barrow Street in Greenwich Village. The personnel were constantly changing, but early on the Workshoppers included trombonist Eddie Bert, pianist Waldron, drummer Willie Jones, alto saxophonist Jackie McLean, and a classically trained French horn player named David Amram. Mingus managed to get the band into a rehearsal space near Times Square for a few meetings, but as Amram recalls, not everything the band played on the first night at the Bohemia was what had been rehearsed. Instead, as he put it, "You just opened up and let the telepathy flow."[132]

What did Mingus have in mind for the Workshop? Eddie Bert remembered it this way: "You'd just go up to his house and he'd play things, like 'Jump Monk,' and he'd say, 'Learn it, because if I write it out, you're gonna play it different. If you learn it in your head, you play it like you play it like you want to play it.'"[133] At one point he asked his musicians to improvise on a drawing he'd made of a coffin.[134]

Mingus himself tells a story that explains much of what he was trying to achieve with the Workshop. In the late 1940s, when Mingus and Fats Navarro were both members of Lionel Hampton's big band, Mingus took a bass solo. Practically no one was taking bass solos back then, and Mingus was especially proud of the way he "played his ass off." But Navarro told him, "You didn't play shit. You played all the right notes. You got the theory right. But you didn't tell me anything. You didn't play what you felt. You didn't say, 'Hello Fats, I love you.'"[135] Mingus says that he learned a great deal from that one statement.

The idea of creating music in the moment, with musicians finding their own unique voices, however, was a risky proposition. It was even riskier doing it nightly in front of a live audience. When Mingus did not like what he was hearing, he would not hesitate to stop the band mid-performance and insist they start a number over again. When I began collecting anecdotes from people who saw him in clubs, this was a consistent theme. Not only were audiences essentially paying to watch a group rehearse on stage, but Mingus had the habit of firing musicians in the middle of a set.

On at least one occasion, he *hired* a musician during a performance. Howard Johnson was on his way home from a gig with his tuba when he stopped in to hear Mingus at the Five Spot. Mingus was complaining from the bandstand that his old friend Red Callender wouldn't be able to play tuba at a forthcoming event. When pianist Jaki Byard saw Johnson in the back of the room with his tuba case, he said, "Well, look. There's your tuba player over there." Mingus asked Johnson what tunes he knew, but Johnson didn't understand the question. He responded, "What tunes do you want to hear?" Johnson told the rest of the story to an interviewer: "The audience went, 'Whoaaaaaaaaaaa.' Mingus said, 'Oh, you're bad, huh? Come on up here. We're going to see about this.'"[136] Johnson played several tunes while the audience looked on. He got the job.

Just as Mingus felt free to stop his musicians if they did not meet his standards, he expected club owners and even audiences to be on their best behavior. From the bandstand Charles would denounce an owner for nonfunctioning toilets or dirty dressing rooms (on the occasions when the club actually had such things). And he regularly instructed audiences on how to conduct themselves. One night he spontaneously delivered an elaborate address to his audience. His then-lover and publicist, Diane Dorr-Dorynek, was there to take it all down. Here is an excerpt:

> I listen to your millions of conversations, sometimes pulling them all up and putting them together and writing a symphony.... You haven't even heard the conversation across the table, and that's the loudest! Have you heard the announcement of a single song title during the night? Or a pause in between tunes, hoping you'd hear yourselves, then quiet down and listen? ... You're here because of jazz publicity, jazz is popular, the word jazz, and you like to associate yourself with this sort of thing. But it doesn't make you a connoisseur of the art because you follow it around. You're dilettantes of style. A blind man can go to an exhibition of Picasso and Kline and not even see their works. And comment behind dark glasses, Wow! They're the swingingest painters ever, crazy! Well so can you. You've got your dark glasses and clogged up ears.[137]

A few years later, on a night when Mingus and his band faced a noisy, inattentive crowd at the Village Vanguard, he stopped playing and handed a newspaper to his pianist and a chess set to the drummer and saxophonist. Mingus himself set up a rabbit-ear television set and began watching. Soon the audience stopped talking and stared at the musicians in silence. Only then did Mingus resume his set.[138]

On another night at the Village Vanguard, he took matters into his own hands, tearing the door off the entrance to the club because the sign on the street did not say "Jazz Workshop." Then he shouted down the stairs at Max Gordon, who ran the Vanguard, "And it's Charles, not Charlie."[139] Many found this behavior to be delightful and a complete departure from the usual performance practice. Gordon even speculated that people showed up in hopes that Mingus would "rage and fume."[140] As a rule, however, Mingus's behavior did not help him sustain regular employment in clubs.

THE ATLANTIC YEARS

In 1956 Mingus signed a contract with Atlantic Records, a small but up-and-coming label thanks to innovative and aggressive management by the Ertegun Brothers, Ahmet and Nesuhi. Mingus's first LP for Atlantic, *Pithecanthropus Erectus*, featured alto saxophonist Jackie McLean, drummer Willie Jones, and J.R. Monterose, a tenor-player most indebted to an earlier generation of saxophonists such as Coleman Hawkins.[141] The pianist was Mal Waldron, who would go on to a distinguished career in jazz, most notably as Billie Holiday's accompanist toward the end of her life but also as the leader and co-leader of several important ensembles, including a dec-ades-long collaboration with soprano saxophonist Steve Lacy.

The erudite title *Pithecanthropus Erectus* was not unusual for Mingus. Along with Raymond Scott, who composed "New Year's Eve in a Haunted House," "Dinner Music for a Pack of Hungry Cannibals," "War Dance for Wooden Indians," and "Reckless Night on Board an Ocean Liner," Mingus was one of the great namers of songs and albums. Consider "All the Things You Could Be by Now if Sigmund Freud's Wife Was Your Mother," "If Charlie Parker Was a Gunslinger, There'd Be a Whole Lot of Dead Copycats," and "Oh Lord, Don't Let Them Drop That Atomic Bomb on Me." As for *Pithecanthropus Erectus,* the term was coined by a Dutch anthropologist in 1891 after he found fossilized skeletons in Indonesia of what he believed to be the ancestors of *Homo sapiens. Pithecanthropus* is Greek for "apeman," and *erectus* is Latin for "upright," though Mingus probably did not use the title for its phallic intimations. In fact, in his liner notes to the LP, Mingus adopts an apocalyptic tone as he charts the history of mankind and its inevi-table decline. The tune on the LP titled "Pithecanthropus Erectus" has four parts, reflecting Mingus's vision: Evolution, Superiority-Complex, Decline, and Destruction. He asked his musicians to improvise around what each term meant to them. Along with this ambitious program, which had grown out of the Workshop sessions, Mingus recorded George and Ira Gershwin's "A Foggy Day," adding "non-musical" effects to create the sounds of a harbor.

An even more important LP was his second effort for Atlantic, *The Clown,* recorded in 1957.[142] This would be the first time that Mingus recorded with both drummer Dannie Richmond, who joined the Workshop late in 1956, and trombonist Jimmy Knepper, who joined early in 1957. The addition of these two artists marked a new direction for the Mingus sound. On the title track, "The Clown," Mingus invited Jean Shepherd to impro-vise commentary around a story of a clown—clearly an allegory of the artist's predicament, especially the *jazz* artist's predicament. Though on the recording, trombonist Knepper does such a brilliant impression of a clown pantomiming and taking prat falls that the narration was practically unnec-essary. Scott Saul has special praise for what Mingus achieved with this tune: "While Mingus elsewhere labeled crowd-pleasing entertainers as Uncle Toms and traitors to the black community, he took their dilemma seriously enough to endow it with sympathetic psychological depth."[143]

Knepper was equally brilliant on "Haitian Fight Song," a composition that celebrated the slave rebellions in Haiti led by Toussaint Louverture in the late eighteenth century. The tune grew out of a number of sources, including the Afrocentric messages Mingus was getting from Max Roach and pianist Randy Weston, two of the first jazz artists to make Africa an essential part of their musical universe. Mingus also recalled visiting his stepmother Mamie a few years earlier on the cross-country trip with Roach and Miles Davis. He remembered her moving from room to room singing spirituals and said that "Haitian Fight Song" was inspired by the music of the Sanctified Church, where she used to take him. With this tune, rather than assuming a negative outcome for man, as he seems to have done with "Pithecanthropus Erectus," Mingus looked to a more heroic outcome for black Americans by citing an event in which slaves overthrew their masters. This dramatic change in the program for his work surely reflected his response to the burgeoning civil rights movement and the rise to prominence of such individuals as Martin Luther King, Jr.

In the mid-1950s, Mingus had a contract with a major booking agency, Willard Alexander, for whom his second wife Celia worked as a secretary. That was the good news. He was also involved with a number of women besides his wife, assuming that at least a portion of the capacious sexual history he recounts in the *Beneath the Underdog* is true. His marriage to Celia was definitely in trouble. And because of mounting debts, both Mingus and Roach gave up on Debut Records in 1957. Several recordings in the production process were never released, and other recordings, even a few by the brilliant pianist Hazel Scott, never sold enough to cover the royalties the artists had been given up front.

By 1957, however, Mingus had won the attention of another of the major players in his career, Gunther Schuller. He invited Mingus to submit a composition for the Brandeis Jazz Festival, the key event in the brief history of what Schuller called "Third Stream Music," an attempt to make equal partners out of jazz and classical music. Only six artists were invited.[144] Schuller had known about Mingus at least since the late 1940s, but the only recording that he knew at this time was *Pithecanthropus Erectus.*[145] Schuller surely heard something unique in this LP. On many levels, it would have been natural for Mingus to jump at the opportunity to explore the relationship between jazz and classical music. He had, after all, grown up with both, and much of his musical experimentation in the 1940s and early 1950s involved pulling together elements from both strains. In the end, however, he did not fall in line with the Third Stream project, as "Revelations," his contribution to the Brandeis festival, reveals (see part III). Miles Davis and the Modern Jazz Quartet had their Third Stream moments at roughly the same time as Mingus, and Dizzy Gillespie made a stab at it as late as 1961. But Mingus seems to have lost interest in the movement after he submitted his composition to Schuller's festival.

Just a few weeks after Mingus and the Brandeis festival ensemble recorded "Revelations," he was back in the studio recording *Tijuana Moods*.[146] In 1957 Mingus was still relatively obscure, but he had landed a session with RCA, one of the most important labels in the music world, to settle a lawsuit he had brought after the company recorded Thad Jones when he was on exclusive contract with Debut. The RCA record with Jones, under the leadership of saxophonist Al Cohn, was part of a series called "Jazz Workshop," though it had nothing to do with Mingus's organization. Mingus would later copyright the term as The Jazz Workshop, Inc., a company that his widow Sue Graham Mingus still manages to this day.

Mingus was extremely pleased with *Tijuana Moods*, even if RCA, doing him no favors, waited several years to make the music available for purchase. Once again he had Knepper and Richmond, but he was also working for the first time with the mysterious trumpeter Clarence Shaw (also known as Gene Shaw), about whom we would know next to nothing had he not worked for Mingus. Shaw was an exceptionally subtle player who rejected the modern trumpet style of filling up a solo with as many notes as possible. Mingus was taken aback when Shaw paused in the middle of a solo to empty the water out of his horn. At first he assumed that Shaw was not taking his job seriously, but later, after the recording was played back, Mingus realized that he was making brilliant use of space.[147]

Shaw himself had a different story about Mingus. On one occasion when he called to say that he had the flu and could not make a recording date, Shaw said that Mingus told him to show up or he would hire people to kill him. On another occasion, Shaw said, he was so upset by Mingus that he physically destroyed his trumpet.[148] But for whatever reasons, the music they made together was always superb.

WITH THE BEATS

In 1958, Mingus became a key figure in the jazz and poetry movement when he recorded *The Weary Blues* with Langston Hughes. Mingus wrote several poems throughout his career, some of which were never meant to be accompanied by music. As a teenager, he had written "The Chill of Death"; when he finally recorded it in 1971, it featured a suitably ominous narrative style.[149] As we've seen, Mingus also worked on "The Clown" with Jean Shepherd, the sage who actually coined the phrase "Day People," a term that the Beats (and I) loved.

Jazz and poetry were an essential aspect of Beat culture. At least, that's the way Hollywood saw it. Of course, films—and television programs like

Peter Gunn—were primarily in the business of making fun of the Beats. Indeed, the years 1958 and 1959 were high watermarks for these representations. In *I Want to Live* (1958), *Bell Book and Candle* (1958), *Visit to a Small Planet* (1959), *The Subterraneans* (1960), and naturally, *The Beat Generation* (1959), we repeatedly see goateed men with berets wielding cigarette holders and reading poetry in dingy clubs with women who have ironed their hair. Invariably, a jazz performance is featured.[150]

What's missing from these films and from much of the coverage of the Beat Generation is the presence of African Americans. Before he was Amiri Baraka, Leroi Jones was a key figure in a group of writers that included Allen Ginsberg, Jack Kerouac, Lawrence Ferlinghetti, and Gregory Corso. In part II, I will compare Mingus with two overlooked black poets, Ted Joans and Bob Kaufman. Also missing from the standard account of the Beat moment is the influence of several black writers who are not usually associated with the Beats, especially James Baldwin. The Harlem Renaissance writers Sterling Brown and Langston Hughes were writing jazz-inflected poetry and poems about jazz long before it was fashionable for Beat poets to free-associate while someone improvised on the flute. *The Weary Blues,* the collection of poems that gave its name to the 1958 LP Mingus made with Hughes, was published in 1926.

LOCK 'EM UP

In the late 1950s, Mingus was becoming known as a legitimate bandleader as well as a virtuoso bass player, but his career was still held back by his reputation for being "difficult." His contract with the Willard Alexander Agency was not renewed. In 1958, shortly after their son Dorian was born, Celia walked out on the day of their seventh wedding anniversary. Looking for answers, Charles followed up on his interest in Freud and psychoanalysis and began seeing a therapist. In his first flirtation with the talking cure, however, nothing was working. He soon self-committed at Bellevue.

In *Beneath the Underdog,* he says that he was suffering from insomnia and that all he wanted was a good night's sleep. He attempted to talk the security guard in the "sentry-box" at Bellevue into admitting him, but the guard patiently tried to convince Mingus that he should turn around, go home, and get some sleep in his own bed. Mingus says that he spent more than seven hours trying to convince the guard that he needed help. Finally the guard relented. "He was a big black man and he still spoke polite when he opened the gate and told me to come in. As soon as I got to the second door I could sense the difference—like 'Surprise, stupid! We been waiting on you, a real special case!' My friend the guard said, 'Bill, here's that crazy one,' and two big white guys in white coats, six-footers, over two hundred pounds apiece, had me in a strait jacket before I knew it and I'm telling the guard, 'Maybe you were right, I don't feel so bad after all.'"[151] Once inside Bellevue, Mingus told the admitting physicians that he needed to sleep. He was given a pill. The next thing he knew, a dreadful ringing sound was waking him up at six in the morning.

In her memoir about Mingus, Janet Coleman wrote that he tried to organize the inmates so that they could pool their special talents and skills. But according to Charles, one doctor thought that all black men were paranoid and should be lobotomized.[152] "His request for a blackboard and a workroom was denied," Coleman wrote. "'May I comment,' said the doctor, 'that compulsive organization is one of the prime traits of paranoia.'"[153] Mingus's account of his self-commitment may be true, but Celia Mingus told Gene Santoro that Charles may have been hiding out from the gangster Joey Gallo, whom he considered hiring as his manager after his deal with Willard Alexander fell through. When Mingus discovered that Gallo was a killer and prone to ruthless behavior, he backed out of the deal.[154]

Nevertheless, a case can be made that Mingus was mentally ill. My guess is that he suffered from bipolar disorder or what used to be called manic depression. He had the symptoms: insomnia, sudden violent behavior, and intense bursts of creativity alternating with periods of depression and suicidal thoughts. He was also prone to grand but unattainable plans as well as dramatic changes in body weight, all common symptoms of bipolar disorder.[155] This is of course just a guess. Even qualified clinicians know better than to diagnose from a distance. And there is no information in the Mingus Collection at the Library of Congress that alludes to mental illness. But Mingus was in and out of institutions on several occasions, and he spent many years taking mood-altering, thorazine-like medications in the years before doctors began giving lithium to patients with his symptoms. In spite of the jokiness that Mingus injects into his account of Bellevue in *Beneath the Underdog*, he may have decided that he was in genuine need of psychiatric help. Remarkably, he continued to create great music and just a few years later displayed startling self-knowledge in his autobiography.

After his friend Nat Hentoff went to work to get Mingus released from Bellevue, he came out with a new sense of determination: he would manage himself. He soon met a beautiful blonde painter named Diane Dorr-Dorynek—the inspiration for "Diane," a song that Mingus himself said was the prettiest thing he ever wrote.[156] She became his publicist and personal assistant. Together they moved into an apartment on East 76th Street. This may have been the period when he was associating with the pimps and prostitutes who populate so much of *Beneath the Underdog*. Mingus apparently told some friends that he intended to "turn Diane out," in other words, to put her to work as a prostitute.[157]

DYNASTIES

After the *Tijuana Moods* sessions, Mingus made two memorable LPs for the Bethlehem label, *East Coasting* and *A Modern Jazz Symposium of Music and Poetry,* both released in 1957.[158] *East Coasting* featured the brilliant pianist Bill Evans almost a year before he joined the Miles Davis band and recorded *Kind of Blue,* the best-selling jazz record in history. Both Bethlehem LPs featured trumpeter Clarence Shaw during his brief tenure with Mingus. There was also a third LP for Atlantic Records, this one called *Blues and Roots,* with several more servings of the gospel-infused music for which Mingus had shown a penchant with "Haitian Fight Song."[159] "Wednesday Night Prayer Meeting" is his most successful attempt to fuse the old Sanctified Church with jazz. *Blues and Roots* also contained "My Jelly Roll Soul," one of Mingus's first tributes to Jelly Roll Morton, especially appropriate at a time when Charles was obsessed with pimpdom. Like Mingus, Morton led small bands with big ideas and claimed to have had close relationships with prostitutes. Morton also bragged that he was the true inventor of jazz.

Mingus had contacted Teo Macero shortly after his month in Bellevue. They had played together during the days of the short-lived Jazz Composers Orchestra, and Macero had recorded as a saxophonist for Mingus's Debut label. By 1957, Macero was producing records for Columbia. His projects included Dave Brubeck's *Time Out* (1959) and Thelonious Monk's first album for Columbia, *Monk's Dream* (1963), as well as records by Miles Davis, Duke Ellington, Count Basie, and Louis Armstrong. Macero produced Mingus's *Mingus Ah Um* in 1959, the same year that Columbia released *Kind of Blue.* It was also the year of John Coltrane's *Giant Steps* and Ornette Coleman's *The Shape of Jazz to Come.* Americans were paying little attention to jazz in 1959; most were watching TV shows like *Bonanza* and *The Twilight Zone,* going to see films such as *Ben-Hur* and *Some Like It Hot* at movie houses, and worrying about Fidel Castro establishing a Communist government in Cuba. But for jazz aficionados, 1959 will always be an *annus mirabilis.*

Mingus Ah Um was recorded in two sessions with seven players, one of the many small big bands with which Mingus made wonderful music.[160] Along with the essential Richmond and Knepper, Mingus worked with three saxophonists, John Handy, Booker Ervin, and Shafi Hadi (Curtis Porter), all of whom had been or were in the process of becoming regular Workshoppers. He also brought in pianist Horace Parlan, a bebopper who later made a series of compelling LPs for the Blue Note label in spite of a partially paralyzed right hand. Some familiar tunes were reworked for the session, including "My Jelly Roll Soul," which was now simply "Jelly Roll." Mingus cried out loud on the rousing "Better Git It in Your Soul," which in a 1963 recording became slightly different as "Better Get Hit in Yo' Soul."[161]

In addition, "Fables of Faubus" made an inauspicious debut. Columbia would not allow Mingus to recite the words to his attack on Orval Faubus, the governor of Arkansas who refused to integrate the Little Rock public schools. The lyrics made it onto vinyl only the following year, when the song was recorded for Candid Records, where Nat Hentoff was putting together a jazz series. For me, the most compelling composition on *Mingus Ah Um* is "Self-Portrait in Three Colors." I can't help connecting this piece with the first words of *Beneath the Underdog:* "In other words, I am three." I will have more to say about this connection in part II.

In 1959 Mingus's relationship with Diane was dissolving, and she left before the end of November 1959, when Mingus was recording his second LP with Columbia. The chaos of his personal life had led Mingus to seek institutionalized help in 1958, and in 1966 he would fall into a severe depression that kept him away from recording studios for more than four years. But at least in November 1959, Mingus was able to put aside his inner demons and record yet another remarkable LP, *Mingus Dynasty*.[162] Many consider it even more significant than *Mingus Ah Um*. Perhaps in an attempt to keep Diane from leaving, Mingus made certain that the first tune his tentet recorded was "Diane," made even lovelier by a piano solo by Roland Hanna.

Mingus Dynasty also included two reverential Ellington tributes, "Things Ain't What They Used to Be" and "Mood Indigo," as well as "Far Wells, Mill Valley," a love letter to his old friend Farwell Taylor. Mingus's tenure with Columbia ended shortly after this important session possibly because of conflicts with Teo Macero. Others suspect that John Hammond, Columbia's legendary producer of Billie Holiday, Bob Dylan, and Bruce Springsteen, decided it was time for Mingus to go. Charles would later refer to Hammond as "John Ham-Head" and accuse him of lying about the sales of Mingus's records.[163]

Just after Mingus lost his Columbia contract, he reencountered Eric Dolphy, another of the musicians who was essential to the sound of a Mingus unit. Dolphy grew up not far from Mingus in Los Angeles, and he had played in a large band with which Mingus briefly recorded in 1949. In

1959 Dolphy joined the Jazz Workshop and became part of the band that was working regularly at a New York club called the Showplace. This group also included the trumpeter Ted Curson, drummer Dannie Richmond, and pianist Jaki Byard. The Showplace group regularly featured "conversations" between Mingus and Dolphy.

If the solos of Ornette Coleman recalled the sound of a human voice, Mingus and Dolphy took it to the next level by literally speaking to each other with their instruments. Both succeeded brilliantly in recreating the cadences of human speech in their improvisations. Dolphy's solos were often speeded-up versions of what Charlie Parker had been playing, and Mingus knew it. But he paid Dolphy a high compliment when he said that at least in his ability to make conversation on his instrument Dolphy was more advanced than Bird.[164]

Early in July 1960, Mingus was in Newport, Rhode Island, organizing an "anti-festival" at nearby Cliff Walk Manor to protest the exclusion from the main festival stage of young jazz innovators as well as some of the older, legendary figures from the music's past. Mingus felt that George Wein, who had been at the helm of the Newport Jazz Festival since 1954, was motivated more by commerce than by anything to do with jazz. The purpose of the "Newport Rebels" event was to feature many of the progressive artists who did not fit in with the more commercially viable musicians at the official festival. To publicize the alternative festival, Mingus rode around in the back of a convertible, standing up holding his bass, and shouting at passersby.[165]

There are photographs of Mingus playing with Ornette Coleman at Cliff Walk, but alas, no recordings. Later, however, Mingus recorded an LP called *Newport Rebels* with his friend Nat Hentoff as producer. The "Rebels" included elder statesmen Roy Eldridge on trumpet and Jo Jones on drums, along with Knepper and Dolphy. The pianist for the date was Tommy Flanagan, who accompanied John Coltrane on his breakthrough recording of "Giant Steps," and who would record with Coleman Hawkins and the traditional jazz clarinetist Pee Wee Russell within the next few months. By the time of his death in 2001, Flanagan was regarded by many as the premier jazz pianist of his generation.

The Newport anti-festival was one of many projects that Mingus undertook in hopes of wresting control of the music away from club owners, record producers, and all the others who were making themselves rich off the labor of jazz artists, especially black artists. The founding of Debut Records and Jazz Workshop, Inc., as well as a subsequent plan to open a School of Arts, Music, and Gymnastics, were all evidence of Mingus's entrepreneurial spirit, and part of his lifelong effort to reconcile his aspirations as an artist with his career in the jazz industry.

The concert at Cliff Walk Manor was intended to become an annual event, but like so many of Mingus's grand projects, that did not happen. The event did, however, have other gratifying consequences. In 1962, Mingus and Max Roach performed on the main stage at the Newport Jazz Festival. Mingus was even invited to participate in a panel discussion at the Festival called "The Economics of the Jazz Community." In an important book on the interactions between jazz artists and their critics, John Gennari wrote: "Charles Mingus, Max Roach, and the other rebels were not *just* registering their impatience with a patronage arrangement they deemed condescending or unjust; they were trying to find a serious audience for an artistically adventurous and intellectually challenging music. It was for this reason, in fact, that Mingus and Roach insisted that their effort was less a rebellion than a vindication of Newport's original mission."[166] When Gennari interviewed George Wein many years later, Wein even suggested that he had supported the rebel festival.[167]

A few days after the Newport rebellion, Mingus took Dolphy, Curson, Richmond, and Booker Ervin to the Juan-les-Pins Jazz Festival in Antibes, France. Always fond of working out his ideas on the piano, Mingus moved back and forth between the bass and the keyboard with this group. When they recorded "I'll Remember April" at Antibes, Mingus invited Bud Powell to sit in with the band. Powell was now living the expatriate's life, playing with French musicians. He was still very sick, but he rose to the occasion when he joined the band of his former sideman.[168]

Back in New York, Mingus's tenure at the Showplace came to an end when he arrived one night to discover that his bass had been damaged. He responded by pulling the strings out of the club's piano. At about this same time, Charles called up Gene Lees, the editor of *Down Beat*. In his account of the phone call, Lees does not say what he or his magazine said, but it was enough for Mingus to call him a "dirty white motherfucker" and abruptly hang up. Mingus called back a few minutes later to apologize for his outburst. He then tried to explain in calm, reasonable terms why he was so upset. But in doing so, he became progressively angrier. By the end of the call, he was cursing and hung up again. A few minutes later, he called back for another attempt at apology but again worked himself up to the point of name-calling and a third abrupt hang-up.[169]

Mingus was still "jazz's angry man," but as Lees's story indicates, he had enough self-awareness to know when he had gone too far. In the months just after Diane Dorr-Dorynek left, he found a new female companion, and in his version of their first conversation, he reveals another level of self-knowledge. Judy Starkey was a blonde, twenty-one-year-old nursing student when she met Mingus, and although he was surrounded by women at this time, he definitely favored her. An intense but brief courtship led to marriage in March 1960. Toward the end of *Beneath the Underdog,* Judy is the woman Mingus meets after he flees from an intense ménage with Lee-Marie and a white woman he calls Donna.

In the typescript of the autobiography, Mingus identifies "Donna" as Ina Nesbitt and talks about the time they lived together while she was working as a prostitute. In the published version, he reencounters his first love, Lee-Marie, after he has fallen in love with Donna. When Donna and Lee-Marie hit it off and begin sharing the duty of meeting Charles's economic and sexual needs, he renames them "Donnalee," recalling a composition by Charlie Parker. (In the typescript, Ina and Mary Ellen become "Inella.")

Judy, who appears in the final pages of *Beneath the Underdog,* seems to provide a way out of an arrangement that had been keeping him away from his true love, music. Unlike his first wife, Jeanne, who is called Barbara in the autobiography, and his second wife, Celia, who is not mentioned at all, Judy is identified by her real name. Mingus, the narrator of a sometimes fantasized memoir, tells Judy that he should have become a full-time pimp and never tried to make a living from music. He then would have made sure that he played music only for fun and for friends from the "raceless set." He also tells her that he would never get involved with a woman who talked about "love." But no sooner does Mingus categorically denounce love than he has Judy laughing because "she doesn't believe a word of it."[170]

It's difficult for me to decide if this passage—so typical of Mingus's practice of changing his mood, and his music, on a dime—reflects real regret or an ironic recognition of his own mercurial personality. Scott Saul sees the passage as practically a guide to how *Beneath the Underdog* should be read. For Saul, we should all be like Judy when we listen to his stories. "Mingus is often appreciated best, most generously, when we challenge him back and refuse to take him at his word."[171]

Early in 1961, Mingus was back on the road, this time heading to London to appear in the film *All Night Long.* Mingus biographer Brian Priestley, who was living in London at the time, has chronicled some of Mingus's encounters with various Englishmen while he was working on *All Night Long* and playing in London clubs. One said that Mingus was highly sensitive about racial slurs, even when they might have been in his imagination. He was, for example, offended when people used terms like "black market" and "black mass" in polite conversation.[172]

But the film did bring Mingus into contact with another person who soon played a significant role in his career. The screenplay for *All Night Long* was co-written by Nel King. She had long admired Mingus's music, and she was instrumental in bringing Mingus to England for the filming. Mingus would later enlist her to edit *Beneath the Underdog*. The details of that collaboration are in part II.

WORKSHOPPING

Mingus's career always seemed most promising at the beginning of the decade. Fresh out of high school in 1940, he was sitting in with elite Los Angeles musicians at Billy Berg's clubs. In 1951, he arrived in New York with Red Norvo, started up Debut Records, and began gigging regularly at New York's hippest clubs. In 1960, he was touring with his own groups and selling enough records to catch the attention of the Shaw Artists Corporation, who also contributed to the careers of Miles Davis, John Coltrane, Ornette Coleman, and Art Blakey. After he shook off his depression at the end of the 1960s, everything seemed to be falling into place. In the single year of 1971 he made one of his great Columbia records, his autobiography was published, and he won a prestigious Guggenheim Fellowship. But the years in between were seldom as successful.

Although Mingus led some great bands in the 1950s, the Jazz Workshop was at its peak in the early 1960s. Two new hires reveal much about Mingus's imagination as well as his skills as a talent scout. In 1961, the blind, surrealist multi-instrumentalist Rahsaan Roland Kirk joined the Workshop. Like Eric Dolphy, another master of several reed instruments, Kirk knew the history of the music and honored it, but he was not afraid to venture into the ether during his improvisations. Kirk was born premature and needed extra oxygen to survive, even though it meant severe damage to his corneas. Because he could "see" best when he was dreaming, he made the most of his visions. Although his birth name was Ronald, he moved the letters around to become Roland after the idea came to him in a dream. In 1970, he acquired the new first name Rahsaan following another oneiric revelation.

Kirk also said that he invented the manzello and the stritch after he saw them in a dream. Essentially, he modified an alto saxophone and a soprano saxophone and gave them new names. He would hang these inventions around his neck along with an unmodified tenor saxophone and play them all at once. It was not a gimmick. Kirk was literally a one-man saxophone section. One of his signature effects was to play the three horns simultaneously and then blow an exclamation point on the whistle he also kept around his neck. Mingus saw tremendous potential in Kirk, at one point saying that he would be "my Frankenstein."[173] When the Mingus sisters were asked about the musicians their brother had admired, they singled out Kirk in particular.[174]

Another extraordinary artist whom Mingus brought into the Workshop in 1961 was Toshiko Akiyoshi. A few months earlier, Mingus had begun playing piano on stage and farming out the bass parts to Henry Grimes or Doug Watkins. For a while he liked being his own pianist, but he soon realized that he was also the ideal bassist for his bands. When he began hiring pianists again, one of the first was Akiyoshi, a brilliant Japanese musician and composer who learned about jazz from American GIs in the 1940s. In 1952, Oscar Peterson heard her while club-hopping during a tour of Japan. He brought her to the attention of his agent, Norman Granz, who recorded Toshiko with Peterson's rhythm section. In 1956 she became the first Japanese student ever to enroll at the Berklee School of Music in Boston.

Akiyoshi was briefly married to Charlie Mariano, the alto saxophonist who delivers an affecting impression of Johnny Hodges on the album *Mingus Mingus Mingus Mingus Mingus*. Since 1969, she has been married to the saxophonist and flutist Lew Tabackin, co-leading with him a big band that has consistently made great jazz out of Toshiko's unique combinations of African American and Asian musics. She was gigging around New York in 1961 when Mingus brought her into his band, and she was a regular Workshopper for the next nine months. In interviews, Toshiko has self-deprecatingly suggested that Charles hired her because she was a new face and would get attention as the only Japanese woman anyone had ever seen playing jazz. But there is no question that she brought a vibrant new energy to the band's live performances.[175]

Akiyoshi's tenure with Mingus did not end well, however. According to trumpeter Ted Curson, Mingus once closed the piano while she was playing, smashing the cover on her fingers. He told her she was playing too much like Bud Powell. Curson said, "He could have ruined her whole career. It sure broke her spirit."[176] Regardless, Toshiko and Mingus remained friends right up until the end, and she visited him during his last days in New York. With their big band, Akiyoshi and Tabackin recorded a tribute album, *Farewell to Mingus*, shortly after his death.[177]

GREAT ENCOUNTERS

Mingus was making great music in the 1950s and early 1960s, but in 1962 the masterpieces began to flow. One, a collaboration with Duke Ellington and Max Roach, was the album *Money Jungle*.[178] The session may have reflected a moment in Ellington's career when he was reaching out to his peers, many of them the *éminences grises* of the jazz world. Or perhaps Duke was succumbing to the pressure of producers who wanted to sell "all-star" recordings. In any case, there were some memorable sessions. In 1961, Duke brought his band into the studio with Count Basie and his orchestra for a raucous session that resulted in a Columbia release.[179] In the same year, his management worked out an agreement with Louis Armstrong and his manager Joe Glaser for some recordings that required neither musician to suppress his ego: Duke would play with Louis's working band, but they would only play Ellington's compositions.[180]

In 1962, Bob Thiele, who produced the Ellington/Armstrong collaboration, signed Duke for two extraordinary impulse! sessions, first with Coleman Hawkins, who in the 1920s practically invented the saxophone as a jazz instrument, and then with John Coltrane, who took the art of improvisation to a new level in the 1960s.[181] Neither artist, however, had any difficulty finding a place in the Ellington universe.

On September 17, 1962, one month after the Hawkins session and nine days before the Coltrane session, Ellington recorded with Mingus and his old sparring partner Max Roach. Mingus had not recorded for almost a year—a real shame because his working group at the time included Akiyoshi on piano, Charles McPherson on alto saxophone, Booker Ervin on tenor, and the essential Dannie Richmond at the drums.

The *Money Jungle* session with Ellington, Roach, and Mingus was organized by Alan Douglas, who in 1960 had been hired by United Artists Records to run their jazz division. During his relatively brief career at UA, Douglas produced a superb LP with vocalist Betty Carter, as well as albums that matched Bill Evans with Jim Hall and Jackie McLean with Kenny Dorham.

Douglas's career changed dramatically when he met rock guitarist Jimi Hendrix in 1969. He wanted to move Hendrix toward jazz-oriented projects, and Hendrix seemed to be enthusiastic about new collaborations. Douglas was organizing recording sessions that teamed Hendrix with Miles Davis and Gil Evans when Hendrix died in 1970. For several decades after the guitarist's death, Douglas took previously unreleased Hendrix material and rerecorded his voice and guitar with studio musicians to create what he considered superior presentations of Hendrix's music. The purists in Hendrix's substantial fan base were, of course, scandalized. When Douglas died in 2014, he was still promoting the legacy of Jimi Hendrix with an unfinished documentary film, *Starting from Zero*.

At the *Money Jungle* session, Ellington introduced himself to Mingus and Roach with his carefully constructed pose of humility, telling them, "Think of me as the poor man's Bud Powell." (This was nine years after the Massey Hall concert in Toronto when Mingus and Roach formed a trio with Powell.) But Ellington's pose did not last long. He completely dominated the session, forcing Mingus and Roach to reach deep into their skill sets. He surely challenged them in a way that he did not challenge John Coltrane nine days later—you can hear Coltrane playing at his comfort level throughout that session.

The Ellington/Mingus/Roach album received a mixed reception. When Miles Davis heard a segment of the album in a 1964 blindfold test, he said, "That's ridiculous. You see the way they can fuck up music." He added that the musicians were badly mismatched: "Mingus is a hell of a bass player, and Max is a hell of a drummer. But Duke can't play with them, and they can't play with Duke."[182]

Mingus himself became dissatisfied during the recording session and left the studio. Duke says that he went after Mingus and flattered him into coming back to finish, pointing out that United Artists had taken out a full-page ad in *Billboard* for Mingus; if Columbia had treated him as well, he observed, he would not have left the label.[183] There is no evidence, however, that Duke explained why "Caravan" was on the set list. The tune was written by Juan Tizol, who was involved in Mingus's dismissal from the band, and its inclusion may have been another element in Ellington's strategy for dominating the session.

Nevertheless, Ellington knew that great music was happening and that its continuation merited some delicate handling of Mingus. The session produced several minor masterpieces, most especially Ellington's delicate composition "Fleurette Africaine." Duke was not necessarily engaging in hyperbole when he called the trio's work "one of those mystic moments when our three muses were one and the same."[184] However, Duke certainly made them accommodate his vision of what the music should be.

Mingus's relationship with Ellington was always complicated, and we will likely never know exactly what was said after the bass player's 1953 encounter with Juan Tizol when Duke arranged for Mingus's dismissal. It's quite possible that the conversation reported in *Beneath the Underdog* never took place. There are also several accounts of what happened at the *Money Jungle* session. In an interview with John F. Goodman, Mingus said that he walked out because he hated the way Roach was patronizing Duke by playing in the old-timey style of drummers like Zutty Singleton.[185] For Mingus, Duke was not trapped in some time warp that made him incompatible with contemporary musicians.

Roach gave his side of the story in an interview with National Public Radio.[186] He said that many critics and journalists had come to Soundmakers Studio in New York to witness an event that was, to quote one of the tunes the three recorded, "Very Special." The atmosphere was festive, and liquor was flowing. According to Roach, a slightly inebriated Mingus became irritated by the stride bass line that Ellington was doling out with his left hand, which was interfering with Mingus's own lines. He then began cursing and stormed out of the studio, bass in hand. In Roach's account, Ellington did not go after Mingus right away, but had to be urged. Duke finally went to look for Mingus, who may have been sticking around in hopes that Duke would do what he eventually did—whisper in his ear and say, "Charles, you sound wonderful." According to Roach, Mingus began crying and brought his bass back into the studio. The demanding father figure brought Mingus to tears by suddenly becoming a nurturing spirit.

A bit more of the story comes from Ross Firestone, who spoke with Alan Douglas a few weeks after the *Money Jungle* session. In his office at United Artists, Douglas showed Firestone an envelope that had just arrived in the mail: Mingus was returning the thousand-dollar check he had been paid for the session. (According to Firestone, Roach also received $1,000, and Ellington was paid $3,000.) In the accompanying letter, Firestone explained, Mingus asked Douglas "to scrap the recording and do it over with just Ellington and himself. Charles was probably thinking of an update of the great Ellington/Jimmie Blanton duets of 1939 and 1940. But he was also still furious with Max Roach and told Alan that if he was set on using the trio format, he should bring in Mingus's regular drummer Dannie Richmond. And if Alan insisted on Max Roach, he should hire Ray Brown. 'He'll work with anybody for money,' Mingus wrote in his parting shot."[187] Ironically, Duke did indeed record duets with Ray Brown at a 1972 session for Norman Granz's Pablo label in which they recreated the music that Duke had originally made with Blanton.

WEEPING IN TOWN HALL

Shortly after the reunion with Ellington and Roach, Mingus had something of a windfall when Bob Thiele offered him an exclusive contract at impulse! Records. He even gave Mingus an extremely generous advance of $10,000, to be paid in regular installments. But the *Money Jungle* session was also followed by the unfortunate Town Hall concert of October 12, 1962. Mingus's anxiety about that upcoming event may explain in part his tendentious behavior with Ellington and Roach. He would later tell John

Litweiler that the *Money Jungle* date "ruined" his Town Hall concert; instead of recording with Ellington and Roach, he should have been home composing.[188]

When Mingus told Alan Douglas that he was preparing an ambitious program of new and old music to be played by an expanded big band, Douglas signed on to record the concert for United Artists. The music was to be an extension and expansion of material that Mingus had composed earlier, a summation of his musical career. (Ultimately, what he began composing for Town Hall would become the massive work *Epitaph*, which did not have its official premiere until ten years after his death.) The band for the Town Hall concert included seven trumpets, six trombones, ten reeds (including a classical oboist), a guitar, two pianos, two basses, and three percussionists. Impresario George Wein was brought in to co-produce with Alan Douglas. Mingus felt pressured to come up with elaborately composed music, and as the event drew closer, he felt increasingly unprepared and desperate. To make matters worse, Alan Douglas or someone at United Artists accepted an offer from Town Hall to move the date of the concert up by five weeks.[189]

When trombonist Jimmy Knepper was a member of the Workshop in the late 1950s, Mingus regularly relied on him to turn his scores into parts for individual musicians. Although Knepper admired Mingus and considered him a friend, he left the band in 1961 after Mingus made a series of nasty remarks about him, some directly from the bandstand. By an extremely unfortunate coincidence, Knepper stopped by to see his old boss a few days before the Town Hall concert, and Mingus hired him on the spot to copy out parts. (Knepper had beautiful handwriting, and Mingus had actually paid him to copy out parts when he was a member of the Jazz Workshop.) As Mingus was handing piles of music to Knepper and at least two other copyists, time continued to slip away. Knepper was not producing at the rate Mingus wanted, and when Charles also asked him to compose figures for the band to play behind soloists, he refused. In response, Mingus punched Knepper in the face with such force that he knocked out a tooth. Knepper subsequently brought charges (see part IV.)

With the Town Hall concert imminent, Mingus's psychotherapist, Edmund Pollack, began making regular visits to Mingus's apartment, always without remuneration. Mingus also sought solace from his childhood friend Buddy Collette. Although the band already had ten reed players, including Eric Dolphy, Charlie Mariano, Charles McPherson, Zoot Sims, Pepper Adams, and Jerome Richardson, Mingus told Collette that he needed him in the section as well. "I can't do it unless Buddy is here," Collette recalls him saying.[190]

At a midnight rehearsal the night before the concert, Mingus tried to teach the musicians some background figures by singing them. This method worked for the Workshoppers, who were used to it. But the enormous band that was about to perform at Town Hall needed written music. Shortly before the performance, Charles told Wein to advertise the program as a rehearsal rather than a concert, and he then surprised everyone, most notably Wein, by telling the audience they could get their money back if they had come expecting a concert.

On the night of the performance, some of the music was being put in front of the musicians for the first time while copyists continued working just offstage. Mingus, who had not slept for two days, stopped and started the band on several occasions and frequently apologized to the audience. By the intermission, Gene Santoro writes, Mingus was "inconsolable, crying and raging."[191] At least a hundred audience members asked for their money back.

As the concert drew to a close and Mingus fled from the stage, trumpeter Clark Terry invited the band to join him in a rendition of "In a Mellotone," a tune that Duke Ellington had written in 1940 using the chord changes from the old standard "Rose Room." Terry had sat in the trumpet section of Duke Ellington's orchestra from 1951 until 1960, but he knew no one on stage would have difficulty playing "In a Mellotone." They all joined in. Even Mingus returned to the stage. By midnight, those in the audience were happy they had not left. Terry and baritone saxophonists Pepper Adams and Jerome Richardson took well-received solos, but when trombonist Britt Woodman started his solo, two stagehands began closing the curtains, in accordance with union regulations. After some booing, the audience departed.[192]

But the band did not go home with the audience. As the reissued and expanded CD of the Town Hall concert revealed when it was released 1994, the band stayed around for at least another seven minutes to record an alternate take of "Epitaph, Part One," a piece they had performed earlier in the concert. In fact, much of the music on the CD sounds substantially better than legends about the concert would lead us to believe. In spite of the last-minute hysteria, Mingus did compose a great deal of music for the program, and the band played it beautifully. When *Down Beat* reviewed the LP that was released a few months later, the reviewer gave it a full five stars. Even so, Alan Douglas lost his job because United Artists was unable to pull together more than thirty-six minutes of music for the LP. Six months went by without United Artists paying Mingus what he had been promised, and he sued the company for $18,000.[193]

MASTERPIECES FOR IMPULSE!

A few days after the Town Hall event, Mingus's third wife, Judy, gave birth to a stillborn child. At the same time, the Cuban missile crisis had put the world on the verge of a nuclear holocaust. Mingus was working regularly in clubs, but events during the last months of 1962 had taken their toll, and he was suffering from bleeding ulcers. He left New York with Judy to visit his old friend Farwell Taylor in California. Willingly submitting to a dietary regimen devised by Taylor, Mingus lost twenty pounds and began feeling better, even inspired. When he returned to New York in early 1963, he began preparing the music that he would record for impulse!, music that places his work deep in the heart of the jazz canon.

The first impulse! session was on January 20, 1963. On that single day, Mingus and ten sidemen recorded all of *The Black Saint and the Sinner Lady* and a bit of what would become *Mingus Mingus Mingus Mingus Mingus*. The latter LP was also remarkable for the overdubbing of some of Charlie Mariano's solos. At Mingus's direction, Mariano recorded his solos on "I X Love" and "Celia" a week after the eleven-piece band had finished their recording session.[194] On first hearing, Mariano's alto is sufficiently foregrounded to give the impression that he is soloing in front of an ensemble. But once you know the solo was dubbed in later, you can hear patterns being played by Quentin Jackson's trombone and the reeds of Dick Hafer and Jerome Richardson that could easily stand alone.

Overdubbing was not a novelty in 1963. Ten years earlier, working with Rudy van Gelder, Mingus had overdubbed a new bass line for the recording of the Massey Hall concert with Parker, Gillespie, Powell, and Roach. But with the impulse! recordings, Mingus took what was a finished piece of music, rethought it, and then added a new voice that greatly enhanced the first take. By contrast, overdubbing was hardly the result of second thoughts when Les Paul, Buddy Holly, and the Beatles planned on using the process from the outset.

Mingus was delighted with *The Black Saint and the Sinner Lady*. To make his new album even more distinctive, he asked his psychotherapist, Edmund Pollack, to write the liner notes. The vast majority of therapists at that time would have refused such an invitation, citing the profession's ethics and its proscriptions against what have become known as "boundary violations." But Pollack contributed a long essay in which he tried to connect the man with the music on *The Black Saint and the Sinner Lady*.[195] He emphasized Mingus's predicament as a black man in America and mentioned that he had been charged with assault (by Jimmy Knepper) and locked up in Bellevue. Mingus learned something from all this, wrote Pollack, and he was still trying to "heal." Pollack also said that Mingus was essentially "inarticulate in words" and that he had turned to music to express himself. The author of *Beneath the Underdog* and a great deal of poetry and lyrics can hardly be called "inarticulate"; Pollack was probably referring to the conflicted, perhaps tongue-tied patient who was trying to make sense of his life during their sessions.

In his essay, Dr. Pollack revealed perhaps as much about himself as he did about Mingus. As contemporary musicologists point out, music may not essentially mean anything, but it is extremely easy to *make* it mean something.[196] Pollack assigned some very specific meanings to Mingus's music, stating: "There can be no question that he is the Black Saint who suffers for his sins and those of mankind as he reflects his deeply religious philosophy." In the keening alto saxophone solo of Charlie Mariano, Pollack heard a voice crying, "I am alone, please, please join me!" At the conclusion of his essay, Pollack remarked that Mingus "is still in a process of change and personal development. Hopefully the integration in society will keep pace with his."[197]

Mingus was fascinated by psychoanalysis even before he arrived at the office of his therapist, but Dr. Pollack's influence is evident in the psychoanalytically inflected version of his own story in *Beneath the Underdog*, which he was writing at about the same time that Pollack was putting together his liner notes. However, as I argue in part II, Mingus was not so sure that the various aspects of his personality could ever be integrated into one.

At least at first, *The Black Saint and the Sinner Lady* did not sell well. To make matters worse, shortly after recording wrapped up Mingus had to go to court to defend himself against Jimmy Knepper's charges of third-degree assault. Mingus's long-time friends Britt Woodman and Buddy Collette testified as character witnesses. So did Pastor John Gensel, the "jazz priest" who was celebrated by Duke Ellington as "The Pastor of the Night Flock" and who had recently baptized Mingus and Judy's daughter, Caroline. Woodman admitted to being reluctant and uncomfortable when he testified that Mingus was a gentle man who "wouldn't hurt a fly."[198] Mingus was convicted of assault but with a suspended sentence. However, he lost his cabaret card, which meant he could not perform in New York night clubs for several months.

During what should have been his glory days, therefore, Mingus spent a great deal of time at home, manically writing the first draft of what became *Beneath the Underdog*. He was having trouble sleeping—a condition that had led him to Bellevue five years earlier—but this time he put his insomnia to use. Judy typed the 870 pages of his autobiography while playing housewife and cooking enormous meals for Charles and any guests who might stop by.

During the months that he was banished from the club scene, Mingus also spent more time than ever playing the piano. He made home recordings of some of this music, a portion of which can be heard on reel-to-reel tapes that his widow Sue Mingus gave to the Library of Congress in 2007. Sometimes the music on the tapes suggests that Mingus is simply doodling, perhaps to take his mind off his troubles. At other moments, he is clearly working out ideas and seems to forget that the tape machine is still rolling. Regardless, his time with the piano paid off.

On June 30, 1963, he went back into the studio to make another impulse! LP, this time all by himself. On *Mingus Plays Piano* he exhibits very little of the splashy technique that many of his peers in the world of piano jazz regularly brandished.[199] Instead he makes use of space and dynamics to bring passion and intensity to his solos. Not surprisingly, he shows a preference for lush ballads as well as for jazz standards such as "Body and Soul" and "I Can't Get Started." The piece on the LP of which Mingus was most proud is "Myself When I Am Real." The tune appears first on the LP and may refer to Mingus's self-explorations with Dr. Pollack. It also supplies the title of Gene Santoro's exhaustively researched biography of Mingus.

A few months later, he was back in the impulse! studios to record the rest of the music that would appear on *Mingus Mingus Mingus Mingus Mingus*.[200] With the exception of a few changes in personnel, it was the same eleven-piece band that had recorded *The Black Saint and the Sinner Lady* earlier in the year. One important addition to the band was Eric Dolphy, then on the verge of another brilliant, if brief, tenure with Mingus. Once again, Mingus's music was extraordinary, and once again the sales were not good. Shortly after *Mingus Mingus Mingus Mingus Mingus* was released, producer Bob Thiele found a knife stuck in the chair in his office. On the blade of the knife was a note: "Where the fuck is my money? MINGUS."[201]

Toward the end of 1963, Judy was pregnant again, and Mingus had moved into a hotel. Although they did not divorce until 1970, that marriage was over. So was the life of President John F. Kennedy, believed by Mingus to have been assassinated by the CIA and the Mafia. And in 1964, his autobiography was rejected by McGraw-Hill, despite a contract signed in 1962.

There was some good news, though. When *Down Beat* published its annual poll of jazz critics in August 1963, Mingus was listed first among bass players, replacing none other than Ray Brown, who had won the award for the past five years. Mingus would win the jazz critics' award for three more years. In 1967, the award went to Richard Davis; by then, Mingus was no longer recording and seldom performing.

TOWARD THE "FIRST BAND"

By the end of 1963 Mingus and his Workshop were in clubs again, but he was unable to sustain the larger orchestra he had brought into the impulse! studios. His working band was a sextet, though he regularly invited guest stars to sit in. In early 1964, when he was playing at the Five Spot, Sonny Rollins, Coleman Hawkins, Illinois Jacquet, and Ben Webster all stopped by to play with the Workshop. Sadly, most of these cameo appearances were not recorded, but the sound of the Jazz Workshop is well documented for a crucial period in the spring of 1964. A sextet with Dolphy, Richmond, pianist Jaki Byard, trumpeter Johnny Coles, and tenor saxophonist Clifford Jordan was recorded at a Cornell University concert, an appearance at Town Hall, and then in multiple bootleg recordings from a European tour that George Wein organized in April (figure 5).[202]

The music from April 1964 is all over the place and consistently intense, in spite of or perhaps because of the tempestuous relationships that Mingus had developed with both Byard and Dolphy. You can already hear the tension between Dolphy and Charles on their long exchange during the 1960 recording of "What Love," originally issued on the Candid label.[203] Byard was of the same generation as Mingus and had already been a bandleader in his own right. He knew the Western classical repertoire as well as he knew jazz and was one of the few musicians other than Charles who was comfortable playing in any style—boogie-woogie, swing, bebop, avant-garde, or ironic combinations of them all. As Philip Clark notes, Byard played as though he had James P. Johnson's left hand and Bud Powell's right.[204] Byard's devotion to exploring all of jazz history, sometimes in a single performance, was shared by no one except Mingus, who even encouraged him to insert some old-style stride piano into his improvisations.

As a sign of his respect, Mingus always made sure that Byard had good pianos, even during the European tour when the band played numerous venues. Since Byard had some facility with the string bass, he would occasionally play Mingus's instrument while Charles switched to piano. Nevertheless, the two often quarreled, for example when Mingus objected to Byard's quotation of the Negro national anthem, "Lift Every Voice and Sing," during several moments of a long solo performance in "Fables of Faubus." In a certain regard, it was a brilliant idea to insert some uplift into

Figure 5. Charles Mingus (bass) with Clifford Jordan (tenor sax), Eric Dolphy (bass clarinet), and Dannie Richmond (drums), Paris, 1964. Photograph © Guy Le Querrec, courtesy of Magnum Photos.

a song that ridiculed a notorious racist. But Mingus thought Byard was ridiculing the civil rights movement and told him he didn't like it. Eventually, Charles came around to understanding what the pianist was trying to accomplish. Byard even says that Mingus himself later quoted the song on his bass.[205]

The widely recorded European tour of April 1964 was fraught almost from the beginning. Just a few days into the tour, trumpeter Johnny Coles, who had recently undergone an operation, collapsed. He went directly to a hospital, where he would remain for two weeks. Each night of the subsequent gigs, Mingus placed Coles's trumpet on an empty stool to symbolize his absence.

Before one concert, Mingus confiscated a fan's tape recorder and smashed it. (With so many bootleg recordings emerging after the tour, Mingus had every right to be paranoid.) Someone painted a swastika on the door to Eric Dolphy's hotel room. At another hotel, Charles broke down doors and had to be restrained by police when he pulled a knife. In Copenhagen, Mingus had a reunion with the great tenor saxophonist Ben Webster, who soon settled in Copenhagen and spent the rest of his life there. When Mingus showed Webster the ten shirts he had bought in a Copenhagen store,

Webster told him that he had been overcharged. Mingus went back to the store with a bodyguard and staged an incident that wound up in the newspapers. Worst of all, Eric Dolphy told Mingus that he intended to stay in Europe when the tour was over.

Back in New York and without Dolphy, Mingus was playing regularly at the Five Spot, one of the city's best clubs. In *Beneath the Underdog*, Mingus wrote (referring to himself in the third person): "These days Charles feels wholly free and not only as good as any white people but better than most and he's found a musical home, a place to play for people who really seem to want to hear."[206] The Five Spot was run by the Termini brothers, Joe and Iggy, both of them devoted to uncompromisingly progressive jazz artists. They regularly booked single artists for months, even years, at a time. Thelonious Monk, Cecil Taylor, Ornette Coleman, and Mingus were all in residence during the club's glory days in the early and mid-1960s.

Even though he loved playing there, Mingus brought his residency at the Five Spot to a dramatic end. At the end of June, he received the devastating news that Eric Dolphy had died in Germany. A few nights later, he began yelling at a woman sitting up front who was talking during his set. He swept the glasses off her table, left the stage with his bass, and walked into the club's kitchen. A few seconds later, he threw his bass back out through the kitchen door. When it landed on the floor, he smashed it with his foot. He later apologized to Iggy Termini, telling him, "Maybe it's time to end the job."[207]

The relationship between Mingus and Dolphy had been especially intense, and the loss affected Charles powerfully. At the funeral, Mingus wept and cried out, "I'm sorry, Eric!"[208] Judy had just given birth to a son; they named him Eric Dolphy Mingus.

ENTER SUSAN GRAHAM

In July 1964, shortly after Dolphy's death, Mingus met Susan Graham Ungaro when she showed up one night at the Five Spot. Sue had grown up in Milwaukee, the daughter of wealthy, eccentric parents—though not too eccentric to present her at a debutante ball when she turned eighteen. She attended Smith College and then left for Paris, where she worked in the editorial department of the *New York Herald Tribune*.

I cannot help but think of the American actress Jean Seberg in the film *Breathless* (1960) hawking copies of the *Herald Tribune* on the streets of Paris. Of course, Seberg's character was simply selling the paper, while the real-life Sue was editing it. But like Sue, Seberg was from the Midwest, from Marshalltown, Iowa. When Seberg briefly lived in Paris, she caught the eye of fledgling director Jean-Luc Godard, who cast her in his break-through film *Breathless* opposite matinee idol Jean-Paul Belmondo. Sue Graham and Jean Seberg were in Paris at roughly the same time; both were young beauties with high cheekbones and capacious eyes; and both married European men. Seberg would chart a difficult career path when she returned to Hollywood, dying at the age of forty under mysterious circumstances after the FBI targeted her because of her association with African American radical groups.

Sue Graham also became involved with a radical African American man, but she has lived a long and rich life. Shortly after arriving in Paris, she married the Italian painter and sculptor Alberto Ungaro. They briefly set-tled in Rome, where they had two children. They then moved to the New Jersey countryside and ultimately to New York, where their marriage began to come apart. As would eventually be the case with her and Charles, Sue and Alberto saw each other on and off in the years before Alberto's death in 1967.

Sue and Charles married in 1975, and they remained together when Mingus died in 1979. She has written compellingly of the life they shared in her memoir, *Tonight at Noon: A Love Story.*[209] Taking its title from one of the many clever song titles in the Mingus canon, *Tonight at Noon* is invaluable on multiple levels. For one thing, it provides a detailed account of Mingus's final struggle with amyotrophic lateral sclerosis. It also reveals how Mingus romanced Sue and, by extension, how he might have won the affections of the many women who populate his memoir.

After a few brief but auspicious conversations at jazz clubs, Sue and Charles ran into each other by accident at an even more auspicious event, a Shakespeare in the Park production of *Othello*. Sitting together, they watched the black Othello love and then kill the white Desdemona. It must have been an amazing night, if only because no less than James Earl Jones played Othello. (Perhaps equally amazing, though, was the fact that two years earlier Mingus had appeared in *All Night Long*, Basil Dearden's film that recasts Othello as a black jazz pianist and Desdemona as a white singer.) After the performance, Charles walked Sue to the Plaza Hotel, one of the few places where he believed a black man had a better than average chance of hailing a taxi. Taxi drivers, he said, assumed that anyone standing in front of the Plaza must be rich—even if they weren't white.

Once in the cab, Charles took Sue to the famous whispering gallery outside the Oyster Bar in the lower level of Grand Central Station. By an acoustical quirk, words spoken on one side of an arch can be clearly heard at the other end, even if whispered. Standing at the opposite end of the arch from where he placed Sue, Charles whispered that he loved her and that he wanted her to be his woman.[210]

Very soon after that performance of *Othello*, Sue went to work at Charles Mingus Enterprises. Like Debut Records, this was another project that Charles hoped would release him from servitude to the "Holding Corporation Called Old America," as he put it in one of his compositions. Sue continued working for Charles even when their romance boiled over into anger and violence. She would effectively become his manager as well as his literary agent.

In 1965, although Sue was still married to Alberto and Charles to Judy, the two were "married" by Mingus's old friend Allen Ginsberg. When Mingus and Sue were attending a gathering at the home of the heiress and bohemian socialite Peggy Hitchcock, Mingus ran into Ginsberg, whom he had met in the 1950s when both were inevitable presences anywhere that jazz and poetry were being created. "Marry us," he said on the spot. Ginsberg immediately picked up two small Indian cymbals and struck them together in his palms as he chanted "Hare Krishna Hare Rama" over and over again. "A long time after he looked up and smiled," Sue recalls. "The ceremony was over."[211]

But Ginsberg's ceremony did not bring Sue and Charles any closer, at least not in 1965. After several breakups and reconciliations, Sue and her children moved into an apartment on West 87th Street. Charles managed to rent an apartment in the building directly across the street. He filled it with all sorts of light bulbs, wires, and timing devices. For weeks he staged elaborate light shows for Sue, delighting many in the neighborhood, some of whom put thank-you notes in Mingus's mailbox. She described the light shows: "Sometimes they splattered bright, rude, and incessant through the dark. Other times he gently staggered the rhythms of his bulbs. He invented fresh images, sacred and obscene: shining crosses, ejaculating phalluses. And all the while, beneath the wild activity of his window, the conductor lay concealed in his bunker behind the sill."[212]

During these early, stormy months of their relationship, Charles composed a tune he called "The Taming of the Sioux." When his sidemen Howard Johnson and Jimmy Owens told him that the phrase was insulting to their Native American brother and sisters, he changed the title to "They Trespass the Land of the Sacred Sioux."[213] Assuming that Sioux is in some ways a reference to Susan Graham, then we have an excellent example of how Mingus the poet could work out his ambivalence toward a lover with nothing but song titles. If at some point he felt that Sue must be "tamed," at another point he felt as if he was "trespassing" when he got too close. Or that she regarded herself as a sacred being. Or any number of other possibilities that the two titles suggest when placed in chronological order.

When Sue and Charles were together, Mingus would sit at the piano and talk to her about his first love Mary Ellen and how he found solace from a single chord he played on the piano. "I was caught in his struggle now, no longer outside, trapped in the middle of his vast appetites and imagination, his sexuality, his angry intelligence, his nonsense and his pain."[214] I am intrigued that Mingus would tell Sue about Mary Ellen. (In *Tonight at Noon*, Sue identifies her as Mary Ella. Although the typescript of Mingus's autobiography refers to her as Mary Ellen, the Mingus sisters also call her Mary Ella.) Regardless of how much myth Charles sowed into his account of his long relationship with Mary Ellen, there is no question that she had a powerful and lasting effect on him. His willingness to talk about her with Sue at an early stage in their relationship also says something about his need for honesty and openness.

Two months after Mingus and Sue watched *Othello* in Central Park, Mingus and his group were back home in California, where he experienced one of his first great triumphs, at the Monterey Jazz Festival. A crowd of more than seven thousand rose to their feet to cheer the twelve-piece ensemble when it concluded a rousing performance of "Meditations on Integration." Ten years later, Mingus would take a portion of the composition and transform it into his greatest tribute to Susan Graham, "Sue's Changes."[215] The music from Monterey was soon released on Mingus's own label and marketed with ads in newspapers, including one ad in the form of a cartoon.[216] "People will read it if it looks like the funnies," he told Sue.[217]

MEET RALPH ELLISON

On September 10, 1965, Mingus had an encounter with Ralph Ellison, a consistently erudite commentator on jazz as well as the author of what is arguably *the* Great American Novel. According to Mario Dunkel, Mingus "cherished" Ellison's *Invisible Man*,[218] but when he read the novel just after it was published in 1952, Mingus could not have guessed that Ellison did not like much of jazz after the arrival of the boppers, whom he called "amateurish."[219]

Ellison definitely knew about Mingus. In 1957, his friend Albert Murray—a novelist and critic every bit as devoted to jazz as Ellison and every bit as wary of bop and its aftermath—described Mingus for Ellison in a letter. Referring to him as a "young mose," meaning a generic African American man, and calling his fans "fay"—short for "ofay," a contemptuous term that blacks used for whites—Murray wrote: "The young mose who keeps the fay boys all shook these days is a bass fiddle player named Charles Mingus, who can out talk, out analyze, out intellectualize, and out fiddle just about anybody around. His best stuff is straight out of Duke, of course, but he also seems to out conservatory all the post-boppers and Juilliarders and Milhauders together. He is really the wildest Academician going these days."[220] I do not know to what extent Ellison shared Murray's view of Mingus in 1957, but as the host of a television program about contemporary jazz in 1965, he seemed to be coming to terms with Charles's Juilliardering and Milhaudering.

Broadcast from the Village Gate, a showcase for jazz in Greenwich Village where Mingus had played more than once, the program, titled "The Experimenters," was an episode in the series *USA: Music,* a production of National Education Television (NET) shortly before it became the Public Broadcasting Service (PBS). The jazz writer Martin Williams also appeared on the show, though he scrupulously avoided engaging with jazz except as a set of stylistic variations. He even managed twice to refer to Mingus as "Charlie." Ellison, however, was magisterial, intellectual, and much more expansive about the culture in which jazz had developed and thrived. What was surprising was that the program featured groups led by Mingus and Cecil Taylor. I cannot imagine how the executives at NET convinced Ellison to present the post-bop band of Mingus and the aggressively avant-garde music of Taylor. Equally mysterious is why they chose such challenging artists, even in a program called "The Experimenters."

From his youth until his death, Ralph Ellison was devoted to Duke Ellington, Charlie Christian, Jimmy Rushing, and most especially Louis Armstrong. In the first pages of *Invisible Man,* Ellison pays tribute to Armstrong when the unnamed narrator says he would like to have five phonographs in his underground lair, all of them simultaneously playing Armstrong's version of "What Did I Do to Be So Black and Blue?" Later Ellison would tell Robert G. O'Meally, "My strength comes from Louis Armstrong."[221] And this at a time when Armstrong was widely regarded as an Uncle Tom by most black Americans.

For Ellison, who played the trumpet as a young man, Armstrong was not simply the genius who invented the art of the jazz soloist. He saw Armstrong as the quintessential American trickster, who knew much more than he let on when he performed. Mistaken as a clown, Armstrong could be, as Ellison suggests, invisible and thus free to take his art in any number of directions without worrying about whether his fellow Americans considered him to be a "serious" artist. "He's made poetry out of being invisible."[222]

Mingus, of course, was never mistaken for a clown. And he had always disliked Armstrong's self-presentation. Mingus actually parodies the trumpeter's voice in his 1961 recording of "Eat That Chicken."[223] But Ellison and Mingus did have much in common when jazz was considered outside of an arena where artists and stylistic moments are judged. As Scott Saul puts it, for Ellison, "the wonder of cultural forms like jazz came in part from their resourceful blending of white and black idioms past the point where the two might be separated."[224] Mingus regularly expressed anger at white racism, and he frequently used the language of black nationalism, but he was also committed to integration. And like Ellison, he had always been intrigued by the prospect of erasing the separation between jazz and European classical music.

On "The Experimenters," with Mingus and his group in the background, Ellison tells the NET cameras that jazz "attempts to humanize the world in terms of sound" and to "impose an American Negro sense of time upon the larger society and upon the world of nature." He even acknowledges the value of jazz's new legitimacy as serious art, referring to "a musical route to social respectability and to a wide acceptance among the cult of jazz intellectuals." And in a statement that no doubt intrigued Mingus, he added that jazz musicians must strive to absorb Western traditions without losing touch with the origins of their own music. Even before jazz became the music of white intellectuals, Mingus had many positive interactions with these aficionados. If nothing else, his performance of *Revelations* at the Brandeis Third Stream event in 1957 was all about gesturing toward classical music without giving up his roots in the blues and the old Sanctified Church (see part III).

The Mingus group that appears on camera for the NET broadcast includes Charles McPherson (alto sax); Dannie Richmond (drums); Hobart Dotson, Lonnie Hillyer, and Jimmy Owens (trumpets); Julius Watkins (French horn); and Howard Johnson (tuba). They play ambitious music that Mingus may have written specifically for the program. Unlike earlier incarnations of the Jazz Workshop, the musicians are clearly reading music that has been laid out in front of them. The first piece is "The Arts of Tatum and Freddie Webster," a composition Mingus recorded only once, in 1965, when this same group played at Royce Hall at UCLA. The music was released on the self-distributed LP *Music Written for Monterey 1965. Not Heard . . . Played in Its Entirety at UCLA.*[225] "The Arts of Tatum and Freddie Webster" is especially memorable for Mingus's ingenious reference to Tatum—back-to-back quotations from Dvorak's "Humoresque" and Johnny Green's "Body and Soul," two of the tunes that Tatum regularly performed in his own dazzling fashion.

Later in the program Martin Williams introduces Cecil Taylor, who also makes no compromise for the television audience. In his first number, Taylor stands up from the keyboard and bends deep into the piano to strike the strings with percussion instruments. He prefaces his second number with a typically allusive prose poem, the conclusion of which deserves to be quoted in full: "The philosophical premise that this music is based on is that man begins a transliteration of the mean fact toward symbolic representation when mind and body move, recognizing their singularity, therefore their unity, and therefore their sanity. The question is, where the economic and social factor determining an artist exist, those which permit the expression of time through time to one whose consumption is unlimited or were they the producers for others? The name of the piece will be 'Octagonal Skirt and Fancy Pants.'" Taylor and his group—Jimmy Lyons on alto saxophone, Sunny Murray on drums, and Henry Grimes on bass—then play an intensely dissonant composition in which Taylor displays his muscular, quicksilver agility as a keyboard artist.

The NET program continues with Ellison speaking briefly about the meeting of European and black American experience as essential to the uniqueness of jazz, after which he reintroduces Mingus. In his final number, Mingus sits at the piano while his group plays an ominous preface. He then reads "Don't Let It Happen Here," his own adaptation of a poem by the German antifascist Lutheran pastor Martin Niemöller.[226] Mingus presented the composition with its narration on several occasions during the mid-1960s. Niemöller's German text can be translated as follows:

First they came for the Socialists,
and I didn't speak out because I wasn't a Socialist.
Then they came for the trade unionists,
and I didn't speak out because I wasn't a trade unionist.
Then they came for the Jews, and I did not speak out—
because I was not a Jew.
Then they came for me,
and there was no one left to speak for me.[227]

In his own version of the poem, Mingus substitutes Communists for Socialists and inserts a couplet about Catholics. He also adds, "I could say nothing because I was as guilty of genocide as those who killed the eighteen million people along with me." Mingus concludes by urging the viewer to speak out: "don't let it happen here."

It is difficult to imagine a major television network broadcasting this kind of politically charged material today. PBS is much too controlled by corporate money to allow any such thing. Even then, Mingus may have capitulated to a certain extent when he was on television. In the only other recorded version of the composition—from the Royce Hall concert at UCLA—he adds a few phrases: "I was as guilty of genocide as you, all of you, for you know when a man is free, and when to set him free from slavery. So I charge you all with genocide."

When I asked Howard Johnson, who played tuba on the program, if he spoke with Ellison when they were both on the set, he said, "No, he was more interested in Mingus."[228] It would be grand to know what Mingus and Ellison discussed that day in September 1965. In spite of their differences and in spite of the radical nature of Mingus's art, Ellison surely found him fascinating.

But it may not have been a good moment for them to have a serious discussion. For this was the beginning of a severe downward spiral for Mingus. Lack of work and the rapidly declining popularity of jazz were taking a toll on his financial and mental health.

DEPRESSION AND DECLINE

In 1966, when George Wein offered Mingus the opportunity to tour Europe with Max Roach and Sonny Rollins, he declined. Instead he chose to appear in a documentary film that was proposed to him by Thomas Reichman, the son of a New York doctor who was a serious fan of Mingus's music. Mingus had always been fascinated by the movies. He even worked as an extra on a few occasions when he was growing up not far from Hollywood in Watts. In 1962, in *All Night Long,* he briefly appeared as a slightly altered version of himself. And of course, he appeared on television in the NET program with Ralph Ellison and Cecil Taylor. By 1966 he had acquired a few ideas about how to play to the camera. The opportunity to display himself was apparently more attractive than the more remunerative tour with Roach and Rollins, especially because he was still at odds with Max Roach.

Mingus also knew that the film, released in 1968 as *Mingus,* would help him make the case that he should be treated as a serious artist and teacher rather than as an intruder being expelled from the loft where he was hoping to start up a school. In 1963, he had sought funding from Harlem Youth Opportunities Unlimited for another of his grandiose plans, a School of Arts, Music, and Gymnastics. He planned to bring in some of his colleagues from the jazz world to teach music and an ex-cop who had worked as his bodyguard to teach self-defense. Mingus was also hoping to enlist the services of his friend Katherine Dunham, perhaps the most eminent African American dancer of her time. The funding for the school did not materialize. In 1966, he moved many of his belongings into a loft in lower Manhattan on Great Jones Street, where he said he would again try to establish a school.

It is not clear just why Mingus was evicted from the loft on Great Jones. Mingus told John F. Goodman it was because the woman from whom he was subletting had not paid the rent.[229] In any case, Mingus received an eviction notice and was given a date when he would be required to vacate the premises. Thomas Reichman filmed Mingus surrounded by boxes in the loft the day before the eviction, and he came back with his cameras and sound equipment on the morning when the eviction actually took place.

Mingus was expelled on November 22, 1966, exactly three years after the Kennedy assassination. That event was clearly on Mingus's mind during the filming. In what may be the most memorable scene in the film, Charles fires a rifle into the ceiling of his apartment, for no apparent reason other than to impress the filmmakers. He holds up the rifle and says that it is the same model that killed Kennedy, then adds, "Or one of them. There must have been several." He has no skill with the rifle, however, managing to get a bullet into the chamber only after several awkward attempts. He tells Reichman that he acquired the gun because the loft had been burgled shortly after he moved in.

Knowing that the presence of a child makes for good cinema, Mingus also made sure that his four-year-old daughter Caroline, or "Keki," was present as the cameras rolled. She is an especially charming, even precocious child, listening to her father play the piano and reminisce about the days when he was well off, living on Fifth Avenue and driving a Cadillac. Caroline remarks that she wishes that she and her little brother, Eric, could go back there.

The one-hour documentary mixes in a bit of footage of Mingus and his group playing "Take the A Train," "All the Things You Are," and "Peggy's Blue Skylight" at a club called Lennie's on the Turnpike, outside Boston in Peabody, Massachusetts. Before the club burned down in 1971, it was an important venue for many established jazz artists. But it was a long way from New York City. In 1966, with jazz at a low point in American entertainment, fewer and fewer clubs were hiring jazz artists, since pop stars could bring in more paying customers.[230]

In Reichman's documentary, Charles was not exaggerating when he described his dismal financial state, especially in contrast to a few years earlier when he had regular employment in clubs like the Five Spot and contracts from Columbia and impulse! In the last sequences of the film, Mingus breaks down crying as his possessions are being carted away. We then learn that the police are taking him off to jail because they found hypodermic needles in the loft. Sue Graham is present in several scenes, including some shot before the eviction. In what was clearly a high point in their early history, Charles and Sue walk hand in hand through Central Park and Harlem. At the end of the film, Reichman's camera creates a striking image as it zooms in on the face of a devastated Sue, watching as Charles rides off in a police car. The camera then cuts to his bass, unattended and leaning against a bookshelf on the street. Although Charles and Sue appear to be a couple in Reichman's film, their relationship was still very much in flux. The light-skinned Carolyn, moreover, was Mingus's daughter by Judy and not Sue's child, as the film seemed to suggest.

After his arrest, Mingus was able to convince the police that the hypodermics were for vitamin C injections and that his gun was properly licensed. Fortunately for Mingus, no drugs were found in the loft. Mingus even tells the camera that he never used heroin: "That's not my style." But Mingus had been taking other drugs, most of them prescribed by doctors and designed to reduce psychotic behavior.[231]

After his eviction, he would not be in a recording studio again until 1970. At one point he spent three months in a hospital after a nervous breakdown, and he was taking a variety of mood-altering drugs during these years. Nat Hentoff, who remained one of Mingus's closest friends, wrote, "Mingus rarely appeared in public, and when he did his music was wearily retrospective. In the daytime I'd see him occasionally wandering around the lower East Side, uncommonly subdued, abstracted."[232]

Mingus was taking photographs during this period, and at moments he considered retirement. He thought he could live off the royalties from the catalog of Debut recordings that had been purchased by Saul Zaentz, the producer who had married Mingus's second wife, Celia. Zaentz had taken over Fantasy Records, an important jazz label in the 1950s and 1960s. Celia had almost singlehandedly kept Debut records going for several years, and Mingus knew it. He was not at all reluctant to sell the entire catalog to Zaentz, even granting him the right to issue material that Mingus had previously tried to distribute on his own. The music that Celia and Saul Zaentz purchased became one of the sacred documents of jazz history when all of it appeared in 1990 as *Charles Mingus: The Complete Debut Recordings*. In the 1960s, however, royalties from the Debut catalog could not even pay Mingus's rent.

If Mingus played at all, his heart was not in it. On the bandstand he gave up his voluble, sermonizing stage persona and asked Dannie Richmond to announce the tunes. But Charles turned a corner in April 1969 when he was invited to the University of California at Berkeley to attend a seventieth birthday celebration for Duke Ellington, still the musician he most admired. Ellington must have known that Charles needed help because he announced that he would play Mingus's "The Clown," with Duke himself narrating.

Ellington seldom programmed the work of other jazz composers, and so far as I can tell, Mingus himself had not performed "The Clown" since the Atlantic recording of 1957. Although Ellington invited Mingus to conduct the orchestra, he ended up hiding in the balcony, still not well enough to face an audience or his idol.[233] Ellington, however, was game. He led the band *and* performed the narration. The unusual amount of attention that Duke directed toward the man and his music helped lift Mingus out of his depression, at least temporarily. His recovery was gradual.

A DUKE ELLINGTON FELLOW

In 1970 Mingus played the Jazzmobile, a series of concerts held in various locations throughout the five boroughs of New York. The Jazzmobile had been presenting the best jazz artists since 1964, but this was the first time Mingus had been aboard. He was surprised to see so many young people at the concert who were genuinely enjoying themselves. He later told Nat Hentoff that even though he had been warned that kids in central Harlem would not like his music, he went ahead and "took it as far as I could."[234] To his delight, the kids wanted more. Mingus said that this experience gave him the title for his great 1971 LP, *Let My Children Hear Music.*

With new energy, Mingus toured Europe in late 1970 and Japan in 1971. Shortly after he returned from Japan, he appeared with Rahsaan Roland Kirk on *The Ed Sullivan Show,* a Sunday night television program popular since the early 1950s. Sullivan had introduced his massive audience to Elvis Presley and the Beatles, not to mention an assortment of comedy acts, classical musicians, ventriloquists, circus performers, and so forth. Kirk, meanwhile, was one of several musicians in an organization called the Jazz and People's Movement. In an effort to get more jazz on television, the group had already disrupted *The Tonight Show* and *The Dick Cavett Show* by approaching the stage and protesting the programs' neglect of jazz artists. The brass at CBS may have been sympathetic when Kirk complained that the Sullivan show had been neglecting black artists for far too long, but it's more likely that they wanted to avoid a similar disruption. The deal was sealed when the talent coordinator said that he was a fan of Kirk's version of the Stevie Wonder tune "My Cherie Amour." Sullivan's people told Kirk that he would have five minutes to play the song on air.

CBS should have seen trouble brewing when Kirk arrived with the outspoken tenor saxophonist Archie Shepp along with Mingus and drummer Roy Haynes. According to Kirk's biographer, Rahsaan grew excited just before the band went on camera, shouting, "We're gonna burn the place down."[235] Once the band was on stage, they did not play "My Cherie Amour" but instead launched into a raucous version of Mingus's celebration of slave rebellions, "Haitian Fight Song." Perhaps coincidentally, perhaps not, *The Ed Sullivan Show* went off the air a few weeks later, ending its twenty-three-year run.

Shortly after the *Ed Sullivan Show* appearance, Mingus joined the Jazz and People's Movement in picketing the John S. Guggenheim Foundation. Although that organization had been generously funding artists and educators since 1925, jazz musicians were seldom among the beneficiaries. It is unclear whether the Guggenheim people heard the protests or if their grant-giving policies were actually affected. Nevertheless, the foundation awarded a grant to Mingus less than a month later. He immediately went to work writing music, some of which he recorded for *Let My Children Hear Music*. In a sense, this LP was everything that the Town Hall event of 1962 was meant to be. Once again featuring a large jazz orchestra—this one augmented by cello, French horn, three pianos, and three basses—the LP presented old and new music, much of it as adventurous as anything Mingus had ever written.[236]

The drummer on *Let My Children Hear Music* was Dannie Richmond, the one artist on whom Mingus had depended for an extended period of time. Richmond had only been playing drums for six months when he became Mingus's drummer in 1956. The rapport between the leader and his drummer was virtually telepathic from the start. But as so often, there were conflicts; Richmond was often in trouble for drug use and ceased to be Mingus's regular drummer late in 1970. He later played with several pop groups, most notably a jazz-inflected soft-rock band called Mark-Almond (see part IV).

In the same year, 1971, that Mingus appeared on *The Ed Sullivan Show*, won a Guggenheim, and recorded *Let My Children Hear Music*, the African American choreographer Alvin Ailey took nine of his tunes, had them arranged for full orchestra, and presented the music with dancers at New York's City Center. The year ended with Mingus being elected to *Down Beat*'s Hall of Fame, a rare acknowledgment for a living artist. But the most significant event of 1971 was the publication of his memoir, *Beneath the Underdog: His World as Composed by Mingus*. No other jazz artist had ever written anything so unbridled, so confessional, and so erotic. Regardless of whether we regard the book as fiction, nonfiction, or some hybrid, it gives us a much more complex Mingus than the music alone could ever reveal.

By 1972 he was flourishing. He was no longer on medication. The Whitney Museum of American Art invited him to set a poem by Frank O'Hara to music. A comeback party with a big band playing old and new music at Lincoln Center's Philharmonic Hall in February, with no less than

Bill Cosby as master of ceremonies, was a success.[237] Another European tour followed in August with a front line of Dizzy Gillespie's pupil Jon Faddis on trumpet and Charles McPherson and Bobby Jones on saxophones. McPherson had been with Mingus since 1965 and was the only musician other than Dannie Richmond who stayed close to Mingus during his years of depression. Bobby Jones had joined the band early in 1971 but did not stick around long. During one performance, Mingus pelted him with onions and cucumbers, and later he threw him down a flight of stairs at Ronnie Scott's club in London.[238] After these and similar outbursts, Faddis and McPherson left too. Mingus was fortunate that great artists like Dizzy Gillespie, Ben Webster, and Dexter Gordon were all either passing through or residing in many of the cities on the tour, and each took a moment to sit in with Mingus's band.

Although he had seemed securely on the road to recovery only months earlier, Mingus suffered another breakdown after this European tour. After an evening of bar-hopping, he took off his clothes in Central Park and began throwing hundred-dollar bills into the air. The police knew a man in need of hospitalization when they saw one, and they took him to a Mt. Sinai facility, where he remained for at least a week.[239]

At this moment in September 1972, Sue believed that she had definitively ended her relationship with Charles. Nevertheless, Mingus had given her telephone number to a psychiatrist at the hospital where he was institutionalized. The psychiatrist called to tell Sue that Charles was concerned about a paper bag. Mingus could remember precisely the name of the bar— the Kettle of Fish on McDougal Street—where he had left the bag. Sue dutifully made her way to the bar, where the bartender told her that he remembered the bag and that he had moved it to a hat rack. There it was, looking rumpled and unimposing. Inside was $10,000 in cash.[240] Mingus was never too depressed or manic to lose track of his finances.

Some might argue that Mingus was still not *compos mentis* later in 1972 when he played at a Yale event organized by Willie Ruff. Mingus was one of the nearly forty distinguished jazz musicians designated Duke Ellington Fellows at a ceremony that October. At a concert during the event, Mingus was on stage with Ray Brown, Milt Hinton, George Duvivier, Joe Benjamin, and Slam Stewart, all of them playing string bass, jamming with saxophonists Benny Carter, Lucky Thompson, and Sonny Stitt. In the midst of joyous improvisation, a police captain came backstage to announce that someone had called in a bomb threat.

Everyone left the concert hall except Mingus. He continued to play his bass alone on stage. When the police insisted that he evacuate along with everyone else, he said, "I'm staying right here! I've got to die sometime, and it ain't ever gonna get better than right now. Racism planted the bomb, but racists ain't strong enough to kill this music; if I'm going to die, I'm ready. But I'm going out playing 'Sophisticated Lady.'"[241] He continued playing alone for the next twenty minutes before the bomb scare was declared a false alarm and the concert resumed. According to Willie Ruff, Charles played beautifully. Duke Ellington was there, standing close enough to the open doors to hear him perform what was surely his most dramatic tribute ever to Duke's music. Ruff says that Ellington was smiling.[242] In his own larger-than-life, death-defying fashion, Mingus had repaid Duke for the well-timed 1969 invitation to Berkeley to hear Ellington play Mingus's "The Clown." He was also repaying Duke for inspiring him over the decades as no one else could. And Mingus was finally resolving a troubled father-and-son relationship that had lasted almost twenty years.

TOWARD THE "SECOND BAND"

By 1972, both Mingus and jazz had survived the late 1960s. He was again making a good living.[243] But it was not because he was reaching out to a larger audience like so many other jazz artists in the early 1970s with their electrified instruments and elephant-footed backbeats. When Mingus hired baritone saxophonist Hamiet Bluiett to join his band, he was reaching out to one of the more uncompromising members of the jazz avant-garde. After he left Mingus, Bluiett would become best known for his work with the World Saxophone Quartet, a collection of four saxophone colossi who seldom if ever played with a rhythm section. Since 1977, Bluiett has been providing a smooth and steady bass line beneath that long-lasting band's twists and turns. With Mingus he often played in the upper register of his instrument when he soloed, squealing as aggressively as the most outré reedmen. But Bluiett had a special appeal for Mingus because he could also quote from older forms of jazz, often with the same parodic spirit that Mingus exhibited in tunes like "My Jelly Roll Soul" and "Eat That Chicken."

Perhaps to balance the extremes of Bluiett, Mingus also hired trumpeter William "Cat" Anderson, for many years the high-note specialist with Duke Ellington's band. When a number ended with an impossibly high note from Anderson's trumpet, Ellington would tell the audience, "That last note was a high C above Hyannis Port." But like Bluiett, Anderson knew his jazz history—born in 1916, he had after all been part of it. When Anderson played with Mingus, he seldom screeched in the stratosphere, instead building his solos in the middle register where he could smear notes and talk with a plunger mute in ways that recalled Cootie Williams and King Oliver.

In 1973 Mingus began putting together what may have been his greatest quintet, and most certainly the best band he led during the last decade of his life. Most crucially, Dannie Richmond returned to the band that year. Mingus then hired pianist Don Pullen and the tenor saxophonist and vocalist George Adams, artists with powerful ties to the avant-garde. Strangely enough, in that same year Mingus published "An Open Letter to the Avant-Garde" in *Changes,* the art and politics tabloid that Sue was editing.[244] Just as he had been profoundly suspicious of bebop thirty years earlier, Mingus now charged that many of the avant-garde musicians of the late 1950s and early 1960s were unable to play with the discipline of their predecessors and thus not entitled to play a music free of structure and tonal patterns. Nevertheless, Don Pullen would frequently abandon rhythm and melody and attack the piano with the same intense energy as Cecil Taylor, and George Adams would regularly squeal hysterically through his saxophone. But both musicians had powerful lyrical streaks as well, they knew the blues, and they had a real talent for seamlessly cycling from gentle to fierce and back again. And Adams could sing the blues with as much panache as he exhibited on the tenor sax.

Just as he was highly ambivalent about the music of Ornette Coleman, Mingus may have had mixed feelings about the excesses of Adams. Early in 1974, Mingus brought his group into Carnegie Hall. A portion of that concert was issued on the Atlantic LP *Mingus at Carnegie Hall.*[245] Mingus's former sideman and comrade-in-arms Rahsaan Roland Kirk was a guest artist. Kirk took a solo shortly after George Adams had blown a few choruses of avant-garde excursions. As Mingus later said, Kirk began "listening his ass" when Adams was soloing. When it was his turn, Kirk started his solo by parodying Adams and then took the music in a direction well beyond what Adams had attempted. According to Peter Keepnews, "Mingus grinned like a rotund Cheshire Cat through the whole thing."[246] Nevertheless, Adams stayed with Mingus for several years and never restrained himself when he felt the need to play "outside."

The final member of the distinguished quintet was trumpeter Jack Walrath, who signed on in 1974. He had graduated from the Berklee School of Music, one of the best places to learn jazz technique, and he subsequently took apprenticeships with Ray Charles and various Latino bands. Walrath was less flamboyant than Adams or Pullen, but he was one of those artists who constantly reinvented himself on the bandstand, never playing the bebop clichés that drove Mingus to distraction. He seemed to have a positive effect on both Adams and Pullen, and like them, Walrath was able to

Figure 6. Charles and Sue Mingus, New York, spring 1969. Photograph by Teppei Inoguchi, courtesy of Sue Mingus.

follow the elaborate musical alchemy that took place between Mingus and Dannie Richmond.

Mingus was now leading a band that would stay together throughout the last months of 1974 and nearly all of 1975. This quintet would record *Changes One* and *Changes Two,* LPs that contain some of the best music Mingus ever composed as well as solos as exciting as anything he had recorded since the departure of Eric Dolphy in 1964.[247] Dannie Richmond said that if the 1964 band with Dolphy, Jaki Byard, and Clifford Jordan was "the first band," the 1975 quintet was "the second band."[248]

Significantly, at the same time that he was keeping a first-rate band together for more than a few months, Mingus was finally settling into comfortable domesticity with Sue (figure 6). According to Santoro, Mingus had become much less the womanizer, in spite of the fact that he was on the road almost constantly.[249] When Charles was home, he got along well with Sue's son, Roberto. He would soon compose "Sue's Changes," a song with some of his most beautiful writing (as well as some of his most cacophonic). When Charles and Sue were "married" by Allen Ginsberg in 1965, both were still married to other people. But in August 1975, after Sue was widowed and Charles had divorced Judy, the two were married at City Hall. The many years of fights, brief reconciliations, and long silences had finally found a resolution.

Mingus had always been on the heavy side, and his eating habits could be prodigious. As the poet William Matthews put it,

> You could say, I suppose, that he ate his way out,
> like the prisoner who starts a tunnel with a spoon . . .[250]

Charles would eat a huge steak for lunch, follow it with a half-gallon of ice cream, and then go out for a multi-course "snack" at a Chinese restaurant. At one point he weighed more than 300 pounds. But there were numerous moments throughout his life when he dropped down to a more normal weight. In 1964, when he was filmed with a large band in Toronto by the Canadian Broadcasting Corporation, he was slim and vigorous, smiling as he led the band with his bass.[251] Add the slightly suggestive body language with which he played his instrument, and you can see why so many women found him intriguing. He was much heavier two years later when he appeared in Tom Reichman's documentary film, *Mingus*.

In one of his many efforts to lose weight, Mingus teamed up with the comedian and activist Dick Gregory, a veteran of many hunger strikes who had learned how to stay healthy with practically no solid food. At Gregory's health farm in Plymouth, Massachusetts, people could lose two pounds a day—in a month, that's sixty pounds. According to Dannie Richmond, Mingus stuck with Gregory's regime for a week. But when he heard that Rahsaan Roland Kirk had a gig in Boston, he told Gregory that he'd drive down for the night and return the next morning. Next to the club in Boston was a Chinese restaurant. Richmond said that "Charlie saw it, hesitated for a moment, then walked in. He didn't come out for a week."[252] Perhaps because of his weight, he began to have physical problems. More ominously, his hands and feet were numb, and in 1975 he was hospitalized with back trouble.

In 1976 he worked with flamenco dancers he had met through Ysabel Morel, who played castanets and sang on the *Tijuana Moods* LP. Mingus had honored her by writing "Ysabel's Table Dance" for that record. When the dancers performed to his music at Carnegie Hall, Mingus was so pleased that he leapt on stage and danced with them during the curtain call. The audience gave him a standing ovation. This could have been the beginning of a prolonged series of similar triumphs, but it was not to be. In August and September of 1976, during a European tour, he began showing signs of exhaustion and weakness. It was probably the first evidence that he had acquired amyotrophic lateral sclerosis, the disease that would lead to his death in January 1979. Not knowing that they were adding pathos to a moment that should have been one of pure triumph, Nesuhi Ertegun and Raymond Silva of Atlantic Records offered him a lucrative contract that was exceptional for a jazz musician without a portfolio of hits. The contract allowed for the bigger orchestras with which Mingus had recorded so memorably. But Atlantic also wanted more marketable music.

In March 1977, a large group of musicians was in the studio when Mingus recorded new versions of "Goodbye Pork Pie Hat" and "Better Git It in Your Soul," old tunes that were as close to hits as anything he had ever written. Although Mingus would never have allowed it even a year earlier, the electric guitarists Philip Catherine, John Scofield, and Larry Coryell recorded with his regular band at these Atlantic sessions. A new composition by Mingus, "Noddin' Ya Head Blues," was also dominated by the electric guitarists.[253] Although they played with great skill, the plugged-in guitarists turned the tune into the kind of straight-ahead, feel-good blues with which the typical rock 'n' roll fan could feel comfortable.

Mingus was on tour when *Three or Four Shades of Blues* was assembled track by track from the several recording sessions. He was either too sick or too distracted to pay much attention. When the LP was released, Mingus hated it.[254] Soon, though, it outsold all his other LPs by a comfortable margin. While the superior *Changes* LPs never sold more than 10,000 copies in their first few years, *Three or Four Shades of Blues* sold 50,000 copies in just two months.

Although recorded mostly at the same sessions as *Three or Four Shades of Blues*, the LP *Cumbia and Jazz Fusion* was a different story.[255] Presenting another chapter in Mingus's romance with Latin music, the title track, which took up an entire side of the LP, represented some of Mingus's most ambitious composing. Thanks to the largesse of the Erteguns and Silva, the Mingus small group was expanded to include flute, oboe, bassoon, and a quartet of Latin percussionists. Jimmy Knepper made a guest appearance and took a typically virtuoso solo on trombone. There were no electric guitars. The band played a music that was inspired by cumbia, a genre of Latin music that emerged from songs and dances of Colombia and Argentina.

As so often in his music, Mingus did not stay in the cumbia groove for long. Toward the end of the long composition, he began singing an old minstrel tune, "Shortnin' Bread." The original lyrics present stereotypical black folk singing in pidgin English: "Put on de oven an' putt on de led / Mammy's gwineter cook som shortnin' bread." Mingus revised the lyrics, telling us that "Mammy's little baby" likes caviar and truffles. Several members of the band contributed vocal statements recalling the minstrel travesty Mingus recorded in 1961 with "Eat That Chicken." What any of this has to do with cumbia is never explained, but this may be an especially good example of how Mingus Music can have a logic of its own.

The flip side of the *Cumbia and Jazz Fusion* LP is "Music for *Todo Modo*," *Todo Modo* being an Italian film directed by Elio Petri and featuring such well-established stars as Gian Maria Volonté, Marcello Mastroianni, and Mariangela Melato. Released in 1976, the film was a dark satire of Italian politics in the mid-1970s when the ruling Christian Democratic party was in an unholy alliance with entrepreneurial forces within the Catholic Church. None of Mingus's music made it into the film, despite an opening section that, recalling the first minutes of *Revelations* (1957), suits the ominous segments with which Petri's film begins. But, typically, whatever is happening at the beginning of Mingus's composition bears little resemblance to what happens later, in this case some straight-ahead swinging with solos by George Adams on tenor and flute, Dino Piana on valve trombone, and Mingus vibrantly on bass.

Mingus's arranging for the ensemble sections of "Music for *Todo Modo*" is as brilliant as ever, but this was not what the filmmakers wanted. The music that is heard throughout the film ended up being composed by Ennio Morricone. An extremely busy composer in the Italian film industry, Morricone is best known for the signature music he wrote for the "spaghetti westerns" of Sergio Leone, a few of which crossed over to American screens in the 1960s with the presence of Clint Eastwood. As of this writing, Morricone has 525 credits on the Internet Movie Database (www.imdb.com).

THE DIAGNOSIS

Sometime in early 1977 Mingus began walking with a cane. It was becoming difficult for him to play his bass, and in another dramatic departure from his old ways, he began using electronic amplification so that his weakening fingers would not have to exert as much force on the strings. His doctors were not certain what was wrong with him, and many in his circle thought that he simply needed to lose weight and get some rest. Even though Mingus was now stipulating that any venue where he played must have an electric amplifier for his bass, Sue booked an ambitious tour of Europe and South America for May, June, and July 1977. On tour, he seldom soloed, and he regularly yielded center stage to his sidemen. His audiences were larger than ever before and consistently enthusiastic. But by the end of the tour, on at least one occasion he was unable to get out of bed.

The last time Charles Mingus was recorded playing bass was late in 1977 at a session put together by his old employer Lionel Hampton.[256] Saxophonist and arranger Paul Jeffrey, who worked regularly with Mingus during his last years, created arrangements of Charles's compositions for a group that included not just Hampton's vibraphone but also two trumpets, three saxes, and a French horn. Mingus wanted to include a composition he had recorded on one of the *Changes* LPs, "Remember Rockefeller at Attica." The title referenced the disastrous handling of a prison revolt when Nelson Rockefeller was governor of New York. Rockefeller's reckless decision to send state police into a situation that could have been resolved without force resulted in the deaths of many inmates as well as prison guards. Hampton was not only a lifelong Republican; he was also friends with Rockefeller. Mingus told Hampton that the tune was called "Just for Laughs." Jeffrey's arrangements for the session capture the old Mingus tonalities and melodies, and the solos by guest artists Woody Shaw and Gerry Mulligan, not to mention Lionel Hampton, are superb. That session took place on November 6, 1977. On November 23, Mingus was diagnosed with ALS.

As of this writing, public awareness of amyotrophic lateral sclerosis may be at its highest thanks to an extremely successful campaign called "the ice-bucket challenge": videos of people dumping ice water on their heads to raise ALS awareness that went viral on Facebook. Hundreds of thousands of people who may never have heard of ALS until recently are contributing funds to sponsor research into the disease. The connection between a crippling disease and a cold water dousing is unclear, but the results of the challenge are making serious research toward a cure much more possible.

The illness is commonly known as Lou Gehrig's disease, after the baseball Hall of Famer Lou Gehrig (portrayed by Gary Cooper in the 1942 film *Pride of the Yankees*) who succumbed to ALS in 1941 at the age of thirty-seven. Chairman Mao Tse-Tung, Senator Jacob Javits, the actor David Niven, and the blues singer Leadbelly all died of ALS as well.

One way to understand ALS is through the etymology of its medical name. In ancient Greek, an "a" before a word makes it negative, as in *atheist.* "Myo" is from the Greek word *myon,* meaning muscle, and "trophic" is from *trophe,* or nourishment. A muscle without nourishment "atrophies," or wastes away. "Lateral" is Latin for belonging to the side, in this case the places along the length of the spinal cord where cells that control muscles are located. With ALS, the cells near the patient's spine atrophy and die, as do the brain cells that send messages to the spine telling it to activate muscles. The affected areas along the spine begin to congeal, developing "sclerosis," from the ancient Greek word *sclerotes,* or hardness. The disease progresses slowly, first resulting in weakness in the muscles. As the body gradually loses its ability to activate the muscles, the victim has difficulty moving, talking, swallowing, and breathing. Complete paralysis often precedes death when the body's essential functions shut down.

Although the windfall in the research budget after the success of the ice-bucket challenge is a cause for hope, there is still no known cause or cure for ALS. Doctors have only been able to develop drugs that slow the progress of the disease. Every case of ALS is different in terms of which areas of the body are most affected and in what order they begin to atrophy. Stephen Hawking, the theoretical physicist and author of the 1988 best-seller *A Brief History of Time,* has survived since the late 1970s with ALS, but he is completely paralyzed and can communicate only with the help of a speech-generating device.

As of this writing, there is no record of anyone recovering from the disease and regaining control of their muscles. Sooner or later, the patient dies, usually from respiratory failure. To make matters even more complicated, the disease is difficult to diagnose. This was the case in 1977 when it struck Mingus. Then as now, patients are almost always approaching full paralysis when an accurate diagnosis is made. Most cruelly, the mind remains fully alive, as do the eyes and ears. Gene Santoro summarizes the progress of the disease thus: "The patient watches himself die, slowly and inevitably buried alive in his decaying body."[257]

After the diagnosis, doctors wanted to keep Mingus in the hospital indefinitely, but Sue arranged to bring him home in secret. She could not, however, take him to their fourth-floor apartment on East 10th Street because it had no elevator. So she took a suite in the Plaza Hotel and eventually an apartment in Manhattan Plaza on the west side of Manhattan, a federally subsidized building that provided comfortable but inexpensive housing for artists. Dexter Gordon, who had recently returned from a long stay in Europe, was a neighbor. So was a young pianist named Armen Donelian, who got to know the couple and helped Mingus with his final projects. Donelian was there when Sue threw Charles a party on his fifty-sixth birthday in April 1978. By this time he was already confined to a wheelchair. One of the people who dropped by was Sonny Rollins. Although the two never recorded together, Rollins and Mingus were friends. Rollins walked over to Mingus and sat down next to his wheelchair. Donelian said that the two sat for at least eight minutes just looking into each other's eyes. Neither man said a word.[258]

His next studio date would have been with the jazz/rock bassist Stanley Clarke, but it never happened. Mingus was too weak to perform at the session, but he also regarded Clarke with contempt, saying "He's not a musician, but he's a superstar. I don't need that shit, man."[259] Nevertheless, Atlantic continued pushing his music toward the popular mainstream, even hiring the Brecker Brothers, excellent musicians who had crossed over to a successful career with jazz/rock. Mingus was still composing, often singing or whistling a tune to Jack Walrath or Paul Jeffrey when he could no longer hold a pen or pick out a tune on the piano.

Charles was physically present at the three recording sessions in January 1978 that resulted in two more LPs, *Something Like a Bird* and *Me, Myself an Eye*.[260] Once again Atlantic Records paid for a large orchestra, with at least twenty-five musicians at each of the sessions. Mingus sat in his wheelchair to watch a band that included an electric piano as well as an acoustic piano and no less than four electric guitars. Although he never spoke, he may have entered into the spirit of the music at one point. In an issue of *Jazz* magazine published shortly after his death, there is a heart-breaking photo of Mingus in his wheelchair wearing a neck brace to hold up his head. He has lifted his left hand into the air and curled his fingers. Sy Johnson, who took the photograph, said that he was playing an imaginary bass along with the band.[261]

Throughout the last months of his life, Sue did everything she could for Charles and sometimes more. She researched the disease thoroughly, looking for a way to at least postpone the inevitable outcome. Less than a month after the diagnosis came down, she took him to a clinic in Montreux, Switzerland, to undergo a treatment that involved embryonic lamb cells. The doctors there did not believe that the treatment would cure him, but it might, they thought, fortify his system. After undergoing a three-hour operation in which serum from numerous organs of unborn lambs was injected into his body, Sue said that he looked as if he had been crucified. When he saw that Sue was looking at him, Charles let out a low sound: "Ba-a-a-a-a-a-a-a-a-a."[262] He would not always be so ready with a joke. For the next year he would be suicidal, demanding, and pathetic. When he was funny, he was often at his most mordant.

Back home, Sue made sure that he got massages, herbal medicines, and biofeedback—anything that might ease the pain. She also saw to it that he ate well, regularly taking him out to Manhattan's best restaurants. Buddy Collette has said that Sue may have been hoping that plenty of food was the best thing for him. When he saw Mingus during his last days, Sue and his son Eugene were feeding him great quantities of food, even though much of it was running down his chin.[263]

A CHAIR IN THE SKY

With mounting medical bills, Sue was desperate for money. Even though Daniele Sanatore, the producer of *Todo Modo*, had been unable to get Mingus's music into his movie, he suggested that some money might be forthcoming if Sue reached out to Joni Mitchell. This was the beginning of an extremely unlikely collaboration that produced what may have been the final statement of Mingus's music.

For most of Mingus's admirers, Mitchell's *Mingus* LP was far from satisfying.[264] I have difficulty listening to more than one track at a time. But I greatly admire Mitchell for her devotion to the project. She persevered in spite of the real damage that the record inflicted on her career.

Born in Fort Mcleod in Alberta, Canada, in 1943, Joni Mitchell took piano lessons for a year when she was seven. She says that she subsequently forgot how to read music. She did, however, have an original, often startling talent as a songwriter. She began making a living singing her own songs in night clubs and church basements in Toronto, Detroit, and New York when she was in her early twenties. Even before Mitchell began recording on her own, Judy Collins had a hit in 1967 with Mitchell's "Both Sides Now." Mitchell began her recording career in 1968, at the same time that a depressed Mingus was languishing in obscurity. With songs like "Big Yellow Taxi" and "Woodstock," Mitchell was becoming a central figure in a youth culture that embraced politics as vigorously as pop music, even though Mitchell considered herself to be apolitical at the time.

Mitchell had always been a jazz fan, with a special fascination for Miles Davis, Duke Ellington, and the vocal group Lambert, Hendricks, and Ross. Although she was widely considered a folk artist, she began moving her music toward jazz when she found that the session musicians in Los Angeles could not give her the sounds and rhythms she wanted.[265] In the 1970s she began working closely with bassist Jaco Pastorius and saxophonist Wayne Shorter.

She knew very little of Mingus's music before he reached out to her. In fact, Mitchell had never collaborated with anyone before. On all of her records she is the only person listed as a producer, except on her LPs from the 1970s where only the engineer is listed. With only two exceptions before the Mingus LP, she never recorded anyone else's music, the exceptions being "Twisted" and "Centerpiece," both recorded in 1959 by Lambert, Hendricks, and Ross. "Twisted" represents an especially brilliant work of vocalese by Annie Ross, who recorded the tune on her own in 1952, taking an improvised solo by the tenor saxophonist Wardell Gray and composing lyrics that precisely fit his notes.[266] The LP with Mitchell's version of "Twisted" was a hit in 1974. At least at that point in her career, she could display substantial jazz chops without alienating her fan base.

But the Mingus project was different. Her management team and people at her record label were appalled. They told her that the music would not sell and that her records would never again be played on AM or even FM radio, especially after her previous LP, *Don Juan's Reckless Daughter,* disappointed so many of her fans. Mitchell's biographer David Yaffe believes that the partially paralyzed Mingus was nevertheless able to turn on the old charm, though he adds that Mitchell took "pride in her jive detector, and she knew that she was in the presence of the real thing."[267] That Mingus was dying may have made her all the more devoted.

Mingus first approached Mitchell asking her to participate in something he had been planning for a while: setting T. S. Eliot's "Four Quartets" to music. She read Eliot's poems, then told Charles she might as well as sing the King James Bible.

That could have been the end of it. But Mingus later called Mitchell to say that he had written six tunes for her. He called them "Joni 1," "Joni 2," "Joni 3," etc. One of the compositions became "Chair in the Sky," a tune that gave its name to the first LP by Mingus Dynasty, a group of Mingus veterans who began performing his music within months after his death. The title came to Mitchell when she saw Mingus in his wheelchair silhouetted against a window in his fortieth-floor apartment at Manhattan Plaza.

Mitchell took the first parts of "Sue's Changes" and created "Sweet Sucker Dance." She also created "God Must Be a Boogie Man" out of phrases in *Beneath the Underdog.* The most memorable track on Mitchell's LP is her version of "Goodbye Pork Pie Hat" with her own lyrics. The song becomes the story of Mingus as much as of Lester Young, the great saxophonist with the signature hat to whom Mingus was paying tribute. As Yaffe points out, however, the song was also about Joni. Like Mingus, Lester Young had a white wife. At the time of her Mingus LP, Mitchell was living with the black percussionist Don Alias.[268] In the early 1950s, Mingus had written "Eclipse," another song about interracial romance.[269]

Mingus had ideas about how Mitchell's songs should be accompanied, but he was not able to see them through. Dannie Richmond and a large orchestra did record some backgrounds for the songs, but no one can tell me what happened to the tapes. Nor have I been able to find out what became of some arrangements for the Mitchell record that Jimmy Knepper wrote. Knowing that Mingus was ill, Knepper called him in early 1978 to wish him well. Mingus immediately began complaining about the arrangements that were being put together for the Mitchell project. Knepper told Santoro that he provided arrangements for two of the songs that Mingus had written.[270]

Knepper's arrangements appear to have vanished along with the recordings in which Dannie Richmond participated. Apparently Joni did not like them. Eventually, the backgrounds for the Mitchell LP were supplied by a group of musicians associated with the jazz/rock group Weather Report.

Herbie Hancock, one of the great accompanists as well as soloists in the jazz of the 1960s and 1970s, was called in late to participate; he played electric piano on all the sessions. There are no instrumental solos on the LP, and the band played exactly the kind of bland fusion music that Mingus regularly denounced. In particular, Mingus would have hated the mechanically augmented sound of Pastorius's electric bass. Mitchell had sent Mingus a tape of herself singing "Chair in the Sky" with only a rehearsal pianist. Mingus said that it was so good it should be put into a time capsule. But when he heard the whole band playing "Goodbye Pork Pie Hat," he was furious.[271]

The people who told Joni Mitchell that her Mingus project would ruin her career were right. Mitchell's recordings have not been heard on AM or FM radio since, in spite of her efforts to promote the LP. (*Mingus* was not a complete financial failure, however. According to Wikipedia, it peaked at number seventeen on the Billboard charts.)[272] She even broke her boycott of *Rolling Stone* magazine, eight years after an obnoxious piece about her sexual history with various pop stars that labeled her "Old Lady of the Year." Putting her anger aside, she gave an interview to Cameron Crowe, hoping to sell the Mingus LP.[273] To her credit, after the LP and her career went nowhere, Mitchell expressed no regrets. When a Canadian journalist asked her if she was jumping on the "jazz band wagon," Mitchell replied that it was more like a "jazz donkey." She knew that her career had not been helped by a flirtation with jazz that stretched through several records before *Mingus*. But asked if she would do the Mingus project all over again, she said without hesitation, "Oh yeah," and added, "I would not trade that experience for anything."[274]

Mitchell did, however, have some intense arguments with Mingus about how the LP should sound. She said she was relieved that he was too ill to take a swing at her. But when all was said and done, she felt most comfortable with the rock-fusion sound and went ahead on her own. Nevertheless, she continued to express real admiration for Charles, telling an interviewer in 1991, "If I learned anything, he was really able to discern purity of intention. He could tell when people were playing a phony note or faking an orgasm. All of those things were apparent to him. He is the only person that I ever met that could perceive certain things—certain sensitivities—in all the musicians I ever met."[275]

A FAILED MERCY KILLING AND AN AFTERNOON WITH THE PRESIDENT

Charles did not live to hear the Mitchell LP. It was released late in 1979, several months after his death. When he was diagnosed with ALS in

November 1977, the doctors at Columbia Presbyterian Hospital told Sue he would live for three to six months. He lasted longer than that, despite moments when he no longer wanted to live. In *Tonight at Noon,* Sue Mingus recounts the night when she almost ended Charles's sufferings with an overdose of Doridon, one of the brand names for Glutethimide, a powerful sedative that is seldom prescribed today. Charles had said that he would cut his wrists if he were able. He repeatedly told Sue that he would rather die than go on living with the pain and the paralysis. Sue acquired fifty tablets of Doridon from two different doctors. She consulted three lawyers to find out the legal status of mercy killing, speaking to them in person so that there would be no paper trail.

In conversation with her son Roberto, Sue devised a plan involving three strong but, by themselves, nonlethal doses of Doridon. One dose would be administered by a male nurse who did not have to be part of the plan. In quick succession, Sue and then Roberto would then give him the rest of the drugs. Together the three doses would be fatal, but no one could be found guilty because each of the three would swear they were unaware that others were also giving Charles his pills. Mingus declared himself ready: "Another dimension. And then the pearly gates! Only trouble is, the Devil's out there waiting."[276] After the nurse gave him eight pills and left the room, it was time for Sue and Roberto to administer their doses. At the last minute, Sue decided that she could not do it. Afterward, neither Charles nor Sue ever again discussed the idea of a quick death. This may have been because a ray of hope appeared just a few days later.

In one of the finest moments in the history of the American presidency, on June 18, 1978, Jimmy Carter invited a large group of jazz musicians to perform on the White House lawn, in celebration of the Newport Jazz Festival, which George Wein had kept going for twenty-five years. But it was also an occasion when President Carter praised jazz as "vivid, alive, aggressive, innovative on the one hand; and the severest form of self-discipline on the other. Never compromising quality as the human spirit bursts forward in an expression of song." More dramatically, he also said that "jazz has never received the full recognition it deserves in America—because of the racism in this country."[277] No other president had ever said anything comparable. In 1969, Richard Nixon had brought Duke Ellington to the White House on his seventieth birthday, but the most controversial thing he said was, "In the royalty of American music, no man swings more or stands higher than the Duke."[278]

The 1978 festival at the White House was remarkable. President Carter accepted Dizzy Gillespie's invitation to sing along with his group. To everyone's amazement, Carter delivered a note-perfect vocal on Gillespie's eccentric composition "Salt Peanuts." (Carter was, after all, a peanut farmer before he began his political ascent.) Cecil Taylor gave a typically riveting performance, then, scarcely acknowledging the applause, skittered off into the bushes behind the bandstand. Secret Service agents suddenly had to jump into action as Carter went running after the pianist to thank him. When the president caught up with Taylor, he asked, "Does Horowitz know about you?"

At one point George Wein, who had known and worked with Mingus since the early 1950s, took the microphone and encouraged the audience to give Mingus "as great a round of applause as he's ever had in his life." Carter went over to Mingus in his wheelchair and leaned over to say something in his ear. Still at the microphone, Wein said, "C'mon, Mingus. Stand up, will you? God bless you, Charlie Mingus." In his autobiography, Wein says that the enthusiasm for Mingus among his peers should have been enough to bring him up out of his wheelchair.[279] It did not. Mingus wept.

Max Roach was among the several jazz artists at the White House that day, but when Sue told him that Charles wanted to say hello, he demurred. They never saw each other again, much to Max's deep regret.[280]

Gerry Mulligan was also there, just back from a tour of South America with Lionel Hampton. Mingus had originally been scheduled for the tour, but Mulligan took his place. With great excitement, he told Mingus about a seventy-two-year-old Indian woman in Mexico who had healing powers that could not be explained by modern medicine. Known as Pachita, the woman had treated a friend of Mulligan's named Vincenzo who, according to Mulligan, had the same disease as Charles. After the treatments, Vincenzo was recovering!

Within three days, Charles and Sue were on a plane to Mexico City.

CUERNAVACA

Pachita was a large, imposing woman who claimed to be the reincarnation of the last Aztec emperor, a nephew of Montezuma. In her estate in the slums of Mexico City, she was surrounded by people who told stories of her marvelous cures. During the several days that Charles and Sue waited for an audience with Pachita, one man told of the day she cured a retarded child by cutting open his head and placing her hands inside his skull. Within days, the man said, the child had recovered.[281]

When Charles finally had his audience with Pachita, she stared at him for a long time. Without examining him more closely, she declared that

Charles had "a living nerve virus" and that he was going to be all right.[282] According to Sue, Pachita prescribed buckets of herbal mixtures, "bitter teas, exotic creams, and an enchanted wine that needed to ripen three days and three nights on our hotel terrace under the sun and the stars."[283] Pachita also recommended that Charles move from his hotel in Mexico City to Cuernavaca, seventy miles south of the capital, where the climate was better for him.

In the early stages of his treatment, Mingus suffered from a plague of boils and ran a temperature of more than 105 degrees. The Mexican doctors who wished to take him to the hospital had made their peace with the local witch doctors and those who believed in them. They understood when Mingus declared his faith in Pachita. Even though Sue saw every sign that he was in the final stages of ALS, he awoke after one difficult, feverish night, lifted himself out of bed for the first time in months, and stood on his feet.

But Mingus did not stand again. Attended by Sue, nurses, maids, and his son Eugene (figure 7), Mingus and his wheelchair were fastened with chains inside a van so that he could ride through the streets and countryside to take the rarefied air. The jostling seemed to ease his pain. Often he would ask to be driven over the bumpy Mexican roads throughout the night. Pachita had told him that she could not operate on him until he lost weight. After two weeks in their villa in Cuernavaca, Sue and Charles returned to Mexico City for the operation. Pachita brandished a large knife, and Mingus said that he felt the pain of incisions. He added that he admired her talent with the implement: "I'd like to have her cut *my* steak," he said.[284] But there was no sign of blood under the bandages the morning after the operation. According to Eugene Mingus's son Kevin, everyone knew that Pachita was a fraud. But Eugene also knew that some degree of faith in her could maintain the routine that was effectively sustaining the Mingus family and its entourage in Mexico.[285]

Mingus still had his voice and was mostly talkative throughout the months they spent in Mexico. Joni Mitchell came to visit. She had updated her lyrics to "Goodbye Pork Pie Hat" to include the line, "Now Charlie's down in Mexico with the healers." Celia, his second wife, also came to visit. She later told Ira Gitler that after sitting quietly in the car for a while, Mingus began to sing something she had never heard before. Then he asked, "What do you think of that?" Celia replied, "It's beautiful." Celia told Gitler, "I thought, 'God, he hasn't stopped. It's still going on.' Music was just part of him in a way that I have never seen with anyone else."[286]

Pachita insisted that he eat snails. Escargots were not part of the normal Mexican diet, so Sue and her staff had to go out into the country to find the

Figure 7. Charles Mingus at the piano with his son Eugene, Châteauvallon (France) Jazz Festival, 1972. Photograph © Guy Le Querrec, courtesy of Magnum Photos.

snails and bring them home in a burlap bag. Then they laboriously cleaned and cooked the snails. Meanwhile, the floors and walls of the villa were littered with the snails that had not yet been consumed. Pachita also prescribed that cow dung mixed with parsley be spread over his stomach. Mingus consented and sat outdoors, where the stench was more bearable, while a nurse wrapped gauze around his stomach to keep the scat close to his flesh. Dung to be used for subsequent treatments was wrapped in plastic and placed in the crisper in the refrigerator. Sue once again contemplated mercy killing.

Pachita had promised that he would be healed fifty days after the bloodless operation. Although on some days his spirits were better than on others, there was no real sign of improvement. As the fifty days drew to a close, Pachita was recommending faith. Mulligan's friend Vincenzo, who had been treated by Pachita, made an appearance when they were all in Mexico City. Obviously, Vincenzo did not have ALS. But the legends around Pachita and the hope she engendered surely made a difference. For better or worse, they extended Mingus's life, perhaps by months.

Very near the end, Buddy Collette got a call from Mingus: "If you're going to come, you better come. I've got to see you."[287] When Sue and Charles picked Buddy up at the airport, Mingus managed a smile but little else. By this time he could barely speak. When Mingus asked when he was going to leave, Collette told him he had to leave the next day, then added, "'Don't worry'—he looked so sad when I said that—'I'll come back.' Then the tears streamed down from his eyes, and I saw a little kid, just like a flashback. There he was, this little kid who wondered about playing the bass. As the tears came down, he said, 'Don't come back. Take me with you.'"[288]

Although Sue initially resisted, she eventually agreed with Buddy and Mingus's sister Grace that Charles should return home to Los Angeles to die. They would find a house in Los Angeles where Charles could be closer to his family and his old haunts. On January 5, 1979, Sue went to the American consulate in Mexico City for visas for the trip back to Los Angeles. While she was out, Charles died of a heart attack in the arms of his second son, Eugene.[289]

SUE'S CHANGES

The emotional and physical strains on Sue Mingus and Charles's family are unimaginable except by those who have themselves struggled for many months with the imminent death of a family member. Sue has written about this time compellingly in *Tonight at Noon*. After his death, she did not collapse from exhaustion and grief. Instead, she immediately went to work on Mingus's legacy.

First, she took his ashes to India and scattered them on the Ganges, as he had requested. The Mingus sisters said that their brother once told them that he had not been happy on earth. He said that he had "been here a couple of times, and he didn't want to come back" and that he believed cremation would get him off the wheel of reincarnation.[290] The man who cried out to Jesus in the middle of a performance and who studied Buddhism and meditation was also a true believer in the Hindu concept of Samsara, the repeating cycle of birth, life, and death.

Mingus also knew that in Hindu mythology the Ganges descended from heaven and anyone who bathes in its water will be cleansed of their sins. The spirit of one whose ashes are scattered in the river will likewise quickly ascend to heaven. But he especially liked the idea of having his ashes scattered someplace far away. He knew about the ill will that surrounded the burial of Charlie Parker, whose legal wife, Doris, insisted that he be buried in Kansas City even though his common-law wife, Chan, said that he did not want his body to end up there.[291]

Just a few months after she returned from India, Sue began working with a small group of musicians, many of whom had played with Charles. The group was called Mingus Dynasty, and they recorded and performed frequently. On their first recording in July 1979, the drummer was Dannie Richmond and the trombonist was Jimmy Knepper. Perfect casting. By 1991 Sue had formed the Mingus Big Band, a group with a revolving cast of the best jazz musicians in New York who performed one night a week in a club called Fez in a neighborhood just north of Houston Street known as Noho. The band has since performed weekly at a variety of clubs in Manhattan. As of this writing, the band has an unbroken streak of twenty-three years of once-a-week-performances, most recently at the Jazz Standard, one of the finest music venues in New York City.

In 2008, Sue connected with Justin DiCioccio of the Manhattan School of Music to develop a nationwide competition for high school bands who play Mingus Music. Every February since 2009, large groups of children with musical instruments have been descending on New York for workshops, master classes, and concerts as well as the competition itself.

A few days after one of the high school competitions, my wife and I were, as so often, at the Jazz Standard on a Monday to hear the Mingus Big Band. At a nearby table, a group of teenagers were drinking Cokes and enjoying the barbecued ribs that are a specialty at the club. They listened politely as the big band played through some obscure compositions by

Mingus. Sy Johnson, who played with and arranged for Mingus, has spent many years crafting arrangements for the big band; like Sue, he wanted the band to resemble the old Jazz Workshop bands that were always trying out new material, even on the bandstand.

That night, the band suddenly broke into a rousing interpretation of "Better Git It in Your Soul." All the high school kids at the nearby table jumped out of their chairs and began applauding. When I was their age and discovering Mingus for the first time, I thought I was alone. Thanks to Sue Mingus and her devotion to Charles's memory, there are now young people throughout America who have not only heard Mingus's music and loved it; they have played it.

Mingus lives.

PART II Poet, Lyricist, Autobiographer

I devote the second part of this book to Mingus the writer, for indeed, his achievements were not entirely musical. His written work includes poems, letters, manifestos, liner notes, and lyrics, but he will be most remembered for *Beneath the Underdog*. With this book, Mingus proved himself to be a master of literary form, switching back and forth from first to second to third person, usually as a means of telling his story in the most engaging fashion. The characters in *Beneath the Underdog* emerge as distinct individuals, even the ones who pass through the narrative only briefly. And even though he speaks with a variety of voices, Mingus is always a powerful presence as he expresses love, anger, disappointment, and trust. At times he introduces characters who may seem to speak for him, especially Fats Navarro and the pimp Billy Bones. But Mingus is careful to distinguish his own feelings from those of the handful of outspoken men with whom he carries on a series of dialogues.

Mingus built his life story around a set of themes that unite this jazz musician's predicament with sexuality and ultimately with prostitution. As a result, there is plenty of erotic writing in *Beneath the Underdog,* but very little of it is pornographic. The sex is always part of a larger tale that needs to be told, especially Mingus's own development as a man seeking truth in the flesh as well as in the spirit. Frequently the sexual passages are connected to a critique of an entertainment business that requires serious musicians to prostitute themselves. And although sections of the book can only be fantasy, and his memory is not always completely accurate, Mingus is completely in control of this remarkable work of self-mythology.

"MYSELF WHEN I AM REAL": MINGUS AND POETRY

Mingus showed a rich understanding of a poet's work in 1972 when he created a deeply sympathetic musical setting for a poem by Frank O'Hara.[1] A few years later, his request to Joni Mitchell that she join him in setting T. S. Eliot's "Four Quartets" to music surely reflected his appreciation of a difficult and highly allusive set of poems. Mingus's own poetry and lyrics are frequently as impressive as his autobiography. Scott Saul, for example, has made the case for reading "Fables of Faubus" as an effective response to the white racists who, using the rhetoric of high school cheerleaders, taunted black students as they attempted to enter all-white schools: "Two—four—six—eight, we don't want to integrate." When his band performed "Fables of Faubus," they sang out some of these same patterns. As Saul put it, "If the segregationist had decided to mine the rhetorical register of the schoolyard—a register of dumb and cruel logic—Mingus would deal back in kind: he would use his music partly as a playground for theatrical idiocy, and he would do so with the knowingness that comes from absorbing the form and switching the message."[2]

Mingus always had the touch of a poet. His second wife, Celia, says that he courted her with poems.[3] I would even argue that Mingus's survey of human history in the liner notes to *Pithecanthropus Erectus* is a prose poem. Consider the phrases about early man rising up and "pounding his chest and preaching his superiority over the animals still in a prone position. Overcome with self-esteem, he goes out to rule the world, if not the universe, but both his own failure to realize the inevitable emancipation of those he sought to enslave, and his greed in attempting to stand on a false security, deny him not only the right to ever being a man, but finally destroy him completely."[4]

Consider also a passage from *Beneath the Underdog*, one of his many conversations with his close friend Fats Navarro. Navarro's nickname was "Fat Girl" because of his high-pitched voice but also because of his tremendous girth. At one point he may have weighed as much as 350 pounds. Late in the book, Fats has lost an enormous amount of weight because of tuberculosis combined with substance abuse. He knows he is dying, and at least in his conversations with Mingus, he rejects all religious faiths and embraces death. Mingus tells Navarro, "There's no need to kill yourself—*think* yourself to death. Go ahead, Fats, you know you're right, there ain't no God. You know more than Christ, Buddha, Socrates, Plato, Mohammed, Bird, Judas, Mingus, Casals, Stravinsky, Benjamin Franklin, Swami Vivikananda and Norman Mailer! You know there ain't no God, you know more than anyone except some of them dumb agents, critics and congressmen."[5]

The litany of sages that begins with Christ and ends with Norman Mailer could only have been constructed by a man who knows his world and its absurdities but who also possesses a profound sense of irony. By placing Ben Franklin, a swami, and Mailer at the end, he shows that he is only half serious. And we are not taken aback when he audaciously lists his own name immediately before Pablo Casals, for this seemingly egotistic display is undermined by the placement of his name immediately after Judas. Like a serious poet, Mingus knows that the ironist can say much more by suggesting than by declaiming.

Mingus had played a role in the jazz and poetry moment in the 1950s, performing with Kenneth Patchen, whose poetry he quotes in *Beneath the Underdog*. He recorded jazz and poetry with Melvin Stewart and Lonnie Elder in 1957 and with no less than Langston Hughes in 1958. The Beats knew him and sent their books to him. The walls of his apartment were lined with volumes by Ferlinghetti, Patchen, Rexroth, Corso, and Ginsberg.[6]

We might even consider Mingus's song titles as examples of a poet's work, beginning with "All the Things You C Sharp" and "All the Things You Could Be by Now if Sigmund Freud's Wife Was Your Mother." Other titles that reveal a poetic sensibility include "Reincarnation of a Love Bird," "No Private Income Blues," "If Charlie Parker Was a Gunslinger, There'd Be a Whole Lot of Dead Copycats," "Ecclusiastics," "Please Don't Come Back from the Moon," "Love Is a Dangerous Necessity," "The Shoes of the Fisherman's Wife Are Some Jive Ass Slippers," and "Noddin' Ya Head Blues." If not all of these titles are worthy of a T. S. Eliot or even an Ogden Nash, they reveal Mingus's witty take on oral and literary traditions, all of it tied to his personal and political convictions.

As an inspired, often funny commentator on American racism who expressed himself in different venues, Mingus has much in common with several black poets of his generation, most notably Bob Kaufman and Ted Joans. They were a few years younger than Charles (Mingus was born in 1922, Kaufman in 1925, and Joans in 1928), but all three have a good deal in common. We might also compare Charles to LeRoi Jones (Amiri Baraka), who was born even later, in 1934.

Both Mingus and Baraka, however, would have had serious objections to the comparison. In some ways, Mingus had a more advanced political sense than Baraka, who educated himself in the 1950s in what was then considered the Western intellectual tradition. In his autobiography, Baraka would characterize his education this way: "I was being drafted into the world of Quattrocento, vers libre, avant-garde, surrealism and dada, New Criticism, cubism, art nouveau, objectivism, 'Prufrock,' ambiguity, art music, rococo, shoe and non-shoe, Highbrow vs. Middlebrow, and I didn't realize the deeper significance of it."[7]

Baraka would later become an outspoken critic of America's racist politics and eventually a Marxist, but in the 1950s, immersed in the formalist aesthetics of T. S. Eliot, William Empson, and Martin Williams, he criticized Mingus for being too political. Like many intellectuals at midcentury, Baraka believed that works of art were separate from the hurly-burly of history and politics. Mingus, however, was under no such illusions.

Baraka also chided Mingus for leading a band that could not swing, calling him "the black Stan Kenton."[8] Mingus and Baraka actually came to blows at one point at the Five Spot. In his autobiography, Baraka says that Mingus pushed and slapped him, calling him "a goddamn punk" and excoriating him for being too positive about avant-garde musicians in something he had written. When Mingus came at him again, Baraka went into his "Newark Sugar Ray stick and run, jab and duck, and started popping him side his fat head."[9] In Baraka's version of the story, Charles realized that he was no match for the smaller but quicker Baraka, so he held out his hand and apologized. Max Roach was present during the altercation and told Gene Santoro that Baraka knew karate but that Mingus kept coming after him anyway. "We could hear his feet thudding against Ming's chest."[10]

On a tape recording in the Mingus collection at the Library of Congress, Charles mentions Baraka briefly when an unidentified interviewer asks him about getting into fights. After saying that he only ever beat up two people, Jimmy Knepper and "Hampton", he then points out that Tommy and Jimmy Dorsey came to blows, suggesting that when white jazz musicians hit each other, it's not reported as evidence of a violent streak. Mingus then adds, "What's that black writer? Little bitty guy." He comes up with the name LeRoi Jones and observes, "Didn't like me anyway. I don't know why."[11]

If the center of the action for Mingus had not been music, he might have become the peer of Joans and Kaufman. Ted Joans was born in Cairo, Illinois, to a family of riverboat entertainers. He played the trumpet and, like Mingus, was fascinated by the surrealists. He paid tribute to jazz artists in his poems and was deeply schooled in black history. He dedicated poems to both Charlie Parker and Malcolm X. Just as Mingus would write "Haitian Fight Song" to honor Toussaint Louverture, Joans dedicated a poem to Crispus Attucks, who, as either a slave or a freeman, may have been the first American casualty in the Revolutionary War. Like Mingus, Joans arrived in New York in the early 1950s. Whereas Mingus immediately took up with the boppers on 52nd Street, Joans sought out the Beat poets in Greenwich Village.[12] Joans wrote a fantastical set of autobiographical poems, *Black Pow-Wow,* published in 1969, two years before Mingus's own book came out.[13] In fact, with its explicit sexuality and violence and with passages of parody alternating with documentary, Joans's book has much in common with *Beneath the Underdog.*

Like Mingus, Bob Kaufman was a self-mythologizer, rewriting his ancestry to include both German Jewish and Caribbean voodoo backgrounds. Although none of this may have been true, Kaufman was making common cause with marginalized people everywhere while emphasizing his own roots in the African diaspora. James Smethurst associates Kaufman's revised account of his family history with what he calls the aesthetics of "the late Popular Front," the leftist art and politics of the Cold War years of the late 1940s and early 1950s. Along with a strong commitment to racial justice, this aesthetic involved "a self-conscious cultural mixing of 'high' and 'low,' of 'popular' and 'literary,' of Whitman and Eliot, of folk culture and mass culture."[14] Invoking jazz, we could add Stravinsky and Charlie Parker, Debussy and the blues, to this list of dyads, not to mention Mingus's "Fables of Faubus" and "The Chill of Death."

Like the younger Baraka, Kaufman was reading the formalist, apolitical criticism of the 1950s, but he had much more in common with Mingus. For one thing, neither man lost sight of the racial politics within the mix. Mingus was just as devoted to combining genres, politics, and aesthetics as anyone in the late Popular Front. And he was just as obsessed with his complicated racial heritage and his place in America. When Kaufman coined the term "A-Bomb-u-nism" to describe American culture, he was clearly thinking along the same lines as Mingus when in 1961 he recorded "Oh Lord, Don't Let Them Drop That Atomic Bomb on Me."

Kaufman saw bebop and its immediate aftermath as the best example of black artistic production, a history that stretched from ancient Egypt to Charlie Parker. Like the boppers, Kaufman was devoted to a style that was cosmopolitan and international. Kaufman admired the boppers for their embrace of European art music, but he was also intrigued by other forms of African influence in jazz, most notably by what Jelly Roll Morton called the "Spanish tinge." The Caribbean, Afro-Cuban flavor of some early jazz became central to the development of bebop shortly after Dizzy Gillespie sat down next to the Cuban trumpeter Mario Bauza in the Cab Calloway band in 1939.

In 1947, after Gillespie had formed his own big band, he prominently featured percussionist Chano Pozo and would make Afro-Cuban rhythms an important part of his music for the rest of his life. Along with the Trinidadian-influenced music of Sonny Rollins, the Cuban bebop of Gillespie provided a model for "Kaufman's spiritual and artistic connection to a larger diasporic sensibility."[15] Mingus was just as fascinated by Latin rhythms. His 1957 masterpiece *Tijuana Moods* was as much an attempt to connect with other marginalized people as it was a celebration of his legendary orgy in the city's brothels. On at least one occasion he returned to his birthplace of Nogales, crossed the border into Mexico, and played for the locals in small restaurants.

"MUST I READ YOUR BOOKS AND YOUR PHILOSOPHIES?"

The lyrics that Mingus wrote for his songs show off different facets of his poetic facility. He writes of lost love in "Weird Nightmare," the paranormal in "The Chill of Death," transcendence through music in "Duke Ellington's Sound of Love," the absurdity of racism in "Fables of Faubus," and artistic inspiration in "Portrait."[16] In "Eclipse," he ingeniously creates an extended metaphor for interracial romance. Mingus has said that he wrote "Eclipse" with the hope that Billie Holiday would sing it.[17] Although her recording of "Strange Fruit" was never a success with the public, it quickly became an anthem for Popular Front liberals in the 1940s. Throughout her career, Holiday took Tin Pan Alley songs and made them her own, often finding new resources of romance and drama in the work of journeyman songwriters. Appropriately, "Eclipse" recalls Tin Pan Alley songs in both its chord progressions and lyrics.

Holiday never sang "Eclipse," but Mingus recorded the song three times—in 1953, 1960, and 1972—always as a slow ballad.[18]

> Eclipse, when the moon meets the sun,
> Eclipse, these bodies become as one.
> People go around, eyes look up and frown,
> For it's a sight they seldom see.
> Some look through smoked glasses hiding their eyes,
> Others think it's tragic, staring as dark meets light.
> But the sun doesn't care, and the moon knows no fear,
> For destiny's making her choice.
> Eclipse, the moon has met the sun.
> Eclipse, two lovers joined as one.

For Scott Saul, with this song Mingus "universalizes" interracial romance. The song's moon and sun are "star-crossed lovers" brought together by fate. They are "victims not of racial prejudice (an issue that might demand a race-sensitive solution) but of narrow-minded conformism, a kind of suburban groupthink."[19] And when Mingus recorded the tune, each of the vocalists sang with a matter-of-fact sweetness that reaffirmed the natural attraction between lovers of different colors.

The sense that the lovers are made for each other by forces beyond their control recalls the early sections of *Beneath the Underdog* in which Charles and Lee-Marie are telepathically and tragically linked well before society sees them as capable of making a serious commitment to each other. "Eclipse" also recalls a poem in the typescript of his autobiography when Charles first meets Ina, the white woman who is called Donna in the published book. They have barely met before Charles gives Ina the keys to his car and to his apartment, where he tells her to wait for him. When he walks into his apartment, he finds that Ina has filled it with the smell of incense and the sounds of a recording of *Images* by Debussy, one of Mingus's favorite composers. At that moment he realizes that what he has with Ina is not about romance with the forbidden other. Rather than describe their lovemaking in straightforward prose, he expresses himself in poetry:

> Pillows of hair that knead . . .
> Mouth not so dry as first
> ????? [*sic*]
> As lips forget
> Their muscles have a grip
> That closed them so
> Then not so
> Until the warm wetness
> Binds them to a oneness
> As tongues
> Joyful at each plight
> Find pleasing similarity
> In their natural unlikeness
> Hers so soft and smooth
> His so firm hot and impatient.[20]

Perhaps Mingus had second thoughts about this passage because he ultimately worked with his editors to translate the poem into more straightforward prose before it was published in *Beneath the Underdog*.[21]

Mingus regularly recited or chanted along with music. Like his lyrics, his recitations seldom resemble one another. With "Freedom," recorded in 1963 during the impulse! *Mingus Mingus Mingus Mingus Mingus* session (though it was not included on that LP), he combines an Aesopian fable with a surrealist account of the Ku Klux Klan and his own sense of anomie. The recording begins with members of the band chanting wordlessly. Then Mingus speaks:

> This mule ain't from Moscow,
> This mule ain't from the South.
> But this mule's had some learning,
> Mostly mouth-to-mouth.

This mule could be called stubborn, and lazy,
But in a clever sorta way.
This mule could be workin', waitin' and learnin' and plannin'
For a sacred kind of day—
A day when burnin' sticks and crosses
Is not mere child's play,
But a madman in his most incandescent bloom
Whose loveless soul is imperfection, in its most lustrous groom.

So stand fast there, old mule
Soothe in contemplation
Thy burning hole and aching thigh
Your stubbornness is ever-living
And cruel anxiety is about to die.

[The last four lines are chanted three times by a chorus on the recording:]

Freedom for your daddy
Freedom for your momma
Freedom for your brothers and sisters
But no freedom for me.[22]

Mingus is again mixing genres, combining black vernacular ("workin', waitin' and learnin' and plannin'") with imagery that recalls high modernism ("a madman in his most incandescent bloom"). And as so often with Mingus's writing, he brings it back to the racial constraints with which he must live ("but no freedom for me").

Mingus had written a somewhat different version of "Freedom" and published it in *Down Beat* in 1956, calling it "This Mule Ain't from Moscow."[23] He felt strongly enough about the poem to recite it at the beginning of his Town Hall concert in October 1962.[24]

With the delicately expressive singing of Jackie Paris on the *Changes Two* LP, we hear Mingus's poetry at its most elegiac in "Duke Ellington's Sound of Love." In the lyrics he assigns to Paris, Mingus turns confessional:

I was young and carefree,
Not a song had found my soul.
Lost in blues, jazz and ragtime,
no sound had got to my mood.
I was searching for my melody,
love blues that gets me wooed.[25]

The lyrics trace out Ellington's impact on the young Romeo: "Taught me how to hear music out of love." Mingus's surrealism and racial protest never surface in this song, which he wrote at least a decade after "Freedom" and "Fables of Faubus." But it is also among his most autobiographical lyrics, chronicling his youthful astonishment when he first heard Ellington's music on his father's crystal set.

One of the poems in the typescript of the autobiography is more polemical and surreal. This untitled work, clearly based on the patriotic song "America," was not included in *Beneath the Underdog*.

> Nigger, it's your country 'tis of thee
> Go out and fight for me
> 'Cause you can't see.
> Land where yo fathers died,
> Their necks all stretched out wide,
> And from our pilgrims' side
> That's how they died.
> "Our Second verse:
> You thought we couldn't see.
> Those bombs aren't liberty.
> That's gone too far.
> You've stomped us long enough,
> You ain't so big and tough.
> You've had your bluff and fluffed.
> We're leaving you.
>
> We're not about to hide
> That you're filled with stupid pride.
> We're leaving you.
> Your need of Homocide
> Is greed of suicide
> From every mountainside
> We will abide.
>
> So good tidink,
> Signed Little Red Ridink."[26]

The intense rhyming within the tirade against American racism and militarism suggests the work of black rappers several decades into the future. It also recalls Joans and Kaufman as well as their mentor, Langston Hughes, who brought black vernacular into his racialized poetics. And Mingus the draft-dodger joins Dizzy Gillespie and several other beboppers, not to mention Malcolm X, in refusing to embrace military service.

Mingus also seems to have picked up some of Hughes's modernist aesthetic, as in this remarkable poem I found among the several hours of undated audiotapes in the Library of Congress collection:

> And so they come, a few steps farther and farther
> Into a fool's life.
> Eating flesh and bones with the vultures.

They bleed and they sigh
They kiss and mourn before they die
They lust for what they live
And this we know is living
And yet it's not life.

A funny sort of death to walk alone
Alone by yourself on a crowded street
Only in faces you've seen before,
Reflecting in view,
Reflecting in view,
Your past and your present and your future
To heed no man's words
To listen to life's song
And this my soul I'll begin to frown
To bend deep in search for the needle they say lay in the haystack
Somewhere there is an answer to nothing.

Insanity. Insane insanity.
But humane humanity has forbidden that the cross be ridden
Across or around and back and forth
Until you have a circle of life's own sweet pleasant dream
To dream as the she-wolf would have my soul in passion
For the woman I knew
Who could not ration.

Her panties she flew
She blew on the floor
She blew
But the panties she blew
Who knew who knew who knew oh no who knew

[sound of tape machine clicking]

This time it's magic
Magic from a white man's words
Tragic
From the black man's turds
To the white man's herds
I know the answer, you know the answer
We all shit together!

There is no doubt in my mind
Or in any true-thinking lexic mind as to how to follow the goal
Of the prejudiced soul
That has no roundness
No full firm masculinity or femininity
This I say is looseness [unclear]
To waste time with a tie around your neck

To look good for the day
That you might want to pray
Only for this day do you stay
Because your suit is gray, clean, and untorn
And your shoes are trussed [unclear].

But when you leave
To take your final shift [unclear]
You take no bath
You comb no hair
You brush no teeth
You go square
You are dead
And so are we all
Until the day we hear our
Beckon call.

I myself have died a million deaths in a row
I myself have died more than you could ever know
Killed at the white man's stake
And beaten and burned.
I'm no saint or Joan of Arc or Christ
I'm no devil either
I'm the beginning and the ending
I've seen all and done all
And I am no saint
I ain't sayin there ain't no saints
But maybe there ain't, but I sure ain't.

Saint, give me the answer to your life long plan
Lend me your helping loving hand
As for me and my madman's prayer
Cast me not aside from the streets [tear in his voice]
Or from the shadows that you call dark laughter
And dark lost and the Black ball
Black market
Black magic
Black beauty I call it all.

Poor white sanity
Running pure humanity
Pure poor or aura
You earning me
I could be mad
I make no rhetoric sense at times
But for some reason I seem to reach a goal
With the wandering pondering words
And the funny noises and sounds

You turn your voice around
And you get some place or other

[Guttural throaty noises, gasping]

I'm talking to you

[Sounds like a tape running too slow]
[Barely intelligible]

Living heaven is the beginning
Hell is the beginning, . . . is the ending
Oh god take away this foolish pride of mine
Set aside mine soul from this
Let me be a separate man in my way of living
Let me find the goal by myself
Teach me how to walk thy pathway
Onward to the goal straight ahead straight ahead they say.

But might I relax in the meantime?
Can I not find my own sort of sane word?
Must I read your books and your philosophies?
Must I follow your pathway or your gold?
Can I not become a man of my own true self?
Can I not grow inside and fear nothing on my own?
Must I follow you?
NO!
You follow ME!

And I will lead you gently away from your hidden prejudiced self to
    beauty
A little kindness
And maybe love if we grow together
Love
The final, the ultimate goal of all
Pure, not innocent, not childlike
Well-developed and well-recepted
Analytic, all-knowing love
Sort of easy, easygoin' love.[27]

The poem is still another example of the multiple modes in which Mingus expressed himself. It is often a condemnation of the white bourgeoisie with their gray suits and gray lives, a common target of the Beats in the 1950s. But Mingus's dominant theme is the unwillingness of whites to accept the oneness of all peoples ("We all shit together").

He is amazed that whites cannot grant the full weight of humanity to a black man, especially one whose inner life is as complex, if not more complex, than anyone's. The poem includes vernacular word games ("I ain't sayin there ain't no saints"), an allusion to the Psalms of the King James Version ("Teach me how to walk thy pathway"), and a radical questioning of the received wisdom of his culture ("Must I read your books and philosophies?"). Mingus drops in references to his sexuality and to his fear of insanity, but ultimately he offers to lead people of different races toward a new understanding of love. His "well-developed and well-recepted love" would be less fraught with the fear that interracial love inevitably arouses in a racist society.

I would attempt to analyze this poem more thoroughly if I had some idea where it came from. There are no marks on the box with the tape to suggest a date or an origin. I don't know if he wrote it out and then recorded it or if he was improvising as he spoke into the tape recorder. He most definitely uses a different style of address on this one recording, abandoning the fast, high-pitched voice in which he most commonly spoke. When he recites the poem on the tape, he lowers his pitch and slows down dramatically, sounding a bit like Orson Welles or Duke Ellington at his most oratorical.

The drama of the poetry and Mingus's voice are complemented in intriguing ways by the recording technology. Dawn Frank, one of the technicians who digitized the tapes in the Library of Congress's Mingus collection, told me that almost all of the tapes contained material recorded at different speeds, including one section that was recorded at the highly unusual speed of fifteen-sixteenths of an inch per second.[28] I have no idea if Mingus intended for his recording of this poem to contain "tape-recorder effects," but having listened to it several times, I think it is a performance that needs to be not just read, but heard. For whatever reason, Mingus left this poem behind. He might have considered including it on one of his LPs, but perhaps he thought that people who bought his records would be disturbed by interruptions in the flow of music. Nevertheless, the poem stands as a powerful, even learned expression of Mingus's anger, confusion, and hope.

MINGUS AMONG THE AUTOBIOGRAPHERS

Regardless of what we make of his poetry, Mingus the author will be most remembered for *Beneath the Underdog*. The list of jazz autobiographies was already long enough in 1995 for Christopher Harlos to speak of jazz literature being "inundated" with autobiographies.[29] The list has grown substantially in the years since Harlos's pioneering article, but *Beneath the Underdog* still stands out among texts by Louis Armstrong, Miles Davis, Duke Ellington, Sidney Bechet, Hampton Hawes, Art Pepper, Jelly Roll Morton, Mezz Mezzrow, Buddy Collette, Buck Clayton, Horace Tapscott,

Rex Stewart, Bob Wilber, Milt Hinton, Joe Darensbourg, Pops Foster, Joe Wilder, and Dizzy Gillespie, to name just a few. Not much has changed, however, since 1995 when Harlos wrote, "As autobiographers, jazz musicians tend to be much more conservative than Mingus in conforming to established practices of self-representation."[30]

Before surveying the autobiographies that ought to be considered alongside *Beneath the Underdog*, I should dispel an old myth about jazz artists. In spite of the ubiquitous image of the inarticulate musician mumbling insider jargon, large groups of jazz musicians have possessed substantial verbal skills. Ron Mann's 1981 documentary film *Imagine the Sound* places several jazz musicians in front of the camera, including Archie Shepp, Paul Bley, and Bill Dixon, all of them remarkably expressive and quick-witted. Eric Porter has exhaustively refuted the stereotype of the tongue-tied black jazz artist in *What Is This Thing Called Jazz?*, an intellectual history of jazz based entirely on utterances by the musicians themselves. Think also of the witty, often learned lyrics that Jon Hendricks set to improvised jazz solos that were often so convoluted as to seem beyond the reach of vocalese.[31]

In spite of the many jazz musicians who have expressed themselves clearly and forcefully in words, it is nevertheless true that many came to self-narrative at a disadvantage. The beginnings of the practice of carefully reflecting on one's life and turning it into a coherent account are usually dated to the fourth century C.E. and *The Confessions* of St. Augustine. As the genre of autobiography developed, it was colonized by white European males, a breed very different from twentieth-century black jazz musicians. Even the best writers among jazz artists confronted a genre with built-in rules demanding a clear narrative arc and a set of incidents illustrating the lessons to be passed on. Few African Americans, especially African American jazz musicians, have had the luxury of the orderly life that is suited to this kind of writing.

Nevertheless, virtually all jazz autobiographers have tried to make their work conform in some ways to the dominant model, and almost all have worked with an editor, usually a white editor. (The major exceptions are Miles Davis and Count Basie, who worked with, respectively, Quincy Troupe and Albert Murray.) Even Rex Stewart, the distinguished cornettist and composer who played with Duke Ellington and Fletcher Henderson among many others, prominently thanks editor Claire P. Gordon in the first pages of his autobiography, despite having written regularly for jazz periodicals throughout his career.[32] Stewart also published a highly readable collection of his journalistic pieces in a book called *Jazz Masters of the Thirties*.[33]

Kevin McNeilly suggests that Stewart consulted an editor for his autobiography because he wanted to avoid the vernacular chattiness of Louis Armstrong, whose *Satchmo: My Life in New Orleans* (1954) would have been the paradigm for the kind of book Stewart was writing.[34] In order to distinguish his book, Stewart and his editors made what McNeilly has called "a self-conscious effort at a crafted, 'professorial' and neutral style."[35]

Albert Murray has been candid about exhaustively researching the career of Count Basie before interviewing Basie himself for a few piquant comments and then sitting down to write *Good Morning Blues: The Autobiography of Count Basie.*[36] Joking that he was "Basie's Basie," Murray pictured himself sitting at his typewriter just as Basie sat at his piano. When he was performing, Basie would periodically raise his head and look at a musician, letting him know it was his time to solo. Similarly, Murray would look up from *his* keyboard to ask Basie to "solo" by dropping a few notes into Murray's stream of words.[37] Basie himself, however, was reluctant to open his life to a thorough examination, so Murray agreed to overlook a great deal of material that might have made the book more interesting. At one point Murray has Basie saying, "Now as for what was happening with me and the ladies during those early days in Kansas City, I figure that ain't nobody's business."[38] Of course, in *Beneath the Underdog*, Mingus repeatedly and abundantly made "what was happening with me and the ladies" the business of anyone who picked up the book.

Novelist Don Asher was sufficiently intrigued by the music of Hampton Hawes to interview him extensively, listening carefully to the cadence of the pianist's speech. The result is *Raise Up Off Me*, a startling account of Hawes's life as a jazz musician and heroin addict, told in the first person but basically written by Asher.[39]

Writing in the afterword to the updated edition of *Straight Life*, Laurie LaPan Miller Pepper speaks of her delight at the stories the white alto saxophonist Art Pepper told her when they first met in Synanon, the legendary rehabilitation center where both were recovering from their separate addictions. As the two drew closer, eventually marrying in 1974, Laurie noticed that Pepper's stories took on new, often contradictory details as he retold them. When she decided to write her husband's autobiography, she asked to hear his stories again and again, regularly stopping him for clarification and insisting that he avoid exaggeration and embellishment.[40] *Straight Life* is a fascinating, often harrowing account of a self-destructive musical genius. Journalist Lili Anolik, however, persuasively argues that Art Pepper himself had little of the self-discipline necessary to write a book as heartfelt and as carefully constructed as *Straight Life*. The book only happened because Art the seasoned raconteur and Laurie the obsessed compiler found each other.[41]

Billie Holiday's *Lady Sings the Blues* has remained in print since its publication in 1956.[42] Long before it was made into a film in 1972, the book's instant popularity may have inspired Mingus to begin working on his own autobiography. Recently, in *Billie Holiday: The Musician and the Myth*, John Szwed presents evidence that Holiday was much more involved in the writing of *Lady Sings the Blues* than many have believed.[43] When Holiday later suggested that she never read her own autobiography, she was apparently concealing her disappointment about a book that never became what she had wanted it to be.[44] According to the story that subsequently emerged, the book was cobbled together by the journalist William Dufty, who was married to one of Holiday's close friends, out of a few conversations with the singer but mostly from newspaper interviews and Dufty's own speculations about what was in Holiday's mind at various moments in her life.

Szwed, however, has found a large cache of material that was edited out of the published book, much of it involving Holiday's extraordinary encounters with celebrities such as Orson Welles, Tallulah Bankhead, and even President Franklin D. Roosevelt. Holiday wrote the book in large part to assert that she was no longer a drug addict and that she was ready to go back to work with a reinstated cabaret card. She hoped to make her case more forcefully by cataloging her encounters with important people, almost all of them white. But when the editors at Doubleday excised much of this material for fear of legal reprisals, the book became something very different.[45]

Robert O'Meally, however, has suggested that Holiday might have been pleased with *Lady Sings the Blues* in its presentation of her as a nobly suffering artist; in this regard, he calls it "a dream book, a collection of Holiday's wishes and lies."[46] On a certain level, this is surely true: Holiday was not above creating fictions about herself if it made the book more distinctive (and more marketable). Consider the book's elegant and forceful opening sentences: "Mom and pop were just a couple of kids when they got married. He was eighteen, she was sixteen, and I was three."[47] None of this is accurate, if only because Holiday's parents never married.

Self-mythology, however, was only a small part of what the book was designed to be. Szwed argues that Holiday wanted to recount her many mistakes without blaming anyone else. The material she gave Dufty was designed to give her dignity while redeeming her in the public's eyes. Even without the material that was excised, the book is not entirely the sensationalized story of still another drug-addicted jazz artist—though that is mostly how it has been understood for the past sixty years.

As for the two giants who dominated twentieth-century American music, both Duke Ellington and Louis Armstrong had a way with words. We know that letters flowed profusely from the portable typewriters that Louis Armstrong carried everywhere, beginning in 1922 when he first arrived in Chicago to join King Oliver's band. Only a small selection of these letters, some of them running to several pages and many addressed to people that Armstrong only knew as correspondents, have been published.[48] Armstrong's first autobiography, *Swing That Music*, was extensively edited and rewritten, and legitimated with a foreword by Rudy Vallee, still a valid spokesman for "jazz" among Armstrong's likely readers in the 1930s.[49] When Armstrong sat down to write his second autobiography, *Satchmo: My Life in New Orleans*, he may have been reluctant to tell it all, recalling how his words had been taken away from him the last time. In this sense, Armstrong's experience was similar to Holiday's; had she lived a bit longer, she might have followed his path and written a second memoir that was not so heavily edited.

Armstrong's second autobiography did indeed please his editors. They cleaned up his spelling and punctuation but made few substantive changes. William Kenney has argued, however, that Armstrong found subtle ways of expressing himself *in spite of* the pressure he felt to make *Satchmo* more acceptable to mainstream readers.[50] For example, he speaks adoringly of Bix Beiderbecke, even calling him godlike. At one point we read, "Whenever we saw him our faces shone with joy and happiness, but long periods would pass when we did not see him at all."[51] Kenney suggests that Armstrong— who may in fact have regarded Beiderbecke and his cult with something less than total reverence—managed to construct an account that did not rouse his editors to take up the red pencil at the same time that it contained a telling trace of ambiguity.[52] If left to his own devices, Armstrong was clearly capable of writing his own story with wit and clarity. This was definitely the case when he produced a long, handwritten document in a hospital bed the year before he died.[53] But if Kenney is right, anyone who delves into *Swing That Music* and *Satchmo: My Life in New Orleans* must read between and around the lines to get a better idea of all that was in his mind.

Duke Ellington's autobiography must be read between the lines as well. My admiration for Ellington is boundless, but I must be straightforward about his limitations as an author. To be fair, he was constantly on the road and always composing music. He had little time to read, and unlike Armstrong, he seldom took time to write. Ellington's debonair stage presence and his *faux* English accent were part of a carefully constructed persona. In fact, Ellington suffered from stage fright and tended to repeat a handful of formulaic phrases from the stage. When forced to improvise his announcements, he was capable of calling the Swedish singer Alice Babs "the essence of [pause] musical [long pause] epitome" (being careful to use the French pronunciation of *essence*). And as James Lincoln Collier has ruefully observed, even a casual reading of the lyrics that Ellington wrote for his songs and sacred concerts suggests that he did not have a natural gift as a lyricist.[54]

Ellington continually postponed the writing of his autobiography, even after he had set aside time to conduct interviews with his devoted supporter, the journalist Stanley Dance. After a concert or a tour, the two would sit down for an interview session, but Ellington would turn away, silently watching old movies on television.[55] Nevertheless, Dance managed to collect statements that Duke made on and off the record, with and without requests for specific information, much of it scrawled on napkins and the backs of envelopes. He then stitched it all together to produce *Music Is My Mistress* in 1973, a year before Ellington's death. The book is full of glowing praise for family and friends in several sections called "Dramatis Felidae," alluding to the Latin phrase *Dramatis Personae*, or Persons of the Drama. Because *Dramatis Personae* is more commonly translated as Cast of Characters, "Dramatis Felidae" is meant to be translated as "Cast of Cats," but it is essentially gibberish. Trying to put some Latin into an autobiography is typical of Ellington in particular and of the "professorial" turn in jazz autobiography in general.

The consistent eulogizing of friends throughout the "Dramatis Felidae" sections of *Music Is My Mistress* has inspired critics to sniff out a bit of damning amidst faint praise as well as a few significant omissions. His very brief section on tenor saxophonist Ben Webster, for example, with whom he had some nasty quarrels, begins with the usual encomium but ends with Duke remembering a photograph of Webster on skis and wondering why the skis "were pointing *up* the mountain."[56] There is no mention in *Music Is My Mistress* of two women who were in fact his mistresses, Beatrice "Evie" Ellis and Fernanda de Castro Monte, both of whom he supported for many years during his life.[57] Nor does Ellington mention Edna Thompson, the wife he never divorced.

But Ellington does recall one of the more notorious figures in jazz history, Joe Glaser. Ellington devotes two pages not just to Louis Armstrong but to Armstrong *and* his manager, Glaser. Acknowledging that Glaser took half of everything Armstrong earned, Duke nevertheless says that Glaser took good care of his client. "Louis Armstrong was the epitome of jazz and always will be. He was also a living monument to the magnificent career of Joe Glaser."[58] Like Armstrong on Beiderbecke, Ellington praises Glaser so excessively that one suspects less than total sincerity.

Mingus, by contrast, refers to Glaser in the typescript as "Joe Iceberger" and "Sam Glacier." Mingus knew Glaser well, and not just from the days when he played with Armstrong. Glaser had also managed Red Norvo when Mingus was in his trio, and for a period in the early 1960s Glaser managed Mingus himself. Mingus knew that Glaser had mob connections and that he was not afraid to bring his gangster friends into a situation if he considered it necessary. Charles was never comfortable with Glaser, who could affect an icelike demeanor when he laid down the law. But Mingus may not have known that Armstrong had real love for Glaser and that Glaser returned that affection in his management of Armstrong's career, even facilitating his dealings with the women he met on the road and with whom he would, to use Armstrong's own phrase, "wail." Thanks to Glaser, Armstrong was free to make music with the musicians he liked and to carry on with whomever he wished when he was offstage. Glaser, however, did nothing to dispel the illusion that Armstrong was working for Glaser and not the other way around.

While composing *Music Is My Mistress,* Ellington was clearly reluctant to open up his private life, to Dance or to anyone who was likely to read the book. Not only does he neglect to mention his love life or his encounters with racists, but the one story he tells about the gangsters he encountered in Chicago seems carefully chosen to minimize the dangers in which he may have actually found himself at moments in his career. The story involves a failed attempt by some small-timers to shake him down for a few dollars and ends with Al Capone himself putting out the word, "Duke Ellington is not to be bothered in the Loop."[59] Again, a comparison with Mingus's autobiography is revealing. Mingus fills pages with rapturous accounts of lovers as well as invective against the gangsters, club owners, and entrepreneurs who took advantage of him.

Ellington always wore a mask in public, setting it aside only for a handful of intimates. (The members of this inner circle called him Edward rather than Duke.) Ellington may have learned his lesson early when, in an unguarded moment in 1935, he sharply criticized George Gershwin's *Porgy and Bess* because it failed to capture the real spirit of black South Carolina and because it sounded nothing like African American music. A reporter for the periodical *New Theatre* was present when Ellington made these remarks, and a minor scandal ensued when he published Duke's words.[60] The article put Ellington in a difficult position with people who both admired Gershwin and were in a position to help Duke's career. (He later showers Gershwin with unironic praise in *Music Is My Mistress.*)[61]

For the rest of his life, Ellington preferred to speak only with humor and urbanity in public and conscientiously avoided candor, even when he surely had strong feelings about an issue. For example, when an interviewer told Duke that an English critic had praised his compositions for recalling "the opalescent subtleties of Debussy," Ellington replied, "Don't those London fellows push a mean pen?"[62] He probably found the critic's comments a bit absurd, but knowing that he would be quoted, he responded with his trademark insouciant humor. With statements like this, Ellington revealed his real talent with words.

Ellington's reluctance to disclose his inner self in his autobiography may also have stemmed from an African American man's disinclination to relive the humiliations and dangers he faced throughout his career. Even so, *Music Is My Mistress* was part of a tradition that begins with slave narratives and includes efforts by black authors to alert the world to their sufferings and to reclaim the personhood that had been denied them. Hampton Hawes and a handful of other black jazz artists can readily be understood as part of this tradition, but many more—Armstrong and Ellington most prominently—tended to put a happy face on their encounters and soft-pedal the dark side of their experiences as African Americans.

Hampton Hawes, however, was never invited to the White House, let alone by Richard M. Nixon. Mingus was on the White House lawn in 1978, but that was—in many ways—a very long time after Nixon honored Ellington in 1969. From 1969 until 1973, during Nixon's first term as president, the United States government was aggressively punishing African Americans for two decades of civil rights demands. Nixon's "Southern strategy" and the FBI's multifaceted attempts to undermine the African American agenda were unprecedented in the twentieth century. That Ellington was embraced by Nixon himself during these same years is a striking testament to his success in setting himself apart from race and politics.

Ajay Heble has argued that *Music Is my Mistress* is consistent with Ellington's goal of "moving contentedly" through the corridors of white power, even when state-sanctioned schemes to disempower black Americans were being devised in those same corridors. Heble demands that we read the book not in terms of what is omitted or downplayed but rather in terms of how it reflects Ellington's ability to achieve "power, credibility, and autonomy." Ellington understood his precarious position as a black American and thus competed "for access and public legitimacy not by explicitly challenging dominant structures of knowledge production but by improvising *within* an already constituted system."[63]

Ellington essentially let his public persona write his autobiography. Comparing Ellington and Mingus as autobiographers, Daniel Stein has said that Ellington's upper-class ambitions led him to "cast himself beyond race, politics, and sexuality in ways almost directly opposed to Mingus's angry stance toward these issues."[64] If Duke sought to project a single, aristocratic self throughout his autonarrative, Mingus turned loose several selves, including many that grew out of his search for a coherent identity.

On the first page of his autobiography, Mingus characterizes one of his personae as a "frightened animal that attacks for fear of being attacked." We see that figure in action in one of the most powerful moments in *Beneath the Underdog*—the confrontation with Lee-Marie's father, Joe Spendell. Even though he had made a life for himself and Donna and might have given up on ever seeing Lee-Marie again, Mingus decides to seek her out after he learns that she is in Sausalito working at her father's fish-and-chips place.[65] Many years after Joe Spendell had shot Mingus, aborted Lee-Marie's child, and seen to it that she was given a tubal ligation, Mingus takes his revenge. One reads in horror as Lee-Marie takes a gun she thinks is loaded. When Mingus tells her to point it at her father and pull the trigger, she does.[66]

This moment when Lee-Marie definitively demonstrates that her love for Charles has no bounds is in both the typescript and *Beneath the Underdog*, yet it was almost certainly invented. Mingus must also have invented the scenes when Lee-Marie joins Donna as a high-priced call girl. (Mingus told Regina Ryan that Mary Ellen Kelly never worked as a prostitute.)[67]

But putting aside the melodrama of the love plot, when Mingus gives an unloaded gun to Lee-Marie and tells her to pull the trigger, he is engaging in a much more familiar autobiographical practice: settling a score. He has never forgiven Mary Ellen Kelly's father, who apparently did keep young Charles away from his daughter. The search for revenge that runs through his account of Joe Spendell in *Beneath the Underdog* is paralleled by the passage when he remembers his own father, who beat him for bed-wetting, never suspecting that his son might have a medical condition. The son writes, "The very act of recalling those early images makes me dwell on getting revenge."[68] Watching Lee-Marie think she is killing her father is surely a fulfillment of that revenge, only slightly displaced from one father to another.

MILES TO GO

Miles Davis brags about abusing his women in *Miles: The Autobiography*,[69] inspiring the poet Pearl Cleage to wonder how she ever could have been so enraptured by the music of a man capable of such violence against women.[70] But there is nothing in Davis's book like the incident when Lee-Marie is prepared to kill her father. And surprisingly, Davis seems to be less interested in settling scores and more intent on portraying himself as an elder statesman offering a hand-up to younger jazz artists.

When Simon & Schuster approached Davis's agent with a contract for an autobiography, Davis chose Quincy Troupe as his collaborator. Troupe had won Davis's respect when he interviewed Miles a few years earlier for a long piece in *Spin* magazine.[71] After the contracts for *Miles: The Autobiography* had been signed, Troupe and Davis spoke for many hours, engaging in disjointed, almost stream-of-consciousness conversations. Neither man seemed intent on constructing a chronological narrative. At some point in his conversations with Troupe, Davis lost interest and refused to continue. He had, of course, taken the publisher's advance money, but this did not stop him from walking away. In desperation, Troupe appears to have dipped into Jack Chambers's two-volume biography of Davis to fill in the gaps. In an article in the *New Republic,* Stanley Crouch thoroughly documented Troupe's borrowings from Chambers by juxtaposing several pairs of passages from both books.[72]

Most of *Miles: The Autobiography,* however, is a heavily edited version of what Davis said to Troupe. Who did most of the editing is unclear. Chambers says that Troupe told him "a whole committee" of editors worked on the book after he turned it over to the publishers.[73] But the transcripts of Troupe's interviews with Davis suggest otherwise. Troupe gave the recordings of his interviews to a typist who transcribed them. The transcripts, often marked up with extensive changes by Troupe, constitute a large stack of papers at the Schomburg branch of the New York Public Library in Harlem. They show how Troupe edited his own questions out and then rephrased Davis's statements so they read like what Troupe believed the authorial voice of Miles Davis ought to be. On some level, he got it right. Many critics who reviewed the published text actually remarked that the book really *sounded* like Miles.

On another level, though, it seems as if he was preventing Davis from speaking in his own voice. For example, when Davis recalls hearing Billy Eckstine's band in 1944 when it included Charlie Parker, Dizzy Gillespie, and Sarah Vaughan, Troupe added some colorful descriptions to Davis's account of Sarah Vaughan's voice. He also changed certain passages to give Davis's language more of a vernacular feel. Troupe may have been trying to make Davis sound like an urban black man speaking casually, even in passages where the transcripts show Davis speaking with perfect grammar. In one instance, Troupe initially revised Davis's entirely grammatical phrase "she used to sing" to "she be singing"; this was later changed again, either by Troupe or by an editor at Simon & Schuster, to "she'd be singing." Davis no longer sounds illiterate, but he does sound more vernacular.[74]

In another passage, Davis speculates about how his voice acquired that distinctive whispery, raspy sound in the 1950s. In his actual statements in Troupe's transcript he appears uncertain, but he does seem willing to allow that, as with Louis Armstrong and Dizzy Gillespie, playing the trumpet transformed his voice. He firmly denies, however, that his voice changed when he yelled at Morris Levy at Birdland after a benign polyp was removed from his vocal cords and he was told not to speak for several days. Many journalists had dutifully reported that Davis ruined his voice by speaking truth to power.[75] It's a useful story, even if Davis was determined to debunk it. In the end, though, the published book has him acting against his better judgment the day after he was released from the hospital and raising his voice to "this guy in the record business" who was trying to talk him into some sort of a deal.[76]

An intriguing aspect of *Miles: The Autobiography* is its close attention to the discographical details of Davis's career. The book regularly tells us who Davis was playing with at a recording session or a club date; very few of the people who performed with Davis, even for brief periods, are left out of the narrative. So far as I can tell, the information is always accurate, even if the narrator regularly adds "I think," "I forget," and "I'm not sure" when personnel are listed. Troupe or an editor probably took the initiative on this, but it's also possible that it was Davis's doing. At some stage in the process, he may have instructed Troupe to look up all those discographical details and add them to the narrative, with "I think" and "I forget" included so Davis didn't sound like a jazz nerd who can recite session personnel the way an obsessed baseball fan can rattle off batting averages. Miles thus retains both a devil-may-care attitude and an image as a benevolent mentor to young musicians.

Davis also seems to have liked some of the stories that Troupe made up, including one about Frances Taylor, Davis's first wife. When Taylor came back into his life, Miles-as-narrator says that everyone loved her, including Marlon Brando and Quincy Jones, and he adds that Jones gave her a ring, presumably an engagement ring.[77] In an interview with Gerald Early, Quincy Jones says that he told Davis, "Miles, you know that's bullshit," to which Davis responded, "Man, that fucking sounds good." Jones added, "Miles was a serious dramatist, you know."[78] Davis may have walked away from the project because he had lost interest, but it is also possible that he was simply content with how Troupe was filling in the gaps.

The oral feeling, whether real or constructed, of *Miles: The Autobiography* strongly connects it to African American literary traditions. However, the book is too ploddingly thorough to have the focus and piquancy of which *Beneath the Underdog* can boast. Indeed, the two books constitute a study in contrasts. As the Quincy Jones anecdote suggests, Miles may indeed never have read *Miles: The Autobiography*, whereas Mingus wrote out everything himself and was a looming presence when *Beneath the Underdog* was being edited. And unlike the Miles Davis created by Quincy Troupe, Mingus seldom talks about the individuals with whom he played. When he does mention an artist, it's almost always because he has an extramusical relationship with that person. And when Mingus has bad memories of musicians, he simply doesn't acknowledge them by name, as when he refers to Red Norvo only as "the Redhead."

Nel King, who edited *Beneath the Underdog*, asked Mingus to put more about his life in music into his memoir, and many agree that too much of Mingus's playing career has been left out. Burt Korall's comment in *Saturday Review* was typical: "It would have been preferable if Mingus had concentrated on music, its makers and the business—about which he has a depth of specialized knowledge."[79] Mingus did in fact have a great deal to say about music, but he was more committed to expressing in words the thoughts and feelings he put into his music. He always insisted that music was the most essential aspect of his life, so essential that he ended his relationships with Lee-Marie and Donna because he wanted to get back to playing and composing.[80] Playing the music was clearly more important to him than writing about it in some systematic fashion.

BRAS COUPÉ, OMAR, AND SIDNEY BECHET

One other jazz autobiography has been as enthusiastically received as *Beneath the Underdog*, and that is *Treat It Gentle* by the New Orleans–born Creole clarinetist and soprano saxophonist Sidney Bechet.[81] Unfortunately, the extent to which the book presents the actual words of Bechet is unknown. Although there is evidence that Bechet was recorded extensively so that his words could be transcribed for *Treat It Gentle*, almost all of the tapes are missing. Jessica Teague has suggested that the tapes were treated "like scrap paper," not considered important enough to be preserved. The tapes may even have been recycled and Bechet's words taped over. So far as we know, there is no way to compare the tapes to what is in the published book.[82]

To further complicate questions of attribution, *Treat It Gentle* went through three editors and two publishers before reaching print. We do have two hours of taped interviews that Desmond Flower, the book's final editor, conducted with Bechet in Paris in 1957. The tapes are now in Tulane University's Hogan Jazz Archive and offer a unique opportunity to hear Bechet's own voice. But the tapes were clearly made after most of the book had been drafted and "served primarily to fill in gaps and bring the story up to date from where it left off around 1936."[83]

Like Mingus, Bechet the writer produced more than just an autobiography. He also wrote short fiction intended for either stage or screen. The Bechet section of the Charles Delauney Collection in Paris contains a screenplay from 1951 based on the popular song "Frankie and Johnny," called *Wildflower (or, The Story of Frankie and Johnny)*. In about 1955, Bechet wrote another treatment for a film or a novel, a four-page story about a jazz musician living in Paris who reminisces about a love affair from twenty years earlier. Like *Treat It Gentle*, the story is vaguely autobiographical.[84]

Actually, parts of *Treat It Gentle* are not even *vaguely* autobiographical. The most memorable chapter in the book is about Omar, an escaped slave whom Bechet claims as his grandfather. In fact, Bechet was Creole on both sides of his family tree, and if some of his relatives were slaves, it would have been several generations previous. More intriguingly, Bechet appropriated the story of Omar from a figure in African American folklore known as Bras-Coupé.

In the earliest versions of a story that dates to the 1830s, Bras-Coupé is the leader of a group of ex-slaves hiding in the swamps near New Orleans. From there they make raids on stores and plantations. He supposedly lost his arm—and so gained his name—when a police officer amputated it after an early attempt to escape from slavery. In an exhaustive and thoughtful account, Bryan Wagner has shown that Bras-Coupé's legend was put to use by New Orleans police officers in the early nineteenth century to increase their own power.[85] When New Orleans passed from French to American hands after the Louisiana Purchase of 1803, citizens were profoundly suspicious of a police force that had previously been employed by the King of France and that was accustomed to making full use of that power. Policemen made the extremely clever decision to embellish the Bras-Coupé story, turning him into a black monster with almost supernatural powers. They then spread the story in hopes of terrifying the population into giving them more guns and sanctioning their use of force.

The legend of Bras-Coupé was substantially enhanced when the white American writer George Washington Cable heard the story from a black porter and decided to create his own version. Cable's novel was eventually published in serial form in 1879 and 1880 in *Scribner's* magazine. The novel added several elements to the story that made it important to Bechet, especially a scene in which Bras-Coupé joins the slaves dancing in Congo Square, distinguishing himself as the most graceful and athletic of the dancers.[86]

With Cable's additions, Bras-Coupé becomes a key figure in the history of jazz, at least as it was conceived in the early years of the twentieth century when Congo Square became known as the place that marked the continuity between blacks in Africa and blacks in America. Early jazz historians were invested in finding strong African precedents for jazz, so Congo Square was perfect for them. Some went so far as to argue that Buddy Bolden, the unrecorded cornettist who may have been the first African American musician to play what we now call jazz, only began to play the music after he heard the drums in Congo Square. This claim was refuted when researchers turned up evidence that slave meetings in Congo Square ceased in the 1840s, at least thirty years before Bolden was born. Contemporary jazz scholars have also argued that what took place at Congo Square was almost entirely African American rather than African. In any case, it seems clear now that the music and dancing had little impact on early jazz.[87]

Sidney Bechet nevertheless accepted the importance of Congo Square and claimed Bras-Coupé/Omar as his grandfather in order to place his own bloodline at the origins of jazz history. Early in *Treat It Gentle*, Bechet asserts that Congo Square "was my grandfather's square. He never had to hear it from a distance. It was there in his mind even before he got to the square and began performing it. It was *his* drums, *his* voice, *his* dancing."[88] Bechet extends the story of Omar with various borrowings that may have come from oral tradition but more likely came from Cable's novel as well as from a version of the Bras-Coupé story in a collection of New Orleans folktales, *Gumbo Ya-ya*, published in 1945.[89]

Bechet's retelling of the Bras-Coupé legend takes up a full fifth of his autobiography. The rest appears to be a more straightforward account of a musician's career. The entire story is told in a colloquial but authoritative fashion that probably came from his editors more than from Bechet. John Ciardi, who worked on the text after it had been transcribed and edited by Bechet's secretary, Joan Williams, has said that his main goal was to restore some of the flavor of Bechet's speech.[90] How much access Ciardi had to Bechet's own words is unknown, as is the extent to which Ciardi himself added to the text. After Joan Williams threatened to sue Bechet and his publishers, claiming that she was the true author of Bechet's autobiography, Ciardi's text was shelved.[91] A few years later, the text was rediscovered by the art collector and jazz enthusiast Desmond Flower. He worked with Bechet to bring the story up to date before editing and publishing it with his own press, Cassell & Co.[92]

We will probably never know precisely how Bechet's stories moved from his mouth to the printed page. For our purposes, it is enough that he wanted to create a history of jazz by forging an existential connection between a highly musical slave and his own origins. "The music, it's my whole story," Bechet wrote. It was also the story of a mythical grandfather who literally embodied the music. As Wagner argues, the men who punished the escaped slave could cut off his arm, but they could not disconnect him from the music.[93] Regardless of what we think of Bechet's self-mythologizing, *Treat It Gentle* is an especially beautiful artifact in the literature of jazz.

MINGUS AMONG THE EDITORS

Mingus told friends that he was inspired by Billie Holiday's autobiography not because he felt the need to tell his own story but because he wanted to make some money. This may explain why *Beneath the Underdog* often reads like a potboiler. Yet the book is much too ingenious to be regarded as hack work. Mingus was an uncompromising artist who rethought the role of the autobiographer, just as he constantly rethought the art of musical performance. He was incapable of grinding it out for a paycheck.

At first, Mingus wanted to call his book *Memoirs of a Half Yellow Schitt-Colored Nigger*. In a long letter to Regina Ryan, the editor at Alfred A. Knopf who acquired the book in 1969, Nel King tells the story of how the book took shape. The letter, dated June 14, 1971, is now part of the Knopf archives at the Harry Ransom Center, University of Texas in Austin. King says that Charles wrote the entire book over the space of six months in 1963. If this is true, Mingus was exceptionally creative in a year when he was also making his superb recordings for impulse! King says that Charles mostly wrote late at night when he was having trouble sleeping. She adds that he also spoke some material into a tape recorder.[94]

Mingus probably wrote in a hurry because he had a contract and a substantial advance from McGraw-Hill (see below). In a 1971 interview with Whitney Balliett, he said that he had been working on the book for twenty-five years.[95] In another interview, he said that he had started writing the book in California but that Celia lost what he had written.[96] He may have had some notes and sketches going back to the 1940s, and this may have been the material that Celia "lost." King, however, says that Mingus had nothing on paper when he first approached her in 1962 to ask for her help with his autobiography.

Today, Regina Ryan is a literary agent living in Manhattan. She remembers Nel King as a petite blonde with a pageboy haircut.[97] In the 1940s, King worked as an apprentice editor in Hollywood,[98] and in the 1950s she wrote a few short pieces for the *New Yorker* as well as scripts for various television program. In a grant application for funds to help defray expenses while editing Mingus's book, she notes that many of these television programs were documentaries about jazz musicians.[99] Nel King knew Mingus's work well enough to insist in 1961 that he be brought over to England to participate in the making of the film *All Night Long,* for which she had co-written the screenplay. Her co-author was Paul Jarrico, a busy Hollywood screenwriter who struggled in the 1950s after he was blacklisted. On the release print of *All Night Long* he is identified as "Peter Achilles."

In *All Night Long,* Mingus plays a character named "Charles Mingus," who looks exactly like Charles Mingus and speaks sentences that the real Mingus might have said, but probably did not.

Gary Giddins was just beginning his distinguished career as a journalist when he interviewed Nel King in her apartment shortly after *Beneath the Underdog* was published. She was moving to California and had packed up most of her records, but she had left out a few LPs by Mingus and Dave Brubeck, the two American jazz stars who appear in *All Night Long.* King told Giddins that she and Charles regularly spoke on the set of *All Night Long,* and when they returned to New York, she would often go hear his bands in clubs. When Giddins asked her to talk about *Beneath the Underdog,* she did have some anecdotes about working with Mingus, but she would not allow them to be published for fear of upsetting Charles. Every time she began talking about her encounters with Charles, she would motion for Giddins to turn off his tape recorder. "After this happened half a dozen times, I threw in the towel, turned off the recorder, and listened to a score of anecdotes, none of which I could convey then or remember now."[100] The young journalist did not get his story. My guess is that many of the anecdotes that Giddins forgot can be found in the correspondence in the Knopf archive.

In her 1971 letter to Ryan, King says that she was away for the several months in 1963 when Mingus was writing. When she next saw him, he had a manuscript of 870 pages. Mingus wrote out his story and his convictions on yellow legal paper, which he then gave to his third wife, Judy, a skilled typist. This typescript is now available to researchers as part of the Mingus Collection at the Library of Congress.

An editor at McGraw-Hill offered Mingus an advance of $5,500 in August 1962. A letter in the Knopf archive says that a book with the working title "Mingus Autobiography" was contracted to be co-written by Mingus and Louis E. Lomax, an African American journalist who had recently published a fairly successful book, *The Negro Revolt.*[101] But any working relationship between these two quickly dissolved when Charles began to suspect that Lomax was only interested in taking his money.

Regardless, with the promise of $5,500 up front, Mingus announced in August 1962 that he was retiring and moving to Majorca, Spain, "perhaps forever," where he would write a symphony.[102] An article in *Jet* magazine, also published in August 1962, said that Mingus was moving to Majorca "to work on his autobiography and composition."[103] In any event, he probably had very little to show McGraw-Hill in 1962.

The McGraw-Hill editors canceled the contract in 1964 at least in part because they did not like what Mingus had written in his burst of activity in 1963. They may also have objected to his demand that the book be bound in white with the title in gold lettering so that it would resemble the Bible.[104] Mingus himself said that the book was rejected because it had too many dirty words. But he had also used the actual names of many people in his life, which meant that lawsuits and reprisals were inevitable. Some of the people he named in the book had read sections of the typescript after the book was rejected by McGraw-Hill. They would walk up to him on the street to complain. Mingus suspected that Louis Lomax had given the typescript to people who had put the book "on the fucking market."[105]

After McGraw-Hill canceled the agreement, Charles said he would publish the book himself and sell it door to door. He ended up carrying the typescript around New York on and off between 1964 and 1969 in search of a publisher. His inability to find one surely contributed to his severe psychological problems during this period.

After Sue Graham met Mingus in 1964 she maintained a professional relationship with him, serving as his literary agent even when their on-again-off-again romance was at its nadir. During this period Sue was editing a journal called *Changes*, devoted to avant-garde culture and politics. In the third issue of the magazine, dated August 1968, Sue published a segment of what Mingus was still calling *Memoirs of a Half Yellow Schitt-Colored Nigger*.

Regina Ryan did not see the issue of *Changes*, but the magazine may have given the book enough buzz that she began hearing rumors about it. She was definitely intrigued. Then a friend who was a Mingus fanatic wanted to play the *Mingus at Monterey* LP for her, and when he pulled the record out of its sleeve, a little piece of paper came fluttering out. Mingus (or someone) had put the paper in with the record to ask people to send him money so that that he could publish his book. In February 1969, Ryan wrote to Mingus at the post office address she found on the piece of paper.[106]

After several years of carrying the book around in boxes and suitcases to publishers who were never interested, Mingus suddenly heard from an editor he had not even approached. But by this time Mingus had become gun shy; he refused to let Ryan see the book for fear that she or someone in her office would make copies and share them with friends, which is what he assumed Louis Lomax had done. Just as Mingus had formed his own record companies to avoid being ripped off by corporate masters, he now wanted to keep people from reading his book in "pirated" form.

But Ryan persisted. After several months of back-and-forth, mostly between Sue Graham and Ryan, an agreement was reached: Ryan could see the manuscript, but only if Sue was present while she read it. In a 1972 interview Ryan said, "We had one day, and she brought this thing in—in Pan Am bags, I mean dripping with paper, you just couldn't believe it—and for about four hours I sat there and read. He doesn't know this, but I put her in another office . . . I would grab up a handful and I'd run into our editor-in-chief and say, 'Look, this is pretty exciting stuff. What do you think?'"[107]

Bob Gottlieb, who was then editor-in-chief at Knopf, was as impressed as Ryan. They bypassed the usual acquisition process and immediately offered Mingus an advance against royalties of $25,000. When Ryan suggested that a third party be brought in to do the bulk of the editing, Mingus told her that he had already asked Nel King to help him edit the 870-page manuscript. In a letter to King signed by Mingus and dated September 1, 1969, he promises her one-half of all advances against one-third of the royalties. The letter also indicates that the title of the book had already been changed to *Beneath the Underdog: His World According to Mingus*.[108] The contract that Mingus, Nel King, and Sue Graham eventually signed with Regina Ryan states that 45 percent of the advance should go to Charles, 45 percent to King, and 10 percent to Sue. If the book made back its $25,000 advance, royalties would be split 60/30/10, respectively.[109] Ryan told me that this was the largest advance she ever offered anyone during her career at Knopf, which began in 1964 and ended in 1975.

King worked diligently during the latter part of 1969 and the early months of 1970 to edit the book down to a little more than half its original length. Making sure that she regularly checked in with Charles for his approval, she skillfully rearranged the material to follow a more coherent chronology. At some point King made the excellent decision to move the segment beginning with "In other words, I am three" to the opening chapter. (The typescript begins with "Baby had just turned two" and the story about young Charles falling on his head that now constitutes chapter 2 of *Beneath the Underdog*.)

Regina Ryan wanted the book to be more linear and to begin early in Mingus's life, just as it does in the typescript. King, however, liked the conversation between Mingus and his psychotherapist that appears much later, on

CHAPTERS	PAGE NOS.	CONTENTS	SOURCE
XXIII	277-283	Nessa again. Stars of Swing; bandstand talk	696-708
XXIV	284-299	Talk with Brother and Bess. Getting ready to go to San Francisco with Donna.	287-309
XXV	300-314	Arrival in San Francisco. Bobby Bell and Babe	NM 18; 309-332
XXVI	315-323	Visiting Spendell's Bar. Taking Lee-Marie away.	332-344

Figure 8. Excerpt from letter by Nel King to Charles Mingus explaining the editing of *Beneath the Underdog*. Knopf Archive, Harry Ransom Center, University of Texas at Austin.

page 688 of the typescript. Eventually, she convinced Mingus that the "I am three" section should be moved to the beginning of the book. When Mingus later signed a document authorizing King's edited version for publication, he added a handwritten note saying that his signature was "valid only if" the book began, as King wanted, with the "I am three" passage.[110]

The correspondence among Mingus, King, and Ryan in the Knopf archive is voluminous, and revealing. Ryan is concerned primarily that the writing be clear and accessible and that there be no question of anyone named in the book filing legal charges. King is more focused on preserving Mingus's voice and making sure that he is comfortable with the editorial changes. After King and Ryan produced a draft on which everyone could agree, King wrote a letter to Charles dated September 6, 1970, asking him to go over the text as carefully as possible and to make notes where he thought changes should be made.[111]

Along with the letter she sent a guide to how sections of the original typescript had been moved around to create the new, edited draft. The entire guide runs to five pages, all of it as detailed as the sample shown in figure 8. The numbers in the column on the right refer to page numbers in the typescript, and those on the left to King's draft. "NM" stands for new material that was not in the typescript but that Mingus wrote at King's request to fill in missing information.

In the letter of September 6, King told Mingus to read the new draft carefully and make whatever changes he wanted. "When we've done this, you and I will get together with your notes for a last and final polish. It is extremely important that you do it, Charles. It may take you a couple of days (and don't under-estimate the time it will take), but you must be completely satisfied before the book goes to type-setting. Please don't let anything interfere with your doing it: plan on setting aside the time you will need immediately after September 22. This will be our last chance to make the book as good as we can."[112] King's language suggests that Mingus was reluctant to devote more time to a project that was still dragging on long after he had finished the draft of 1963. But the letter also reveals how determined King was to make sure the book really was Mingus's. And Mingus did indeed send in the letter approving her draft three weeks later.

One of the documents in the Knopf archive is a forty-seven-page letter from King to Ryan in which King responds page-by-page to the many changes that Ryan had made to King's first edit of *Beneath the Underdog*. King agrees to many of Ryan's suggestions, but she frequently states that Charles wishes her to reject or modify others. Like the letter from September 6, 1970, this document also reveals the extent to which Mingus was responsible for writing his own book, even if King had to coax some of it out of him. There are plenty of lines in King's long letter that begin, "CM says insert . . .," as well as several instances where Mingus rejects Ryan's editing of passages she considered unclear. For example, "Mingus says this makes perfect sense to him, and he likes it exactly the way it is."[113]

Mingus occasionally appears to have given in on certain changes. For example, Ryan asked that the names of the pimp Bobby Bell and his girlfriend be changed in order to avoid lawsuits. King responded, "CM believes that true pimps and whores will never come forward and sue anybody for calling them such and maybe he's right. (It's not a chance I care to take.) So we've changed his name to William Bones, known as Billy Bones, and changed his description."[114] Mingus may have resisted, but he saw the logic of what Ryan was suggesting. He also knew that changing a name hardly changes the story or the multilayered account of pimping that runs through a large portion of the book.

The correspondence reveals that Mingus had a variety of reactions to his editors' requests for more material. When I read the typescript for the first time, I was surprised that I did *not* see three of the most memorable passages in *Beneath the Underdog*: the sexual advice from Pop Collette, the story of Mingus's self-commitment to Bellevue, and his encounter with Juan Tizol during his days with the Ellington orchestra. King would later explain that these and other anecdotes "were extracted from him in conversation, and sometimes it took a number of his infrequent visits to get enough for a rough which was slowly converted to Mingus-ese."[115]

When King told Charles that stories of his professional and musical life were essential to give the book "some balance," he replied, "I don't want that stuff in, Nel—the book is about sex and religion."[116] The book was indeed about sex, but it was only slightly about religion. At least at that point in the writing and editing process, Mingus was not prepared to talk about those aspects of his life that ultimately made the book so distinctive, including his long conversations about politics, economics, and spirituality with Nat Hentoff, Fats Navarro, and Billy Bones.

The many months of the editing process took its toll on everyone involved. In her own correspondence, Ryan is consistently reasonable, professional, and occasionally firm in her convictions. Mingus and King both had their outbursts. In a letter written a few months after her forty-seven-page response to Ryan's edits, King writes about a phrase that Ryan wanted her to "bring up with Charles once again." Mingus had written "c.p. time" as an abbreviation for "colored people's time," a phrase that black people used to joke about their tendency to be less punctual than white people would like them to be. Ryan had apparently asked on more than one occasion that it be changed or omitted. Here is what King says happened after she did in fact bring it up again: "Boy! Did my boy react with rage! He said, 'I told you I didn't want to explain it. The whole fucking book has been destroyed by your making me explain on every page to WHITE PEOPLE what things mean. Either leave it the way it is or fuck it! —Take it out!'"[117]

Increasingly irritated by the many calls he was getting from King, Mingus followed his usual practice of lashing out in racial terms. Although the book was his work, Mingus was becoming disenchanted with the process of getting it published. And despite the period of generally successful collaboration with King, he ultimately grew disenchanted with her as well. A good deal of correspondence in the Knopf archive addresses the question of how King should be represented in the front of the book. At first she insisted that "With Nel King" be placed immediately after Mingus's name. Ryan and Gottlieb talked her out of that, saying that "with" indicated the work of a second-rate ghostwriter. At one point she asked to be listed as co-author. She eventually agreed that the phrase "Edited by Nel King" appear below the subtitle, "His World as Composed by Mingus." She then began asking for a larger share of the advance against royalties, finding ambiguities in the wording of the contract she had signed.

As Mingus's manager at this stage, Sue was caught in the middle. In her correspondence just before and after the book was published, King consistently refers to Sue as "Mrs. Ungaro," her previous married name. By the time the book finally came out, Nel was pointedly not invited to the publication party. She came anyway.

Nel King passed away in California in 1977. An obituary in *Variety* states that she was in her mid-fifties and that she had written for television shows such as *Mike and Buff* and *Look Up and Live.*[118] Regina Ryan says that she once encountered her working as a sales clerk at Gimbels department store during Christmas sales. She also recalls that King pitched a book about director/screenwriter Preston Sturges to Bob Gottlieb when he was at Knopf.[119] King apparently worked with Sturges in the 1940s, but the book never happened.[120]

In Knopf's promotional literature, *Beneath the Underdog* is called "the wild, shocking, anguished, dirty, sexy, funny, and above all, profoundly moving autobiography of the great black jazz composer and bassist."[121] Whoever wrote the "Fact Sheet" for the book also says that it would attract the same kind of reader who had bought Claude Brown's *Manchild in the Promised Land,* another autobiography by an African American that had been published a few years earlier and sold several million copies. *Beneath the Underdog* did not sell nearly as well. Ryan, who left Knopf in 1975, told me that the hardback version of the book probably did not earn back its advance against royalties.[122] However, the paperback edition has sold steadily for more than forty years now.

Beneath the Underdog proves that Mingus—with or without editors—had a genuine gift as a writer. He fought with editors who wanted to change his work, and sometimes he had to give in, but his commitment to every aspect of the book's genesis affirms that the book is truly his.

"SELF-PORTRAIT IN THREE COLORS": MINGUS AND AUTOBIOGRAPHY

Unlike almost all the other autobiographies of important jazz musicians, *Beneath the Underdog* was not written or heavily rewritten by someone else. Nor was Mingus speaking from behind a carefully constructed mask like Ellington, or providing only traces of his real self like Armstrong. And he did not massively appropriate the work of others like Bechet. Also keep in mind that Mingus wrote the book on his own and did not, like Art Pepper or Hampton Hawes, collaborate with someone who decided to "set the story straight" by interviewing him extensively.

Nel King was not a highly motivated interviewer like Laurie Pepper, nor was she a mythologizing collaborator like Miles Davis's Quincy Troupe or a patient palace guardsman assembling jottings like Ellington's Stanley Dance. King strived at every step in the process to make sure that her edits were acceptable to Mingus. After expressing enthusiasm about collaborating with King early on, however, Mingus began to find the months working with her and Regina Ryan to be tedious. Janet Coleman said that he referred to the book during this period as his "pick and shovel autobiography."[123] Regina Ryan, however, said that Mingus was "delighted, thrilled" at what she and King did with his book. "I think sometimes out of self-defense, he'll say, 'Oh, well, the best part of it's gone,' or that kind of thing. But it's not."[124] Shortly after the book was published, Mingus told interviewers at radio station WKCR that he liked the book: "Yeah, it's good."[125]

Charles's older sister, Vivian, never read more than a few pages of *Beneath the Underdog*. She said that she could not get past the passage where Charles says that he had sex with a houseful of Mexican prostitutes.[126] His younger sister, Grace, said that she read about a third but stopped because she was so "disgusted with that book." When the sisters told him how shocked they were by stories of their beloved brother consorting with pimps and prostitutes, Charles told them, "They had to commercialize it in order to sell it."[127] But there was even more about pimps and prostitutes in the typescript. Alfred A. Knopf, who had retired from running the company that bore his name but still read what the new editors were publishing, exclaimed: "That sweet Ryan girl did this!"[128] Mr. Knopf had no idea how hard Ryan had worked to make the book less raunchy!

Having read the typescript in the Library of Congress more than once, I can confidently say that almost all of what was edited out was not essential. Mingus was surely sincere when he added a note to the first pages of *Beneath the Underdog* that praised King and Ryan: "I would like to express my deep thanks to Nel King, who worked long and hard editing this book, and who is probably the only white person who could have done it. And my thanks to Regina Ryan of Knopf—who heard about my book, came looking for me, and was responsible for its publication."[129] He knew that he had left a substantial portion of himself inside the covers of the book. He must also have known that he had accomplished in literature what he had so brilliantly achieved in his music, what Eric Porter has called an "aesthetic Romanticism and the heartfelt attention to romance."[130]

Thanks to the insight of Nel King, *Beneath the Underdog* begins with what we soon discover to be Mingus speaking to his psychotherapist, later identified as "Dr. Wallach." Here are the first words of the book:

In other words, I am three. One man stands forever in the middle, unconcerned, unmoved, watching, waiting to be allowed to express what he sees to the other two. The second man is like a frightened animal that attacks for fear of being attacked. Then there's an over-loving gentle person who lets people into the uttermost sacred temple of his being and he'll take insults and be trusting and sign contracts without reading them and get talked down to working cheap or for nothing, and when he realizes what's been done to him he feels like killing and destroying everything around him including himself for being so stupid. But he can't—he goes back inside himself.[131]

This passage recalls an especially beautiful composition that Mingus had recorded a few years before. "Self-Portrait in Three Colors," first released on the 1959 Columbia LP *Mingus Ah Um*, is so tightly composed that there is no need for the musicians to improvise after a brief piano introduction.[132] The composed portion begins with saxophonists Shafi Hadi (Curtis Porter) and John Handy playing a lilting line for fifteen bars. They repeat the line as Willie Dennis adds a new melody underneath with his trombone. On the third time through, Booker Ervin's tenor saxophone adds still another voice while the other horns repeat what they had just played. And then the recording ends, clocking in at barely three minutes. At moments the three voices mesh well within the chord changes. At other points, the lines seem to be going off in different directions, creating dissonant harmonies. The song is a lyrical ballad, and we should take Mingus at his word that this "Self-Portrait" represents how he saw himself, at least at this moment in his life. Mingus signals the three figures' incompatibility in the moments when the three lines fail to mesh according to the familiar conventions of the popular song.

Mingus's "I am three" also anticipates his habit of speaking as "I," "you," and "he" at different points in *Beneath the Underdog*. When speaking in the third person, he calls himself "my boy Charles," "Chazz," "my man," and just "Mingus." Early on, too, he refers to himself as "Baby," the nickname his stepmother and two older sisters gave him.

The practice of name- and pronoun-shifting by autobiographers intrigues literary critic Laura Marcus. In her book *Auto/biographical Discourses*, Marcus praises the "autobiographical criticism" of many female writers who carefully phrase their perceptions of works of art within their own histories.[133] For Marcus, autobiographical criticism is every bit as important as the canonized self-narratives of the great dead white males. She argues that certain female writers fortuitously transgress against the familiar, lofty style of "classic" autobiographies that aspire to universal truth. Writers who ground their criticism in their own lives do not imagine that their truths are so powerful that they transcend time, place, and the writer's subjectivity.[134]

Late in her book, when Marcus brings her theoretical models to bear on a number of texts, she devotes several pages to André Gorz's *The Traitor* (1989): "One of the most striking aspects of *The Traitor* is Gorz's use of pronominal forms to chart the move from alienation to a kind of self-affirmation."[135] In other words, at different moments in the book the author refers to himself as "I," "we," "they," and "you." Marcus is also intrigued by the "shifting temporalities" of the autobiography as well as the lack of a "secure standpoint from which the past can be recounted as something already known and complete, nor any obvious starting point for the analysis."[136]

Twenty-five years before Gorz wrote *The Traitor*, Mingus was telling his story in multiple voices, exactly the technique that Marcus finds so fascinating about Gorz's book. Also like Gorz, Mingus switches from past to present tense at various points in the narrative. Both Mingus and Gorz make it clear that there is no "secure standpoint" from where they can conduct a valid analysis of who they are. In the final section of Marcus's book, "Autobiography and Ethnicity," she looks at slave narratives and the writings of African American women who have attempted to remake for themselves a literary genre that had been carefully constructed by white European men. At no point in her book, however, does she mention Mingus, who confronted many of the same problems as the black female authors she cites. At the risk of seeming unfair to Marcus, whose work I admire, I would point out that the omission of *Beneath the Underdog* from her survey of autobiographical writings is part of the long history of neglect that has, until very recently, deprived jazz music and jazz artists of sustained and thoughtful attention.

TRIPLE CONSCIOUSNESS

Mingus's "I am three" should also be read alongside W. E. B. Du Bois's famous concept of African American's double consciousness:

> Born with a veil, and gifted with second-sight in this American
> world—a world which yields him no self-consciousness, but only lets
> him see himself through the revelation of the other world. It is a
> peculiar sensation, this double consciousness, this sense of always
> looking at one's self through the eyes of others, of measuring one's soul
> by the tape of a world that looks on in amused contempt and pity. One
> ever feels his twoness,—an American, a Negro; two souls, two thoughts,
> two unreconciled strivings; two warring ideals in one dark body, whose
> dogged strength alone keeps it from being torn asunder.[137]

Mingus may have read Du Bois and liked the idea of irreconcilable forces within his own spirit. But if he did know the work of Du Bois, he began writing long after many black American writers had found their own voices and were fully capable of "measuring one's soul" by their own standards and not by those who look on "in amused contempt and pity." Of course, Mingus knew the work of Langston Hughes, perhaps the earliest and most eminent writer to use black vernacular to tell real stories about African Americans. Thomas Carmichael has argued that Mingus's multiple selves confirm "the true force of the contingent formations of racism and exclusion."[138] But even if Mingus never stopped talking about race, he realized that his own predicament was more than just racial. With his insistence on irreconcilable threeness, he argued that his situation was more complex than what Du Bois described.

In addition, that first paragraph of *Beneath the Underdog* must be read as direct address to a psychotherapist. Immediately after Mingus says that he is three, the therapist asks, "Which one is real?" Mingus replies, "They're *all* real." The book thus begins with a clear acceptance of the value of psychoanalysis, not to mention the value of his therapist, who is treated extremely sympathetically throughout the autobiography, very differently from the "Nazi-thinking Jew called Dr. Bonk or something" he meets at Bellevue, who insists that all black men are paranoid and should be lobotomized.[139] The private psychotherapist, Dr. Wallach, is based on Dr. Edmund Pollack, who was treating Mingus while he was working on the first complete draft of *Beneath the Underdog*. Like the Dr. Wallach of the autobiography, Dr. Pollack was interested only in helping his patient and did not even want his money.

Mingus expresses enthusiasm about psychoanalysis in an early passage in the typescript, writing: "So maybe Freud is right."[140] And throughout the published autobiography, Mingus refers to his unconscious, accepting one of the foundational notions of psychoanalysis. We might even compare his "I am three" to Freud's map of the mind: the man who sits and watches could be the superego, the frightened animal the id, while the one trusts too much and then strikes out is the ego. Psychoanalysis gave Mingus a template with which he could search for an inner self rather than simply lay out the events of his life.

Yet despite Mingus's fascination with psychoanalysis, the book begins by rejecting one of the principal goals of the talking cure—the need to integrate different aspects of the self into one. Mingus understands psychoanalysis well enough to critique it from the inside. In the liner notes to *The Black Saint and the Sinner Lady*, Dr. Pollack himself concludes by hoping that "the integration in society will keep pace with [Mingus's]."[141]

Dr. Pollack is of course aware of the ambiguity of the term *integration,* which refers both to the process of making blacks full partners in the American experience and to the process of making all aspects of a personality work together. In extreme cases, when a patient has dissociative personality disorder, or what used to be called "split personality," the possibility of turning all of the "alters" into one is abandoned and the therapist tries to help the patient designate one as the "executive personality." But Mingus did not suffer from dissociative personality disorder, and his therapist was working to help him combine all his selves into a single positive identity.

Still, the book begins with Mingus telling his therapist that all three of his selves are "real" and cannot be so easily integrated. He is also providing a compelling explanation for why so many people have found his behavior to be erratic. Each one of the three can come forward at any time. There is no question, however, that Mingus wishes it could be otherwise. Christopher Harlos was right when he wrote that Mingus's decision to tell his story within the context of psychotherapy represents "an attempt to find out how he is *supposed* to feel about himself."[142] In an interview for the Jazz Oral History Project in 1977, Sy Johnson told Charles that he would have turned out to be a very different person had he not grown up with so much adversity. "But that's because I didn't know what kind of person I am," Mingus replied. When Johnson asked, "What kind are you?" Mingus said, "I don't know, man."[143]

In this context, David Yaffe was on to something when he compared *Beneath the Underdog* to Philip Roth's 1969 novel *Portnoy's Complaint.*[144] Both books were written in the 1960s when America's fascination with psychoanalysis may have been at its peak. All of *Portnoy's Complaint* is one long therapy session in which the protagonist pours out his stories and his anxieties to his therapist, Dr. Spielvogel (translation: the bird who plays the game). Spielvogel even delivers the "punchline" at the end of the novel, "Now vee may perhaps to begin. Yes?"[145] Mingus's first draft of *Beneath the Underdog* preceded *Portnoy* by several years, but it also has something of a punchline at the end. In the very last sentences of the book, Mingus tells Fats Navarro that he will not be ready to die until he writes up his story. Like Portnoy in Roth's novel, Mingus ends his story with the promise that he, too, is about to begin a writerly voyage of self-discovery, the finished version of which the reader is holding in her hand.

SURROGATES AND CONFESSORS

This powerful need for self-knowledge leads the Mingus of *Beneath the Underdog* to seek the help of a psychotherapist. It also leads him to a number of other figures to whom he can confess and from whom he can seek advice, including not just Dr. Wallach but also the pimp Billy Bones, the critic Nat Hentoff, and even the autistic chess master he meets in Bellevue. But in both the typescript and the published book, his most intense conversations are with Fats Navarro. At least one of these conversations is set just days before the trumpeter's death in 1950.

In *Beneath the Underdog*, Mingus's conversations with Navarro range widely through religion and racial politics. When Mingus asks him why he won't go to a doctor to stop his internal bleeding, Navarro responds, "Mingus, I'm bleeding 'cause I want to bleed. I got T.B. intentionally and I'm hoping there ain't no heaven or hell like you say there is. Think how drug I'd be to get there and find the white man owns that too and it's rent-controlled in heaven and hell's like the slums. I'd tell them, 'Kill me, white faggot cocksucking angels, like you did down on earth, 'cause you sure ain't gonna get no work or rent from my soul.'"[146]

Both the typescript and *Beneath the Underdog* end with Mingus bidding farewell to the dying Navarro. (The end of chapter 1 of the published book, in which Mingus bids farewell to his psychotherapist, rhymes elegantly with the book's conclusion.) His identification with a man who failed in spite of immense talent and political conviction is an especially poignant finale. On some levels, Mingus may have also seen himself as a failure, a brilliant musician who was nevertheless unable to find his way in a world where gangsters, pimps, and corporation men succeed when an artist cannot. On another level, Mingus may have admired Navarro for at least knowing himself, something that the Mingus of *Beneath the Underdog* is constantly striving after.

Kevin McNeilly points out that Mingus writes about confessor figures such as Navarro, Billy Bones, and Dr. Wallach "because, as pimp, musician, or healer, they represent unassimilated aspects of himself, life-strategies through which he has tried at various points to gain access to his own sense of who he is."[147] The Mingus of *Beneath the Underdog* also spends a great deal of time in intense, confessional dialogue with Lee-Marie, Donna, and even Barbara, the first wife who moved back in with her mother shortly after the marriage. And as Sue Mingus's *Tonight at Noon* reveals, Charles had equally intense moments of confession with her. But McNeilly is careful to distinguish these kinds of conversations from the man-to-man dialogues in which he was searching for his own identity outside of the sexualized context in which he appeared to be so boastfully confident of himself.

Like the autobiography, the biographies of Mingus include long lists of female lovers, but none of the women received his attentions for an extended period of time. He was with Celia for seven years, but he was consistently unfaithful. He does not even mention her in *Beneath the Underdog*. He was with Jeanne and Judy for even less time. Even during the last few years of his active life, when he had finally settled into a comfortable marriage with Sue, he was traveling most of the time. Perhaps because he found the most pleasure in the sexual aspects of his relationships, the erotic writing in *Beneath the Underdog* is powerful. Indeed, his portraits of Lee-Marie and Donna are marked by the same intense romanticism and erotics with which his music is saturated, especially in the compositions he named after women, "Celia," "Diane," "Peggy's Blue Skylight," and most especially, "Sue's Changes."[148] The scene with Judy toward the end of the book, when he is impressed by her amusement at his declaration that he is through with love, suggests the possibility that he can still bring the romance of his music into his life.[149]

Nevertheless, Nel King was right to complain about the paucity of musical detail in *Beneath the Underdog*. There is not much more in the longer typescript. When Mingus does write about playing with other musicians, he often lets onomatopoeia fill in for the music, as when he adds a bird sound to his description of a solo by Charlie "Bird" Parker: "Chirp da la da la!"[150] When the musicians on the bandstand speak to each other, it's seldom about music, and even when it is, the musicians are mostly engaged in some sort of verbal jousting as, for example, in this exchange when vocalist Dan Grissom tells Mingus what he is about to sing:

"Take it out, Charlie. I'm now going to sing 'Diane,' key of A flat."

Mingus says, "I think you mean the relative minor B natural. Haw!"[151]

As McNeilly points out, the music is often replaced by ellipses, as in a scene when the young Charles is playing with legendary pianist Art Tatum, who tells him, "All right, here's how I do 'All the Things You Are.' One, two, three, four . . . . . . Now let's take it again."[152]

Mingus knows that the music cannot be captured in words, so he lets the rhythms and verbal eccentricities in the conversations among musicians stand in for the music. As Nichole T. Rustin has written, Mingus "intimated that, as a language, music possesses a greater capacity than verbal communication to express the depths of one's consciousness about the world in which one lives."[153] When verbal communication is all that he has, Mingus tries to express the spirit of his music rather than its mechanics. The "I am three" passage that begins the book is an attempt to say in words what he is also saying in "Self-Portrait in Three Colors."

ALLEGORIZING THE PIMP

Pimping is an important theme in Mingus's writing from the outset. There is no denying the profound misogyny in *Beneath the Underdog*, and it is crucial to any understanding of how pimping functions within the book. Virtually all of the young women in the book are interested almost exclusively in sex and eager to annihilate themselves in a relationship with the man they desire, regardless of how they are treated. Otherwise the women in Mingus's book are angry and/or manipulative wives. Early in the typescript, Fats Navarro tells Mingus that his wife "tricks" with gangsters.[154] Later, Fats makes a connection that is crucial to the polemic that runs through all of Mingus's autobiographical writings: "My old lady turned me out. I'm a pimp. I know better than to try and make out on these dirty gang-mob ruled streets and expect success without selling out like a slave, which I'm not going to do because I still love playing music better than money."[155] Navarro thus provides a direct statement of Mingus's dilemma throughout the book.

Well before Mingus meets Bobby Bell/Billy Bones, the theme of prostitution and pimping has been established. In his very first conversation with Cindy, a sexually aggressive woman who approaches him at a club on Central Avenue and who turns out to be a madam, he demands that she give him money, which she does. Then he asks for more.[156] The conversations with Fats Navarro are much longer and more discursive in the typescript, involving gangsters, American politics, the exploitation of black men, spirituality, and prostitution, all of which circle around each other as if they were a single phenomenon.

Eric Porter is especially sensitive to the importance of the pimp in Mingus's book. "As at least a symbolic alternative to the wage labor system and the artistic compromises facing African Americans in the jazz industry, pimping in *Beneath the Underdog* is an attempt to reclaim masculinity in these spheres of activity by exercising domination over women, reaping economic rewards, and affirming the homosocial bonds of the jazz community."[157] Especially in the typescript, how well Mingus can negotiate this world—and in what capacity—is the essential question in his self-narrative.

For much of the last two-thirds of *Beneath the Underdog*, Mingus lives in a world of pimps and whores, but he never fully commits to being a pimp himself. Drummer Dannie Richmond, who worked with Mingus for most of the last twenty-two years of his life, told Max Gordon of the Village Vanguard, "Charlie was no pimp. He was a ladies' man, like I said. It was good to have a broad around who could bring in a few bucks when things got tough. And Charlie had 'em. Dig?"[158] In *Beneath the Underdog,* Charles meets Cindy after a gig at Bobo's on Central Avenue. She quickly takes him home, where they make love.[159] The next morning he discovers that Cindy is a madam with at least two girls working for her. When Cindy sets up one of her girls to be arrested because Mingus is paying too much attention to her, Mingus leaves her in disgust.

When Mingus first meets Donna, she tells him that she has lost custody of her son and wants him back. Knowing that neither she nor Mingus has the money they need to successfully live together, Donna herself suggests that she go to work as a prostitute. There is real pathos in the scene when Mingus takes Donna to have sex with her first customer. At least in Mingus's telling, both are deeply ashamed but desperate to keep their love alive in a culture that has no place for them outside of prostitution.[160] Mingus has feelings for Donna, but he also knows that her prostituting her body for money is no worse than him prostituting his art for whatever commerce allows.

Later, when Donna becomes a successful call girl and Mingus is living off her wages, he contemplates his situation: "Pimps are usually pretty calm people, cool but lively, full of laughs and jokes, and some are even intellectuals. Surely they could never feel like this. To be a pimp, one would have to lose all feelings, all sensitivity, all love. One would have to die!"[161] Billy Bones surrounds himself with women who will do anything for him. He claims that one even ate horse shit to allow him to win a bet. He didn't even have to ask. But Mingus is not a good pimp. Donna herself makes the decision to sell her body. When Pam, the naive young woman he calls "a poor man's Hedy Lamarr," offers to enter into a formal whore/pimp relationship with him, he can't bring himself to do it.[162] He is incapable of being a pimp, just as he is incapable of being a gangster, a faithful husband, or a money-making musician. To paraphrase one of his song titles, *Beneath the Underdog* is about all the things he could be by now if he really knew who he was.

Navarro, who speaks most frequently and eloquently throughout the book—and who comes closest to being Mingus's surrogate—can only answer Mingus's questions about self-realization with self-destruction. Mingus is definitely tempted by Navarro's nihilism, but he is determined to find his true self, make music, and look for love. The other character with a powerful voice is Billy Bones, who explicitly makes the connection between pimping and being a jazz musician.

The extent to which Billy Bones is, like Navarro, speaking for Mingus is especially evident in a speech Billy makes that uses the phrase "Pithecanthropus

Erectus"—a passage that is very similar to Mingus's liner notes for the LP of the same name.[163] And in a long speech in which he lays out how wealth is the greatest aphrodisiac, capable of stripping any man or woman of integrity, Bones mentions Jelly Roll Morton, whom he claims to have known: "By any reckoning a good jazz musician has got to turn to pimpdom in order to be free and keep his soul straight. Jelly Roll Morton had seven girls I know of and that's the way he bought the time to write and study and incidentally got diamonds in his teeth and probably his asshole."[164]

Mingus paid tribute to Morton in several compositions, most notably "My Jelly Roll Soul," as well as the two variations on the tune, "Jelly Roll" and "Jelly Roll Jellies," he recorded in 1959.[165] Gunther Schuller has called Morton—who in 1938 dictated what is essentially his autobiography while sitting at the piano with Alan Lomax—the "First Great Composer" in jazz history.[166] Mingus and Morton were composers, autobiographers, and sharp dressers. Even if Mingus never actually worked as a pimp, there is no denying his fascination with Morton's music and life. When he praises Morton, Billy Bones is functioning as still another of the selves circulating within the mind of Mingus.

The long speech in which Billy Bones connects Morton, pimping, capitalism, and jazz begins with Bones instructing Donna on how to extract expensive favors from a wealthy client. The speech culminates in a pornographic frenzy as Bones exhaustively describes abusing a woman by fucking all of her orifices, urinating on her, and finally beating her with "this big black French douzzie jumbo dummy bull's dick" and a "Brazilian horsewhip."[167] At this point, Bones is Mingus's surrogate only to the extent that he is venting desires that Mingus has succeeded in repressing. In spite of his reputation as the Angry Man of Jazz, Charles never indulged in this kind of violence against a woman. He tells Bones that he wants nothing to do with his business practices. Although he takes advantage of the lavish surroundings and free-flowing cash that his life with Donna and Lee-Marie makes possible, he eventually walks away from both, determined to pursue his music.

Although his last conversation with Navarro touches on Mingus's religious awakening, there is no real evidence that Christianity is the answer either. Perhaps in an effort to sell the book to publishers, Mingus insisted that *Beneath the Underdog* was about a man's search for God. Both Nat Hentoff and John F. Goodman, who spoke with Mingus extensively, deny that he was a religious man. "Spiritual, certainly, but not religious."[168] For me, a telling moment comes when Mingus writes, "I only call on God in an emergency or to solve some selfish material problem."[169] Immediately after this passage he meets Cindy, the madam who becomes his benefactor and, at least briefly, gives him the satisfaction of practicing what he learned from Pop Collette.

In the late 1960s, when he was still looking for a publisher for his autobiography, Mingus was in and out of depression and seldom performing or composing. A moment during those lost years is well documented in Tom Reichman's film *Mingus* (1968), the portrait of a man who has quite literally lost his place in his society. He doodles on the piano, talks in circles about days when he was wealthy, and randomly fires a rifle into the ceiling. Sue Mingus deserves great credit during those years for publishing a portion of his autobiography and for continuing to serve as his manager despite their personal troubles.

The resurrection of his autobiography came at a crucial moment in his life, just as he was reemerging as an important artist. *Beneath the Underdog* was published in 1971, the same year he received a Guggenheim Fellowship, held the Slee Chair in Music at the State University of New York at Buffalo, and saw Alvin Ailey choreograph several of his compositions. Also in 1971, he released one of his most ambitious LPs, *Let My Children Hear Music,* with a large jazz orchestra playing some of his earliest compositions and more recent work.[170] The LP summed up his career. The year 1971 ended with the readers of *Down Beat* voting him into the magazine's Hall of Fame.

The reviews of *Beneath the Underdog* were not good, but they were written at a time when the critical establishment was not ready to listen to a serious jazz artist tell his own story in his own way. In fact, Mingus deserved an award for his book every bit as much as he deserved one for his music.

Third Stream Music and the Rest of Jazz History

In *Beneath the Underdog,* Mingus portrays himself as a complex individual searching for self-knowledge. We should not, therefore, be surprised by the many contradictory statements that have been attributed to him. An especially astonishing moment came in a 1964 radio interview with Nat Hentoff, when he said: "I'm probably the world's worst lover there is."[1] Yet in his autobiography he consistently portrays himself as irresistible to women, only partly because of the skills he learned from Pop Collette. And as recently as the year before the interview he had written about having sex with twenty-three Mexican prostitutes, all in one night.[2]

Similarly, he told Nel King that he had "never read a book—any book—since his religious readings at about age sixteen,"[3] but the evidence of his reading is everywhere, both in his writings and in his song titles. Mingus did not want to be pigeonholed or associated with only one aspect of his career. He would even object when someone labeled him a "jazz musician."[4] And when he speaks on the *Charles Mingus Presents Charles Mingus* LP, he introduces "All the Things You Could Be By Now if Sigmund Freud's Wife Were Your Mother" by carefully pronouncing the entire title twice and then saying that it means nothing. His almost perverse set of disavowals, at one point or another denouncing even *Beneath the Underdog* as well as his superb impulse! recordings, was surely related to his search for an identity that might suit him.

When it came to race, Mingus was just as unwilling to be classified, occasionally speaking of his desire to associate with "the raceless set."[5] He knew that white people in the United States had convinced themselves that they had no race but that African Americans did. For better or worse, African Americans have built communities—or have been forced into communities—because of this racial divide. Because of his mixed race background, however, Mingus was never able to settle comfortably into either white or black society. He often denounced white people, but he had close friends who were white, and he hired many white musicians.

Most of all he hated racism, regardless of where it came from. On this point at least he was consistent. Trumpeter Jack Walrath has spoken eloquently about the time Mingus revealed his commitment to integration when the band was touring in 1975 and Walrath was the only white member of the group. "He always wanted to go to Africa, and some people wanted him to play in a festival there but told him to leave the 'white boy' (me) at home. He promptly told them to go fuck themselves.... He denounced racism, whether it came from Orval Faubus or Idi Amin."[6]

Mingus was also consistent in his conviction that "it's all one music," a statement he made in a letter to Ralph Gleason in 1951, just after settling in New York at the age of twenty-nine.[7] Mingus knew that jazz and classical music were kept separate by racist notions of virtuosity and genius. He was also aware of how critics had broken down jazz into a set of separate schools. As Geoff Dyer elegantly phrases it, Mingus's "music was pledged to the abolition of all distinctions: between the composed and the improvised, the primitive and the sophisticated, the rough and the tender, the belligerent and the lyrical.... The most future-oriented music would be that which dug deepest into the tradition: his music."[8]

With these convictions, Mingus was willing and able to navigate effortlessly among seemingly incompatible musical styles. Although this chapter focuses on the Third Stream movement in which Mingus played an important role, I also want to concentrate on his place in the entire story of jazz. In a mere forty years as a working musician he managed to touch almost every major moment in that history, and he never seemed to let go of something once he made it his own. Here I retell the story of Mingus's life, but this time entirely in terms of his music.

HISTORY AND A HARLEM BROWNSTONE

In August 1958, when Mingus was thirty-six, he and fifty-six other musicians posed in front of an apartment building on East 126th Street in Harlem (figure 9). The photograph, taken by Art Kane, was intended for a special issue on jazz in *Esquire* magazine. It has now become an index for twentieth-century jazz greats, on different instruments and from different eras. Those present are playing out little dramas, such as a flamboyant attempt by Dizzy Gillespie to break the composure of his mentor, Roy Eldridge. Count Basie is the only artist sitting on the sidewalk, at one end of a long line of children from the neighborhood who insisted on inserting themselves into the photograph.

We know from an excellent documentary about the photograph, *A Great Day in Harlem* (1994) directed by Jean Bach, that Thelonious Monk spent so much time choosing the right wardrobe for the photograph that he almost missed the photo shoot. Eventually he decided on a yellow sports jacket, assuming that it would make him stand out among his peers with their conservative dark jackets. He then took additional steps to make sure he was noticed by standing next to the two beautiful pianists, Marian McPartland and Mary Lou Williams. But if Monk was hoping to be the center of attention, he had to compete with many other jazz artists who were every bit as charismatic and photogenic.

Looking at the photograph today, we may find it solemn, almost ceremonious. That feel may have been there from the beginning. The weathered faces of older jazz artists such as Willie the Lion Smith, Miff Mole, Zutty Singleton, Lucky Roberts, and Red Allen give the photo an austere look, in spite of the clowning going on between Gillespie and Roy Eldridge on the far right.

With few exceptions, the artists in the photograph represent the music's past rather than its future. John Coltrane and Miles Davis, busy changing jazz history in 1958, are absent. So are Duke Ellington, Louis Armstrong, and Benny Goodman, whose long and distinguished careers might have given a "timeless" dimension to the photograph. But the carefully composed black-and-white photography and the nineteenth-century brownstone in Harlem where the musicians posed make even devout modernists like Gerry Mulligan and Sonny Rollins seem like part of an ancient tradition.

In the photograph Charles Mingus stands halfway up the stairs, directly behind two grand old men of the jazz clarinet, Buster Bailey and Pee Wee Russell. On his left is drummer Osie Johnson, and pianist Jimmy Jones is to his right. Trombonist Tyree Glenn is directly behind him. All of the musicians around him are smiling. Mingus is not. He is scowling, a cigarette dangling from his lips. Thelonious Monk was not the only person in the picture who was trying to stand out. Mingus knew how to play to the camera.

In the photo he is playing a tough customer who has little connection to the men near him, and not just because they come from a tradition where jazz musicians were supposed to grin and mug. (Both Buster Bailey and Tyree Glenn would join Louis Armstrong's All Stars a few years later.) Of course, he may have been scowling because he was depressed. Shortly after the photo was taken, he self-admitted to Bellevue, where, at least according to *Beneath the Underdog*, he narrowly escaped being lobotomized. Nevertheless, looking at the photo today, a student of jazz history might

Figure 9. "Harlem 1958." Photograph © Art Kane, courtesy of Holly Anderson.

argue that Mingus stands out because no one else in the photo can lay equal claim to roles in both the ancient and modern traditions of jazz, not to mention traditions that the photograph could not foresee.

APPRENTICESHIPS

I begin this account of Mingus's many places in jazz history by connecting him with what might be called the music's "prehistory." In 1942, Mingus played with Edward "Kid" Ory when they were both members of a band led by clarinetist Barney Bigard.

Bigard had played with Duke Ellington since 1928, but left the band after many exhausting years of almost constant touring. He had fallen in love with a woman in Los Angeles and was ready to begin a new life. He gave Duke his notice when the band was playing at the Trianon Ballroom in Los Angeles in April 1942. He married his sweetheart and settled in LA, where he hoped to get work in the busy world of studio musicians.

As a light-skinned Creole from New Orleans, Bigard was able to pass for white—until someone informed a union official that he in fact had African blood. He was expelled from the rigidly segregated LA music union, and his chances for getting the best studio jobs came to an end.[9] Although he makes no mention of this incident in his autobiography, *With Louis and the Duke*,[10] Bigard gave up on the studios and began playing in clubs where colored Creole musicians were still welcome. In the fall of 1947 he would go back on the road when Louis Armstrong gave up his large swing band and formed a group of six "All Stars" who mostly played the old New Orleans music that was gaining an audience of revivalists or "moldy figs" in the 1940s.

Five years before he left Los Angeles to go on the road with Armstrong, Bigard took a job at Billy Berg's Capri Club, forming his own "All Stars." Two of his first hires were Mingus and the trumpeter Red "Mack" Morris. In his autobiography, Bigard mentions Mingus only briefly, but he praises his work, describing him as "a disciple of Jimmy Blanton."[11] Shortly after opening at the Capri, Bigard ran into trombonist Kid Ory, who was living in LA and earning twelve dollars a day sweeping out the city morgue.

Ory, too, was a Creole from Louisiana and a much more important figure than Bigard in the early history of jazz. In the late 1910s, he led a band that featured King Oliver, surely the most prominent jazz trumpeter of that moment. Buddy Bolden, widely credited with being the inventor of what we now call jazz, had been a star in the New Orleans music scene until 1907 when he had a mental breakdown. Bolden spent the rest of his life in an institution, where he died in obscurity in 1931. Ory and Oliver were making music when Bolden was in his prime, and although they were surely inspired by him, they should be considered his peers rather than his disciples.

When King Oliver left New Orleans and Ory's band in 1919 for greener pastures in Chicago, Ory hired none other than Louis Armstrong as Oliver's replacement. Ory recorded prodigiously in the 1920s but then left the music business. By 1942, when he ran into Bigard, he had not picked up the trombone for many years. Bigard took a chance on what he called "the old man" (Ory was fifty-six) and brought him onto the bandstand.[12] Thus Mingus, barely out of high school, found himself in the company of two jazz icons, one from the origins of jazz, the other from the music's greatest flowering, the Duke Ellington orchestra.

Mingus has never spoken about what he learned from Bigard or Ory, but as an already seasoned bass player, he knew that his job was to create a sense of time that brought out the best in the hornmen on the front line. Even if the two veterans never took him aside to give him pointers, Mingus surely learned a great deal as he figured out how best to complement their musical offerings.

Mingus's association with Bigard and Ory brought him to the attention of Louis Armstrong, who stopped by the Club Alabam one night when he knew that his two old friends would be performing. Armstrong was so impressed by Mingus's playing that he invited him to join his big band in either late 1942 or early 1943. At this point in his career, Mingus could have made a name for himself as a young revivalist, playing in styles originated decades earlier by Ory and Armstrong and growing in popularity during the war years. Riding that wave, Kid Ory would rise from obscurity to a solid career, playing and recording for the rest of his life. In 1956 Ory even played himself in *The Benny Goodman Story*, a fascinating film that is an almost complete compendium of naive myths about jazz.[13]

Charles Mingus, however, was no moldy fig. He was still fascinated by Debussy and Ravel, not to mention that most eminent of modernists, Duke Ellington. He also had problems with Armstrong's stage persona. A few years later, black jazz artists like Charlie Parker and Bud Powell would adopt stone faces and comport themselves like bank presidents rather than mug and laugh like Armstrong. Miles Davis, who notoriously turned his back on audiences, wrote in his autobiography, "I loved Satchmo, but I couldn't stand all that grinning he did."[14] In *Beneath the Underdog*, Mingus regularly refers to Armstrong as "King Spook."

Mingus toured with Armstrong for two months. But when Armstrong announced that he was taking his band on a tour of the South, Mingus quit. He had never been to the southern states, but he had heard enough to know that it was not a place for him, even in the company of a respected star like Armstrong. In 1962, he told Nesuhi Ertegun that if he had gone south, "I knew I'd get killed."[15]

BEFORE AND AFTER BEBOP

Only a few months after Mingus ended his brief career with the musicians of old New Orleans, Charlie Parker and Dizzy Gillespie came west for the first time. In 1945 they played Billy Berg's club, but the patrons were not impressed. At least in their first appearance on the West Coast, Parker and Gillespie were failures. Mingus was not impressed either. Although he would later say that Parker had as powerful an influence on his own ideas about music as did Duke Ellington, at this stage in his career Mingus was still immersed in Ellington, and he was trying to bring classical music and many of its formal properties into his own compositions. When he first heard the boppers, it sounded to him as if they had abandoned the essentials of tone and rhythm.

Also in 1945, Mingus was making connections with two musicians who might be regarded as "pre-boppers," Coleman Hawkins and Howard McGhee. Through the network of LA musicians being hired by Norman Granz for his Jazz at the Philharmonic concerts, Mingus had an opportunity to play with Hawkins. Charlie Parker did things with jazz improvisation that no one could have imagined, but Coleman Hawkins had been pointing in the same direction for several years. Howard McGhee was living in Los Angeles and had already established himself as an exciting trumpet player when he and Mingus played several gigs together. Like Dizzy Gillespie, McGhee was a veteran of swing bands who began playing in a new style after hearing Parker. In Scott DeVeaux's *The Birth of Bebop*, an essential history of the music's beginnings, Hawkins and McGhee are both central figures.[16]

Born in 1904, Hawkins had starred with the Fletcher Henderson Orchestra in the 1920s and early 1930s. He sat in front of Louis Armstrong during the trumpeter's fourteen months with Henderson in 1924 and 1925. From Armstrong, Hawkins learned a great deal about how to solo and how to swing. Listen to the drama, tension, and emotion he brings to his 1933 recording with Henderson "It's the Talk of the Town."[17] Shortly after he recorded that tune, Hawkins left New York and spent several years in Europe, always as a featured performer with various ensembles. He returned triumphantly to the States in 1939 and soon recorded "Body and Soul," an extraordinary three-minute solo that practically sums up the state of jazz improvisation at that time.[18] Many jazz musicians, old and young, can still play it by heart today. Unlike other musicians of his generation, Hawkins was intrigued by bebop and gave musicians such as Thelonious Monk, Gillespie, and McGhee an opportunity to play high-profile gigs with an established master of the music.

While playing in the straight-ahead swing band of Andy Kirk, trumpeter McGhee was twenty-four years old when he heard Charlie Parker for the first time in 1942. Bird was still an unknown alto player in Jay McShann's big band, but when he took a solo, McGhee realized immediately that he was bringing new harmonic sophistication and rhythmic complexity to jazz.

In Los Angeles, when it became clear that Parker and Gillespie were not going to make any real money, Gillespie decided it was time for the group to return to New York. He was also becoming increasingly concerned about Parker's drug habit and unreliable behavior. Gillespie bought airline tickets for everyone in the band but made the mistake of giving Parker his ticket a few days before their scheduled departure. Brian Priestley speculates that Parker sold his ticket for money so that he could buy drugs. He was left stranded in Los Angeles.[19]

While Bird struggled to reach West Coast audiences, McGhee regularly played trumpet in his groups. McGhee was the trumpeter at a recording session for the Dial label in July 1946 at which Parker could barely play. His solo on "Lover Man" is all the more heartbreaking for its sudden flashes of beauty amid the fumbles.[20] At the time, Parker was drinking heavily and suffering from the news that the woman with whom he had been living was pregnant with another man's child. After the session, he went back to his hotel and set his room on fire.

Having spent a few days in police custody, Bird was committed to a mental hospital in Camarillo, where he stayed six months, ultimately deciding to devote himself to relaxation and a full recovery. Shortly after he was released, cured of his heroin habit (at least for the moment) and with all his faculties intact, Parker recorded "Relaxing at Camarillo," with McGhee on trumpet.[21] It was during this time in early 1947, when Parker was playing gigs and sitting in on jam sessions in Los Angeles, that Mingus began to revise his opinion of Parker. Meanwhile, he was getting regular work with the increasingly boppish McGhee.

Sadly, no recordings have turned up to document Mingus's tenure with either Armstrong or Bigard. Early recordings of Mingus, however, do allow us to hear what he sounded like with McGhee and Hawkins.[22] We can understand why older artists like Armstrong and Bigard would be every bit as impressed with his skills as were the emerging beboppers. His beat is rock solid, and his sound bristles with authority. He is completely comfortable with swing era ensemble rhythms, in part, no doubt, because of the careful attention he paid to the work of Jimmie Blanton when he was with Ellington.

Also during this time of prolific recording in 1945 and 1946, Mingus began to work as an arranger. He had played with saxophonist Lucky Thompson, who introduced him to the vocalist Dinah Washington, a jazz singer with enough feel for rhythm and blues to cross over to larger audiences. Mingus scored several blues numbers for Washington and a backup group led by Lucky Thompson.[23] The band featured a trumpet, several reeds, and a young Milt Jackson on vibraphone. The arranging he did for Washington is more than adequate, but for Mingus at this time, married with a child and a second one on the way, it was mostly about money. As was the case throughout the late 1940s—indeed, for the rest of his life—he was hoping for a hit record. He had too much integrity, however, to dumb down his music in hopes that it would sell a lot of records.

Just five years after he was discovered by Bigard, and two years after he first played with Coleman Hawkins, Mingus joined up with another old master of the big band era, Lionel Hampton. After beginning his career in 1930 as a drummer in a band led by Louis Armstrong, in 1936 Hampton won a starring role with Benny Goodman's small ensembles. He made a series of small-group recordings in the late 1930s, consistently uniting the most advanced jazz artists and creating some of the best music of the swing era. In 1939, on the celebrated "Hot Mallets" session, Hampton brought together Dizzy Gillespie (trumpet); Benny Carter (alto sax); Coleman Hawkins, Chu Berry, and Ben Webster (tenor sax); Charlie Christian (guitar); Milt Hinton (bass); and Cozy Cole (drums).[24] Gillespie, who would soon remake himself as the greatest of all the bop trumpeters, was playing as well as anyone in jazz in 1939, but in a state-of-the-art swing style. So were the other members of the band. In these recordings, the proximity of swing to bop is so clear that one can argue that bop was not so much a dramatic departure as it was a set of variations on swing rhythms and harmonies.

After leaving Benny Goodman in 1940, Hampton started up a big band that met with constant success throughout the 1940s and early 1950s. As always, he knew to hire the most promising musicians. The Hampton band's biggest hit was "Flying Home," recorded in 1942 and driven by an uproarious tenor saxophone solo by Illinois Jacquet.[25] Like Louis Armstrong, Hampton was an old-school black performer, much too eager to please for the tastes of younger musicians like Mingus. And the band was managed by Gladys Hampton, one of the most notoriously parsimonious figures in jazz history. She was a competent businesswoman and an ideal mate for Lionel, but she made sure the musicians in the band were paid as little as possible.

If you listen to the recordings that Hampton made just before the arrival of Mingus and also when Mingus was one of the band's two bassists, you mostly hear good-time rhythm and blues and boogie-woogie. Sometimes the music is a bit more in the jazz mainstream with hip arrangements and adventurous improvised solos. Hampton also played a good deal of what is now called "Jump Blues," the kind of backbeat dance music heard in contemporaneous recordings by Louis Jordan and a handful of other musicians that helped usher in rock 'n' roll.

Hampton must have known he had someone special when Mingus joined his organization because he consented to record Charles's composition "Mingus Fingers."[26] Nothing in the Hampton repertoire sounds even remotely similar. For one thing, the piece has a more boppish feel than was typical for the Hampton band. But the piece is also full of weird modernist harmonies, sudden changes in tempo, and some commanding solos by Mingus that include an *arco* passage where, departing from standard big-band practice, he applies his bow to his bass.

Mingus stayed with Hampton for almost a year, even though he never earned a cent from "Mingus Fingers." He briefly considered a lawsuit.[27] But the Hampton band was another important stop on Mingus's journey through jazz history. The funkier rhythms that Hampton brought to the late big-band era may have set the stage for some of Mingus's more soulful compositions, such as "Better Git It in Your Soul," "Slop," and "Wednesday Night Prayer Meeting." He may also have recalled his work with Hampton when he recorded "Boogie Stop Shuffle" in 1959.

Mingus left Hampton in hopes of finding success as a band leader, calling himself "Baron Mingus." But at this stage, he was destined for a few more apprenticeships. He had to adopt a completely different approach to jazz when he joined Red Norvo's trio in 1950. Born in 1908, Norvo began his career playing xylophone and marimba on the vaudeville circuit. In 1931 he joined the band of Paul Whiteman, the incredibly successful white entrepreneur who called himself the "King of Jazz" while almost entirely denying the existence of black jazz musicians. Whiteman deserves credit, however, for regularly hiring the best white jazz artists, including Bix Beiderbecke, Frankie Trumbauer, and Joe Venuti. He also made a star of no less than Bing Crosby. While working with Whiteman, Norvo met and married vocalist Mildred Bailey, another notable white jazz artist.

Norvo and Lionel Hampton were among the first percussionists to develop an affinity for the vibraphone, a sort of electrified xylophone with metal keys. In 1936 Norvo started his own big band, with Mildred Bailey and his vibes up front. The band broke up after a few years, but Norvo was able to land a good job with Benny Goodman in 1945. At about this time he embraced bebop and arranged a recording session with Dizzy Gillespie, Charlie Parker, and, in a choice for pianist that worked surprisingly well, Teddy Wilson.[28]

Throughout the late 1940s Norvo worked regularly in a jazz world where bop, swing, and the music of the New Orleans revival coexisted. The critics would champion or vilify one music over another, but the musicians took whatever jobs they could find. A good example was the Woody Herman band of 1946, in which Norvo was a regular. After forming "The Band That Plays the Blues" in 1943, Herman began moving toward a more African American sound, and by the time he formed "Herman's Second Herd" in 1947 he was hiring boppers, including "The Four Brothers"— saxophonists Stan Getz, Zoot Sims, Herbie Steward, and Serge Chaloff. The band played ambitious arrangements by Ralph Burns and Jimmy Giuffre that married the innovations of the boppers with the conventions of big-band swing.

After Norvo left Herman and began gigging regularly in older and newer styles, he undertook a tour with Billie Holiday in 1949. Norvo and Holiday may have heard Mingus in San Francisco, which by this time had become his second home. After the tour with Holiday ended, Norvo found himself back in Los Angeles playing with guitarist Tal Farlow and looking for a bass player. The pianist Jimmy Rowles, who had played regularly with Norvo, reminded him of his admiration for Mingus. Fortunately, Norvo ran into Buddy Collette who told him he could find Mingus working at the post office. The Red Norvo Trio was born.

Norvo could not have found a better bassist for playing the music of the transitional years following World War II. Both had played with traditional and modernist groups throughout the 1940s, and both had learned how to create a rhythmically infectious music that was more than the sum of its parts. Critics have suggested that Norvo's trio, in which a vibraphonist, a guitarist, and a bassist mostly played standards and bop tunes, was inspired by the trios of Nat King Cole (piano, bass, and guitar) and the quintets of George Shearing (piano, vibes, guitar, bass, and drums). Others have suggested that the band was more interested in pleasing crowds than in advancing the music.[29] To my mind, these criticisms are unfair to a group that found highly original approaches to playing without a pianist. Not until a few years later would Gerry Mulligan and then Ornette Coleman play small-group jazz without a pianist. Norvo's trio had neither a drummer nor a pianist.

By not confining the missing drummer's role of keeping time to a single instrument, Norvo, Farlow, and Mingus functioned as equals. Norvo regularly soloed, but at other moments Farlow would play a walking bass figure on his guitar, and Mingus would take the melody by bowing his instrument in the upper register. Behind solos by Farlow or Mingus, Norvo would create rhythmically solid patterns, laying down chords to keep the changes moving. And all three would create unusual textures by exploring the possibilities of their instruments both in isolation and in combination.

Gary Giddins has said that the Norvo Trio was perfectly positioned between prewar and postwar jazz. The only group of the time that was comparable, according to Giddins, was Artie Shaw's 1953–54 small group with Hank Jones and the essential Tal Farlow.[30] Both bands could swing like the best groups of the 1930s, but they were also incorporating the new sounds and rhythmic eccentricities of bebop. What was important about the Red Norvo Trio, in terms of both jazz history overall and Mingus's role in that history more specifically, was the beginnings of what, for want of a better term, can be called "cool jazz."

Bebop was an exhilarating music built around altered chords, unpredictable rhythms, and virtuoso solos, often played at breakneck speeds. The best bebop artists—Charlie Parker, Dizzy Gillespie, Fats Navarro, Bud Powell, Thelonious Monk, Max Roach, Kenny Clarke—performed high-wire acts that few musicians could even imagine, let alone play. The critics loved the music and declared it the next step in the evolution of a uniquely American art form. But audiences, by and large, never got it.

Realizing that the boppers were dragging down jazz as a popular music, *Down Beat* magazine tried to dispense with the name "jazz" altogether, hoping that a more danceable music with some middle-brow artistic goals (think Stan Kenton) would bring audiences back. In 1949, when bebop was at its most popular and even Benny Goodman was fronting a boppish band, *Down Beat* held a contest, inviting readers to suggest a new word for this music. The winner was "crewcut music," acknowledging the hair style of musicians like Kenton but also separating it from classical, or "long-hair music."[31] Needless to say, the word *jazz* is still with us, and crewcuts have long since become associated primarily with men in the military.

By the early 1950s, when several calypso songs were hits, some journalists suggested that calypso would soon replace bebop. But cool jazz was already established and would keep the best traditions of the music alive.

Meanwhile, bebop eventually become part of what Marshall Stearns named "main stream jazz."[32]

The contrapuntal music of New Orleans as well as the call-and-response between brass and reeds in the swing bands was all about ensemble playing. The boppers had their moments of ensemble collaboration, but their music fundamentally foregrounded the soloist. Miles Davis, who had befriended Mingus and his West Coast peers in the late 1940s, came back to New York and made a series of recordings with a nonet in New York, mostly in collaboration with Gil Evans. If nothing else, the "Birth of the Cool" nonet brought back the felicities of ensemble playing. The Norvo Trio was doing the same in a small-group setting.

The Miles Davis nonet recordings from 1949 and 1950 were collected on a Capitol LP in 1957 titled *Birth of the Cool*.[33] The recordings on this exceedingly popular album took a great deal from bebop, but mostly they slowed down the music so that the beauty of what was in the best solos could be appreciated. Once the music had been deaccelerated, it could be voiced. Cool jazz was not a whitening of the music, as many have charged, nor was it an attempt to commercialize jazz. Those charges are as unfair to Davis's nonet as they are to the Norvo Trio.

Listen to the Standard Transcriptions that Norvo, Farlow, and Mingus recorded in late 1950 and early 1951.[34] Whether they are playing familiar ballads such as "September in the Rain" and "Where or When," or bop tunes like "Budo" and "Good Bait," the excitement of bop and the openness of cool are always present. Within a year the Modern Jazz Quartet would continue in this vein, but by this time cool jazz was clearly defined with its conventions firmly in place. The MJQ made great music, and I regularly go back and marvel at their interactions. But the Norvo Trio was the laboratory where many of the first experiments took place and where the elements were combined most ingeniously. I seriously doubt that the band would have been as successful without Mingus. Listen to the magic slipping away when Red Mitchell replaces him on Norvo's trio recordings from 1952.

"THIS IS THE BAND YOU DON'T QUIT"

Mingus left Norvo and settled in New York with Celia in 1951. For the next several months he worked on and off with boppers, most notably Charlie Parker and Bud Powell. Late in 1952, Parker invited him to join his group, but a steady gig did not materialize. Of course, Parker and Mingus would play on the stage of Massey Hall in Toronto a few months later alongside Dizzy Gillespie, Max Roach, and Bud Powell. "The Greatest Jazz Concert

Ever" will always be remembered as a high-water mark in the history of bebop, but it was a one-off affair and had nothing to do with Mingus's regular employment.[35]

Late in 1952, at roughly the same time that he was hoping to make a living as a Charlie Parker sideman, Mingus went into a recording studio with pianist John Mehegan to make the LP *From Barrelhouse to Bop: A History of Jazz Piano*.[36] Mehegan narrated the history as he played different styles of piano jazz. The only other musician at the session was Mingus. As Priestley points out, Mingus was fascinated by the jazz theorist and pianist Lennie Tristano, who could play the music as well as he could analyze it.[37] Tristano was devoted to the work of J. S. Bach as well as to twentieth-century composers who dabbled in atonality. He was in fact playing a jazz-based music without a tonal center several years before Ornette Coleman. Like Tristano, Mehegan was an accomplished jazz pianist who taught the principles of improvisation. He even wrote several books on the subject.

Both Mehegan and Tristano were white, but Mingus was able to put aside his knee-jerk suspicion of whites and learn from people who were thinking as seriously about music as he was, especially if they were, like him, listening to European classics *and* jazz. The LP with Mehegan also allowed Mingus not only to capitalize on his unique experience as a sideman with so many key artists in jazz history but also to further explore the earlier jazz with which he was intrigued. On *From Barrelhouse to Bop*, Mehegan played New Orleans, boogie-woogie, ragtime, bop, and what he called "classic swing" (Earl Hines and Fats Waller), "modern swing" (Teddy Wilson and Art Tatum), and "society" (Cy Walter).

Duke Ellington may or may not have heard the Mehegan/Mingus LP, but he did know that Mingus was available and abundantly talented. The offer from Ellington came late in 1952. In *Beneath the Underdog*, Mingus wrote, "This is The Hero, and this is the band you don't quit."[38] Mingus would be subbing for Wendell Marshall, who had been with Duke since 1947 and who had briefly left the band to get married. Mingus might have been able to stay with Duke, who had kept two bass players in his band from time to time. But Mingus's temper and his powerful convictions about music made such an arrangement impossible.

Mingus may also have been unwilling to simply copy Jimmie Blanton and fold himself into the sound of the band. More importantly, Duke honored loyalty and discretion. Harry Carney, who was with Duke from 1926 until the end, was probably his most trusted friend in the band. When, in 1938, a young Billy Strayhorn approached Duke in his dressing room and greatly impressed him with his piano skills, Duke said to a companion, "Go get Harry."[39] He would not invite Strayhorn into his entourage without Carney's advice. For many years, Carney also functioned as Duke's driver. Just the two of them were in a car while the rest of the band took the bus or the train. When Duke wanted to talk, Carney was his confidant. When Duke did not want to talk, Carney kept quiet.

Tenor saxophonist Paul Gonsalves joined the Ellington organization in 1950 and remained until 1974, the year both he and Duke died. Ellington loved his playing and kept him in the band even though Gonsalves was sometimes too drunk or stoned to perform. Vince Prudente, who played trombone in the Ellington orchestra during the last months of Ellington's career, told me that one night he was trying to sleep on the bus between gigs when Gonsalves woke him up to say, "Hey man. Do you realize how lucky we are? We are playing with The Maestro!"[40] While many sidepeople tired of the long hours traveling with Ellington and always playing the same music, Gonsalves never lost his enthusiasm.

In spite of his massive respect for Ellington, Mingus could not offer him Carney's reliable counsel or Gonsalves's profound devotion. The episode with Juan Tizol made this clear much too soon during Mingus's career with Ellington. Mingus may also have been caught in an oedipal struggle with Ellington, who was, more than any other artist, his essential father figure. Just as he devotes several pages of *Beneath the Underdog* to a dialogue in which he berates his biological father, in 1953 he could not bring himself to play exactly the kind of music he most certainly knew Duke wanted. Later, at the *Money Jungle* session in 1962, Mingus walked out in part because Duke had become the stern patriarch, totally dominating his two accomplished sidemen, both of whom were a full generation younger.

Nevertheless, Mingus paid tribute to Ellington throughout his career. His 1946 recording of "Make Believe" is clearly inspired by Duke's "Everything But You."[41] In 1957 he recorded one of his most beautiful ballads, "Duke's Choice," on a Bethlehem LP.[42] Parts of the song would also appear as "Open Letter to Duke" on *Mingus Ah Um* in 1959.[43] The most engaging version of "Duke's Choice," here called "I X Love," was recorded in 1963 for the *Mingus Mingus Mingus Mingus Mingus* LP. This rendition takes only the most lyrical section of the tune and features Charlie Mariano soloing in the style of Johnny Hodges—at the specific request of Mingus.[44]

In the 1959 recording of "Open Letter to Duke," the same beautiful melody is followed by a new theme that picks up the tempo with a Mexican flavor. Although Ellington recorded music with a strong Latin tinge, most notably "Flaming Sword" from 1940, Mingus's coda to "Open Letter" is decidedly non-Ducal. Ellington's great recordings of the 1940s often ended with splashy, driving crescendos. Mingus's "Open Letter," by contrast, has a strangely abrupt, low-energy ending.

In 1960, a Mingus band would record up-tempo versions of "Do Nothin' Till You Hear from Me" and "I Let a Song Go Out of My Heart" on top of each other, revealing that each of these two Ellington tunes is the counter-melody of the other.[45] I could fill up several pages cataloging the large and small traces of Duke's influence throughout the Mingus discography. Instead let me argue that many of Mingus's overt references to Ellington's work can be considered contested homages. Like many great African American performers, Charles was "signifying" on the work of an eminent predecessor by simultaneously honoring it, parodying it, and/or revising it.[46] Much the same can be said of Mingus's rich and strange tribute to Charlie Parker, "Reincarnation of a Love Bird," which sounds much more like Mingus than Parker.[47] In both cases, Mingus was working out his conflicted relationships with the musicians whose artistry he most admired.

Anyone who knew Mingus's work before 1963 would have been surprised by the sudden openness of his debt to Ellington on *The Black Saint and the Sinner Lady* and *Mingus Mingus Mingus Mingus Mingus*, both recorded for impulse! Along with "Open Letter to Duke," the music includes a fairly straightforward rendering of "Mood Indigo," written in 1930 by Ellington and Mingus's old boss Barney Bigard. The impulse! LPs feature growling trombone solos by Quentin Jackson, several alto solos by Mariano designed to recall Hodges, and an arrangement of saxophones that put the baritone sax and the lead alto closer to the microphone, replicating the many years when Hodges and baritone saxophonist Carney dominated the Ellington reed section.[48] And yet the solos were in the modal style that Mingus had developed in the 1950s; tempos would change within a single phrase; and the solos of Mariano were dubbed in a week after the original recording date. Priestley wrote that this music was Mingus's "most Ellingtonian piece and his least Ellingtonian."[49]

By the tender age of thirty-one, Mingus had already played in bands led by Louis Armstrong, Barney Bigard, Dinah Washington, Lionel Hampton, Howard McGhee, Red Norvo, Charlie Parker, Miles Davis, and Duke Ellington. But one more canonical figure belongs in this list. In 1954 Charles got a call from Art Tatum, with whom he had sat in years before when both were in LA. For some time, Tatum had been the pianist's pianist. As his earliest recordings from 1932 reveal, Tatum possessed a complete mastery of the art of jazz improvisation and displayed it with dazzling technical facility.

When Mingus joined guitarist Everett Barksdale as the third member of Tatum's trio, Norman Granz was in the process of bringing Tatum into the studio repeatedly from 1953 through 1956 to cement his legacy. (Tatum died shortly after the last session.) The results were collected in the 1970s in two large boxed sets.[50] The solo collection contained an astounding 123 songs, as many as 34 of which were recorded in a single day!

The group recordings featured several sessions, each of which matched Tatum with a different ensemble of experienced musicians, most of whom had a reasonable chance of keeping up with him. The musicians included Lionel Hampton, trumpeters Roy Eldridge and Harry Edison, drummer Jo Jones, and alto saxophonist Benny Carter. The final session brought Tatum together with drummer Bill Douglass, bassist Red Callender, and the virtuoso tenor saxophonist Ben Webster, who wisely underplayed. On many selections, Tatum would rip through a ballad with his usual tenacity, after which Webster soulfully and deliberately blew a miniature masterpiece. Surprisingly, Mingus appears on none of the Tatum group recordings.

With his light touch, his rhythmic stability, and his unimaginably elaborate flourishes, Tatum had many admirers but few imitators. It was simply not possible to play like him. Tatum would take a familiar standard and then run it through a set of variations, sometimes using two different techniques on top of one another. Mingus would signify on Tatum in 1965 when he wrote "The Arts of Tatum and Freddie Webster" by inserting a phrase from Dvořák's "Humoresque" and immediately following it with a phrase from "Body and Soul."[51] Tatum regularly performed both of these tunes, and he would quote from them in his improvisations even when he was in the middle of a completely different tune. Mingus was having some perverse fun with his memories of Tatum when he directed his musicians to play the quotations at a speed substantially slower than Tatum ever played them.[52] Surely Mingus was not the only musician to play with Tatum who would have preferred that the pianist pull back from his wild-ride tempi. But placing a bit of nineteenth-century European classical music next to a fragment from a song deep in the heart of the jazz tradition was entirely consistent with Mingus's convictions about the compatibility of jazz and classical music, especially when, as here, there was wit in the connection.

Freddie Webster, the other legend referenced in "The Arts of Tatum and Freddie Webster," was a highly respected trumpeter and one of the artists who inspired the young Miles Davis. Mingus told Sy Johnson that Freddie Webster and Fats Navarro were playing complicated bebop-like lines before Charlie Parker got around to it.[53] Perhaps Mingus put tributes to Tatum and Webster in the same composition to remind us that both musicians were, like Mingus himself, playing an advanced music before critics had a name for it. Like Navarro, Freddie Webster died much too early, at the age of thirty, of a heart attack after injecting himself with heroin. Mingus salutes Freddie Webster by featuring Hobart Dotson's trumpet throughout almost all nine minutes of "The Arts of Tatum and Freddie Webster."

Art Tatum never worked from a written score. His vision was so poor that, to play a game of poker, he had to hold his cards up to his one good eye one at a time. Mingus therefore had to rely on his ear and his skills as an improviser to keep up. During his brief tenure with Tatum, Mingus may already have started thinking about composing without writing anything down. By the time he was regularly creating music for the members of his Jazz Workshop, he would sing parts or pick out melodies on the piano to convey what he was looking for. The musicians then had to apply their own skills as jazz players to the compositions. As so often, Mingus did not walk away from his most recent employer empty-handed.

MODAL, FREE, AND SOULFUL

Before he formed the Jazz Workshop in 1955, Mingus's musical story was primarily about the distinguished musicians with whom he had performed. Contemplating Mingus in the early stages of his career, John McDonough wrote, "By the mid-50s he was an honored virtuoso of virtuoso music, but not a ground-breaker."[54] After 1955, and especially after *Pithecanthropus Erectus* (1956), his musical story began to revolve around his own work as a composer and leader. But it was also about his reactions to jazz history and its transformations over the next twenty years. For example, he insisted that he had been playing modal jazz—so essential to Miles Davis's hugely popular *Kind of Blue* LP—several years before Miles.[55] Listen to Mingus's "Pithecanthropus Erectus" and "Love Chant," recorded in 1956, and then to "So What," recorded in 1959 for *Kind of Blue*. In both, the musicians create modal, scale-based improvisations around two and only two chords, each of which may persist for extended periods before giving way to the other chord. As Stanley Crouch points out, Mingus believed that the blues, which is built around three chords, "could be reduced even further and, with an appropriately charismatic rhythmic foundation, a piece could avoid monotony and achieve incantation, a force he was attracted to in musics as far removed as those of the sanctified Negro church and flamenco."[56]

Improvisation with just two chords or two scales has been practiced by many artists who appreciate its simplicity as well as its challenges. Mingus himself said that Jelly Roll Morton was doing it in the 1920s.[57] (He is probably referring to Morton's 1927 recording of "Jungle Blues."[58]) But also keep in mind that Mingus hired Bill Evans as his pianist one year before

Evans went to work with Davis.[59] Bill Evans wrote the liner notes to *Kind of Blue* and definitely contributed to the modal concepts behind that music. Miles made a fortune with Bill Evans, *Kind of Blue,* and modal jazz, but Mingus was there first.

Mingus bands in the 1950s also anticipated the "free" jazz of the late 1950s as practiced by Ornette Coleman, Albert Ayler, and Cecil Taylor. Mingus's first experiments with the Jazz Workshop granted an immense amount of freedom to his sidepeople. A soloist had the license to move away from the familiar structures of the popular song if it felt right—especially if it felt right for Mingus. When he wrote the liner notes for the Savoy LP *Jazz Composers Workshop* in 1954, Mingus specifically said that he wanted the group improvisations to be "tonal," but he also said that he was prepared to "delve a little more into the so-called dissonance of free-form improvisation—which one may then label atonal."[60]

ORNETTE AND AFTER

A powerful *conservative* streak was always part of Mingus's thinking, especially when it came to other people's art. Consider, for example, the experimental filmmaker Stan Brakhage, who, for one project, collected wings from moths and petals from various flowers, careful to choose items through which light could easily pass. He pressed the wings and petals between two strips of splicing tape and then made a print that could be projected through a movie camera. He called this one-minute, decidedly nonnarrative film *Mothlight* (1963). He made many other films that were every bit as startling and innovative. Although Brakhage has his detractors, his defenders find structural intricacy in his films and call him a poet of the cinema. Mingus, however, did not agree. According to Janet Coleman, when she and Mingus went to see a Brakhage film at the Bleecker Street Cinema in the West Village, he screamed, "Fraud!" at the screen.[61]

In addition to publishing "An Open Letter to the Avant-Garde," in which he reproached jazz artists who departed from tradition without really knowing the tradition,[62] Mingus also criticized John Coltrane, who was one of the most revered figures of the jazz avant-garde when he died in 1967. But Charles believed that Coltrane was stuck in India, repeatedly playing "Indian-type pedal point music." According to Sue Mingus, at some point in 1965 he wondered out loud to a journalist who had asked about Coltrane, "Why doesn't he do other things too?"[63]

By contrast, Charles always had great respect for Jelly Roll Morton, singling him out for special praise in his liner notes to *Let My Children Hear*

Music. After discovering Duke Ellington's music as a young man, learning to love the recordings of Morton, gradually coming around to admire Charlie Parker, and then playing with so many giants from the music's history, Mingus moved through the rest of his career highly suspicious of any musician claiming to have something new to say.

Mingus was especially ambivalent about what Ornette Coleman was playing. In 1959, Coleman was attracting a great deal of attention, especially with his long residence at the Five Spot, one of the most visible jazz venues in New York. Coleman was leading a piano-less quartet that created music with no discernible tonal center but with a powerful emotional impact that was rooted, however obliquely, in the blues. The aspirations of Coleman's music are evident in self-consciously titled LPs such as *Tomorrow Is the Question, Change of the Century,* and *The Shape of Jazz to Come.* Mingus had been slow to respond to the challenges of bebop, and he was suspicious of the "free jazz" of Coleman, which was perhaps even more radical in its rejection of much of what was considered essential to good music.

To Coleman's great fortune, jazz criticism as a discipline was coming into its own at this time. Some of the more learned critics compared Coleman's music to the Viennese avant-garde of the 1920s and 1930s. Others heard it as a natural development in jazz history, with Ornette looking back at his predecessors and taking their music to a new level. Coleman was considered to be every bit as revolutionary as the young Louis Armstrong or the mature Charlie Parker. The influential critic Martin Williams made this case, both in his book *The Jazz Tradition* and in his *Smithsonian Collection of Classic Jazz,* a box set of six LPs that was the most widely available version of the jazz canon from the 1970s until Ken Burns constructed a slightly different canon in 2001.[64] One wonders if Coleman would have been as successful had Williams and a handful of others not made such grandiose claims for his music. Regardless of how we now place Ornette in jazz history, he had solid roots in the vernacular, and he possessed what Francis Davis has called a "keening, vox humana" resonance on his saxophone that was both new and authentic.[65]

At least at first, Mingus was not impressed. In his "Open Letter to the Avant-Garde," Mingus pointed out that Coleman did not and perhaps could not play in tune. At the "Newport Rebels" event in 1960, Mingus and Coleman played in a band that also included Kenny Dorham and Max Roach.[66] In Mingus's account of the gig, "Kenny Dorham and I tried to get Ornette to play 'All the Things You Are' straight, and he couldn't do it."[67] But in a "blindfold test" for *Down Beat* with Leonard Feather, Mingus admitted that Coleman's playing sounded so fresh that it made all other jazz, even Mingus's, "sound terrible."[68] Later, Mingus would say of Coleman, "It's like not having anything to do with what's around you, and being right in your own world."[69]

He eventually came to like Coleman as a person as well. When Mingus stopped by the Five Spot one night to hear him and his band, he ended up sitting in on piano, perhaps testing the artists' musicianship, perhaps hoping to find out what it felt like to play in Ornette's world. He would later return with members of his quartet, Eric Dolphy and Ted Curson, and ask if they could play in the style of Ornette and his trumpeter, Don Cherry.[70]

In Shirley Clarke's 1985 documentary *Ornette: Made in America*, he comes off as a naif, almost Candide-like. Most remarkably, Coleman says that he contemplated castration because he was uncomfortable with the women who approached him after performances, even going so far as to consult a physician. The doctor suggested that Coleman first try circumcision and then reconsider castration. Coleman says he did not like being circumcised, so he decided not to continue on to castration. The affectless style in which he tells this story, like much of his behavior in the film, may have been a pose or a ruse, much the way Thelonious Monk toyed with the public's idea that he was crazy by in fact acting crazy. Nevertheless, there was definitely an element of naiveté in Coleman's music.

Although he was capable of talking in vaguely—and naively—musicological terms about his "harmolodic" theory of musical improvisation, Coleman did manage to bypass much of the preparation that Mingus insisted an avant-garde musician should acquire. There is something fundamentally instinctive about the improvisations Coleman's groups recorded in the early 1960s. This was even more evident in 1965 when Coleman began playing violin and trumpet, instruments he was still a long way from mastering. Mingus must have felt vindicated when Ornette was roundly denounced by critics.

At the same time that Coleman's quartet was attracting so much attention at the Five Spot, Mingus was leading a group with the same instrumentation, and both groups were playing what could be called "free jazz." But Mingus's quartet with Dolphy, Curson, and Dannie Richmond was playing a very different kind of music. As Michael Cuscuna has written, that band had "the impact of something traditional and avant-garde performed with calculated thought and complete freedom."[71]

After hiring Dolphy, who moved Mingus closer to free jazz, he would bring musicians like Don Pullen, George Adams, and Hamiet Bluiett on board, who absolutely belonged to the free-blowing avant-garde. Mingus had come a long way from the bands of Barney Bigard and Louis Armstrong, but in no way was he jumping on each new bandwagon as it came along. He struggled to understand every new advance, and unlike the avant-garde players of whom he was so critical, he never let go of what he had already learned.

To my knowledge, Mingus never played klezmer music, and there are surely other exceptions to his near omnipresence in jazz history. But to complete my catalog of Mingus connections, I will point out that he was on the ground floor of the jazz and poetry movement, recording with Lonnie Elder and Melvin Stewart in 1957 and with Langston Hughes in 1958. He ingeniously incorporates elements of both Mexican popular music and flamenco into the material on *Tijuana Moods,* and for *Cumbia and Jazz Fusion* he looks to the patterns and tonalities of a vernacular music from South America.

I would add that Mingus is rarely associated with the "soul jazz" that had some crossover success in the 1960s. The music had a funky rhythmic feel and some gospel infusions. Jazz writers include recordings such as Lee Morgan's "The Sidewinder" (1963), Herbie Hancock's "Cantaloupe Island" (1964), Horace Silver's "Song for My Father" (1964), and Cannonball Adderley's "Mercy, Mercy, Mercy" (1966) in this genre. Mingus was critical of soul jazz early on, and specifically denounced the music that Adderley was making in the mid-1960s. According to Eric Porter, he feared "a music that spoke of racial pride but also of a narrowly conceived marketing strategy."[72] But there is no question that the key components of soul jazz were already in place in "Haitian Fight Song," which he recorded in 1957, not to mention "Better Git It in Your Soul" and "Wednesday Night Prayer Meeting," both from 1959.[73]

For me, Mingus brought it all together with the great quintet of 1974 and 1975, with George Adams, Jack Walrath, Don Pullen, and Dannie Richmond, a group I was fortunate to hear in a club when the band was on tour. By this time Mingus was writing out his music and not asking his musicians to interpret a sketch or something he sang to them. Musicians were still expected, however, to be original and to listen carefully to one another. This was especially important when Mingus and drummer Richmond were perfectly in sync as they accelerated or decelerated.

Adams, Walrath, and Pullen were always able to go with the flow as they moved from composed segments to boppish improvisation to full-throated free-blowing and then back again. The blues regularly circulated through the music, as when George Adams sang "Devil Blues," channeling Screamin' Jay Hawkins. The Ellington influence was also there, as in the almost reverential "Duke Ellington's Sound of Love" and "For Harry Carney," a composition by Sy Johnson that moves the baritone saxophonist into a slightly Asian mode. When the band performed in a club, each set would end with a parody of music from the 1930s and 1940s, such as "Cherokee" or "Tea for Two," always played at lightning speed.

And there was a political cast to this music. Even tunes with elegant melodies might be given names such as "Remember Rockefeller at Attica" and "Free Cell Block F, 'Tis Nazi USA." The band would also revive "Fables of Faubus," first as "Fables of Nixon" and then as "Fables of Nixon, Rockefeller, and Ford." Shortly after two failed assassination attempts on Gerald Ford in 1975, Mingus announced a piece as "Remember Rockefeller at Attica, and Look Who's Blastin' at Ford."

In a typical set with "The Second Band," the longest tune was often "Sue's Changes," based on a reworking of "Celia," a lovely piece that Mingus had first written for his second wife in 1957. In 1972, his musicians would play the melody to "Celia" in all its beauty, then gradually work up to squealing improvisations before slowing down and returning to the original softness.[74] By 1974, after he had reached a level of domestic comfort with Sue, Charles gave the same treatment to "Sue's Changes," but both the beauty and the chaos were even more dramatic.[75]

With this last great band, Mingus had come to terms with the avant-garde and made it part of his own musical identity. When Don Pullen left the band, he was replaced by Hugh Lawson, then with Danny Mixon and finally with Bob Neloms. George Adams was replaced by Ricky Ford. All of these musicians made great music with Mingus. If we had more recordings of Mingus with these musicians, we could develop a fuller account of Mingus's experience with the avant-garde. What we do have suggests that toward the end of his career Mingus was more interested in large-scale composition than in small groups with aggressively avant-garde improvisers.

The records with "The Second Band" did not sell nearly as well as the later ones in which the dying Mingus barely participated while producers moved his music toward jazz/rock fusion. Had Mingus cast his lot with one and only one style, he might have received more recognition from critics and audiences. If, for example, he had decided to stick with the boppers and become the "Charlie Parker of the bass," he would have had a much better shot at fitting into the narrative that drove Ken Burns' documentary *Jazz*, shown on American television in January 2001.

As Scott DeVeaux points out, in *Jazz* Burns creates a story about a steadily developing art form pressed ahead by a handful of magisterial improvisers and composers, all working from their own unique places in the music's history. The narrative culminates in a patriotic flourish with America's participation in World War II: jazz had become "a symbol of America's special mission abroad."[76] Mingus, of course, wrote many songs with distinctly anti-American titles, most notably "Once There Was a Holding Corporation Named Old America."[77] When jazz began to lose its popular audience in the 1950s and could no longer be associated with American triumphalism, Burns argues, jazz artists lost their way, finding it again only when Wynton Marsalis and other neo-revivalists arrived to show them that embracing older styles of jazz is the only solution.

According to Burns, in Marsalis and his music, the spirits of Armstrong, Ellington, and Charlie Parker were once again alive. Without question, Marsalis is a prodigious talent who deserves great credit for using the cultural force of Lincoln Center to celebrate the legacy of his great predecessors. He has even staged concerts to showcase the music of Mingus!

But the most grotesque misrepresentation in *Jazz* is its portrayal—or what DeVeaux calls the "near-complete erasure"—of the music in the 1970s. In Burns's narrative, the music was in a drastic decline and could only be saved by the arrival of Marsalis, who began recording in 1980. But DeVeaux provides a long list of great artists he saw performing in the 1970s.[78] The list includes Mingus, who made some of his most exquisite music during that decade. It should come as no surprise that Burns and his staff granted Mingus less than three minutes in their seventeen-and-a-half-hour history of jazz. It was Mingus, not Marsalis, who was busy preserving the spirits of Armstrong, Ellington, and Parker—as well as Morton, Tatum, and the best of the jazz avant-garde—throughout the 1970s. Mingus the anti-American revivalist, the conservative hyper-modernist, and the jazz composer who hated the word *jazz* could have no place in Burns's narrative.

REVELATING AND SIGNIFYING

Among the many jazz movements in which Charles Mingus participated, the most likely and the most *unlikely* was Third Stream Music. Gunther Schuller coined the term, describing Third Stream as "the fusion and cross-fertilization of two musical mainstreams, classical and jazz."[79] Schuller—composer, performer, conductor, critic, entrepreneur, and musician—was responsible for a great deal of the music that emerged from the project when it was at its height, from approximately 1956 until 1961.

Like Nat Hentoff and George Wein, Schuller was a crucial figure in Mingus's career. Several years after Mingus died, the musicologist Andrew Homzy was cataloging the music Mingus left behind and discovered the score for a massive work for jazz orchestra, much of it written for the infamous Town Hall concert of 1962 but parts of it from even earlier. The composition, appropriately titled *Epitaph*, was performed by thirty musicians on the stage of Avery Fischer Hall at Lincoln Center in 1989. *Epitaph* had eighteen movements and took more than two hours to perform. Schuller reconstructed and edited the music and then conducted it. But Schuller had been part of Mingus's world at least since the early 1950s when Charles was establishing himself as a New York jazz musician.

On the one hand, Mingus was right for Schuller's Third Stream dreams. Charles had a profound connection with classical music and had always insisted that there should be no distinction between jazz and classical. In 1971, when he gave a long interview to student DJs at WKCR, the radio station of Columbia University, someone asked what recording they should play after the interview was over. After suggesting music by other jazz artists—Art Tatum, Sonny Rollins, Charlie Parker, and Bud Powell—Mingus shifted gears and told the DJs to play music by Zoltán Kodály or, being more specific, Bartók's second violin concerto, "the B side." Even more pointedly, he asked for Isaac Stern as violin soloist, then changed his mind to Yehudi Menuhin. He also suggested Beethoven's Ninth Symphony and Stravinsky's *Firebird Suite.*[80]

As a child, Charles was sufficiently devoted to the symphonic repertoire to risk violence at the hands of neighborhood toughs every time he crossed the mean streets of Watts with a cello case on his back. Many of his early recordings, such as "God's Portrait" (1949) and "Extrasensory Perception" (1952), display a dedication to the art of the classical composer, as do many of the recordings he produced for his Debut label.[81]

On the other hand, by the mid-1950s Mingus had in some ways moved on from classical music. Although he spoke highly of the European masters, his composing style bore little resemblance to theirs. If Mingus did not simply sing a tune for the early Jazz Workshoppers, he would give them a bit of written music that was more of a sketch than a score.

His major influences in jazz, Ellington and Parker, knew how to swing, an element that has seldom if ever been important to classical composers, certainly not in the 1950s. Along with everything else, Ellington was a great bluesman, and once you get past Parker's exquisite technical prowess, you realize that his music was saturated with the blues as well. Likewise Mingus, who knew his way around African American rhythms, was immersed in the blues. The classical music of Mingus's time had no use for any of this and certainly not for the kind of improvisation that Mingus was encouraging among his Workshoppers. Most importantly, Mingus was almost perverse in his resistance to formal constraints and to any and all separations thrown up between one kind of music or another. From the outset, Third Stream was in danger of becoming yet another genre that had to be distinguished from the others in spite of the fact that "it's all one music."

Gunther Schuller, however, was uniquely qualified to create a new genre by fusing jazz with classical music in a systematic fashion. Born in 1925, Schuller, whose father played violin with the New York Philharmonic, was a child prodigy on both flute and French horn. At age seventeen he sat first chair in the horn section of the Cincinnati Symphony Orchestra. By eighteen he was composing symphonic works, including concerti for cello and French horn. Schuller discovered jazz at an early age and became even more devoted to the music than the many jazz enthusiasts who give equal time to the classics. In fact, Schuller had exactly the same experience as the young Mingus when, at age eleven, he was transfixed by his first exposure to the Duke Ellington orchestra. Like Mingus, he first heard Ellington on a radio broadcast.

In 1944, the nineteen-year-old Schuller sought out Ellington after his orchestra gave a concert in Cincinnati. Pleased by how much of his music Schuller seemed to know, Ellington invited the young man to come back and play something for him on his French horn, assuring Schuller that he didn't care whether he played jazz or classical music. The next time Ellington was in town, Schuller did indeed bring along his horn. When he had Duke's full attention, he replicated the alto saxophone solo that Johnny Hodges played on the Ellington band's 1940 recording of "Warm Valley." Schuller told Duke that he had also arranged the tune for symphony orchestra. Ellington was so impressed that he invited Schuller to join his band as its only French horn player.[82]

In his autobiography, Schuller speculates that Ellington was probably joking when he asked him to join the band. After all, it would have been impossible to rewrite all of the band's music to accommodate a French horn. Just as impossible would have been the addition of a white musician to an all-black orchestra in the 1940s—the logistics of touring in America's racist heartland would have been a nightmare. Regardless, Schuller's ideas for Third Stream Music were related to his conviction that Ellington was as serious a composer as any old master from Europe.

The Third Stream idea began to come into focus when Schuller met the young pianist and composer John Lewis in the late 1940s. They became fast friends, regularly talking on the telephone for hours at a time. Lewis, who grew up in New Mexico and studied composition and orchestration at the Manhattan School of Music, was the pianist for Miles Davis's nonet as well as one of the band's several composers and arrangers. The band was nominally led by Miles Davis, who, having made some useful connections during his stint with Charlie Parker, was able to book the band into the better venues. In some ways, the nonet was a laboratory where Gil Evans continued working out musical ideas he had been developing as writer and arranger for Claude Thornhill's big band in the 1940s. Arrangers like John Lewis, Gerry Mulligan, and John Carisi were happy to join in as well. Unlike most groups that played modern jazz, the nonet included a French horn and a tuba, instruments that gave Evans's arrangements their rumbling, signature sound.[83]

In 1950, Lewis was instrumental in bringing Schuller to play French horn at the third and final recording session of the nonet, his first time recording with jazz artists. (Junior Collins or Sandy Siegelstein had played the French horn in earlier sessions.) Schuller had actually heard one incarnation of the nonet when he was a regular at the Royal Roost, a jazz club on Broadway near 52nd Street. Several months after the recording session, he played with the band at Birdland to a small audience. Schuller recalls seeing Mingus in the club and says that he "left after one set, without saying much."[84] As always, Mingus was not easily converted.

By the early 1950s, when they were both living in New York, Schuller and John Lewis regularly went out together to hear classical music and jazz. Afterward they would go to the Carnegie Hall Tavern, where Mingus occasionally joined them. Sadly, Schuller makes no mention in his autobiography of what Mingus added to their conversations. In 2013, when I asked him what they talked about, he said simply, "Everything."[85]

Thanks to the G.I. Bill, John Lewis was able to study piano as well as composition and orchestration at the Manhattan School of Music. In 1951, he was a founding member of what would become the Modern Jazz Quartet. Schuller says that Lewis invited him to the band's recording sessions as early as 1953.[86] By the mid-1950s, the MJQ was playing classically tinged pieces like "Little David's Fugue," "Versailles," and "Concorde," surely written under the influence of Schuller.[87] Soon Schuller was contracting for Lewis's recording dates and bringing in classically trained musicians to record with Lewis and the MJQ.

The Third Stream project was fully realized with the Columbia LP *Music for Brass,* released in 1956. On the album cover, "The Brass Ensemble of the Jazz and Classical Music Society" was prominently credited, along with the composers, conductors, and soloists. The LP comprised four works: Lewis's "Three Little Feelings," J.J. Johnson's "Poem for Brass," Jimmy Giuffre's "Pharaoh," and Schuller's own Symphony for Brass and Percussion, a long, atonal, nonjazz piece he had written a few years earlier. On "Three Little Feelings" and "Poem for Brass," Miles Davis soloed elegantly on trumpet and flugelhorn while Schuller conducted.[88]

As even the most casual jazz fan knows, the practice of "jazzing the classics" has a long history. We could trace the appropriation of European music by African American performers back to the black churches of the nineteenth century. Many of the early jazz performers had no conservatory training, but they always had opportunities to hear classical music. In New Orleans during the late nineteenth and early twentieth centuries when jazz was being born, brass bands gave public concerts in parks virtually every weekend. The bands were sponsored by civic associations, fraternal organizations, and loose assemblages of ethnic groups. Bands assembled from German, Polish, and Italian populations in New Orleans regularly made the classics an important part of their repertoire. None of this was lost on the first jazz artists.

And of course, jazz musicians also heard classical music when radio became an important part of American culture in the 1920s. Not surprisingly, jazz artists have long quoted motives from classical compositions, sometimes with tongue in cheek. As Joshua Berrett points out, Louis Armstrong was a great fan of Caruso and occasionally inserted a quotation from an opera in the middle of a solo.[89] Duke Ellington referenced Chopin's "Funeral March" at the end of his "Black and Tan Fantasy."[90] Working with Billy Strayhorn in 1960, Ellington transformed Tchaikovsky's *Nutcracker* and Grieg's *Peer Gynt Suite* into extended jazz pieces.[91] Art Tatum regularly performed his version of Dvořák's "Humoresque." Stan Kenton recorded "Chorale for Brass, Piano, and Bongo."[92] And Hazel Scott, who would eventually record with Mingus on his Debut label, made a career of playing a classical composition with conservatory virtuosity before launching into a jazzed-up version. In the late 1930s and early 1940s, the John Kirby Sextet regularly jazzed themes by Grieg, Schubert, Chopin, and Beethoven.[93]

Meanwhile, European composers who were enchanted by jazz experimented with African American patterns of syncopation and blues tonalities. Darius Milhaud's "Creation of the World" (1922–23) may be the best example.[94] In 1945, the same year that Boyd Raeburn's jazz orchestra recorded "Boyd Meets Stravinsky," Stravinsky himself wrote the "Ebony" Concerto for Woody Herman.[95]

Schuller's Third Stream project, however, was something else. If "jazzing the classics" meant the use of jazz to comment on a classical piece, his idea was to integrate the two in such a way that neither genre was eclipsed by the other. A classical piece would not simply be quoted in a jazz piece or vice versa. Even when the music was closest to jazz in its rhythmic groove, it would be through-composed with elaborate chordal structures and a wider variety of timbres than a jazz piece typically included.

You can hear Schuller's designs successfully carried out in the pieces by Lewis and J.J. Johnson on the *Music for Brass* album. In Lewis's "Three Little Feelings," for example, motives are introduced, developed, and recalled as in a symphony. But as in most arrangements for big-band jazz, there are call-and-response patterns between different groups of instruments, and Lewis regularly makes use of a flatted fifth, so essential to the blues idiom. Often the music has no rhythmic pulse, but sometimes it shifts to an unmistakable jazz beat with a walking bass or a drumstick tapping a cymbal. Even when the rhythm is not jazz, there is a great deal of syncopation, especially the familiar "Charleston" pattern.

When Miles Davis solos on "Three Little Feelings," he improvises as often as he plays exactly what is written. In a sense, Davis was the perfect choice to solo on a Third Stream composition, being among the first well-known jazz artists to have rigorous conservatory training. When he was in high school, Davis's well-to-do father saw to it that he took lessons from Joseph Gustat, the principal trumpeter with the St. Louis Symphony.[96] During his first year in New York, when he was regularly attending classes at Juilliard, Davis studied with William Vacchiano, the first chair trumpeter with the New York Philharmonic and for several decades one of the most revered trumpet teachers in New York.[97] But with their warm timbre and bent notes, Miles's solos on "Three Little Feelings" were clearly fashioned on 52nd Street, not at the conservatory. He is playing jazz even as he is faithfully executing written music.

John Lewis uses tympani and French horns to add gravitas as well as a familiar orchestral resonance to "Three Little Feelings." In jazz, tympani function as novelty instruments, if at all. As for the French horn, there are good reasons why it has never become a standard jazz instrument, in spite of the best efforts of Gil Evans, not to mention Gunther Schuller, Julius Watkins, Tom Varner, Vincent Chancey, John Clark, and a few other brave souls who have brought the instrument to jazz venues. Jazz musicians must be loose and agile with their instruments, as when Louis Armstrong moved beyond the boxy solos of his cornet predecessors and played arpeggios in the style of clarinetists. It took a great deal of practice and imagination, but as Ralph Ellison famously observed, Armstrong transformed the trumpet from a "military instrument" into a "lyrical beam of sound."[98] No one, however, can play the French horn like a clarinet, and its sound is most easily associated with stately passages from the symphonic repertoire. Lewis surely understood this when he made the French horn and the tympani important elements of his ensemble. Throughout "Three Little Feelings,"

Lewis tries a variety of approaches to combining the sound of a symphony with the sound of a jazz combo.

If Third Stream came of age with *Music for Brass* in 1956, it reached its zenith at a festival at Brandeis University in 1957. Schuller was surprised when the festival organizers, who had been presenting classical music, dance, and poetry annually since 1952, asked him to put together a special jazz concert at the 1957 event. Seizing the opportunity to contribute new music to the Third Stream repertoire, Schuller invited three jazz artists and two classical composers to write music for the festival. He contributed a new piece of his own to the mix, thus creating a balanced program with three pieces by jazz artists and three by university and conservatory composers.

Schuller, who had now known Mingus for several years, was impressed with the just-released *Pithecanthropus Erectus* and invited him to participate in the Brandeis festival. Mingus contributed what may be the most remarkable piece of the six, a twelve-minute composition called "Revelations (First Movement)."[99]

The other two composers with roots in jazz were George Russell and Jimmy Giuffre. Russell had made his mark in 1947 when he wrote the ambitious "Cubana Be, Cubana Bop" for Dizzy Gillespie's big band.[100] He was already foreshadowing Third Stream with "A Bird in Igor's Yard," a tribute to Charlie Parker and Igor Stravinsky that Buddy DeFranco recorded with a large jazz orchestra in 1949.[101] Russell was also a good choice for the festival because of his work with music theory. Although musicologists may have reservations about its basic theses, Russell's 1953 book *The Lydian Chromatic Concept of Tonal Organization* was widely read by jazz musicians looking for new approaches to improvisation.[102] (There is no indication that Mingus read Russell's book, but he was surely aware of it in the 1950s when he was looking around for musical ideas.) As a leader, Russell made well-received LPs with pianist Bill Evans and trumpeter Art Farmer, both of whom appeared in the orchestra that Schuller assembled for the Brandeis Festival. Like Mingus, Russell also later employed Eric Dolphy.

Before the Brandeis event, Jimmy Giuffre had already worked with Schuller when he contributed "Pharoah" to the *Music for Brass* sessions. And as with Russell, 1947 became his breakthrough year when the big band known as Woody Herman's "Second Herd" recorded "The Four Brothers," composed and arranged by Giuffre.[103] (One could make the case that Mingus also had his first breakthrough in 1947 when Lionel Hampton recorded "Mingus Fingers.")

Giuffre, who is featured in Bert Stern's documentary about the 1958 Newport Jazz Festival, *Jazz on a Summer's Day* (1959), is now remembered primarily as a West Coast player of the cool school. He was an appropriate choice for the Brandeis festival if only because he modeled some of his music on the work of the American composer Aaron Copland. In fact, Copland had been infusing his compositions with flavors from jazz and the blues since at least the 1920s, and in 1968 he would single out the work of Giuffre and Ornette Coleman to argue that jazz was taking more from "serious music" than the other way around.[104]

To represent the academic side of Third Stream, Schuller first commissioned Harold Shapero. As the founder and chair of the Brandeis music department, he was an essential choice. Shapero graduated from Harvard in 1940 and won the Prix de Rome the following year. In 1947, he would watch as Leonard Bernstein conducted the premiere of his *Symphony for Classical Orchestra* with the Boston Philharmonic.

Schuller also invited Milton Babbitt, at that time a professor of music at Princeton University. Babbitt became interested in jazz and popular song at an early age, and both the songwriter Stephen Sondheim and the jazz guitarist Stanley Jordan are among his former students. But Babbitt was mostly attracted to more formalist musics such as the twelve-tone compositions of Arnold Schoenberg and Alban Berg. He wrote a number of pieces for synthesizer and electronic instruments that allowed him to create an absolutely precise rhythmic pulse. Not surprisingly, his father was a mathematician, and Babbitt himself once contemplated entering that same profession.

The music from the Brandeis festival was first released on an LP called *Modern Jazz Concert* in 1957. In 1963, Columbia Records rereleased the music as part of a double LP that also included a three-part suite by Duke Ellington, *Idiom '59*, as well as the pieces by Lewis, Johnson, and Giuffre from the *Music for Brass* LP. Columbia gave the set the formidable title *Outstanding Jazz Compositions of the Twentieth Century*.[105]

At the time Third Stream Music made its first appearances, jazz was losing its association with youthful hipness and rebellion. The flappers and jitterbuggers who had scandalized their parents by dancing to music created primarily by African Americans were now raising children who were in turn scandalizing their parents by dancing to an even more black-inflected music, rock 'n' roll. Jazz was becoming associated less with those who defied bourgeois notions of decorum than with middle-aged connoisseurs and the professorate. Third Stream did nothing to dispel that notion.

In the film *Jailhouse Rock*, Elvis Presley plays an independent-minded young man imprisoned for beating up an obstreperous stranger in a bar. In jail, he becomes serious about music, crooning to the other prisoners with a borrowed guitar. Barely out of prison, he is discovered by a young female record producer who takes him to a recording studio and then brings him home to meet her father, a college professor.

Presley's character arrives as the professor is entertaining a room full of middle-aged bourgeois who speak authoritatively about jazz as they listen to the latest recording of a fictional musician named Stubby Wrightmeyer. When one white-haired matron asks Presley if he thinks that "atonality in jazz is merely a passing fancy," he replies, "Lady, I don't know what the hell you're talking about" and storms out of the house. Like the music festival at Brandeis University, *Jailhouse Rock* dates to 1957. Unlike the other festival participants, Mingus might have reacted as Presley did if a jazz dilettante had posed such a question to him.

Along with Schuller, the Brandeis festival was put together and promoted by George Avakian, an executive at Columbia Records who had recently brought Miles Davis to the label. In 1956, he had produced the *Music for Brass* LP that featured Davis on "Three Little Feelings" and "Poem for Brass." Earlier, in 1940, Avakian produced the first reissues of Louis Armstrong's classic recordings from the 1920s. He would go on to produce records by Ellington, Thelonious Monk, and Dave Brubeck at Columbia. He recorded Armstrong in several configurations, including a date with the German actress Lotte Lenya.

Avakian was also one of the three visionaries who created the Columbia Record Club, at a time when the Sears and Wards catalogs and the Book of the Month Club were the only choices for mail-order shoppers. I seldom encounter people of my generation whose parents did not join the Columbia Record Club and receive a deeply discounted copy of *Johnny Mathis's Greatest Hits* as part of the introductory offer. Mathis was discovered by Avakian, who hired no less than Gil Evans to write arrangements for his first recordings at Columbia.

Avakian was intrigued by Schuller's Third Stream initiative at least in part because he was a lifelong enthusiast of both jazz and the classics. For many years he was married to the classical violinist Anahid Ajemian.

By participating in the Brandeis festival, Avakian and Schuller were taking part in a debate about jazz and what it said about American culture. As John Gennari has shown in his thorough account of jazz writing in America, in the 1950s the most adamant defenders of jazz cast the music as part of the American mainstream, not as a subculture of prostitutes, junkies, and gangsters. Within a few years, however, white critics would be obsessed with the music's connections to the black freedom movements of the early 1960s.

But at the time of the Brandeis Festival, many believed that the interplay of musicians in a performance was a profound expression of American democracy.[106]

At the same time, with the rise of cool jazz and a West Coast scene that was mostly populated with white artists, many thought that jazz was losing its soul. More specifically, cool jazz seemed to be invested in denying the music's vernacular roots. The term *vernacular* actually comes from a Latin word meaning slave. In my interviews with Avakian and Schuller, both assured me that they were in no way trying to move jazz away from its roots in African American traditions.[107] But they did embrace the democratic and totally admirable vision of a future in which white and black artists would participate as one in creating a new music.

Although he would later condemn white interlopers in African American music, Mingus made it clear in the 1950s that he too hoped to see the boundaries between jazz and classical dismantled, most famously in the letter to critic Ralph J. Gleason published in *Down Beat* in 1951.[108] Mingus even commented on the music of the white bandleader Stan Kenton, who actually did admit that his ambition was to remove jazz from its African American roots: "If Kenton can change the music, then he can play Carnegie, not just as the representative of jazz, but as a modern composer of American music."[109]

For better or worse, Third Stream advanced an agenda that had been part of jazz discourse at least since the 1920s, one very different from the bagatelles of jazzing the classics. Paul Whiteman, of course, sought to make a lady out of jazz, whether or not he knew that he could then be charged with demasculinizing the music. Other musicians and many critics did not necessarily hope to feminize jazz, but they did seek to strip the music of its primitive roots in country blues, field hollers, and the groans of the Sanctified Church.

Third Stream was also devoted to foregrounding the art of composers and arrangers over the improvising soloist. The "bodiliness" of early jazz, along with what Nathaniel Mackey has called "the telling inarticulacy" of the blues and the emotional immediacy of black music generally, was at this time working its magic for rock 'n' roll.[110] Even without Third Stream, the jazz of the 1950s had been cultivating a more refined and restrained clientele. Although there was plenty of grit in what he played, one could also argue that Mingus helped create a kind of intellectual "chamber jazz" during his tenure with the Red Norvo Trio in 1950 and 1951. The stuffy jazz connoisseurs at the faculty party in *Jailhouse Rock* would probably have admired that band's recordings.

Mingus was not an inevitable choice for the Brandeis Festival. Although he was roughly the same age as Russell and Giuffre, Mingus had had a much more varied career as something other than a composer. Listening to the Brandeis compositions by the African American Russell ("All about Rosie") and the white Giuffre ("Suspensions") today, I do not hear a real fusion of jazz and classical; rather, both sound like straight-ahead jazz pieces. Neither composer shared Mingus's broader vision of what music could be.

Both Russell and Giuffre would soon become pedagogues at the Lenox School of Jazz, directed by John Lewis between 1957 and 1960. Although the school was devoted to expanding the boundaries of jazz, its mission may have been too modest for Mingus. And Mingus may have been not modest enough for Lenox. He was in fact invited to speak at the Lenox School, but he did not stay long after he tangled with "a Texas cop kind of cat" and had to be restrained.[111]

Like the music of Giuffre and Russell, the works by the three classical composers were not especially daring examples of classical/jazz fusion. Harold Shapero's title, "On Green Mountain," puns on the name of Claudio Monteverdi, whose 1632 chaconne is the piece's starting point. After several out-of-time flourishes and some fairly literal renditions of what Monteverdi had written, trumpeter Art Farmer and guitarist Barry Galbraith improvise deftly over the centuries-old chord changes. The same basic pattern continues with out-of-time and regular rhythms alternating. The familiar Monteverdi motif is almost always present while various instrumentalists solo. Most of the musicians who played at the festival and who appear on the recording were based in jazz, but almost all of them had some conservatory training. Truth be told, with a jazz rhythm section of Bill Evans, Barry Galbraith, Joe Benjamin, and Ted Sommer, even Shapero's sedate rendering of Monteverdi does sound a bit jazzy.

Babbitt's piece, by contrast, does not swing at all. "All Set" is rigidly structured around a twelve-tone row, or "set." According to Schuller, pianist Bill Evans had no problem playing what Babbitt had written. (Evans would later embrace twelve-tone music on his own when he recorded "T.T.T. [Twelve Tone Tune]" in 1970 and "T.T.T.T. [Twelve Tone Tune Two]" in 1973.)[112] When the other jazz musicians saw the music, however, "they nearly freaked out" at parts that resembled nothing they had ever seen before.[113] Babbitt could easily have written the same thing for a nonjazz venue. Once again, the piece fits in because it is played by jazz artists who give the piece a looser feel.

With "Transformations," Schuller contributed a work that recalls the sound of the Birth of the Cool band more than any of his modernist atonal compositions. Although much of it is composed and elaborate, Schuller sticks with an infectious rhythmic groove throughout. And unlike most of the other music from the festival, he allows for some moments of pure jazz improvisation, at one point leaving space for a solo by Bill Evans that recalls Bud Powell and Art Tatum rather than anything from the classical repertoire.

In short, the six pieces that premiered at Brandeis had very little in common besides the composers' stated intention of fusing jazz and classical music. On one level, this is exactly what Schuller and the proponents of Third Stream had in mind: a new musical genre that could be stretched in many different directions by enterprising composers. But the music from the Brandeis festival was not well received. Jazz purists were put off, and classical critics were mostly confused. Writing in the *New Yorker*, Whitney Balliett's characterizations of the compositions were typical:

> one fairly successful jazz composition (Russell's "All about Rosie");
> an obtuse atonal contrapuntal classical piece (Babbitt's "All Set");
> a concoction in which, through sheer cleverness and compositional
> strength, jazz and classical music are forced together (Schuller's
> "Transformation"); a watery work that never, except in one brief
> instance, makes up its mind where it belongs (Shapero's "On Green
> Mountain"); and a couple of pieces (Giuffre's "Suspensions" and
> Mingus' "Revelations, First Movement") that are variations on jazz
> material that their composers have handled better elsewhere.[114]

In this assessment, Balliett refuses the basic premise of Third Stream, arguing that Mingus and Giuffre had contributed inferior versions of what they had already done in jazz. I would argue that Mingus and Giuffre certainly recorded a great deal of music that Balliett (and I) might prefer, but Mingus deserves credit for what is surely the most successful combination of jazz and classical performed at the festival.

Even before black people began putting their bodies on the line to achieve equality and before jazz artists began playing with new, politically charged intensity, Mingus had his own ideas about civil rights and the canons of the concert hall. When Mingus wrote to Ralph Gleason in 1951, he was demanding cultural legitimacy for jazz. But he was not entirely interested in granting the status of classical music to jazz. He wrote, "Charlie Parker is in his own way creating complex, clearly thought-out compositions of melodic line every time he plays a solo, as surely as one as ever written down by Brahms or Chopin or Tchaikovsky. . . . Those who have always separated the two into jazz and classical will finally see that it's all one music we're playing and what they've been buying is just the confusion out of the separation of the two."[115]

In his letter, Mingus was also aware that the decline in popularity of bebop had forced musicians to choose between a classical world that disdained them and a jazz audience that favored the liveliness of rhythm and blues. His convictions about the oneness of all music derived in part from his strong convictions about the absurdity of racial distinctions. He usually self-identified as black, beginning with his realization at age fourteen that he would have a better career as a black musician playing jazz bass than as a classical cellist.

But Mingus's father told the young Charles Jr. that he was not one of the "niggers" of Watts, and Mingus would later speak frequently of his Chinese and European grandparents. In the 1998 documentary *Charles Mingus: Triumph of the Underdog,* Dorian Mingus, Charles's son with his white wife Celia, recalls one of his last conversations with his father. "You have no color," Mingus told him. Dorian had become part of the "raceless set," the people for whom Mingus wanted to play a music that transcended race as well as genre.[116]

MINGUS HAS HIS SAY

During the first two minutes of Mingus's "Revelations" we hear ominous rumblings from the string bass and tuba, sprinkled with accents from Ted Sommer's triangle. The opening moments recall the dark chromaticism of Richard Strauss, Wagner, and Bartók. Soon the orchestra drops out to make room for unaccompanied solos for three brass instruments: Jimmy Buffington's French horn, Louis Mucci's trumpet, and Jimmy Knepper's trombone. When the orchestra returns, a walking bass and tympani lead to some brass crescendi.

With the brief addition of a percussive sound that suggests bongos or even African tribal drums, Mingus sends the piece off into a completely new direction by crying out, "Oh yes, my lord. Hmm mmm." He has audaciously brought his music back to the Sanctified Church and to the "telling inarticulacy" of the blues and other black musics. And yet it is not clear to what he is assenting when he addresses "my lord." At this point, "Revelations" does not yet contain a rhythmic or melodic gesture that we might associate with the black church. And what are we to make of his "Hmm mmm"? Regardless, his cry is radically inconsistent with Third Stream's (unacknowledged) project of stripping jazz of its primitive roots. The cry is, however, consistent with Mingus's immense appetite for all kinds of music and with his fascination for the spiritual. It may also be Mingus signifying—having a joke at the expense of Schuller, Avakian, and the pretensions of Third Stream.

About four and a half minutes into the piece, Mingus turns the music over to Bill Evans and the rhythm section, who make the composition sound much more like modern jazz. But as is so often the case with Mingus, nothing stays in one groove for long. Within a minute the piece drops its jazz rhythm and become an almost dreamlike reverie for flute, harp, horn, and *arco* bass that recalls French impressionists such as Debussy and Fauré. After a symbol crash, Evans leads the full orchestra into a section that moves in and out of melodic passages, often with generous helpings of the blues. At eight minutes, "Revelations" jumps into its most accessible moments with upbeat jazz harmony and rhythm, now having little apparent connection to the ominous opening segment and Mingus's cry. But the composition soon returns to deeper matters.

Jennifer Griffith has pointed out that Mingus's title does not refer simply to the last book of the Bible. "'Revelation' is the revealing or disclosing through active or passive communication with a supernatural or a divine entity. Mingus's *Revelations* expresses his spiritual beliefs by dismantling generic boundaries, and unifying musical expression, the principles of universal brotherhood."[117] Mingus may have hoped that in "Revelations" the interplay among musicians—their "brotherhood"—would also recall the worship services of the Sanctified Church.

At approximately eight and a half minutes, Art Farmer and alto saxophonist John LaPorta both solo, first independently and then together. They are soon joined by trombonist Jimmy Knepper. Mingus's pizzicato bass drives the music as the three improvise on top of each other. Little by little the entire ensemble enters, each of the brass and reed players improvising on their own. Suddenly there is chaos with trumpets screaming in the upper register. Just as suddenly, instruments begin to drop out.

Then, as if to unite this spirit with the darker strains of European art music, Mingus returns to the rumblings of bass and tuba with accents from the triangle that we heard in the opening section. But he is not repeating himself. Timbres, rhythms, and moods continue to shift. For closing gestures, flutist Robert DiDomenica and vibraharpist Teddy Charles improvise over Fred Zimmerman's bowed bass. In the final section the bass stands alone, slowly fading away. Our revels and revelations are over. Mingus was proud of this remarkable composition and of the recording he made of it. Sue Mingus wrote that when Charles was dying in Cuernavaca, he listened regularly to "Revelations."[118]

Max Harrison deftly distinguishes Mingus's piece from the other pieces written for the Brandeis Festival: "Mingus takes greater risks than the other composers. The unity of his works depends not on their technical organization, as with Babbitt's *All Set,* nor on a highly personal musical language, as does *All About Rosie,* but is largely of an emotional order. . . . [*Revelations*] extends itself as a succession of moods, feelings, atmospheres, melting into and out of each other. This was something which had not then been widely attempted in jazz."[119] With "Revelations," as with so much of his work, Mingus was continuing to forge "a language for emotions."[120]

In the liner notes for the first issue of the Brandeis music, Schuller describes the culminating free-for-all with several musicians improvising on top of each other as a "paroxysm" that threatens to make the interplay "virtually unbearable."[121] But as Griffith has suggested, is this collective climax perhaps unbearable only for Apollonian folk unwilling to lose themselves in Dionysian wholeness?[122]

The Dionysiac oneness that concludes "Revelations" reflects Mingus's philosophical and spiritual knowledge, especially his childhood experiences in the Sanctified Church. But there was a political dimension as well. If Mingus sought to dismantle boundaries, he knew from his career in the music industry that discrimination excluded African American musicians from pursuing jobs in the classical world and elsewhere. And he knew that the industry kept genres separate in order to sell records. Debut Records was one attempt to solve this problem. A great deal of superb music was released on the Debut label, but it folded in 1957, the same year as the Brandeis Festival of Third Stream Music and the fatal parody of jazz enthusiasts in *Jailhouse Rock.*

"Revelations" was in some ways Mingus's response to the loss of the jazz audience reflected in the demise of his record company and Presley's cinematic outburst. His unifying of the full range of jazz expression with a modernist classical tradition was also an act of protest against those who might continue to segregate the two genres. Mingus saw Third Stream as still another genre that could be distinguished from jazz *and* from classical music.

Several excursions into Third Stream Music followed the Brandeis festival, many of them with the participation of Schuller. In 1958, Miles Davis soloed on Gil Evans's transformations of Gershwin's *Porgy and Bess* for jazz orchestra, with Schuller in the French horn section.[123] On the *Sketches of Spain* LP of 1960, Davis and Evans pushed even harder against the Third Stream envelope when they collaborated on Evans's reconceptualization of Joaquin Rodrigo's *Concierto de Aranjuez.*[124] In 1961, J. J. Johnson wrote an LP's worth of material called *Perceptions,* with Dizzy Gillespie soloing and Schuller conducting.[125] Also in 1961, with arrangements for string orchestra by Eddie Sauter, Stan Getz recorded *Focus,* an ambitious project that Getz numbered among his favorite records.[126] In 1964, at the urging of

Schuller, the Modern Jazz Quartet put their mark on a fugue by Bach. Schuller and John Lewis were the conductors and Avakian the producer of several performances and recordings by "Orchestra U.S.A." in the early 1960s, an invention of Lewis dedicated to elaborate arrangements inflected with Third Stream principles.

In 1972, Mingus had an even closer encounter with classical music when the Whitney Museum of American Art commissioned him to write a musical setting for a poem by Frank O'Hara. Mingus wrote a work for voice, two cellos, violin, and viola and called it String Quartet, No. 1. The composition was apparently performed exactly once for an audience of mostly young concertgoers, many of whom sat on the Whitney's floor. As with "Revelations" fifteen years earlier, he was still testing the boundaries between high art and popular art, between black music and white music, and between his passion for classical music and his profound suspicion of these same boundaries. As Vilde Aaslid has written, the music could be heard "as both aspiration and resistance."[127]

In that same year that Mingus wrote his string quartet, Gunther Schuller helped establish a Third Stream Music department at the New England Conservatory, with Ran Blake as its director. In 1992 the name of the program was changed to Contemporary Improvisation, and it is still attracting students today. But by the time Schuller had begun institutionalizing Third Stream at the NEC, Miles Davis and Gil Evans had plugged in and were playing what sounded more like rock 'n' roll than classical music.

Third Stream is now confined to a few paragraphs in the jazz history books. In 1988, when Wynton Marsalis was at his most combative about what was and was not jazz, he went so far as to dump Third Stream into the same subgenre where he put rock and pop—"nonjazz."[128] Ultimately, Third Stream did not succeed in transforming jazz, and it certainly did not bring back the audiences that had drifted away after the decline of the big bands and the rise of bebop in the late 1940s.

Nevertheless, Schuller and the old Third Stream enthusiasts should be gratified that jazz and classical are now profoundly intertwined in at least some quarters of contemporary music. For most of us, jazz and classical are clearly defined musics, if only because nothing in classical music ever swings. But there are a few artists who, like Mingus, have problematized the old distinctions. The career of George Lewis is an excellent example of a new genreless turn in music history. Although Lewis started his career playing with jazz artists in the Association for the Advancement of Creative Musicians in Chicago, he has moved toward styles of composition that can be called neither jazz nor classical. Wikipedia, with its bland delivery of received wisdom, reveals a great deal when it opens its article on Lewis with: "composer, electronic performer, installation artist, trombone player, and scholar in the fields of improvisation and experimental music."[129] Significantly, there is no mention of jazz in this description.

Anthony Braxton is another artist with deep associations with jazz but for whom that label is inadequate. And as early as the 1980s composers such as Witold Lutosławski were including improvisation in their work, although it was more likely to be called "aleatoric" music. John Zorn may be the composer who has exerted the most pressure on genre boundaries. He has performed free-jazz improvisation in both clubs and concert halls and also written for string quartets.

Mingus might have applauded these trends. In the end, however, he saw Third Stream as just another attempt to separate one aspect of music from all the others. For Mingus, there was only one stream, and he swam in it. Because he refused to identify himself with a single, sanctioned style of jazz, he never gained the stature he deserved—or the pigeonhole that would have made him more marketable. Mingus knew this as well as anyone. He also knew how harmful this need for genre boundaries has been to the music itself. In 1971 he wrote, "It's too bad that so many musicians started separating themselves into 'modern,' 'old-time,' and 'bop' camps. If we had all continued together, the music would have developed into a much richer language than it has."[130]

PART IV

On and Off the Bandstand with Richmond, Dolphy, and Knepper

Any mature jazz artist with the ability and the desire to succeed will have shared the stage with a long list of musicians. But Charles Mingus seems to have played with everyone from Kid Ory to George Adams and at every stop along the paths of jazz history. Once he became a leader, he hired and fired a long list of sidepeople. Some stayed longer than others. Many were quickly discarded because Mingus did not always like what he heard. And there were plenty who left on their own, unwilling to engage with Mingus's music or with Mingus himself. The genial tenor saxophonist Jimmy Heath, for example, says in his autobiography that he "never wanted to work with Mingus because he often hollered at his musicians on the bandstand and wouldn't hesitate to stop a performance. I loved his music, but I didn't want to play with him because I was intimidated by him."[1]

At least one musician continued working with Mingus even after a nearly murderous confrontation. Jackie McLean had already recorded several times with Miles Davis when he joined the Jazz Workshop in 1956. Within a few days he was in the studio with Mingus to record *Pithecanthropus Erectus*, the first of the many great LPs that Charles would make with Atlantic Records. At this early stage in their relationship, Mingus was sufficiently impressed by McLean to record a tune called "Profile of Jackie."[2] On the bandstand, however, Mingus regularly berated McLean for sounding too much like Charlie Parker.

When the band was in Cleveland on tour, Mingus was so aggressive in his public criticisms of McLean that, at the end of the set, Jackie announced that he was giving two weeks' notice. According to Derek Ansell, Mingus then punched McLean in the mouth, knocking out two of his teeth.[3] McLean pulled out a knife and would have severely injured Mingus had someone not accidentally bumped his arm. The knife struck Mingus in the stomach, but the cut was not deep. Mingus fired McLean on the spot, leaving him penniless in Cleveland. He had to pawn his saxophone to get back home.

A year later, Mingus invited McLean to join him for a gig at Birdland, and McLean showed up. Mingus hugged him and laughingly showed him the small scar from their altercation in Cleveland. He then invited McLean to rejoin the band, which he did, though only for four months. In spite of the constant stress that Mingus imposed on his musicians, McLean stayed on because the band leader "helped me to discover myself and to become more concerned with being original" and not another Bird imitator.[4]

Like his idol Duke Ellington, Mingus heard musicians in his own way and then made their sounds part of a whole. Those who had a real history with Mingus or Ellington had to put aside much of what they had been playing and dig deep within themselves to find what worked for the maestro. Ellington, for example, loved the romantic bounty in Johnny Hodges's alto saxophone solos, and he and Billy Strayhorn wrote melodies that featured Hodges at his most sublimely lyrical.

And yet when Hodges recorded outside the Ellington organization, he often exhibited a deft mastery of rhythm and blues. He especially liked the chicken-shack sound he could get with a blues-drenched organist like Wild Bill Davis. Ellington continued to give the intense ballads to Hodges, but he ultimately came to terms with the other side of Hodges's style and even invited organist Davis to join his orchestra. But listen to the greasy blues Hodges and Davis recorded on LPs such *Blue Hodge* and *Sandy's Gone*.[5] Then listen to Hodges and Davis as members of the Ellington orchestra on the *New Orleans Suite* album, recorded just before Hodges's death in 1970.[6] Even in their bluesy comfort zone, Hodges and Davis sound like they *belong* with Ellington.

Some of the artists who passed through Mingus's Jazz Workshop not only sounded like they belonged with Mingus; some transformed themselves. For me, tenor saxophonist John Handy was at his most compelling when he soloed on Mingus's 1959 recording of "Goodbye Pork Pie Hat." After taking one blues chorus, Handy begins his second chorus by trilling a series of notes with a single key on his tenor saxophone. Handy only creates this effect for two measures, but it is so memorable that several musicians have attempted it in their own way when they play "Goodbye Pork Pie Hat" (also known as "Theme for Lester Young"). The effect even turns up in Joni Mitchell's 1979 recording of the song.

Mingus inspired Handy to play something so striking that it stands out from everything else he recorded. I have similar feelings about various recordings with Mingus by saxophonist Booker Ervin; pianists Jaki Byard,

Don Pullen, and Roland Hanna; and trumpeters Lonnie Hillyer and Ted Curson—to name only a few. In this chapter, however, I will concentrate on three sidemen who were essential to what many of us hear in our minds when we think of Mingus: Dannie Richmond, Eric Dolphy, and Jimmy Knepper. Each brought something powerful and unique to the Mingus sound, and each had a deep, if often conflicted, relationship with Charles.

Dannie Richmond was born on December 15, 1931, in New York City. He played with Mingus longer than any other sideperson, and his drumming style was practically invented by Mingus. Their connection on the bandstand has been described as "telepathic." Eric Dolphy, born on June 20, 1928, in Los Angeles, played and recorded with Mingus briefly when they were both coming of age in Los Angeles in the 1940s. Dolphy was a fully developed artist when he formally joined the Jazz Workshop in 1960, and his recordings with Mingus reveal a unique set of talents—talents seldom heard in the many recordings he made without Mingus. Jimmy Knepper, born November 22, 1927, also in Los Angeles, actually played with Mingus and Dolphy as a young man. Knepper signed on with Mingus in 1957, shortly after Richmond joined the band. His relationship with Mingus culminated in disaster for both men, but they became friends once again as Mingus's life drew to a close.

DANNIE RICHMOND

The uncompromising, avant-garde pianist Cecil Taylor was playing at a club in Brooklyn in the 1950s. His drummer was Denis Charles. According to Gary Giddins, a fan approached Denis after a set came to an end and asked, "Does Cecil know that you don't know how to play drums?" Denis replied, "Cecil is *glad* that I don't know how to play drums."[7]

Giddins offers this anecdote to explain Mingus's relationship with Dannie Richmond (figure 10). Before he met Mingus late in 1956, Richmond had only been playing drums for six months. Obviously, the man had talent and a powerful rhythmic sense, but very few musicians can master an instrument in a few months. Because Richmond was not yet fully developed as a drummer, Mingus seized upon a unique opportunity to mold Richmond into exactly the kind of player he needed, just as Cecil Taylor seems to have tutored Denis Charles. With Mingus, Richmond proved to be an especially attentive student. No other musician was ever as essential to Mingus's music.

Gene Santoro has compared the slim, compliant Richmond to Sancho Panza, the devoted follower of a corpulent, obsessed Don Quixote.[8] Brian

Figure 10. Dannie Richmond, 1957. Photograph by Francis Wolff, courtesy of Mosaic Images, LLC.

Priestley has gone so far as to suggest that Richmond was to Mingus as Harry Carney was to Duke Ellington.[9] Carney, who played baritone saxophone and clarinet in the Ellington reed section, spent forty-eight years as a member of Duke's orchestra, longer by far than any other player. Carney was still in the band when Duke died in 1974. A year later, he would appear with Duke's son, Mercer Ellington, and Cootie Williams on the cover photo of *Continuum*, an album of music by a reconstituted Ellington orchestra led by Mercer.[10]

Richmond played on and off with Mingus for the last twenty-two years of Charles's life. That is slightly less than half as long as Carney was with Ellington, but Mingus was much younger than Ellington when he died. In their own way, both Carney and Richmond served as anchors for their leaders' bands.

In his teens in Greensboro, North Carolina, Richmond played tenor saxophone in rhythm and blues bands. In high school ensembles he played xylophone and tympani. After he graduated from high school, he moved to New York and studied at the Music Center Conservatory in Brooklyn. At one point, he decided to give up music as a profession and study something more practical. He returned to Greensboro to study at an agricultural and technical college. But he continued to hang out with musicians and sit in at jam sessions. One night when Richmond was playing with some local musicians, the drummer took a break, and Richmond put aside his saxophone to sit down at the drum set. He felt good behind the drums, and the other musicians expressed amazement at how well he played. The next day he went out and bought himself a set of drums.[11]

Shortly after Richmond had made the drums his principal instrument, he encountered Lou Donaldson, who was in North Carolina visiting his mother. Donaldson had already made a name for himself playing alto saxophone with bands led by Milt Jackson and Thelonious Monk. In 1954 he was a member of an Art Blakey band that also included the esteemed trumpeter Clifford Brown, and by 1956 he was an on-again off-again member of Mingus's Jazz Workshop. One night when Donaldson was in a club in New York to hear Mingus's band, Charles counted off "Cherokee" at an unusually fast tempo. Willie Jones, the band's regular drummer at the time, could not maintain the speed, and Mingus expressed his dismay out loud. That night, Donaldson told Mingus that he knew a drummer who could keep up. Donaldson introduced Richmond, but only after Mingus paid the cover charge so that Dannie could get into the club.[12]

Mingus was indeed satisfied, soon discovering that Richmond was more than willing to accommodate his musical ideas. Charles told an interviewer that Dannie "gave me his complete open mind . . . to work with as clay."[13] He would later tell John F. Goodman that from the outset Richmond somehow knew exactly what tempo Mingus wanted just by the way Mingus looked at him. After a while, it seemed, Charles only had to think it, and Dannie would switch to the tempo he wanted. When Goodman asked how this was possible, Mingus replied, "I don't know man. It made me start to believe in God."[14]

Richmond's own statements demystify the relationship. He told Bret Primack that everything was always worked out first in long rehearsal sessions that took place daily, if possible. Richmond said that at the rehearsals, Mingus made sure that everyone was situated just as they would be on the bandstand so that he and Dannie could always see each other's eyes. "With just a look or a glance, we knew if we were going to play two bars apiece against each other, or play free or play six at half time. . . . We had it so that anyone listening would say, how did they do that?"[15] Richmond said that he had begun playing drums with flashy technique, a young man showing off, but that Mingus taught him about dynamics, urging him to play softer at crucial moments. "He would also make a point to drop some of his philosophical things on me," he added.[16]

When Mingus found someone he liked, male or female, he would quickly develop an intense relationship with them. With Richmond he was especially enthusiastic. Soon after Richmond had joined and the band was on a road trip to the West Coast, they had a few days off in California before a gig in Vancouver. Dannie was the only member of the band that Mingus invited to join him in Tijuana, specifically at a brothel that Mingus knew from his time growing up in Los Angeles. The experience inspired *Tijuana Moods,* recorded for RCA Victor a few weeks later in July 1957. In the liner notes to that LP, Mingus mentions the time he spent with Dannie, when he was separated from Celia and desperate to bury his sorrows in all the Mexican city had to offer. This meant tequila, food, and dancing as well as sex. "It actually ends in a contest between Dannie and myself to see who could outdo who. . . . Dannie lost: he was very hungry; I was starved."[17]

One of Richmond's first contributions to Mingus's music was the title for "Fables of Faubus." In 1957, a politician named Orval Faubus was the governor of Arkansas. Although he had been elected a few years earlier as a progressive candidate, when Faubus found himself in some political trouble, the easiest way out was to curry favor with the state's white racists. Defying a unanimous decision by the United States Supreme Court, Faubus refused to allow African American students to attend Little Rock Central High School in the state's capital. He even called out the Arkansas National Guard to stop students from entering the building.

Meanwhile, Mingus's erstwhile employer Louis Armstrong was about to play a concert in Grand Forks, North Dakota. Armstrong turned on the television and saw black children being turned away from school by armed troops just as a young reporter arrived to interview him for the local newspaper. The reporter was astonished when the trumpet player declared that the American government could "go to hell" and that President Dwight Eisenhower, who had yet to begin enforcing the law, had "no guts." Fifty years later, the reporter said Armstrong was angry enough to sing a version of the "Star-Spangled Banner" that began, "Oh, say can you see, by the dawn's motherfucking light," in which vein he continued for several minutes.[18] Even when a sanitized version of his interview was published, Armstrong was attacked for his antipatriotic rant. But he was not deterred. When his publicist gave a press conference declaring that Louis did not really mean what he said, Armstrong fired the publicist and told the press that he *did* mean what he said.[19] Within a few days, President Eisenhower found his guts and ordered the Arkansas troops to enforce segregation.

Jackie Robinson, Lena Horne, and Marian Anderson were among the black Americans who spoke up in support of Armstrong's denunciations of Faubus and Eisenhower. There is no record of Mingus making any public statement about Armstrong at that time. But Faubus's name came up in an improvisation one night when the Little Rock crisis was still in the news. The Mingus band was working on an as yet unnamed tune when Mingus cried out, "Tell me someone who's ridiculous." Richmond shouted out, "Governor Faubus."[20] After the song was enlarged to include lyrics and some chanting, it formally became "Fables of Faubus." When Mingus recorded the song for Columbia in 1959, however, he was not allowed to sing or chant.[21] But the next year, when Mingus recorded the tune for the Candid label, this time calling it "Original Fables of Faubus," he sang the lyrics and even recreated the moment when the tune was christened.[22] On the recording you can hear Mingus say, "Name me someone who's ridiculous. Dannie?"

According to Richmond, Mingus had a tendency to play "on top," propelling the music forward so intensely that there was a tendency to rush. Richmond compensated by laying back a little. Although Mingus is remembered more for changing rhythms within a performance than for a steady, compelling rhythmic feel, there is no question that Richmond and Mingus knew how to swing. With the addition in 1962 of Jaki Byard, one of very few artists as comfortable as Mingus in any stylistic setting, the rhythm section became the "Almighty Three." Mingus had tampered with tempi before, but together Mingus, Richmond, and Byard could slow down and speed up the music as if the entire band were a single mechanism. They knew how to occupy a solid swinging groove when they chose to, but no other jazz group has so successfully negotiated radical tempo changes "in the moment."

An anecdote from Howard Johnson reveals how deeply devoted to Mingus's music Richmond had become by the time of the "Almighty Three." Johnson played tuba in a variety of Mingus ensembles in the mid-1960s and was usually positioned very close to Richmond. On one occasion, Johnson could hear Richmond singing along with Johnson as he played his tuba part.[23]

When I saw Mingus and Richmond in a club in 1975, and in most of the film footage of the band, Mingus looks like a man at work. Although he occasionally cries out, mostly he is all business. But look at footage from 1964 that appears in the 1998 documentary *Charles Mingus: Triumph of*

the Underdog. There Mingus smiles with pleasure as he engages in a musical conversation with Richmond.

Nevertheless, relations between Dannie and the mercurial Mingus could
become frayed. The first time Richmond drifted away from the band was
late in 1957, when he went to record with the legendary pianist Herbie
Nichols and with vocalist Frank Minion. In 1958, Richmond signed on with
Chet Baker, the popular singer and trumpeter. It may have been then that
Richmond began using drugs. Baker was a notorious drug addict who would
often demand payment in cash before a club date and then fail to show up
because he was out looking for a fix. According to Chet Baker's biographer
James Gavin, he began injecting himself in his jugular vein when the larger
veins in his arms were used up; that way, too, the drugs could get into his
system more quickly.[24] Gene Santoro implies that Richmond was arrested
for drug use late in 1958 and that Mingus bailed him out so that Dannie
could rejoin the band for a gig at the Half Note in New York City.[25]

In the late 1960s, when Mingus was dealing with depression and scarcely
working at all, Richmond remained Mingus's drummer, but he left for an
especially long stretch in 1971 even though Mingus was then on the upswing
toward recovery. Shortly after he returned in 1973, he gave an interview at
a Milwaukee television station to Ben Sidran. Richmond told Sidran that he
was surprised Mingus never had a hit record in all the time they had played
together. Although he may have been reluctant to come out and say it,
Mingus's lack of a hit record and the money it would have brought in may
have been one of the reasons Richmond left the band.

Perhaps hoping to make some real money playing with popular artists,
Richmond presented himself to Mark-Almond, a British soft-rock band
with jazz pretensions, when they were playing opposite Mingus at Ronnie
Scott's in London. The band was playing music by the white blues singer
John Mayall, without a drummer. Richmond came up from behind and
began playing a drum set that was on the stage. The band was impressed by
what they heard.[26] Giving his notice to Mingus, Richmond joined Mark-
Almond in the studio to record "The City," which became a hit. Richmond
appeared on two of the band's albums, *Mark-Almond II* (1971) and *Rising*
(1972), but there is little in the music that suggests the presence of such a
gifted musician. He also played with the Ray Charles imitator Joe Cocker,
and with Elton John in the years when he was a conventional rocker and
not an amphitheater act.

Mingus once said, "I'd rather not use a drummer if Dannie weren't
available."[27] In 1961, before Mingus traveled to London to perform in the
film *All Night Long,* he urged the producers not to hire a "lead-foot" drum-

mer to play along with the American and British musicians slated to appear in the film. He even offered to bring Richmond along and pay all the expenses himself.[28] After Richmond left, Mingus told Don Pullen, "Man, everything would be all right if Dannie would just come back."[29] Roy Brooks, who played drums with Mingus for most of Richmond's absence, acquitted himself well, often adding a completely different sound to the band when he soloed on, of all things, a musical saw.

Richmond spent most of 1972 and 1973 touring with Mark-Almond and making good money. One day when the band was playing in New York, Dannie heard that Mingus was performing at the Village Vanguard. He walked down the stairs into the club and ran into Mingus at the doorway to the club's kitchen. "He said, 'I had a dream last night that my drummer was coming back and here he is!' I rejoined him right after that."[30]

Richmond stayed with Mingus until Charles stopped recording in 1978, and he continued playing and recording Mingus's music, most notably on the CD *Dannie Richmond Plays Charles Mingus*.[31] For the next several years, he regularly appeared in groups with Mingus alumni such as Pullen, George Adams, and Jimmy Knepper. He died of a heart attack in 1988, probably related to his drug use. He was fifty-six, the same age as Mingus when he died.

In his memoir *Live at the Village Vanguard*, Max Gordon recalls a conversation he had with Richmond shortly after Mingus stopped performing. Dannie came to the Vanguard to ask Max if he would hire a band made up largely of musicians who had played with Mingus. The bassist would be Eddie Gomez, a mainstay of the Bill Evans Trio for many years. Gordon and Richmond began chatting, reminiscing about Mingus. Gordon recalled some of Mingus's more flamboyant moments at the Vanguard, such as the time he told Max that he needed money right away. When Gordon pulled out a roll of bills and handed them to Mingus, it apparently wasn't enough. "So he threw the whole roll up into the air and grabbed a knife." Richmond remembered the incident and added a detail that goes a long way toward explaining his relationship with Mingus: "Like a good boy," he said, he bent down and began picking up the bills.[32]

Gordon asked Richmond why he stayed on for all those years. Dannie said simply, "It was the music he kept writing. I don't know a greater jazz ballad than 'Goodbye Pork Pie Hat.'" He added, "No, it wasn't always easy," then, changing the subject, began talking about what a ladies' man Mingus was. He mentioned that as a young man Charles was so good-looking that he once got a job posing half-naked with several scantily clad women in "a porno mag." He then told a story about Mingus beating up a pimp who objected to the way Charles was talking to one of the women in the pimp's employ.[33]

In his memoir, Max Gordon's memory is not always totally reliable, but if he is correctly recalling what Richmond told him, Dannie's answers to the question about why he stayed with Mingus are revealing. No doubt the music was an important reason, but it was not reason enough to prevent a very long list of other musicians from leaving, sometimes after just a few days or at most a few years. Yet Richmond gave up the good money he was making with Mark-Almond, not to mention the first-class travel, the best hotels, and the waiting limousines, to rejoin Mingus.

Perhaps the music was his reason for staying, but then he talks about Mingus as an attractive and audacious man. Father figure? Role model? Mentor? Masculine ideal? Charismatic leader? Surely it was all of these in one way or another, and we should celebrate the fact that Dannie stayed for as long as he did. Richmond was good for Mingus's music. He was also good for Mingus himself. And in ways that only Richmond may have understood, Charles was good for Dannie.

ERIC DOLPHY

Most reed players are expected to play more than one instrument. In the big-band era, composers and arrangers asked saxophonists to double on clarinet. And jazz musicians joke that every saxophonist plays "a little flute." Mingus recorded briefly with Rahsaan Roland Kirk, surely the most flamboyant multi-reed player in the music's history. Kirk would play three instruments at once, including the home-grown instruments he called the manzello and stritch. Even after a stroke paralyzed one side of his body, Kirk would solo simultaneously on saxophone and flute. But Eric Dolphy (figure 11) was something else altogether. He is now widely recognized as the most accomplished multi-instrumentalist in jazz history, who exhibited complete mastery of alto saxophone, bass clarinet, and flute. On early recordings, he also played baritone saxophone and soprano clarinet.

Dolphy is also the locus classicus for the transition from bebop to what John Szwed has called "the permanent avant-garde."[34] Like many of the musicians most favored by Mingus, Dolphy mastered the bop vocabulary established by Charlie Parker without becoming beholden to it. Dolphy then took it to the next level and extended the tonal language of the boppers. His playing reveals a thorough knowledge of music theory and jazz history, and once listeners get past the shock of hearing what at first sounds like dissonance, they can detect solid structural principles driving his

Figure 11. Eric Dolphy at the *Out to Lunch* recording session, 1964.
Photograph by Francis Wolff, courtesy of Mosaic Images, LLC.

improvisations. In fact, he was downright conventional in his use of rhythmic patterns, often building his solos around regular series of eighth and sixteenth notes.

Like Mingus before him, Dolphy had his first musical experiences in church. As a youth he sang in the choir and taught Sunday school. He began playing clarinet at age six and switched to oboe in junior high school. Mingus went from the trombone, a conventional band instrument, to the cello, a staple of classical music ensembles, and then took up the bass so that he could play in Buddy Collette's band. Similarly, Dolphy went from a conventional band instrument to a more classical one and then took up the alto saxophone so that he could play in a jump blues band like Louis Jordan's.[35]

Dolphy briefly attended Los Angeles City College but, according to Ted Gioia, lost his desire to continue when a racist faculty member told him to leave the college orchestra, saying that "he ruined the color scheme."[36] Dolphy's father, who had soundproofed the family's garage to accommodate his son's practice sessions alone and with groups, asked why he didn't continue his education so that he might someday become a music teacher. Eric replied, "Dad, I want to be a musician and that's *all* I want to be."[37] Like Mingus once again, Dolphy studied with Lloyd Reese, the distinguished teacher of many black artists, who opened his house in Los Angeles to musicians, old and young alike.

Dolphy had known Mingus at least since 1945, and he played in the rehearsal band that Mingus established in 1949. During this same period Eric played regularly with a West Coast band led by the drummer Roy Porter, who had recorded with Charlie Parker during his stint in Los Angeles in 1946 and 1947. When Porter started a big band in 1948, it was surely the worst possible moment. Most of the big bands that had been so successful in the 1930s and 1940s were long gone by 1949. Even Count Basie briefly gave up his large orchestra and began recording with an octet.

Porter only managed to keep his band alive for a year or so, but during its existence it boasted a distinguished cast of characters: Art and Addison Farmer, Jimmy Knepper, Russ Freeman, and Eric Dolphy. The music was a uniquely West Coast take on big-band bop.[38] After the band broke up, Dolphy remained in Los Angeles where he played in a variety of bop bands, eventually forming a small group, Eric Dolphy and His Men of Jazz. In 1956 and 1957, the group worked regularly as the house band at a popular LA club.

Dolphy's big break came when he joined Chico Hamilton's band in 1958.[39] Before Dolphy joined, the band was playing a kind of chamber jazz, with Fred Katz on cello and Jim Hall on guitar. A version of this band can be seen and heard in the 1957 film noir classic *The Sweet Smell of Success*. When Dolphy joined a slightly different incarnation of this group in 1958, he took over the reed chair that had once belonged to Mingus's good friend Buddy Collette. In 1959 Dolphy moved to New York and joined Mingus's Jazz Workshop for a remarkable ten-month residence at the Showplace.

Even before he went into the studio with Mingus for the first time, in May 1960, Dolphy recorded under his own name with trumpeter Freddie Hubbard, pianist Jaki Byard, and drummer Roy Haynes. The title of this first effort, *Outward Bound*, suggested a departure from the old ways.

Other Dolphy LPs followed suit, with such titles as *Out There, Far Cry,* and *Out to Lunch.*[40]

Some critics hear indications that Dolphy had listened carefully to Bartók and Stravinsky.[41] He did in fact perform the music of Edgard Varèse at a concert in 1962, and he participated in several of Gunther Schuller's Third Stream events. He was also a member of John Lewis's Orchestra U.S.A. But thinking of Dolphy largely as a Third Stream player does not do justice to the impact his solos had. His great achievement was to express a range of emotions—often with stunning immediacy—with what at first may sound like wrong notes and abstractions. He spoke the "language of emotions" as fluently as Mingus.

Dolphy's commitment to music was profound. As Dannie Richmond told an interviewer, "A lot of people don't know that Eric never took off his neck strap. During the breaks, he would go in the back and still be playing, rehearsing, always searching. He practiced out of a harp book. Practicing out of a book like that would give him the facility to be able to play the notes he played and to be able to jump around and play these different intervals that he played, backwards, forwards, and inside out."[42]

By all accounts, Dolphy was a beautiful soul. Mingus named one of his sons Eric after Dolphy, saying, "[He] was a saint—in every way, not just in his playing."[43] When John Coltrane hired Dolphy, he probably knew that Eric was an awkward fit for his group. By the early 1960s, Coltrane seldom played a tune along with another hornman at the beginning and end of a performance like most other jazz artists of the era. There was little room for Dolphy other than as a soloist. Coltrane asked Dolphy to join because of his affection for the man and his respect for his music. After Dolphy's death, Coltrane carried his picture with him when he traveled and would hang it on the walls of the hotels where he stayed.[44]

Dolphy's music spoke to people outside the world of jazz as well. Rocker and satirist Frank Zappa listed Dolphy as an influence in the liner notes to his first LP, *The Mothers of Invention Freak Out!* (1966), and four years later, on *Weasels Ripped My Flesh,* he paid homage with "The Eric Dolphy Memorial Barbecue." In performance Zappa often soloed at length on his guitar, sometimes sounding as much like an avant-garde jazz artist as the strictures of pop music allowed. Zappa had clearly absorbed some of Dolphy's ideas about improvisation.

Dolphy began playing with Mingus just as Ornette Coleman was making his splash in New York. Coleman may have sounded as dissonant as Dolphy, but unlike Ornette, Dolphy was still thinking in terms of chords and form when he performed his edgy improvisations. As Nat Hentoff wrote, Dolphy "became acutely important to Mingus because Mingus could rely on him to understand what Mingus wanted while being able to fulfill that understanding in his own, strongly personal way."[45]

After recording with Mingus for less than two years, Dolphy left the Workshop to play with John Coltrane in 1961. This was the moment when Coltrane was being criticized for straying too far from conventional jazz. Prior to 1961, Coltrane had been pouring out "sheets of sound" improvisations that, though intense, stayed within tonal boundaries. When Dolphy joined, Coltrane was beginning to push the envelope, often screaming with his saxophone and disregarding the chord changes that were traditionally the basis for jazz improvisation.

In many ways Dolphy was even more "outside" than Coltrane, but the critic John Tynan accused both of them of playing "anti-jazz."[46] Various critics had been unnerved by bebop fifteen years earlier; indeed, the eccentricities of that music were surely responsible for jazz losing most of its audience in the 1950s. Although most jazz critics eventually came around to considering bop as just another way of swinging and improvising, the music of Coltrane and Dolphy—often called "the new thing"—was still too much for many of them, and a great deal of ink was spilled in the argument over whether they had essentially left the fold.

When Dolphy and Coltrane were invited to answer the critics in 1961, Coltrane played it straight, describing his music in his own terms and refusing to be drawn into the more fundamental debate about what jazz should or should not be. Dolphy was more specific. He wrote, "I think of my playing as tonal. I play notes that would not ordinarily be said to be in a given key, but I hear them as proper. I don't think I 'leave the changes' as the expression goes; every note I play has some reference to the chords of the piece."[47] But the critics were not mollified. As Ben Ratliff puts it, "To a critic, a musician who does not describe his music in terms of emotion and precise historical precedent can seem a blank slate."[48] Neither Dolphy nor Coltrane chose to speak about emotion or history, and they paid the price of critical censure.

Dolphy's tenure with Coltrane lasted less than a year. At the same time that Coltrane was trying to fold Dolphy's sound into his own music, he was developing the quartet format so essential to many of his most celebrated recordings, specifically the band with McCoy Tyner (piano), Jimmy Garrison (bass), and Elvin Jones (drums). When Dolphy was playing in a Coltrane group, he mostly took a long solo after Coltrane had played his own long solo. Otherwise, there was little interaction between the two. Clearly, Coltrane's affection and respect for Eric were more important than specific musical goals. Only after Dolphy left the band did Coltrane perfect the quartet chemistry we know so well from impulse! LPs such as *Ballads*, *A Love Supreme*, and *Crescent*, not to mention the superb meeting of the quartet with vocalist Johnny Hartman, the only singer with whom the mature Coltrane ever recorded.[49]

Before returning to Mingus in 1963, Dolphy also made several recordings with Booker Little, a trumpet player who managed to have an impossibly distinguished career before dying of uremia at the age of twenty-three. Dolphy also made great music with Oliver Nelson, Gil Evans, and Freddie Hubbard.[50]

With Dolphy, Mingus made some of his most fascinating recordings for the Candid label, a project that was the brainchild of critic Nat Hentoff. Acting as producer, Hentoff sought to create the immediacy of the club dates for which Mingus was famous by allowing him to introduce each tune as if the studio were full of patrons. On the LP originally titled *Charles Mingus Presents Charles Mingus*, we hear Mingus telling the imaginary audience not to applaud or clink the ice in their glasses and instructing the club "employees" not to ring up charges on the cash register. Mingus is clearly enjoying himself, knowing full well he is fooling no one.[51]

When Mingus made his first Candid recordings in October 1960, Dolphy had been a regular in the band for ten months. In addition to the first recording of "Fables of Faubus" with its lyrics restored, the band of Mingus, Dolphy, Richmond, and Ted Curson recorded "All the Things You Could Be by Now if Sigmund Freud's Wife Was Your Mother," a title that connected the Jerome Kern ballad "All the Things You Are," a tune greatly favored by the beboppers, with America's 1960s fascination with psychoanalysis. But the most remarkable recording at that first Candid session was the duet between Mingus and Dolphy, "What Love."

Ever since the emergence of call and response at some distant, originary moment in the history of black music, instrumentalists have engaged in musical conversation. Mingus engaged in vocal-like conversations with his sidepeople throughout his career—as in the film *Charles Mingus: Triumph of the Underdog*, when he and Dannie Richmond talk to each other with their instruments. Shortly after this scene, an interviewer asks them what they were saying to each other. Mingus says, "Fuck you, you dirty motherfucker, you son of a bitch. Uh, sometimes I love you truly. Sometimes Mary had a little lamb." This could just as easily be what Mingus and Dolphy are saying in "What Love."

Browsing through Mingus's collection of scores, Dolphy had found a copy of Charles's 1945 tune based on the changes of Cole Porter's "What is This Thing Called Love." He may have been drawn to it because he could imagine a recording that sounded very much like the music of Ornette Coleman and his group at this time. (Shortly after the Candid session, Dolphy recorded with Ornette as part of the "double quartet" on the LP *Free Jazz.*)[52] But after the band laid down the main melody, amazing things begin to happen in a series of out-of-tempo dialogues. Mingus, who preferred that Dolphy play alto saxophone, may have become angry when he picked up his bass clarinet instead. With his bass, Mingus speaks the word "motherfucker." He then clearly makes his bass say, "Did you hear what I said?" Many restatements of the four-syllable epithet follow. Throughout, Dolphy honks and squawks back, sometimes with pathos, sometimes with anger. Jazz musicians have always been inclined to imitate the human voice with their instruments, but never like this.

According to Nat Hentoff, both Dolphy and trumpeter Curson were by now seriously contemplating leaving the band, and Hentoff had to beg them to stay on, if only to finish the recording session.[53] Dolphy's reasons for leaving Mingus were nothing new. Charles would regularly ask his Workshoppers to play beyond the capabilities not just of their instruments but of their own abilities. And many were challenged by his unwillingness to write out music for them, not to mention his habit of berating and physically threatening musicians on and off the bandstand.

Mingus made Dolphy's work even more difficult by turning his facility with so many instruments against him. Charles would call a tune that required flute, then, once Dolphy had picked up and adjusted his instrument, Mingus would change his mind and name a tune that required alto saxophone; when Dolphy was ready to go with his saxophone, Mingus would change his mind again—and so on. Ted Curson said that when "Dolphy was getting a lot of applause, he [Mingus] made him go into the dressing room and play where nobody could see, just hear[,] the saxophone."[54]

Dolphy did leave to play with Booker Little and John Coltrane, but he came back in late 1963 for several live dates as well as the second *Mingus Mingus Mingus Mingus Mingus* session for impulse! Just before Dolphy and Mingus left for Europe in April 1964, Eric made two extraordinary recordings, *Out to Lunch* with his own band and *Point of Departure* with pianist Andrew Hill.[55] These records show Dolphy firmly establishing his own voice outside the Mingus universe, but tragically, he did not have the opportunity to further develop that voice.

In Europe, trumpeter Johnny Coles was not the only one to miss a number of concerts (see part I). Tenor saxophonist Clifford Jordan also missed a few, leaving the stage to Mingus, Richmond, Dolphy, and pianist Jaki Byard. Little was lost, however, because the range of sounds and timbres that Eric produced on his several instruments kept the music alive and fresh.

Indeed, so much great music came out of that European tour that it's difficult to summarize what the band achieved. The musicians seemed to reinvent both themselves and their repertoire at each concert.

Consider "Fables of Faubus." When the sextet played at Cornell University on April 4, 1964, Mingus begins by announcing the tune as "Fables of FauBOOS."[56] In his solo, Dolphy then quotes "I wish I were in the land of cotton" after a fairly straightforward solo by trumpeter Coles. Skip forward just six days to the first of several European concerts, this one in Amsterdam, where "Fables of Faubus" becomes a political tour de force. The tune now includes a bass solo in which Mingus references "Turkey in the Straw" and a range of other songs associated with minstrelsy and the early history of black entertainment, including "Shortnin' Bread." He also does an extended riff on "When Johnny Comes Marching Home Again." Byard, for his part, quotes from "Yankee Doodle Dandy" in his solo before launching into "Lift Every Voice and Sing," the Negro National Anthem. But beyond these games of quoting, the two versions also display stark differences in mood, tempo, and the arrangement of solos.

One of the most intriguing numbers that Mingus programmed throughout the tour was "Ow," also known as "Parkeriana" or "Dedicated to a Genius." The selection starts out with a brief quotation of "Ow," a tune by Dizzy Gillespie but that Mingus attributed to Charlie Parker. (Parker recorded the tune only once, at a Jazz at the Philharmonic date in 1949, playing a few bars as the band welcomed the vocalist Ella Fitzgerald.) After stating the theme, the band plays a loosely connected medley of tunes associated with Parker, including several that Parker did not write but made his own during his career as a recording artist, including Ralph Rainger's "If I Should Lose You," Willard Robison's "Old Folks," and Rodgers and Hart's "I Didn't Know What Time It Was." After the medley portion of the performance, each musician works various quotations from the Parker canon into his solo. Along with the standards, we hear bits of Gillespie's "Night in Tunisia," "Salt Peanuts," and "Groovin' High," Parker's "Moose the Mooche" and "Parker's Mood," and many others. At one point Jordan throws in a lick from the theme to Walter Lantz's *Woody Woodpecker* cartoons, knowing that many critics used to say that Parker's improvisations sounded like "The Woody Woodpecker Song."

In the various recordings of "Parkeriana" I was fascinated to hear fragments from "Country Gardens," a tune that Percy Grainger wrote in 1918 and that I knew well because my father played it often on the piano in our family room when I was growing up. Sheet music sales of the tune were substantial, giving Grainger an almost instant hit. Indeed, "Country Gardens" soon became the only song for which he was known. Grainger, however, saw himself as a serious composer and eventually came to despise the song.[57]

I was intrigued when I first heard Charlie Parker quote from "Country Gardens" in the middle of a solo. On many recordings, too, he would end a tune by quoting from it in an exaggerated fashion, adding a diminuendo and then a baroque trill on the third-from-last note. In so doing, Bird was asking audiences to differentiate his music from the polite bourgeois music enjoyed in so many American households (including my own).[58]

The nose-thumbing assumes a new level of irony when Dolphy ends a solo on "Parkeriana" by quoting from "Country Gardens" in the same way Parker ended many a number with it. Mingus had written a tune titled, "If Charlie Parker Was a Gunslinger, There'd Be a Whole Lot of Dead Copycats," and even though he was always hard on saxophonists who tried to duplicate Bird's style, with the various versions of "Parkeriana" the band achieved exactly what Mingus says he intended to do for Parker when he introduced the selection: "We're trying to make him live a little here."

The European tour with Mingus was effectively the end of Dolphy's career. After the rest of the band left at the end of April, he stayed on, but died on June 29, 1964. Eric made a few recordings with pickup bands, but nothing that recalls the magic of the music he had so recently made with Mingus. No other collaboration allowed Dolphy to reveal his abilities so thoroughly. His biographers have argued that when Dolphy recorded with Chico Hamilton and even with Third Stream organizations led by Gunther Schuller and John Lewis, he was inhibited by specific compositional choices.[59] At other times, Hamilton or some other leader would ask him to play in a traditional fashion that did not allow the full reach of his imagination. The version of Ellington's "In a Sentimental Mood" that he recorded with Hamilton in 1958 is lovely, but it did not hint at his talents as an improviser.[60] Dolphy bio-discographers Simosko and Tepperman have written, "Even with Coltrane, surely the most spiritually profound association of his career, the modal surroundings imposed limits on the kind of wildly exciting harmonic contrasts his improvisations usually entailed."[61]

There is remarkable film footage of Mingus, Dolphy, Coles, Richmond, and Jordan during a rehearsal for a television broadcast in Stockholm on April 13, 1964.[62] At one point, Mingus has stopped the band and says, "Eric, I'm going to miss your ass over here." Then he chuckles, almost to himself. The camera shows only Charles, and he is looking down as he applies resin to his bow. Now Mingus turns serious and says, "How long you going to stay? You thought about it?" Off camera, Dolphy says, "I don't know. Not long." The camera pulls back so that every member of the band is visible and Mingus says, "What's 'not long'?"

At this point, Dannie Richmond begins laughing and hooting. He is off mike, so it's difficult to understand what he is saying—something about how long a year can be. Mingus ignores Richmond and asks again in exactly the same voice, "What's not long, Eric? What's not long?" Another hoot from Richmond. "What's not long, Eric? A year? A month?" Dolphy says, "No, not a year. Maybe a year; not more than that." Mingus, sounding slightly reassured, says, "Not more than a year." Then the band begins playing "Meditations on Integration."

It's unclear what frame of mind Richmond was in and why he seemed to regard the situation as a joke. Clifford Jordan, meanwhile, sat mute and expressionless throughout, an equally dramatic response to the drama between Mingus and Dolphy. What comes through on multiple viewings of this footage is the great disappointment Mingus feels from the imminent loss of a player for whom he has such respect and affection.

Though he was surrounded by junkies, Eric Dolphy never abused drugs so far as we know. According to one account, he managed to stay aloof from the culture of addiction in jazz circles without being excluded from those circles.[63] In *Jazz and Death*, a well-documented catalog of how jazz artists have died, Frederick J. Spencer, M.D., says that Dolphy probably died of a heart attack brought on by diabetes. It was a common cause of death, especially at a time when diabetes often went undiagnosed, as was probably the case with Dolphy.[64] According to Zan Stewart, Dolphy collapsed in his hotel two days after playing at a club in Berlin. Relying on information from Dolphy's mother, Stewart says that a German doctor diagnosed him as being in a diabetic coma and administered an insulin injection, but it was too strong a dose, and Dolphy died of insulin shock.[65] In the documentary film *Eric Dolphy: Last Date* (1991), Hans Hylkema has still another account: Dolphy, he maintains, collapsed on stage in Berlin and was brought to a hospital. The doctors, not realizing that Dolphy was diabetic but rather assuming that he, like so many jazz musicians they had heard about, was a drug addict and had overdosed, left him in a hospital bed for the drugs to run their course.[66] Mingus was even more suspicious: distraught at the news of his friend's death, he claimed that Dolphy had been murdered by Germans.

The drummer Elvin Jones, who had traveled with Eric in Coltrane's group, wrote, "He was very conscientious and almost meticulous.... Although he rarely spoke about his music and what he was striving for, you could see what he was doing. He was just brimming over with ideas all the time. In fact, that was probably his biggest problem ... he just had too much to say, and this occasionally would get in the way of his saying it."[67]

Shortly after Dolphy's death, Mingus said, "Usually, when a man dies, you remember—or you say you remember—only the good things about him. With Eric, that's all you could remember. I don't remember any drags he did to anybody. The man was absolutely without a need to hurt."[68] Eight years later, when asked by a French jazz magazine to explain the importance of Dolphy for his own music, Mingus said, "I don't want to speak about Eric. It's not that I'm afraid to. ... What do you want me to say about Eric? What I think and what I feel about the life and death of Eric is very personal."[69]

JIMMY KNEPPER

Trombonist Jimmy Knepper (figure 12) joined the Jazz Workshop in 1957, just three months after Dannie Richmond became Mingus's drummer and almost immediately after Charles and Dannie had returned from Tijuana. On Mingus's second Atlantic LP, *The Clown,* Knepper plays the clown to perfection on the title track and then takes an exciting solo on "Haitian Fight Song."[70]

A few months before the *Clown* sessions, the Supreme Court had ruled that bus segregation was illegal, thus granting Martin Luther King, Jr., a solid victory in his thirteen-month-long bus boycott in Montgomery, Alabama. In February 1957, King appeared on the cover of *Time* magazine as its "Man of the Year." The civil rights movement of the second half of the twentieth century had definitively begun.

"Haitian Fight Song" begins with a bass solo; the theme is then played several times by the ensemble, each time more assertively. As the ensemble crescendos, Mingus, for the first time in his recording career, utters one of his signature cries. The intensity of "Haitian Fight Song" and Mingus's cries may have been inspired by the national cry for equal rights. But he may have cried out to encourage Knepper and Richmond, the two sidemen who were giving new energy to his music.

Jimmy was born in Los Angeles, five years after Mingus. Charles first hired him in the summer of 1946 when he was leading a band at Billy Berg's.[71] Even earlier, before he was eighteen, Knepper played in a band with Dean Benedetti, who would later become famous for dragging a tape recorder into night clubs to record every solo by Charlie Parker. In fact, when Benedetti first began making his Parker tapes, he and Knepper were living together with Jimmy's mother. Knepper assisted Benedetti on many of his

Figure 12. Jimmy Knepper, 1978. Photograph © Thomas Marcello, used by permission.

first recording sessions. By 1947, when he was twenty, Knepper had already begun the difficult work of transcribing Parker's solos and studying them.

After he moved to New York in 1950, Knepper and saxophonist Joe Maini rented an apartment on 130th Street in Harlem where musicians, including Parker, would drop by for jam sessions. Knepper made sure that a tape recorder was always in the room when Parker played. As he had done in LA, he would transcribe everything he recorded and transpose it down an octave. He would then practice Parker's solos on his trombone, much as other musicians would play études. Fellow trombonist Sam Burtis says that Knepper also made J. S. Bach's complex cello suites part of his practice regimen.[72]

Needless to say, playing the alto saxophone is very different from playing the trombone: the slide makes Parker's lightning-fast runs almost impossible to achieve. Knepper had long arms, so he could comfortably extend the slide to greater lengths than was typical, but like many jazz trombonists, he had also mastered the art of playing fast and in tune with the slide just a few inches from the mouthpiece. (Many of the best trombonists never even used the fifth and sixth positions toward the end of the slide.) Knepper was therefore a "double threat," able to play at both the top and bottom of the slide. Take a look at film footage of trombonists such as Jack Teagarden and Vic Dickenson, then watch Knepper playing Gordon

Jenkins's "Goodbye."[73] The other players are much more "economical" than Knepper as they keep the slide closer to the top. Knepper, however, makes the trombone say more by expanding the lower register and exploring the possibilities of overtones.

For Knepper, the Parker études clearly paid off. Loren Schoenberg, who regularly worked with Knepper in various ensembles, said, "I know of no other musician who had a greater mastery of Parker's idiom than Knepper."[74] Burtis first heard Knepper in 1966, and said that Jimmy's sound was so complex and so full of overtones that he looked around to see if there were any other trombonists playing in the room. Both Schoenberg and Burtis compare Knepper favorably to such bop trombonists as J.J. Johnson, Kai Winding, Curtis Fuller, and Slide Hampton, indeed insisting that Knepper was more advanced than all of them.[75]

Before he left Los Angeles, in 1948 and 1949, Knepper played in Roy Porter's big band, sitting just one row behind Eric Dolphy. A few years later, in New York, he played in a four-trombone group called Trombone Scene. One of the other trombonists was Willie Dennis, who had played with Mingus on a few Debut recordings in 1953. It was Dennis who reintroduced the two. The rapport was instant. Just three months after the *Clown* sessions, Mingus brought Knepper and Richmond along with alto saxophonist Maini and pianist Bill Triglia to record an LP called *New Faces* on his Debut label.[76] Although Mingus played bass on the recording, Knepper was listed as the leader.

Knepper was a regular with Mingus groups for the next few years while also working in a small group led by clarinetist Tony Scott and in the big band of Stan Kenton. Gil Evans hired Knepper on several occasions, both for his own records and for the large orchestra that Evans conducted behind Miles Davis on the *Live at Carnegie Hall* LP in 1961.[77] Gunther Schuller and John Lewis also discovered Knepper's talents and made him the go-to trombone player on several Third Stream recording sessions.

For several years Knepper and Mingus were good friends. In the late 1950s, when many Americans were replacing their old record players with stereophonic component systems, Knepper was becoming an audio-technophile. In a gesture of friendship he came to Mingus's apartment to set up a system for him. When Debut Records went out of business in 1957, Mingus started up a new company, Jazz Workshop Records. The short-lived venture issued only two LPs, both of them previously unreleased recordings that Knepper had made of Charlie Parker. He gave them to Mingus free of charge.

When the band landed a West Coast gig in the early 1960s, Mingus decided to drive from New York in his Buick. He planned to take several members of the band, leave the Buick with his friend Buddy Collette, and then fly home. Mingus hoped that Collette could sell the car in California, where he thought it would be worth more money. But when a sideman showed up with a wife who was either drunk or stoned, Mingus decided to make the trip with only Knepper, in the new Cadillac limo he had recently purchased. The other band members would take their own cars. After driving for several hours, Mingus asked Knepper to take the wheel, only to learn that Knepper's driver's license had expired. When Knepper observed that he shouldn't be driving, Mingus said it would be all right: "Nobody stops a Caddie limo."[78]

They made the trip in four days, stopping as seldom and as briefly as possible. Mingus was surely uncomfortable traveling with a white person through middle America, and not just because he feared racist reprisals. He may have been just as uncomfortable with being taken for something other than the white man's employer. But so far as we know, the road trip brought both men to LA without incident, and once they arrived, they roomed together. Once, Buddy Collette reports, Mingus told Knepper to sit in the driver seat wearing a chauffeur's hat while Mingus and Collette sat in the back, all of them enjoying the spectacle of a white man chauffeuring two black men around town.[79]

Mingus was not always so chummy with Knepper, however. Patricia Willard tells of a club date when Mingus complained how terrible it was to have a white man in his group, especially when he was touring the South. Mattie Comfort, the vocalist and light-skinned black wife of bassist Joe Comfort, was sitting with Willard and cried out, "Leave that white boy alone. He loves you." Mingus replied, "You're not black enough to talk to me like that." To which Mattie retorted, "You're lighter than I am, Mingus."[80]

Priestley reports the same incident a bit differently. When a fan asked Mingus why he said such terrible things about Knepper, a nice man who contributed so much to Mingus's music and who clearly loved him, Mingus answered, "Don't mess with my act."[81] I will argue shortly that the "act" to which Mingus refers was a kind of reverse minstrelsy and that he found various ways to work Knepper into that act.

By the time the band's West Coast sojourn was over, Knepper had had enough and gave his notice. Back in New York, taking whatever work he could get, he pulled enough money together to buy a house on Staten Island. For whatever reason, Knepper decided to drop in on Mingus in early September 1962, when Mingus was planning his big Town Hall event—and was immediately hired back as a copyist. Charles had a good reason for hiring Knepper to write out parts for the musicians. During the years when Knepper was Mingus's copyist, the music was often arranged differently from what Mingus had originally intended. Mingus clearly liked the kinds of changes that Knepper made to his music although he seldom acknowledged them.

Jazz bassist Bill Crow has speculated that Mingus may have thought Knepper would be his Billy Strayhorn.[82] Strayhorn was Duke Ellington's composing and arranging partner from 1939 until his death in 1967. He was also openly gay at a time when people were regularly losing their jobs because of their sexual orientation. Realizing that he would likely be unable to front his own orchestra, Strayhorn effectively hid both his musical and his personal identity within the Ellington organization. The two men worked extremely well together, and they had deep affection for each other, but Strayhorn was not always happy that Ellington took bows that should have gone to him. As David Hajdu suggests in his biography of Strayhorn, the arrangement with Ellington may have been one reason why Strayhorn effectively drank himself to death, eventually dying of esophageal cancer at the age of fifty-two.[83]

Knepper, however, never intended to be Mingus's Strayhorn. Although he did receive wages for his work as a copyist, Knepper thought Mingus should pay him for his arrangements as well. It all came to a head just before the 1962 Town Hall event. Even as Knepper was busy copying parts, Mingus asked him to write some new figures for the band to play behind soloists. Knepper later told Whitney Balliett, "I told him it was his music and he should do it, it should be his composition, and suddenly he called me a white faggot and punched me." The punch knocked out one of Knepper's teeth. At this point, Knepper chose to fall down so Mingus could not punch him again. Amazingly, he continued copying music and presented a stack of parts to Mingus on the day of the concert, even as he was dealing with the intense pain where his tooth used to be.[84]

As for the epithet Mingus flung at the heterosexual Knepper, I cannot help but wonder if it was an unintentional acknowledgment of his fantasy of making Knepper his Strayhorn.

Because Mingus had damaged his embouchure, Knepper was unable to play for several weeks. When the wounds healed and he returned to the trombone, he found that, at least at first, he had lost some notes in the upper register. At the urging of friends, Knepper eventually sued Mingus for assault. A paragraph in the typescript of Mingus's autobiography that is not in *Beneath the Underdog* adds a detail to the story of the altercation. Mingus is speaking with his friend and confessor Fats Navarro: "Like the latest joke that the white man was telling on studio sets not long ago was that the slogan 'Brotherhood Week' was 'Take a nigger to lunch.' My famed white trombonist, Jimmy Knepper, told me this as though he were an innocent child without the proper mental faculties to place himself in the position of a black man seeking freedom that's long past overdue, having to sit with a stupid white man like him and pay him a salary besides."[85]

Clearly, beneath the affection and profound musical sympathy that existed between Mingus and Knepper, there was unresolved tension. If Nel King is right, however, and Mingus wrote virtually all of the first draft of his autobiography in 1963, the paragraph about Knepper's bad joke may have been written at the same time that Mingus was in court defending himself against assault charges. Before the bench, Mingus told the judge that Knepper had fallen down because he was drunk. He also said that Knepper had called him "a nigger."[86]

Like Jackie McLean, Knepper agreed to play with Mingus again, but not until nine years had passed. When contractor Alan Raph brought him in to play with the large ensemble for Mingus's *Let My Children Hear Music* LP in 1971, the two men did not reconcile. Knepper said that when he saw Charles in the studio, "Mingus didn't say a word. He just sat over in the corner."[87]

According to Santoro, however, Mingus had attempted to reconcile with Knepper in 1969 when he went to the Village Vanguard to hear the big band co-led by drummer Mel Lewis and Mingus's old friend Thad Jones, in which Knepper regularly played. Jones, though, knowing of the bad blood between the two men, told Mingus not to get close to Knepper lest he be "clobbered" by Jones.[88]

They finally reconciled in March 1977, when Mingus asked Knepper to perform at the *Cumbia and Jazz Fusion* recording session. "I wrote this part for you," he said. "You're my trombonist, man."[89] Knepper may also have done some arrangements for Joni Mitchell's *Mingus* project in 1978 when Charles was too ill to write.

Knepper continued to play in the larger ensembles that Mingus or his surrogates led in the last years of his life. He was also regularly employed by Gil Evans, Chuck Israels's National Jazz Ensemble, Gary Giddins and John Lewis's American Jazz Orchestra, and the Smithsonian Masterworks Orchestra. He had a long residency at the Village Vanguard as a member of the Jones/Lewis Big Band. In 1988 he would record memorably with an early incarnation of the Mingus Big Band at a concert at the Théâtre Boulogne-Billancourt in Paris.[90]

PLAYING THE CLOWN

The ethnomusicologist Steven Feld has noticed that jazz history includes three prominent examples of white trombonists playing with black leaders.

First there was Louis Armstrong and Jack Teagarden. They played together on many occasions, most notably when Teagarden recorded and toured with Armstrong and his All-Stars from 1947 until 1951, during which time he was often the only white person in the band. He deplored the fact that he would get to say in a good hotel while the rest of the band was stuck in a mediocre place on the other side of the tracks.[91]

In performance, Armstrong and Teagarden would often sing together and cut up on stage. There is a delightful video of the two of them singing Hoagy Carmichael's "Rockin' Chair" when they reunited for a television broadcast in 1957.[92] They engage in their own brand of call and response, with Armstrong making side remarks after each of Teagarden's phrases, and Teagarden doing the same while Armstrong takes over the song. When Teagarden sings, for example, "Hand me that gin, son, 'fore I tan your hide," Armstrong responds, "My hide's already tan, Fatha."

Teagarden was not as flamboyant a showman as Armstrong and clearly did not mind being upstaged by the trumpeter. Nor did he, or many in the audience, mind that he was employed by a black man. Of the Teagarden/Armstrong collaboration, Feld writes: "Teagarden was the completing complement of Louis Armstrong. Whether he played the shil, the bantering sidekick, the straight man, the co-mugger, the clown, or the swinging hipster accomplice, he was always the ultimate noncompetitive supporter, the consummate accompanying front man, the very definition of a principal second, someone secure enough in his own musical strengths to delight in playing alongside a stylistic powerhouse."[93]

And then there was Roswell Rudd, who in the 1960s made great music in a group led by the avant-garde saxophonist Archie Shepp. Even today, the two are still playing and have staged several reunions.

Shepp was especially militant in the 1960s, frequently denouncing what he saw as the white ownership of jazz: "Give me leave to state this unequivocal fact: jazz is the product of the whites—the ofays—too often my enemy. It is the progeny of the blacks—my kinsmen. By this I mean you own the music and we make it. By definition then, you own the people who make the music."[94] Yet Shepp seems never to have turned this animus against Rudd. In fact, Rudd speaks admiringly about being in the same car with Shepp when they were pulled over by the police and of how Shepp "got the jump on the guy," talking so persuasively that the policeman ended up apologizing.[95] According to Rudd, when people asked Shepp why he had a white man in his band, he would respond: "'Roswell Rudd is in my band because he's a fine trombonist.' Period. Get out of here."[96]

Writing about the John Coltrane song "Naima" on Shepp's 1964 impulse! LP *Four for Trane*, Feld praises Rudd's arrangement for evoking the spirit of both Charles Ives and Duke Ellington: "Forms of musical modernism then largely coded as 'white experimentalism' are allowed to linger and develop eloquently in the theatre of black avant-gardism."[97]

Chronologically, Knepper and Mingus are between these two pairs of white trombonists with black employers—and theirs was by far the most complicated partnership of the three. As Knepper put it, Mingus "had trouble with black and white, and he was childish and all the rest, but he had exuberance and warmth."[98] Mingus's "trouble with black and white" may explain his decision to feature Knepper's trombone on "The Clown" on the very first day they were in a studio together. It may also explain the reverse minstrelsy that was part of Mingus's "act" when Knepper was in his band.

Mingus would return to clowns in 1965 when he performed "Don't Be Afraid, the Clown's Afraid Too" at UCLA, although he claimed to have written the piece much earlier.[99] In 1972 he would compose a string quartet that included a musical setting of a poem by Frank O'Hara that was also called "The Clown." The poem bore a striking resemblance to Mingus's 1957 portrayal of a clown who is essentially at odds with his audience.[100]

There was no trombone in his music for O'Hara's poem, but Mingus's 1957 recording of his own "The Clown" was neither the first nor the last example of a trombone being associated with clowns. Stravinsky's *Pulcinella* (1920), named for the clownlike trickster in Commedia dell'Arte, includes wide glissandi from the trombones to represent his persona. In the 1920s and 1930s, symphony trombonists were loath to use the slide in this way when they played *Pulcinella*, surely because they associated it with the vernacular music played by African American jazz musicians. As Trevor Herbert points out, some flat out refused, and instead of the glissandi played a series of descending sixteenth notes.[101] But when executed as Stravinsky wrote them, the trombone sounds are completely compatible with the composer's gnomish humor and a clown's antics.

In 1934, the French director Jean Vigo made *L'Atalante*, in which a clownlike intruder tries to woo the heroine with his trombone. Federico Fellini's 1954 film *La Strada* has a character called *Il Matto*, or The Fool (Richard Basehart), who works a trombone into his circus act. And *Sequenza 5* (1966) by the Italian composer Luciano Berio features a trombonist who solos in front of the orchestra wearing a clown suit.

Clowns had been important to Mingus for a long time. Like everyone, he had seen paintings by Picasso and circus posters; but his Eastern-flavored religious readings had also led him to see Christ as a "holy fool" and to appreciate lost innocents like the title character of Dostoevsky's *The Idiot*.[102] There is a connection, too, between clowns and minstrelsy, since many of the first minstrels had previously worked as circus clowns. In early nineteenth-century minstrelsy, white men put burnt cork on their faces and acted out stereotypical images of African Americans and their music. By the late 1800s, black people themselves took prominent roles in minstrel shows, and minstrelsy was the dominant form of entertainment in the United States. Well into the twentieth century, many white actors were still performing in blackface in films. Al Jolson was the most famous, but Bing Crosby, Eddie Cantor, Fred Astaire, Mickey Rooney, and Judy Garland all blacked up in movies of the 1930s and 1940s. Even Doris Day appeared in blackface when she imitated Jolson in *I'll See You in My Dreams*, released in 1952. After that, however, blackface disappears almost completely from the screen.[103]

Minstrelsy provided a path into show business for many black performers, including Bert Williams, one of the most popular entertainers of the early twentieth century. Although he was dark-skinned, Williams performed with burnt cork on his face, except for his lips, which he painted white. Long after Williams died in 1922, many black performers retained minstrel mannerisms, though without the burnt cork. Brent Hayes Edwards has called minstrelsy "the historical debris" in a great deal of African American performance.[104] Louis Armstrong's mugging is the most commonly cited example of the survival of minstrelsy, even after many African Americans began referring to Armstrong as an Uncle Tom.

Mingus was certainly aware of minstrelsy, and he parodies it raucously in his 1961 recording of "Eat That Chicken."[105] Jennifer Griffith has found phrases in "Eat That Chicken" that are strikingly similar to passages in a song by the white minstrel Frank Dumont called "Bake Dat Chicken Pie," first recorded in 1907.[106] Mingus may not have known the original recording, but he surely could have heard some version of the tune at a performance or on a record. "Eat That Chicken" also includes references to the verbal asides of Fats Waller and the gravel-voice of Armstrong, all of them performed broadly by Mingus himself. He knew that both Waller and Armstrong had to include minstrelsy in their acts or risk losing their audiences. Mingus was thus simultaneously commenting on white people's stereotypical notions about blacks while "nodding to precursor black entertainers who had had to restrict their overt parodies of these misconceptions to black audiences."[107]

Part of Mingus's habit of lecturing and hectoring his audiences reflected his desire to distinguish black entertainers like himself not only from the old minstrel men but also from more contemporary black performers, like Armstrong and Lionel Hampton, who could not completely abandon minstrel gestures. Mingus was, however, equally unwilling to emulate Miles Davis, whose rejection of minstrelsy meant turning his back on the audience, neglecting to announce the names of tunes, and leaving the stage when a sideperson soloed. Rather than kowtowing to spectators, like Armstrong, or simply ignoring them, like Davis, Mingus in his performances foregrounded racial issues that virtually every other jazz artist scrupulously avoided.

On the recordings of "The Clown" and "Eat That Chicken" and at many performances in the late 1950s, Jimmy Knepper was the only white musician in the band. It would have been unlike Mingus to imitate other jazz artists—white or black—and feign color-blindness. In the liner notes to *The Clown*, Mingus described how he felt about the bass solo with which he begins "Haitian Fight Song": "I can't play it unless I'm thinking about prejudice and hate and persecution, and how unfair it is."[108] And he could not resist turning some of this emotion toward Knepper. In the end, Mingus's anger over America's appalling persecution of African Americans trumped the affection and admiration he had for his trombonist. His racialized treatment of Knepper included enthusiastically presenting his brilliant musical facility *and* calling him a "white faggot" while knocking his tooth out—and everything else in between.

Of course, there are other ways of interpreting "The Clown." It can also be heard as a race-free allegory of the artist's predicament. I would compare it to Kafka's "The Hunger Artist," whose protagonist gives everything to his craft, even putting his life at risk, all for an audience that is stolidly oblivious.[109] Whether or not he had read the Kafka story, Mingus knew that the jazz artist was in just such a predicament. Nevertheless, there is no way around the fact that Mingus, who self-identified as black, was asking a white man to play the clown. That Knepper played the trombone made Mingus's project easier, despite the fact that Knepper was among the most accomplished musicians ever to take up the instrument.

At least at first, Knepper did not mind because he knew he was in on the joke, as when he engaged in another type of reverse minstrelsy and served as the white chauffeur for two black passengers. And he also knew that he and Mingus were making extraordinary music together. Steven Feld, who once took trombone lessons from Knepper, told me that Jimmy "knew Mingus's music as well as anyone could know it—as a player, arranger, rearranger, and historian. That was the bottom line for me. He was such a committed and professional musician that once he was in the music he could put aside the crappy life-with-Mingus chapters and just play his ass off."[110]

All of the people I talked to about Jimmy Knepper expressed great affection for the man. Like Dolphy, he had a degree of inner peace that must have helped him through the difficult moments with Mingus. Although Knepper rarely smiled, everyone mentioned his wry, perfectly pointed sense of humor. Once, traveling to a gig on a bus together, Loren Schoenberg was sitting across the aisle from Knepper. Schoenberg told Knepper that his plans for the evening were simple: he was going straight to his hotel room and curling up with the *New York Times* crossword puzzle. Later that day, when Schoenberg opened his newspaper, he found that Knepper had completely filled in the puzzle—but he did so very lightly in pencil so that Loren could easily erase and start from scratch on his own.[111] Schoenberg was as impressed by Knepper's talents as a crossword whiz as he was by his facetious, intentionally failed attempt to ruin Schoenberg's evening.

Sam Burtis told me that at some point in the 1970s Knepper essentially gave up any hope of being recognized as an important artist, let alone making a good living as a jazz musician. He had purchased a second house on Staten Island, near the one where he lived with his wife. One year, he made more money renting out that house than he did as a musician.[112] Knepper was not too proud to take any number of jobs well outside the domain of jazz. During one stretch of three years and nine months, he played in the pit orchestra for the Broadway show *Funny Girl,* and Jeff Nussbaum says that he once saw Knepper playing in a religious parade in an Italian American section of Brooklyn.[113] It is not too extreme to say that Knepper died in obscurity in 2003.

WHAT *IS* THIS MUSIC?

I conclude this chapter with a few words about a movie in which Mingus and Knepper play small but significant roles. Elsewhere I have written about the Hollywood film industry's habit of keeping the bodies of black artists off the screen while making abundant use of the romantic potential in their music.[114] The list of American films in which white people fall in love to the voices of invisible black musicians playing in the background is long. In *Groundhog Day* (1993), for example, Bill Murray and Andie McDowell fall for each other to the accompaniment of Ray Charles's voice. And at the climax of *Before Sunset* (2004), Ethan Hawke and Julie Delpy are listening to a Nina Simone CD when they realize that they are about to spend the rest of their lives together. Many other films appropriate invisi-

Figure 13. Tom Cruise and Renée Zellweger in *Jerry Maguire* (1999), directed by Cameron Crowe. Tristar Pictures and Gracie Films. Jerry Ohlinger's Movie Materials Store, Inc.

ble black voices for white romance as well, but these examples should not be confused with the scene in *Jerry Maguire*, released in 1996 and directed by Cameron Crowe, where the couple played by Tom Cruise and Renée Zellweger (figure 13) make love while Mingus's 1957 recording of "Haitian Fight Song"—specifically, the trombone solo by Jimmy Knepper—plays in the background.

Before the scene unfolds, it has become clear that Jerry (Cruise) and Dorothy (Zellweger) are going to consummate their relationship. As a working single mother, Dorothy entrusts her child for most of the day to "Chad the Nanny," played by Todd Luiso. Meeting Jerry at the door and knowing what he has in mind, Chad offers Jerry a cassette tape. With a great deal of flourish and detail, he suggests that the couple listen to Miles Davis while they make love. Although Jerry is not the least bit interested, Chad lectures him about the importance of jazz in general and of Miles in particular. He even provides some discographical details, telling Jerry that the music on the cassette comes from a "1963 Swedish concert" in which

John Coltrane was part of Davis's group.[115] As Chad hands the tape to Jerry, we hear him off-camera saying, "I put a little Mingus on there too."

In a 1997 interview with *Entertainment Weekly*, Crowe said that he originally intended to film Jerry and Dorothy making love to "So What" from the Stockholm concert with Davis and Coltrane. "But when I put it on that day, it was too languid and wasn't as good as Mingus' 'Haitian Fight Song,' which sounded like a herd of elephants mating. We'd already filmed the nanny saying the music was on a tape of 'Miles and Coltrane'—so we later dubbed [him] saying 'And I put some Mingus on there too.'"[116] I understand why Crowe was not interested in reshooting. Luiso's portrayal of a proselytizing jazz enthusiast who firmly believes that sex can be enhanced by music is so spot-on that it had to be retained.

Immediately after Chad hands the tape to Jerry and heads home, we see a close-up of Dorothy in her bathroom preparing to join Jerry in the bedroom. We also hear the bass solo with which Mingus opens "Haitian Fight Song."[117] Within a few seconds we see Jerry and Dorothy undressed and in bed together while Knepper's solo plays in the background. At this point, those who don't know Mingus might think "Haitian Fight Song" is just part of the soundtrack and not there for the characters to hear. But then, when Knepper's already amazing solo becomes even more amazing as he breaks into double time, Jerry stops, gives Dorothy an incredulous look, and says, "What *is* this music?" They both begin laughing, even more united now that they share a complete inability to understand what Mingus and Knepper (along with Curtis Porter, Wade Legge, and Dannie Richmond) have achieved.

I have not been able to interview Cameron Crowe, but I have a few questions for him. First, I would like to know why he associates the music of Mingus's stripped-down unit of five musicians with a herd of elephants. Second, did he know how profoundly he was revising, perhaps even ridiculing, Hollywood's conventional use of black music as a romantic lubricant for white couples? And third, did he know that "Haitian Fight Song" celebrates slave rebellions? And if so, how did the song tie in with the relationship between Jerry Maguire and Rod Tidwell, the football player played by Cuba Gooding, Jr.?

In the most famous scene in *Jerry Maguire*, Rod engages Jerry in a long telephone conversation, demanding that Jerry repeatedly shout, "Show me the money." Although Rod has employed Jerry as his agent, the idea of a black athlete making demands on a member of the white power structure that controls his career almost suggests a slave rebellion. David Yaffe has even compared Jerry and Dorothy to the Captain Delano of Herman Melville's short story "Benito Cereno," first published in 1855.[118] Just as the lovers in *Jerry Maguire* cannot make sense of black music (with its intense contribution from a white artist), Delano makes the deadly mistake of not realizing that a group of slaves has taken over his ship. Neither Jerry nor Dorothy nor Delano can hear a slave rebellion taking place.

The "show me the money" scene has even more in common with the recording of "Haitian Fight Song." In both, a white man is performing for a black man. Just as Jerry is required to look ridiculous as he loudly exclaims the phrases that Rod demands, so is Knepper putting all his creativity to work at the request of Mingus—just as much as when he brilliantly played the clown for Mingus.

In my final question for Crowe, I would ask if he knew that Jimmy Knepper was white—the only white member in a group of African American musicians. Crowe did, after all, begin his career as a music journalist, and he most certainly knew the work of Mingus (he was the *Rolling Stone* reporter mentioned in part I who interviewed Joni Mitchell when she was working on her *Mingus* LP).[119] It is possible that he was in fact using "Haitian Fight Song" to comment on the racial dynamics of his film. If so, I salute him.

Nevertheless, *Jerry Maguire* is still a Hollywood film, and so it is no surprise that the white man's story is central at the end. In typical Hollywood fashion too, the black man serves as a role model for the white hero when Jerry, not yet fully committed to Dorothy, witnesses the powerful bond between Rod and his wife Marcee (Regina King). The vaguely racist notion that blacks lead richer emotional lives and that they can give life lessons to whites is much more typical of the post-minstrel era of white/black interaction in Hollywood films. Also at the end of *Jerry Maguire*, the white man is no longer playing the clown for the black man. Jerry has become his own man; neither Rod nor any other black character is asking him to perform.

In "Haitian Fight Song," Mingus asked a great deal of Jimmy Knepper, and Knepper rose to the occasion. Mingus, who did not hesitate to lecture his audiences on how they should listen to his music, must have known that not everyone would get it, certainly not clueless white people like the Jerry and Dorothy of *Jerry Maguire*. I do not think, though, that Jerry's saying "What *is* this music?" would have made him angry. At least Jerry and Dorothy are listening.

Sue Mingus was not at all upset about *Jerry Maguire*. In fact, she was delighted to receive the royalty check. It was the biggest check the Mingus estate had ever received for the use of his music.[120]

There was, of course, no royalty check for Jimmy Knepper. He was still alive when *Jerry Maguire* was in theaters. I do not know if he saw it, but if he did, I hope it at least gave him a chuckle.

EPILOGUE **Mingus in the Movies**

Jerry Maguire was only one of several films that were transformed by Mingus Music. Before I conclude this book with a few words about those films, please allow me to share a fantasy about Mingus in the movies. In 1941, when Mingus was nineteen, his lifelong friend Buddy Collette made a brief appearance in *Citizen Kane,* the film many consider to be the greatest American motion picture ever made. The scene takes place about twenty minutes before the end of the film when the elderly Kane (Orson Welles) tries to give his bored wife, Susan (Dorothy Comingore), a bit of excitement by throwing an elaborate party in the Everglades. The audience's first view of the party is a tight close-up of a round-faced, dark-skinned man singing, "It can't be love, 'cause there is no true love," a phrase from the song "In a Mizz." The song was written by Charlie Barnet and Haven Johnson, and recorded in 1939 by Barnet's big band. A few months later, Duke Ellington's orchestra would record the tune with Ivie Anderson, a vocalist who spent several years with Ellington.[1]

The singer with the big close-up in *Citizen Kane* is Alton Redd, today a forgotten figure in jazz history. He is not listed in the film's credits, nor is Buddy Collette, who is visible for a few seconds playing the alto saxophone along with Raymond Tate on trumpet, Buddy Banks on tenor sax, and the leader of the band, Cee Pee Johnson, vigorously beating the drums. Only recently has the Internet Movie Database (www.imdb.com) begun listing these musicians in the "Soundtracks" section of its page on *Citizen Kane.* And even then, the page incorrectly identifies Redd's song as "It Can't Be Love."

What I find intriguing about this scene is the absence of a bassist in the band that Charles Foster Kane has hired for his party and that Orson Welles hired for his film. Mingus was always fascinated by Welles and would imitate his voice. A long poem that Mingus recorded sometime in the 1960s, now in the Mingus collection at the Library of Congress, sounds very much like his attempt to channel Welles.

Watts is not all that far from Hollywood, and in the early 1940s Collette and Mingus found jobs as extras in films. They both appear in *Higher and Higher* (1943), the first film in which Frank Sinatra had a starring role. They might also have appeared in a Bob Hope/Bing Crosby vehicle, *The Road to Zanzibar* (1941), but the scene was cut from the release print of the film. In *Beneath the Underdog,* Mingus says that he was filmed holding a spear and saying to Hope and Crosby, "Yes, Bwana."[2]

The *Road to Zanzibar* came out just a few months before *Citizen Kane* appeared in theaters. Cee Pee Johnson, the leader of the group in *Citizen Kane,* hired Mingus on several occasions in the 1940s. Was Mingus meant to be in the scene with Redd, Johnson, Collette, and the others but did not show up for the shoot? How different would Mingus's career have been if he had played bass in that celebrated film?

There were other films that should have been on Mingus's resume. When Mingus was a member of the Red Norvo Trio, the band was contracted to perform in *Texas Carnival* (1951) with the queen of the "Aqua Movie," Esther Williams. The film also featured singer/dancer Ann Miller and Red Skelton, a popular movie comedian who had not yet made the transition to television. Norvo's group was to perform in only one scene, but Mingus's color made the producers nervous.

In *Texas Carnival,* when Ann Miller sings "It's Dynamite" and then breaks into a dance number, the camera shows several musicians in the background, all wearing head bands, a typical Hollywood attempt to suggest the Native American presence in the Old West. At the edges of the stage are a pianist and a drummer. In the center are Tal Farlow, the trio's regular guitarist, and Norvo with his vibes, but no Mingus. The bassist is white. Hollywood movies practically never show musicians playing or singing "in the moment." Inevitably the music is prerecorded and then played back while the musicians lip-sync or pantomime as the cameras roll. Listening to the bass on the soundtrack, I believe that Mingus may have been there for the prerecording, but for the usual racist reasons, his participation ended there.

Mingus also did not appear on camera for John Cassavetes's *Shadows* (1959), but not because producers catering to racist audiences kept him off screen. In 1958, Mingus was invited to compose and perform the soundtrack to *Shadows,* now considered a landmark in cinema history. Cassavetes was an intense young actor with a vision of what cinema could accomplish outside the clichés of Hollywood. Shortly after he finished principal photography on *Shadows*, he landed a job as the star and sometime director of a television series called *Johnny Staccato* in which he played a private detective who was also a jazz pianist. Final production on *Shadows* was put on hold.

The twenty-five episodes of *Johnny Staccato*, broadcast on NBC between September 1959 and March 1960, often feature stereotypically posturing beatniks. The jazz, however, wasn't bad. A few episodes presented some of the most eminent West Coast musicians, including the trumpeter Pete Candoli, guitarist Barney Kessel, drummer Shelly Manne, bassist Red Mitchell, and Mingus's erstwhile employer, Red Norvo. The jazz pianist on one episode of *Johnny Staccato* was "Johnny Williams," who would soon become John Williams, today the most widely heard composer in the universe.

Cassavetes now used the money he made on *Johnny Staccato* to pay for the final cut of *Shadows*. The film had a distinctive look. New technologies had made light, portable cameras available at increasingly reasonable prices, and Cassavetes was able to follow his actors through several New York locations with a handheld camera. With its grainy black-and-white texture, the unpredictable reactions on the actors' faces, and the heart-breaking portrayal of racism's effect on the characters, the film delivered more intense realism than American audiences were accustomed to seeing.

Immediately after *Shadows* had its first screening, however, Cassavetes pulled the film from distribution and shot most of it all over again. Whereas the actors in the first version were really and truly improvising, and although the revered film critic Jonas Mekas abundantly praised the first version, Cassavetes was not satisfied. The subsequent version that Cassavetes eventually put into distribution was more carefully scripted, though he instructed the actors to give the impression of improvising.[3] For the rest of his career, Cassavetes would make films in a style that, at its best, presented actors as flesh-and-blood people revealing themselves with such abandon that many audience members felt they were eavesdropping rather than watching a movie.

Cassavetes has said that when he was contemplating music for *Shadows*, he heard that an artist was playing great music in Greenwich Village and that he had made a few records.

> So I listened to a couple and *oh!*—this guy was wonderful! Charlie Mingus. So Charlie said, "Listen, man, would you do me a favor? I'll do it for you, but you have got to do something for me."
>
> "Sure, sure," I say.
>
> "Listen. I've got these cats that are shitting all over the floor. Can you have a couple of your people come up and clean the cat shit? I can't work; they shit all over my music."

So we went up with scrubbing brushes and cleaned up the thing. Now he says, "I can't work in this place. It's so clean, I've got to wait for the cats to shit."[4]

Perhaps Mingus was asking Cassavetes to jump through hoops in the same way that he had tested so many artists before him. This anecdote may also explain why the collaboration never really worked out. Although Mingus eventually completed the music, he delivered most of it well after the film was finished. It was eventually released in the box of Debut recordings issued on CD in 1990.[5]

The prospect of working with Cassavetes on *Shadows* should have been irresistible for Mingus, who shared the film's compassion for black artists trying to survive in a climate that was more about business than art. The blues singer in the film played by Hugh Hurd lands a job as a vocalist in a club only to discover that he is also required to introduce the women who parade through the club, thus ensuring that no one will pay attention to a black male singer. The mulatto Lelia (played by the Italian American actress Lelia Goldoni) confronts a different kind of racism when her white male boyfriend becomes outraged on discovering that her brother is clearly black. Mingus had written "Eclipse" in the 1940s as a celebration of interracial romance, using the meeting of the sun and the moon as a metaphor for the love between a white person (the sun) and a black person (the moon). The scene in *Shadows* was essentially the flip side of "Eclipse."

Regardless of what prevented Mingus from working successfully with Cassavetes, a key collaboration in the avant-garde art of America in the 1950s went unrealized. Mingus claimed he did not have enough time to write the material, but Jimmy Knepper said that Mingus became so serious about the project that he actually wrote out parts for each musician, violating the system he had developed at the Jazz Workshop of singing or playing phrases for the musicians and letting them take it in their own directions. According to Knepper, the music that was to be delivered to Cassavetes sounded stiff.[6]

Although there is not much Mingus in *Shadows*, several scenes do benefit from the saxophone of Curtis Porter (who by then had changed his name to Shafi Hadi), a member of the Workshop, who improvised unaccompanied as the actors went through their paces. Mingus, for his part, went to the second premier of *Shadows* expecting to hear much more of his music. A photographer who attended the screening at the Paris Theater was standing at the back of the auditorium. As soon as the film was over and the applause began, one and only one person walked out: Mingus. The photographer knew Charles and told him how much he liked his music. "Mingus stopped in his tracks, looked him dead in the eye and said, 'Go fuck your-self.' Mingus was furious at Cassavetes's re-editing of the score."[7]

Early in 1961, Mingus answered the call of Nel King and traveled to London to appear in *All Night Long*. Just as he had wanted to be in the "Harlem 1958" photo, and just as he would later agree to let Tom Reichman film him in 1966 in his loft, he wanted to be in this British film. The direc-tor was Basil Dearden, who had a long history in the British cinema, having directed more than forty films in different genres. Several of Dearden's films addressed taboo subjects, including race and homosexuality. In *Sapphire* (1959), a pregnant woman found murdered is assumed to be white until her mixed racial origins are discovered; in *Victim* (1961), Dirk Bogarde plays a gay man threatened with exposure by a blackmailer; and in *Khartoum* (1966), Laurence Olivier plays the Mahdi, a charismatic Muslim leader opposing British colonial forces in the Sudan. I do not know how many of these films Mingus had actually seen, but he was no doubt intrigued by the film's retelling of the Othello story.

The Desdemona character in *All Night Long* is Delia (Marti Stevens), a white singer who has married a black jazz pianist, Aurelius Rex (Paul Chase). The Iago figure is Johnny Cousin (Patrick McGoohan), a drummer who doctors a reel-to-reel tape to convince Rex that his wife is cheating on him. In some ways, *All Night Long* does little to dispel what Thomas Cartelli has called the "Othello Complex."[8] As in Shakespeare's play, Aurelius Rex can only assimilate so far into white society. When his jeal-ousy is unleashed, he becomes the stereotypical black beast. Capable of strangling the woman he loves, the Othello figure reveals his true self. For Shakespeare as well as for many racists today, it is impossible for black men to leave behind their primitive souls, even if they seem to be civilized. But unlike Shakespeare's *Othello*, the film allows the heroine to live and does not portray the Othello character as relentlessly savage.

Early in *All Night Long*, Johnny Cousin asks Delia to join his band, but she says she cannot because it would damage her marriage to Rex. When Johnny aggressively tells her that she absolutely must join, she rebuffs him just as forcefully. The film's Iago then puts his plan into motion, hoping to break up the marriage out of revenge. When, at the party during which almost all of the action takes place, Rex hears the altered tape and becomes convinced that his wife is involved with Cass (Keith Michell), he grabs Delia by the throat.

What should happen when Rex begins strangling Delia was hotly debated as the film took shape. The film's writers, Paul Jarrico and Nel King, told the producers and the director that the marriage of Rex and Delia must survive. Letters in the Paul Jarrico archive at Columbia University reveal that director Basil Dearden, however, did not believe that an interracial marriage could "triumph over the obstacles."[9] He advocated a scene in which Rex is prevented from killing Delia only when several men burst into the room and pull him away. King was especially opposed to a passage in the producers' rewritten draft of the script in which Rex confronts Johnny, who has been revealed as the perpetrator of a deadly scheme. Unrepentant to the end, Johnny calls Rex a "nigger," and Rex runs out of the apartment. Delia then slaps Johnny and goes rushing after Rex.

In response to this passage, Nel King wrote, "You reflect on what Charles Mingus would do if he had been provoked as far as Rex has. The man who has done it to him now spits out the word 'nigger' at him. Can you imagine him rushing out into the night with his feelings hurt? There would be MURDER."[10] Ultimately, King and Jarrico succeeded in convincing the director and producers to accept an ending in which Rex does not need to be restrained before he stops himself from killing Delia. When she tells him that she loves him, he relaxes his grip. Moments later, when he learns the truth, Rex goes after Johnny and puts his hands around *his* throat. He relents only when Delia begs him to stop. In the last moments of the film, Delia and Rex walk away from the party with their arms around each other. *All Night Long* suggests that an interracial couple can keep their love alive even when the odds are very much against them.

Except for a brief prologue and the finale in which the audience sees Rex and Delia walking along the street from a distance, all the action in the film takes place on one night at a party in the townhouse of a wealthy jazz aficionado named Rodney (Richard Attenborough). The occasion is the celebration of Rex and Delia's second wedding anniversary. The plot regularly pauses to feature many of the most prominent and advanced British jazz artists of 1961, including John Dankworth, Tubby Hayes, and Keith Christie, who make music around the townhouse's piano.

Mingus appears in an early scene of *All Night Long*. Casting a large, sharp shadow on a modernist mural in Rodney's apartment, he is plucking his bass and smoking a pipe. Rodney hands him a glass of Scotch just as the other musicians are arriving. One says, "I see you got here first." Sipping his Scotch, Mingus replies, "Yeah, baby, and I'll be the last one to leave." Although Mingus plays a somewhat altered version of himself in *All Night Long*, it is appropriate that he joins Rodney and his guests in toasting the marriage of a black man and a white woman. At this time Mingus had twice married white women, but he did not seem to object to the film's perpetuation of the stereotype of the seemingly housebroken black man reverting to his primitive, murderous self when sufficiently provoked. He was probably more concerned with the music.

Although the film did not do well at the box office, it is worth seeing for the music. Johnny Dankworth and Tubby Hayes take excellent saxophone solos in between the plot machinations. Mingus only makes a few brief appearances, at one point joining Dave Brubeck, the only other American jazz man in the film, for a duet that the two improvised on the spot as the cameras rolled. The music has some of the eccentric rhythmic patterns in which Brubeck specialized, but the rest is pure Mingus. Both musicians clearly enjoyed themselves, and on several occasions they asked to hear a playback of the recording.[11]

Mingus did not hit it off with Philip Green, who was hired to provide background music when the jazzmen were not performing on camera. The correspondence in the Jarrico archive suggests that Mingus was brought in as some kind of music advisor as well as a performing artist. Even though his role was not clearly defined, he regularly complained about the music he was hearing on and off the set and attempted to assert what authority he had as the only African American jazz artist involved in the project. He was even able, over Philip Green's resistance, to get some of his own music onto the background score: "Peggy's Blue Skylight" pops up on the soundtrack for a few moments. Mingus was probably working on the tune when he was in London, because he did not record it until a few months later.[12]

Apparently Green was instructed to heed the words of Nel King. Several years before she would edit *Beneath the Underdog,* Nel wrote the following to one of the producers of *All Night Long:* "Believe me, I'm sorry you're having a hard time with Mingus, but to quote a long-gone line from the script, A-R-T is the key word. Mingus happens to be an artist of a very high order, and whatever it is that makes him[,] *that* makes him 'temperamental'—i.e., unable to compromise about his work."[13] King was charitable in her use of the term *temperamental,* but then who knows if Mingus's contribution to the film would have been more substantial had he been more agreeable on the set.

ELEVATION AND RESURRECTION

Mingus's music shows up now and then in television commercials, and Ira Glass regularly inserts bits of Mingus into his spoken-word radio program *This American Life.* In addition to the bizarre placement of "Haitian Fight Song" in *Jerry Maguire,* Mingus's 1959 recording of "Moanin'" is used to ratchet up the suspense during a scene in another Hollywood genre film, *The Whole Nine Yards* (2000). In Spike Lee's *Mo' Better Blues* (1990) we hear a bit of "Goodbye Pork Pie Hat" while Bleek Gilliam (Denzel Washington) lies motionless in a hospital bed and his father (Dick Anthony Williams) reminisces about the past. And in Oliver Stone's *U Turn* (1997), "II B.S." plays over the opening credits as a drifter (Sean Penn) aggressively drives along a highway in the middle of the desert.

"Boogie Stop Shuffle" and "Better Git It in Your Soul" are put to much more satisfying use in the opening sequence of *Absolute Beginners* (1986), directed by Julien Temple. In versions arranged and conducted by Gil Evans, Mingus Music dominates a six-minute stretch early in the film, including a dazzling three-minute sequence in which a moving camera ceaselessly follows a young photographer through London streets overflowing with scenes of exuberant nightlife, some of which briefly break into dance segments that recall Bob Fosse's choreography.

"Haitian Fight Song," which played a small but important role in Cameron Crowe's *Jerry Maguire,* can also be heard in the 2014 film *Top Five,* starring and directed by Chris Rock. By a strange coincidence, Chris Rock had previously played a character named Mingus in an American film directed by the French actress Julie Delpy, *2 Days in New York* (2012), though no one in the film ever associates him with his namesake. In *Top Five,* Rock plays an actor who has appeared in several crowd-pleasing films as a policeman who wears a bear suit. Now attempting to make his name as a director of more serious and ambitious films, he has directed *Uprize,* an epic about the same slave rebellion that Mingus celebrated with "Haitian Fight Song." On the several occasions when the name of the film is spoken, the audience hears a few bars of the Mingus tune in the background.

The most brilliant use of Mingus's work is in a forty-five-minute film from 1980 called *Stations of the Elevated.*[14] Like Crowe and Rock, director Manfred Kirchheimer used segments of "Haitian Fight Song," but he also included short phrases from other Mingus compositions including "Ecclusiastics," "Fables of Faubus," "Better Git It in Your Soul," "Hog Callin' Blues," and "Percussion Discussion." Mingus's music pops up and fades out repeatedly in a film that is more cinematic poem than conventional documentary. Superficially, the subject is the New York subway system, but only those sections that pass over the city on bridges. With no voiceover narration of any kind, the film documents the extraordinary work of artists, known to each other as "Writers," who spray-painted subway trains in New York City in the 1970s and 1980s. Toward the end of the film, we hear a bit of "Amazing Grace" sung by Aretha Franklin, the only other artist represented on the film's soundtrack. In the film's final moments, we hear Mingus preaching his way through "Ecclusiastics."

Kirchheimer shot the entire film in 1977 without sound. He then gave *Stations of the Elevated* an extremely complex sound design. The audience regularly hears sirens, train noises, and sounds from nature, sometimes competing with the music, sometimes giving way completely to Mingus's recordings. The succession of images is equally complex. At times the gaudy images on the subway cars sharply contrast with the geometric patterns of several trains lined up in the yards, where they sit motionless in the early morning. Kirchheimer includes shots of billboards with tacky images of scantily clad models and Marlboro men, a stark counterpoint to the non-commercial and more engaging images painted on the trains. Shooting from within the elevated trains, the director also includes views of the Statue of Liberty and the New York Correctional Facility at Napanoch as the train passes by. Without emphasizing the comparison, Kirchheimer invites us to link the prison with the iconic image of the liberty that as been denied the inmates.

When we see the commuters on the trains, they are usually motionless and enervated, recalling figures in paintings by Edward Hopper and George Tooker. Along with the Statue of Liberty and the prison, Kirchheimer's moving camera also looks at wooded areas and junk yards. At other moments an earthbound camera looks at young black men, some playing stickball in a devastated neighborhood of the Bronx. At one point, some young men are staring up at the subway and talking about the graffiti that decorates them.

Young urban artists began spray-painting subway cars in the mid-1970s. Many New Yorkers regarded their work as a form of gang violence. Mayor Ed Koch famously said, "Graffiti on the walls of trains or subway stations create bad karma." Koch put MTA employs to work cleaning cars as soon as they were painted and took older trains with extensive markings completely out of service. When not in use, subway cars were carefully protected with angry guard dogs and razored concertina-wire on top of tall fences. On May 12, 1989, the MTA declared a victory over graffiti.[15]

Some commentators saw this moment as a turning point, marking a kind of rebirth for New York City. Many linked the end of spray-painted subways to the Broken Windows thesis, the idea that one broken window inevitably leads to more broken windows, and one painted train leads to another, whereas an intact building or unmarked train is less likely to be vandalized. The advocates of this theory also argued that if minor offenses, such as the possession of small amounts of marijuana, are regularly punished, the overall crime rate would decline.[16]

The Broken Windows thesis has been widely disputed; indeed, some consider it in part responsible for the national catastrophe of a growing prison-industrial complex.[17] It was, nevertheless, dogma during the Koch administration.

In the late 1970s, the *Village Voice*, in a rejection of the theory and a celebration of the art of the Writers, ran a full two-page center spread of photographs showing elaborately painted subway trains with the caption, "Since these pictures were taken, these trains have been defaced by the MTA."[18] Elsewhere, including *Stations of the Elevated*, the work of the Writers has been recognized as legitimate art, even showing up in galleries and art books.[19] By placing the music of Mingus on his soundtrack, Kirchheimer has elevated the achievements of the Writers, implying that their work is compatible with jazz in general and with Mingus in particular. Jazz and subway graffiti are predominantly African American art forms, despised by many but recognized as serious art by those intellectuals, regardless of color, who have found aesthetic qualities in what is otherwise dismissed as urban blight.

Kirchheimer has said that he decided early on that jazz should be on the soundtrack of *Stations of the Elevated*. But when he listened to the jazz recordings in his collection, none of the familiar tunes followed by improvisation seemed to fit. Then he saw Mingus in a club. He immediately went out and bought as many of his recordings as he could find. Instead of recognizable old standards and improvisations, Mingus's recordings feature complex, often beautiful melodies that were not widely known. Audiences would not be distracted by familiar songs; instead they would hear a compelling music that matched up well with the images.[20]

When the film was first exhibited in 1980, many young people told Kirchheimer that he should have put rap music on the soundtrack instead of jazz. But Kirchheimer knew that the words in rap recordings—by far the most interesting aspect of the music—would interfere with the texts the audience is invited to read in the film's images. He also knew that although rap might have a direct connection to the spray paintings, it did not jibe with everything else in the film. Mingus's music, in contrast, could connect with the prison, the commuters, even with the green world that the trains pass by. When *Stations of the Elevated* was rediscovered and exhibited in theaters in 2014, Kirchheimer was pleased that this time around no one told him that he should have used rap music. Audiences got it.[21]

Charles Mingus died in January 1979, shortly before Kirchheimer began mixing sound and image for his film. This may account for the elegiac quality that Mingus's music takes on and the gravitas it sometimes gives to the work of the Writers. But no composition is heard for more than a few minutes, and with the jokey cadences of "Fables of Faubus" and "Hog Callin' Blues" also on the soundtrack, the tone of the film can change as quickly as the tempo in a Mingus song. Of course, in 1979 Mingus was more marginal than he is today. Only a handful of connoisseurs would have recognized his music in the film.

Kirchheimer did not see the subway paintings simply as the work of playful, transgressive free spirits who deserve more respect as artists. He knew that the paintings emanated from and coexisted with poverty and oppression. He drives the point home by contrasting deteriorating black neighborhoods with lovely, pastoral images. Along with the humor, Mingus's music supplies doses of rage as well as pathos that fit with the film's images of urban decay and dehumanizing prisons.

In the end, Kirchheimer connects Mingus's "Ecclusiastics" and his crying out to Jesus with the tragic conditions of inner-city blacks.[22] Being Jewish did not prevent Kirchheimer from using the title *Stations of the Elevated*, with its echoes of the "Stations of the Cross," Christ's journey to the Crucifixion.[23] Kirchheimer has also said that the last station—both in the film and in its allegory—should be "resurrection."[24] In its final minutes, the film twice shows airplanes climbing into the sky. We also see an old automobile on a platform high in the air near a junkyard. Like the trains suspended on bridges, the ascending airplanes and the elevated car suggest escape. Along with the ascension of Christ after his resurrection, the images recall African American stories of people who could fly back to Africa or magically travel through the sky to heaven. Think of the Depression-era gospel song "I'll Fly Away" as well as the enormous concrete sailing ship pointed toward Sam Rodia's home in Italy that sat a block from where Mingus grew up in Watts.

At the end of the film, Kirchheimer overlaps "Ecclusiastics" with Aretha Franklin's performance of "Amazing Grace." Both are devoted to the same project. As the long day closes, transcendence does seem possible in the elegiac images of trains departing and airplanes climbing through the sky. Even more so in the perfect blending of Franklin's intense spirituality with the ridiculous and sublime music of Charles Mingus.

Acknowledgments

First, I thank my editor, Mary Francis, who has been publishing the best books in film and music studies at the University of California Press for more than twenty years now. I thank her for scrupulous professionalism and good will even when my tardiness in delivering a manuscript stretched from months into years.

Sue Mingus has tirelessly and imaginatively devoted herself to the legacy of her husband's music. I thank her first for keeping Mingus Music alive, vital, and available. I am also in her debt for granting me permission to publish writings by Mingus, some of which neither of us knew about until they turned up in the archives. Sue's assistant, Sarah Williams, has also been a treasure.

I owe an especially large debt to Brian Priestley, the first great Mingus biographer. He carefully corrected and annotated an early draft of this book. He generously gave me a great deal of information and saved me from massive embarrassment. Thomas Brothers also read all of an early draft and made numerous corrections and suggestions that have proved to be essential. I also thank two anonymous reviewers who judiciously read and commented on an early draft.

Abundant thanks to John Szwed, who gave me great advice and loaned me a pre-prepublication copy of his superb new book on Billie Holiday. Holly Anderson, Michael Cuscuna, Sy Johnson, Tom Marcello, and Cynthia Sessowere were extremely helpful in my search for the best photos. Shelley Hamilton graciously talked me through the latest research on amyotrophic lateral sclerosis.

Anne Cunningham, Jennifer Griffith, Marty Lee, Kate McQuiston, Mary Morris, Donald Sickler, and David Yaffe read and commented smartly on individual sections of the book. Sincere thanks to George Avakian, Sam

Burtis, Jay Clayton, Janet Coleman, Bill Crow, David Hajdu, Nat Hentoff, Howard Johnson, Manny Kirchheimer, Dick Munich, Jeff Nussbaum, Vince Prudente, Regina Ryan, Loren Schoenberg, Gunther Schuller, Jessica Teague, Jack Walrath, and George Wein, all of whom patiently responded to my questions about Mingus. I had an especially helpful interview with Gary Giddins, who has written brilliantly about Mingus (and who really should write more about him).

In the archives, I enjoyed the seemingly limitless attentions of Larry Applebaum and Zoran Sinobad at the Library of Congress's Music Division. Richard Watson and Andrew Gansky were extremely generous in helping me explore the Knopf Archive at the Harry Ransom Center, University of Texas, Austin. Lewis Porter loaned me a huge stack of CDs with music and interviews that I could never have tracked down on my own, and Aidan Levy shared with me his treasure trove of material from the Paul Jarrico Archive at Columbia University. At the University of California Press, Zuha Khan, Bradley Depew, and Kate Hoffman were indefatigably helpful, and Anne Canright was a superb copy editor.

For crucial bits of information, inspiration, and friendship, I humbly thank Anne Beversdorf, Norma Beversdorf, Rebecca Gormezano Brown, Michael Bushnell, Eric Comstock, Stephanie Stein Crease, Elizabeth Davis, Scott DeVeaux, Armen Donelian, Brent Edwards, Barbara Fasano, Michael Feinstein, Steven Feld, Barbara File, Mike Fitzgerald, Caryl Flinn, Will Friedwald, Bernard Gendron, John Gennari, Fiona Goh, Ruth Goldberg, Maxine Gordon, Pamela Grace, Farah Jasmine Griffin, Philip Brian Harper, Andre Hurni, Travis Jackson, Thomas Jacobsen, Lia Benedetti Jarrico, Kay Kalinak, Peter Keepnews, Robin D.G. Kelley, Deborah Kempe, Bill Kenney, Tom Larson, Peter Lehman, George Lewis, George Lipsitz, Cindy Lucia, Bill Luhr, Joe Medjuck, Russell Merritt, Vera Micznik, Ivor Miller, Marcia Miller, Leslie Mitchner, Stewart Mitchner, Dan Morgenstern, Adrienne Munich, Richard Munich, Carol Oja, Robert G. O'Meally, Guy Ramsey, Jacqueline Reich, Roswell Rudd, Christopher Sharrett, Tad Shull, Mark Spencer, Louise O. Vasvari, Jans Wager, Chris Washburne, Susan White, Tony Whyton, and Carlota Zitreen. If I have somehow left you off this list, please forgive my fading memory and accept my heartfelt thanks for your help.

At Stony Brook University, I thank my chair, Robert Harvey, and Mary Moran-Luba, the absolutely indispensable woman in the office who takes care of just about everything even before I can think of what I need. Alinda Askew was equally indispensable.

My parents, Lucina Paquet Gabbard and Earnest Glendon Gabbard, died before I began working on this book. They were extraordinary people, and

I am still filled with wonder at all they accomplished and at all they did for me over so many years. I wonder what they would have thought of Mingus. I do know that my father, who waged a lifelong battle against what he called "hillbilly English," would not have approved of my title with its flagrant mispronunciation of get. I'm sorry, Gab.

Thanks always to Paula Gabbard: lover, editor, wife, friend, and companion for life.

Discography

This scaled-down, chronological guide to Mingus's recordings concentrates primarily on music that I discuss in the text. Essential items for serious Mingus listeners are asterisked (*). Unless otherwise indicated, every item is (or was recently) available on CD. For a much more complete Mingus discography, go to www.jazzdisco.org/charles-mingus/discography/.

Charles "Baron" Mingus, West Coast, 1945–49 (Uptown UPCD 27.48). Includes most of Mingus's early recordings as a sideman and as a leader.

Illinois Jacquet, *The Complete Illinois Jacquet Sessions, 1945–50* (Mosaic MD4–165).

Dinah Washington, *Mellow Mama* (Delmark DD-451), recorded December 1945.

Ivie Anderson and Her All Stars (Storyville SLP 804) (LP), recorded January 1946.

Lionel Hampton, *Sweatin' with Hamp* (MCA 1331) (LP), recorded 1947–50.

*Red Norvo, *The Red Norvo/Charles Mingus/Tal Farlow Trio* (Vintage Jazz Classics VJC 1008–2), recorded 1949–50.

Billy Taylor, *Jazz at Storyville* (Roost RLP 406) (LP), recorded November 1951.

From Barrelhouse to Bop: A History of Jazz Piano—Narrated and Played by John Mehegan with Charles Mingus, Bassist (Perspective PR 1) (LP), recorded late 1952.

Sonny Stitt, *The Complete Roost Sonny Stitt Studio Sessions* (Mosaic MD9–208), recorded 1952–65.

Charles Mingus, *Trios* (Jazz Door 1213), recorded March 1953 (with Bud Powell) and July 1957 (with Hampton Hawes).

Bud Powell, *Inner Fire* (Elektra Musician E160030) (LP), recorded April 1953.

*The Quintet, *The Greatest Jazz Concert Ever* (Original Jazz Classics OJCCD 044–2), recorded May 1953.

Miles Davis, *Blue Haze* (Prestige Original Jazz Classics OJC 093), recorded May 1953.

*Charles Mingus, *Complete Debut Recordings* (Debut 12-DCD 4402–2). This box set of twelve CDs contains everything recorded for the Debut label between 1953 and 1957.

Charlie Parker, *Bird: The Complete Charlie Parker Recordings on Verve* (Verve 837 141–2), recorded 1946–54.

J.J. Johnson/Kai Winding Quintet, *Complete Fifties Studio Recordings* (Lonehill Jazz [Sp]LHJ10179), recorded 1954.

J.J. Johnson, *The Eminent Jay Jay Johnson,* vol. 2 (Blue Note CDP 7 81506 2), recorded September 1954.

Charles Mingus, *Timeless* (Savoy SVY 17132), recorded October 1954. Also released as *Jazz Workshop* (Savoy SJL 1113).

*Charles Mingus, *Passions of a Man: The Complete Atlantic Recordings, 1956–1961* (Atlantic 72871). Contains all of Mingus's Atlantic records: *Pithecanthropus Erectus* (1956), *The Clown* (1957), *Tonight at Noon* (1957), *Blues and Roots* (1959), *Mingus at Antibes* (1960), and *Mingus, Oh Yeah* (1961), as well as a Teddy Charles session with Mingus, *The Word from Bird* (1956).

*Bill Evans and His Orchestra, *Brandeis Jazz Festival* (Gambit 69214), recorded June 1957. Includes Mingus's "Revelations."

*Charles Mingus, *Tijuana Moods* (RCA Victor Gold Series 74321749992), recorded July and August 1957.

Charles Mingus, *East Coasting* (Essential Jazz Classics 55471), recorded August 1957.

Charles Mingus, *A Modern Jazz Symposium of Music and Poetry* (Bethlehem BCP 6026), recorded October 1957.

Langston Hughes, Charles Mingus, and Leonard Feather, *Weary Blues* (Verve 841 660–2), recorded March 1958.

Charles Mingus, *Jazz Portraits* (Blue Note CDP 7243 8 27325 2 5), recorded January 1959. Also released as *Mingus in Wonderland* (United Artists UAJS 15005).

*Charles Mingus, *The Complete 1959 Columbia Recordings* (Columbia C3K 65145). Edited and unedited versions of the music on two LPs, *Mingus Dynasty* and *Mingus Ah Um*.

Charles Mingus, *Mingus Revisited* (Emarcy 826 496–2), recorded May 1960. Also released as *Mingus, Pre-Bird*.

*Charles Mingus, *The Complete Candid Recordings of Charles Mingus* (Mosaic MD3–111), recorded 1960.

Charles Mingus and the Jazz Workshop All Stars, *The Complete 1961–1962 Birdland Broadcasts* (Rare Live Recordings 88661).

*Duke Ellington Trio, *Money Jungle* (Blue Note 7243 5 38227), recorded September 1962.

Charles Mingus, *The Complete Town Hall Concert* (Blue Note CDP 7243 8 28353 2 5), recorded October 1962.

*Charles Mingus, *The Black Saint and the Sinner Lady* (impulse! IMPD-174), recorded January 1963.

Charles Mingus, *Mingus Plays Piano* (impulse! IMPD-217), recorded July 1963.

*Charles Mingus, *Mingus Mingus Mingus Mingus Mingus* (impulse! IMPD-170), recorded January and September 1963.

Charles Mingus Sextet with Eric Dolphy, *Cornell 1964* (Blue Note 0946 3930712), recorded March 1964.

*Charles Mingus, *The Jazz Workshop Concerts 1964–65* (Mosaic MD7–253).

Charles Mingus, *Revenge!* (Revenge 32002), recorded April 17, 1964.

*Charles Mingus, *Music Written for Monterey 1965. Not Heard . . . Played in Its Entirety at UCLA* (Sue Mingus Music SSC 3041), recorded December 1965.

Charles Mingus with Toshiyuki Miyama and His New Herd Orchestra, *Charles Mingus with Orchestra* (Denon CY 1388), recorded January 1971.

*Charles Mingus, *Let My Children Hear Music* (Columbia CK 48910), recorded September, October, and November 1971.

Charles Mingus and Friends in Concert (Columbia C2K 64975), recorded February 1972.

Charles Mingus, *Stormy and Funky Blues* (Moon MCD 064–2), recorded 1972–77.

Charles Mingus Quintet Meets Cat Anderson (Unique Jazz J20) (LP), recorded November 1972.

Charles Mingus, *Mingus Moves* (Atlantic SD 1653), recorded October 1973.

Charles Mingus, *Mingus at Carnegie Hall* (Atlantic SD 1667), recorded January 1974.

*Charles Mingus, *Changes One* (Atlantic R2 71403) and *Changes Two* (Atlantic R2 71404), recorded December 1974.

Charles Mingus, *Keystone Korner* (Jazz Door 1219), recorded April 1976.

Charles Mingus, *Three or Four Shades of Blues* (Atlantic 1700–2), recorded March 1977.

*Charles Mingus, *Cumbia and Jazz Fusion* (Rhino/Atlantic R2 71785), recorded March–April 1977.

Lionel Hampton *Presents the Music of Charles Mingus* (Who's Who in Jazz WWCD 21005), recorded November 1977.

Charles Mingus, *Something Like a Bird* (Atlantic SD 8803) and *Me, Myself an Eye* (Atlantic SD 8805), recorded January 1978.

Notes

INTRODUCTION: CHARLES MINGUS CHANGED MY LIFE

1. Listen to Previn's totally convincing jazz piano work on *Shelly Manne and his Friends: Modern Jazz Performances of Songs from "My Fair Lady"* (Contemporary CCD-7527–2), recorded August 1956.

2. Tony Whyton, *Beyond a Love Supreme: John Coltrane and the Legacy of an Album* (New York: Oxford University Press, 2013).

3. Scott Saul, *Freedom Is, Freedom Ain't: Jazz and the Making of the Sixties* (Cambridge, Mass.: Harvard University Press, 2003), 147. In 1955 Mingus himself wrote, "Just because I'm playing jazz I don't forget about *me*. I play or write *me*, the way I feel, through jazz or whatever. Music is, or was, a language of the emotions" (Charles Mingus, "An Open Letter to Miles Davis," *Down Beat*, November 30, 1955, 12–13).

4. Charles Mingus, *Changes One* (Atlantic R2 71403) and *Changes Two* (Atlantic R2 71404), both recorded December 1974.

5. Jack Walrath, conversation with the author, June 27, 2013.

6. Charles Mingus, *Beneath the Underdog: His World according to Mingus* (New York: Knopf, 1971).

7. Brian Priestley, *Mingus: A Critical Biography* (London: Quartet, 1982); Gene Santoro, *Myself When I Am Real: The Life and Music of Charles Mingus* (New York: Oxford University Press, 2000).

8. Janet Coleman and Al Young, *Mingus/Mingus: Two Memoirs* (Berkeley, Calif.: Creative Arts, 1989).

9. Sue Graham Mingus, *Tonight at Noon: A Love Story* (New York: Pantheon, 2002).

10. Buddy Collette, *Jazz Generations: A Life in American Music and Society* (London: Continuum, 2000); George Wein, *Myself among Others* (New York: Da Capo, 2003); Clark Terry, *The Autobiography of Clark Terry* (Berkeley: University of California Press, 2011); John F. Goodman, *Mingus Speaks* (Berkeley: University of California Press, 2013).

11. Eric Porter, "Passions of a Man: The Poetics and Politics of Charles Mingus," in *What Is This Thing Called Jazz? African American Musicians as Artists, Critics, and Activists* (Berkeley: University of California Press, 2002), 101–48; Saul, *Freedom Is;* John Gennari, *Blowin' Hot and Cool: Jazz and Its Critics* (Chicago: University of Chicago Press, 2006); Nichole T. Rustin, "Cante Hondo: Charles Mingus, Nat Hentoff, and Jazz Racism," *Critical Sociology* 32.2–3 (2006): 307–31; Jennifer Griffith, "Mingus in the Act: Confronting the Legacies of Vaudeville and Minstrelsy," *Jazz Perspectives* 4.3 (Winter 2010): 337–68.

12. *The Mingus Sisters Speak* (Audio CD), interview by Shelby Johnson (Sacramento, Calif.: Lacecap Records, 2001).

13. Willie Ruff, *A Call to Assembly: The Autobiography of a Musical Storyteller* (New York: Viking, 1991), 378–79.

14. Mingus wrote in 1965, however, that he had been in love "maybe twice." See Charles Mingus, liner notes to *Mingus at Monterey* (JWS 001 and 002).

15. Nat Hentoff, conversation with the author, September 5, 2011.

16. Mingus, *Beneath the Underdog*, 3.

PART I: A CIRCUS IN A BATHTUB

1. Kevin Jackson, *Constellation of Genius 1922: Modernism Year One* (New York: Farrar, Straus & Giroux, 2012).

2. F. Scott Fitzgerald, *Tales of the Jazz Age* (New York: Charles Scribner's Sons, 1922).

3. Ralph Ellison, "Going to the Territory," in *The Collected Essays of Ralph Ellison,* ed. John F. Callahan (New York: Modern Library, 1995), 608.

4. Whitney Balliett, "Mingus at Peace," *New Yorker*, May 29, 1971, 50.

5. Mingus, *Beneath the Underdog*, 8.

6. Charles Mingus, *Tijuana Moods* (RCA Victor Gold Series 74321749992), recorded July–August 1957.

7. Mingus, *Beneath the Underdog*, 128–29.

8. Philip Durham and Everett L. Jones, *The Negro Cowboys* (New York: Dodd, Mead, 1965), 10.

9. I made a pilgrimage to Nogales, Arizona, during the summer of 2013. When I crossed the border into Nogales, Mexico, I was simply waved in by a couple of uniformed officials. Getting back in was not so simple. I had brought my passport, but one of the Americans with whom I spent an hour standing in line to get through customs only had a driver's license. She spent a good twenty minutes talking her way back into the country.

10. Mingus, *Beneath the Underdog*, 66.

11. *Mingus Sisters Speak.*

12. Mingus, *Beneath the Underdog*, 121.

13. Ibid., 8.

14. Ibid., 124–33.

15. Kenneth Scambray, "The Literary and Immigrant Contexts of Simon Rodia's Watts Towers," in *Sabato Rodia's Towers in Watts: Art, Migrations,*

Development, ed. Luisa Del Giudice (New York: Fordham University Press, 2014), 151.

16. Mingus, *Beneath the Underdog,* 32.

17. Guglielmo Bilancioni, "Everybody Knows This is Nowhere: Structure and Performance in Rodia's Watts Towers," in Del Giudice (ed.), *Sabato Rodia's Towers,* 72.

18. Luisa Del Giudice, "Sabata Rodia's Towers in Watts: Art, Migration, and Italian Imaginaries," ibid., 162.

19. *I Build the Tower* (DVD), a film directed by Edward Landler and Brad Byer (2006).

20. Ibid.

21. Mingus, *Beneath the Underdog,* 37.

22. Thomas Harrison, "Without Precedent: The Watts Towers," in Del Giudice (ed.), *Sabato Rodia's Towers,* 93. The reference to the pier is in James Joyce, *Ulysses* (Oxford: Oxford University Press, [1922] 1998), 25.

23. I. Sheldon Posen and Daniel Franklin Ward, "Watts Towers and the *Giglio* Tradition," in *Folklife Annual: 1985,* edited by Alan Jabbour and James Hardin (Washington, D.C.: Library of Congress, 1985), 143–57.

24. John Szwed, *Space Is the Place: The Life and Times of Sun Ra* (New York: Pantheon, 1997), 134.

25. Don DeLillo, *Underworld* (New York: Scribner, 1997), 277.

26. Priestley, *Mingus,* 4.

27. *Mingus Sisters Speak.*

28. "Wednesday Night Prayer Meeting" is on Charles Mingus, *Blues and Roots* (Atlantic SD 1305) and *The Complete Atlantic Recordings, 1956–1961* (Atlantic 72871).

29. Louis Armstrong, *In his Own Words: Selected Writings,* edited by Thomas Brothers (New York: Oxford University Press, 1999), 170.

30. Thomas Brothers, *Louis Armstrong's New Orleans* (New York: Norton, 2006), 36.

31. Quoted in Nat Hentoff, liner notes for Milt Jackson, *Plenty, Plenty Soul* (Atlantic SD1269), recorded 1956 and 1957.

32. Johnny Otis, *Upside Your Head: Rhythm and Blues on Central Avenue* (Hanover, N.H.: University Press of New England, 1993), 12.

33. Mingus, *Beneath the Underdog,* 24.

34. James Weldon Johnson, *God's Trombones: Some Negro Sermons in Verse* (London: Allen & Unwin, 1929).

35. Ira Gitler, "Charlie Mingus—'Mingus Dynasty,'" *Down Beat,* July 19, 1960, 26.

36. Nat Hentoff, *The Jazz Life* (New York: Dial, 1961), 164.

37. Rustin, "Cante Hondo," 320.

38. "Duke Ellington's Sound of Love," sung by Jackie Paris, on *Changes Two* (Atlantic R2 71404).

39. Mingus, *Beneath the Underdog,* 27.

40. Santoro, *Myself When I Am Real,* 27.

41. Mingus, *Beneath the Underdog*, 69.

42. Ibid., 72. In his own memoir, Buddy Collette claims that he never heard his father speak to Mingus in such a way, though he does allow that Pop Collette might have taken his friend aside to dispense his wisdom (Collette, *Jazz Generations*, 24).

43. Mingus, *Beneath the Underdog*, 74 (emphasis in the original).

44. Charles Mingus, liner notes to *Let My Children Hear Music* (Columbia CK 48910). Award-giving organizations are notorious for overlooking the most deserving artists. As we might expect, Mingus was never nominated for a Grammy Award for his music. He was, however, nominated for his liner notes for this Columbia LP.

45. "Half-Mast Inhibition" is on *Mingus Revisited* (Emarcy 826 496–2), recorded May 1960. "What Love" is on *Charles Mingus Presents Charles Mingus* (Candid CCD 79005), recorded October 1960.

46. Santoro, *Myself When I Am Real*, 37–38.

47. Mingus, *Beneath the Underdog*, 25. The Mingus sisters also mention Mr. Arson as one of their teachers.

48. Listen, for example, to the tracks with Callender on Lester Young, *The Complete 1936–1951 Small Group Sessions, Vol. 4* (Blue Moon BMCD 1004), recorded August 1946.

49. Nel King, letter to Regina Ryan, June 14, 1971, in the Knopf Archive, Harry Ransom Center, University of Texas at Austin (hereafter cited as HRC).

50. Peter Danson, "Jimmy Knepper: An Interview," *Coda*, no. 179 (June 1981): 9.

51. Pepper Adams, interview by Gary Carner, *Cadence* 12.2 (February 1986): 21.

52. Collette, *Jazz Generations*, 23.

53. Gitler, "'Mingus Dynasty,'" 30.

54. "Far Wells, Mill Valley," recorded November 1959, is on Charles Mingus, *The Complete 1959 Columbia Recordings* (Columbia C3K 65145).

55. Collette, *Jazz Generations*, 32.

56. Duke Ellington, *Music Is My Mistress* (Garden City, N.Y.: Doubleday, 1973), 175.

57. Santoro, *Myself When I Am Real*, 52.

58. Klaus Stratemann, *Duke Ellington Day by Day and Film by Film* (Copenhagen: Jazz Media, 1992), 170.

59. In 1939, Ellington and Blanton duetted on "Blues" and "Plucked Again," now on Duke Ellington, *The Complete 1936–1940 Variety, Vocalion and Okeh Small Group Sessions* (Mosaic MD7–235). The 1940 Ellington/Blanton material—including the duets "Pitter Panther Patter," "Body and Soul," "Sophisticated Lady," and "Mr. J. B. Blues"—is on a set of three CDs: Duke Ellington, *Never No Lament: The Blanton-Webster Band* (RCA Bluebird 5659-2-RB).

60. Priestley, *Mingus*, 16.

61. Mingus, *Beneath the Underdog*, 110.

62. *Mingus Sisters Speak.*

63. Collette, *Jazz Generations,* 55.

64. Mingus, *Beneath the Underdog,* 108.

65. Gitler, "'Mingus Dynasty,'" 30.

66. Mingus, *Beneath the Underdog,* 122.

67. Collette, *Jazz Generations,* 25.

68. *Mingus Sisters Speak.*

69. E. Porter, "Passions of a Man," 142.

70. Jeanne Page, letter to Regina Ryan, October 10, 1970, HRC.

71. "Eclipse," recorded in October 1953, is on Charles Mingus, *The Complete Debut Recordings* (Debut 12-DCD 4402–2).

72. Santoro, *Myself When I Am Real,* 56.

73. The early Mingus recordings are collected on *Charles "Baron" Mingus, West Coast, 1945–49* (Uptown UPCD 27.48).

74. Miles Davis, *Blue Haze* (Prestige Original Jazz Classics OJC 093), recorded May 1953.

75. All recordings as well as the comments by Homzy are on *Charles "Baron" Mingus, West Coast, 1945–49* (Uptown UPCD 27.48).

76. E. Porter, "Passions of a Man," 109.

77. Daniel Widener, *Black Arts West: Culture and Struggle in Postwar Los Angeles* (Durham, N.C.: Duke University Press, 2010), 66.

78. Charles Mingus, letter to Sonny Rollins, June 20, 1961, Max Roach Collection, Library of Congress.

79. Santoro, *Myself When I Am Real,* 84.

80. Charles Mingus, interview by Nesuhi Ertegun, 1962, www.youtube.com/watch?v=couv9Gshveo.

81. Priestley, *Mingus,* 40.

82. "Story of Love" and "Boppin' in Boston" are on *Charles "Baron" Mingus, West Coast, 1945–49* (Uptown UPCD 27.48).

83. Priestley, *Mingus,* 44.

84. http://en.wikipedia.org/wiki/Morris_Levy.

85. Charles Mingus, interview by unidentified announcers, WKCR, 1971.

86. Nick Catalano, *Clifford Brown: The Life and Art of the Legendary Jazz Trumpeter* (New York: Oxford University Press, 2000), 185.

87. Santoro, *Myself When I Am Real,* 104.

88. Charles Mingus, letters to Max Roach, February 17 and 22, 1961, Max Roach Collection, Library of Congress.

89. Mingus, letter to Roach, October 12, 1961, Max Roach Collection, Library of Congress.

90. Wein, *Myself Among Others,* 92.

91. Santoro, *Myself When I Am Real,* 100.

92. Priestley, *Mingus,* 79

93. Ellington, *Music Is My Mistress,* 56.

94. A.H. Lawrence, *Duke Ellington and His World* (New York: Routledge, 2001), 340.

95. Mingus, *Beneath the Underdog*, 324. Tizol could in fact claim to be white. In 1930, when the Ellington band appeared in the film *Check and Double Check* with the white actors who played Amos and Andy on the radio, Tizol was, like the lead actors, blacked up. So was the band's "Colored Creole," clarinetist Barney Bigard, who would later pass for white and join the segregated musicians' union in Los Angeles before he was "exposed" for having black blood.

96. Mingus, *Beneath the Underdog*, 323–25.

97. Bill Crow, *Jazz Anecdotes* (New York: Oxford University Press, 1990), 315–16.

98. Terry, *Autobiography*, 149–50.

99. Santoro, *Myself When I Am Real*, 103.

100. D. Ellington, *Music Is My Mistress*, 244.

101. Robin D.G. Kelley, *Thelonious Monk: The Life and Times of an American Original* (New York: Free Press, 2009), 153.

102. Geoffrey Haydon, *Quintet of the Year* (London: Aurum, 2002), 83.

103. Ira Gitler, *Jazz Masters of the Forties* (New York: Collier, 1966), 122.

104. Guthrie P. Ramsey, Jr., *The Amazing Bud Powell: Black Genius, Jazz History, and the Challenge of Bebop* (Berkeley: University of California Press, 2013), 113. "The Glass Enclosure" is on Bud Powell, *The Complete Blue Note and Roost Recordings* (Blue Note CDP 7243 8 30083 2 2), recorded August 14, 1953.

105. Haydon, *Quintet of the Year*, 82.

106. Edward Berger, *Bassically Speaking: An Oral History of George Duvivier* (Metuchen, N.J.: Scarecrow Press, 1993), 115.

107. Ramsey, *Amazing Bud Powell*, 118.

108. E. Porter, "Passions of a Man," 112

109. All included in Charles Mingus, *The Complete Debut Recordings* (Debut 12-DCD 4402–2).

110. J.J. Johnson/Kai Winding Quintet, *Complete Fifties Studio Recordings* (Lonehill Jazz [Sp]LHJ10179). The first recordings of the group (with Mingus on bass) were made in August 1954.

111. Mark Miller, *Cool Blues: Charlie Parker in Canada 1953* (London: Nightwood, 1989), 12.

112. Max Roach, interview by Bob Rusch, *Cadence* 5.6 (June 1979): 6. Dizzy Gillespie repeats the story in Dizzy Gillespie with Al Fraser, *To Be or Not to Bop* (New York: Doubleday, 1979), 374.

113. Brian Priestley, e-mail message to the author, November 11, 2014.

114. Mike Hennessey, "Charles Mingus. Changed Man?" *Down Beat*, May 13, 1971, 131.

115. Haydon, *Quintet of the Year*, 106.

116. M. Miller, *Cool Blues*, 72.

117. Ramsey, *Amazing Bud Powell*, 116.

118. Haydon, *Quintet of the Year*, 147.

119. Gillespie, *To Be or Not to Bop*, 375.

120. M. Miller, *Cool Blues*, 94.

121. E. Porter, "Passions of a Man," 114.

122. Charles Mingus, typescript of autobiography, Charles Mingus Collection, Library of Congress, 97.

123. The material is on Charlie Parker, *Bird: The Complete Charlie Parker Recordings on Verve* (Verve 837 141–2), recorded 1946–54.

124. John Szwed, *So What: The Life of Miles Davis* (New York: Simon & Schuster, 2002), 105.

125. The Thad Jones material is on *The Complete Debut Recordings* (Debut 12-CD-4402–2).

126. Rafi Zabor, "Mingus in Europe, Vols. I & II," *Musician* 42 (1982): 71.

127. Nat Hentoff, "Mingus Dynasties," *Village Voice*, March 5/12, 1979, 34.

128. "Mingus on Mingus" (radio broadcast), Mingus interviewed by Greg Gallagher, 1974. The tape is part of the Mingus Collection in the Motion Picture, Broadcasting, and Recorded Sound Division, Library of Congress (hereafter referred to as MPB).

129. John LaPorta, *Playing It by Ear* (Redwood, N.Y.: Cadence, 2001), 111.

130. Ibid., 114.

131. Charles Mingus, *Timeless* (Savoy SVY 17132), recorded October 1954.

132. David Amram, *Vibrations: A Memoir* (New York: Thunder's Mouth, 2001), 223.

133. Santoro, *Myself When I Am Real*, 116.

134. Charles J. Gans, "Ted Curson: Memories of Mingus," *Jazz Forum* 57 (1979): 29.

135. "Mingus on Mingus," MPB.

136. Howard Johnson, interview by Bill Donaldson, *Cadence* 30.7 (July 2004): 11.

137. Diane Dorr-Dorynek, "Mingus," in *The Jazz Word*, ed. Dom Cerulli, Burt Korall, and Mort L. Nasatir (New York: Da Capo, 1987), 16–17.

138. Crow, *Jazz Anecdotes*, 351.

139. Max Gordon, *Live at the Village Vanguard* (New York: Da Capo, 1980), 107.

140. Ibid., 104.

141. Charles Mingus, *Pithecanthropus Erectus* (Atlantic SD 8809), recorded January 1956. Also on *The Complete Atlantic Recordings, 1956–1961* (Atlantic 72871).

142. Charles Mingus, *The Clown* (Atlantic LP 1260), recorded February–March1957. Also on *The Complete Atlantic Recordings, 1956–1961* (Atlantic 72871).

143. Saul, *Freedom Is, Freedom Ain't*, 153.

144. All of the music written for the Brandeis Festival is collected on *The Birth of Third Stream* (Columbia CK64929), recorded June 1957. Miles Davis's Third Stream recordings are also on this disc.

145. Gunther Schuller, conversation with the author, July 13, 2012.

146. Charles Mingus, *Tijuana Moods* (RCA Victor Gold Series 74321749992), recorded July–August 1957.

147. Charles Mingus, liner notes for *Tijuana Moods* (RCA Victor Gold Series 74321749992).

148. Don DeMichael, "Shavina Philosophy," *Down Beat*, January 30, 1964, 16.

149. "The Chill of Death" is on Charles Mingus, *Let My Children Hear Music* (Columbia CK 48910), recorded September–November 1971.

150. Krin Gabbard, *Jammin' at the Margins: Jazz and the American Cinema* (Chicago: University of Chicago Press, 1996), 304.

151. Mingus, *Beneath the Underdog*, 331–32.

152. Ibid., 328.

153. Coleman and Young, *Mingus/Mingus*, 22.

154. Santoro, *Myself When I Am Real*, 133.

155. A good survey of the literature on bipolar disorder can be found on the Mayo Clinic's website, www.mayoclinic.org/diseases-conditions/bipolar-disorder/basics/symptoms/con-20027544. In 2003, psychiatrist Geoffrey Wills wrote that Mingus had a "cyclothymic disorder," a mild form of bipolar disorder. See Wills, "Forty Lives in the Bebop Business: Mental Health in a Group of Eminent Jazz Musicians," *British Journal of Psychiatry* 183.3 (August 2003), available at http://bjp.rcpsych.org.ezproxy.cul.columbia.edu /content/183/3/255.

156. The first recording of "Diane" is on Charles Mingus, *The Complete 1959 Columbia Recordings* (Columbia C3K 65145), recorded November 1959.

157. Santoro, *Myself When I Am Real*, 132.

158. Charles Mingus, *East Coasting* (Essential Jazz Classics 55471), recorded August 1957; Charles Mingus, *A Modern Jazz Symposium of Music and Poetry* (Bethlehem BCP 6026), recorded October 1957.

159. Charles Mingus, *Blues and Roots* (Atlantic SD 1305), recorded February 1959. Also on *The Complete Atlantic Recordings, 1956–1961* (Atlantic 72871).

160. Along with several alternate takes, all the music originally released on *Mingus Ah Um* is collected on Charles Mingus, *The Complete 1959 Columbia Recordings* (Columbia C3K 65145).

161. Charles Mingus, *Mingus Mingus Mingus Mingus Mingus* (impulse! IMPD-170), recorded September 1963.

162. The Music from *Mingus Dynasty* is collected on Charles Mingus, *The Complete 1959 Columbia Recordings* (Columbia C3K 65145).

163. Santoro, *Myself When I Am Real*, 258.

164. Priestley, *Mingus*, 114.

165. Ibid., 115.

166. Gennari, *Blowin' Hot and Cold*, 248–49.

167. Ibid., 248.

168. Charles Mingus, *Mingus at Antibes* (Atlantic R2–72871), recorded July 1960.

169. Gene Lees, *Meet Me at Jim and Andy's: Jazz Musicians and Their World* (New York: Oxford University Press, 1988), xii.

170. Mingus, *Beneath the Underdog*, 353–54.

171. Saul, *Freedom Is, Freedom Ain't*, 179.

172. Priestley, *Mingus*, 127.

173. Santoro, *Myself When I Am Real*, 186.

174. *Mingus Sisters Speak.*

175. Several of Akiyoshi's performances with Mingus are collected on the three-disc set Charles Mingus and the Jazz Workshop All Stars, *The Complete 1961–1962 Birdland Broadcasts* (Rare Live Recordings 88661).

176. Jack Lind, "Ted Curson's Story: Life with Mingus," *Village Voice*, Jazz Supplement, June 10, 1997, 14.

177. Toshiko Akiyoshi/Lew Tabackin Big Band, *Farewell to Mingus* (RCA BVCJ-35007), recorded January 1980.

178. Duke Ellington, *Money Jungle* (Blue Note 7243 5 38227), recorded September 1962.

179. Duke Ellington, *Meets Count Basie* (Columbia CK 65571), recorded July 1961.

180. Louis Armstrong and Duke Ellington, *The Great Summit* (Roulette 7243 5 24547), recorded April 1961.

181. *Duke Ellington Meets Coleman Hawkins* (impluse! IMPD-162), recorded August 1962; *Duke Ellington and John Coltrane* (impulse! IMPD-166), recorded September 1962.

182. www.noisemademedoit.com/miles-davis-blind-listening-test/

183. D. Ellington, *Music Is My Mistress*, 243–44.

184. Ibid., 243.

185. Goodman, *Mingus Speaks*, 142.

186. www.npr.org/2008/04/23/89852381/charles-mingus-fables-of-bass-part-1.

187. Ross Firestone, e-mail message to the author, April 7, 2014.

188. John Litweiler, "There's a Mingus among Us," *Down Beat*, February 27, 1975, 13.

189. Brian Priestley, liner notes for *Charles Mingus, The Complete Town Hall Concert* (Blue Note CDP 7243 8 28353).

190. Collette, *Jazz Generations*, 26.

191. Santoro, *Myself When I Am Real*, 203.

192. Priestley, liner notes for *Charles Mingus, The Complete Town Hall Concert.*

193. Priestley, *Mingus*, 140.

194. Santoro, *Myself When I Am Real*, 210.

195. Edmund Pollock [*sic*], liner notes for Charles Mingus, *The Black Saint and the Sinner Lady* (impulse! IMPD-174).

196. Richard Taruskin, "Defending Classical Music against Its Devotees," *New Republic*, October 22, 2007, 36.

197. Pollack, liner notes for Mingus, *Black Saint and Sinner Lady.*

198. Santoro, *Myself When I Am Real,* 212.

199. Charles Mingus, *Mingus Plays Piano* (impulse! IMPD-217), recorded July 1963.

200. Charles Mingus, *Mingus Mingus Mingus Mingus Mingus* (impulse! IMPD-170), recorded January and September 1963.

201. Bob Thiele and Bob Golden, *What a Wonderful World: A Lifetime of Recordings* (New York: Oxford University Press, 1995), 132.

202. The first recordings of the quartet are on *Charles Mingus Sextet with Eric Dolphy, Cornell 1964* (Blue Note 0946 3930712), recorded March 1964, and Charles Mingus, *Town Hall Concert* (Prestige OJCCD 042–2), recorded April 4, 1964. Music from the European tour of April 1964 appears on multiple CDs, many of them bootlegged. Sue Mingus authorized the release of the Paris concert of April 18, 1964, on *Revenge! The Legendary Paris Concert* on her own Revenge label.

203. "What Love" is on *Charles MingusPresents Charles Mingus* (Candid CCD 79005), recorded October 1960.

204. Philip Clark, "Black Saints and Jive Ass Slippers," *Jazz Review* 28 (January 2002): 22.

205. Priestley, *Mingus,* 156.

206. Mingus, *Beneath the Underdog,* 250.

207. Bill Whitworth, "The Rich Full Life of Charlie Mingus," *New York Herald-Tribune,* November 1, 1964, 41.

208. Santoro, *Myself When I Am Real,* 231.

209. S. Mingus, *Tonight at Noon.*

210. Ibid., 28.

211.. Ibid., 73.

212. Ibid., 56. Shortly after I read this section of Sue's memoir, I was chatting with a female colleague. I told her about the light show that Mingus provided in hopes of gaining Sue's attention. I then asked my colleague, "Have you even been romanced like that?" She replied, "Only by womanizers."

213. Howard Johnson, e-mail message to the author, April 13, 2015. "They Trespass . . ." is on *Music Written for Monterey 1965. Not Heard . . . Played in Its Entirety at UCLA* (Sue Mingus Music SSC 3041), recorded December 1965.

214. S. Mingus, *Tonight at Noon,* 58.

215. "Sue's Changes" is on Charles Mingus, *Changes One* (Atlantic R2 71403).

216. Charles Mingus, *Mingus at Monterey* (Rhino/Atlantic R2–71402), recorded September 1964.

217. S. Mingus, *Tonight at Noon,* 36.

218. Mario Dunkel, *Aesthetics of Resistance: Charles Mingus and the Civil Rights Movement* (Zurich: Lit Verlag, 2012), 29.

219. In 1959, however, Ellison wrote benevolently about the "revolution" created by the boppers in the early 1940s. See "The Golden Age, Time Past," in *The Collected Essays of Ralph Ellison,* ed. John F. Callahan (New York: Modern Library, 1995), 237–49.

220. Albert Murray and John F. Callahan, eds., *Trading Twelves: The Selected Letters of Ralph Ellison and Albert Murray* (New York: Modern Library, 2000), 155.

221. Ralph Ellison, *Living with Music: Ralph Ellison's Jazz Writings*, ed. Robert G. O'Meally (New York: Modern Library, 2001), 265.

222. Ralph Ellison, *Invisible Man* (New York: Vintage, 1972), 8.

223. "Eat That Chicken" is on Charles Mingus, *Mingus Oh, Yeah!* (Atlantic SD 1377), recorded November 1961. Also on *The Complete Atlantic Recordings, 1956–1961* (Atlantic 72871).

224. Saul, *Freedom Is, Freedom Ain't,* 264.

225. Charles Mingus, *Music Written for Monterey 1965.*

226. Priestley, *Mingus,* 167.

227. Martin Niemöller, "First They Came for the Socialists . . .," www .ushmm.org/wlc/en/article.php?ModuleId=10007392.

228. Howard Johnson, conversation with the author, February 14, 2015.

229. Goodman, *Mingus Speaks,* 247.

230. I confess that my devotion to jazz was tested when so many of my college friends were listening to the psychedelia of the Beatles and the topical satire of Frank Zappa and the Mothers of Invention. When Mingus was at his most depressed, I was listening to more pop music than to jazz. I was not the only young person in the late 1960s who was, at least briefly, drifting away from jazz.

231. Santoro (*Myself When I Am Real,* 274) writes that Mingus was taking mellaril, a thorazine-like medication.

232. Nat Hentoff, "Mingus: 'I Thought I Was Finished,'" *New York Times,* January 30, 1972, D17.

233. Priestley, *Mingus,* 179.

234. Hentoff, "I Thought I Was Finished,'" D17.

235. John Kruth, *Bright Moments: The Life and Legacy of Rahsaan Roland Kirk* (New York: Welcome Rain, 2000), 245.

236. Charles Mingus, *Let My Children Hear Music* (Columbia 48910), recorded September–November 1971

237. *Charles Mingus and Friends in Concert* (Columbia C2K 64975), recorded February 1972.

238. S. Mingus, *Tonight at Noon,* 110.

239. Ibid.

240. Ibid., 110–11.

241. Ruff, *Call to Assembly,* 375.

242. Ibid.

243. It was no coincidence that by 1972 I had stopped buying pop music and had returned to jazz. I was assiduously collecting Duke Ellington records, a massive undertaking, as well as the recordings of Mingus, of which there were never enough.

244. Charles Mingus, "An Open Letter to the Avant-Garde," in *More Than a Fake Book,* ed. Sue Mingus (New York: Jazz Workshop, 1991), 119.

245. Charles Mingus, *Mingus at Carnegie Hall* (Atlantic SD 1667), recorded January 1974.

246. Peter Keepnews, "Caught: Charles Mingus and Old Friends, Carnegie Hall, New York City," *Down Beat*, March 28, 1974, 34.

247. Charles Mingus, *Changes One* (Atlantic R2 71403) and *Changes Two* (R2 71404), both recorded December 1974

248. Bret Primack, "The Gospel According to Mingus: Disciples Carry the Tune," *Down Beat*, December 7, 1978, 40.

249. Santoro, *Myself When I Am Real*, 393.

250. William Matthews, "Mingus in Diaspora," in *Search Party: Collected Poems* (New York: Houghton Mifflin Harcourt, 2005), 243.

251. Portions of this broadcast are included in the film *Charles Mingus: Triumph of the Underdog* (1998), directed by Don McGlynn.

252. Gordon, *Live at the Village Vanguard*, 108.

253. This material is on Charles Mingus, *Three or Four Shades of Blues* (Atlantic 1700–2), recorded March 1977.

254. Gary Giddins, *Visions of Jazz: The First Century* (New York: Oxford University Press, 1998), 453.

255. Charles Mingus, *Cumbia and Jazz Fusion* (Rhino/Atlantic R2 71785), recorded March–April 1977.

256. Lionel Hampton, *Presents the Music of Charles Mingus* (Who's Who in Jazz WWCD 21005), recorded November 1977.

257. Santoro, *Myself When I Am Real*, 365.

258. Armen Donelian, interview by Bob Rusch, *Cadence* 11.10 (October 1985): 30.

259. Arnold Jay Smith, "Charles Mingus: Developmental Changes," *Down Beat*, January 12, 1978, 22.

260. Charles Mingus, *Something Like a Bird* (Atlantic SD 8803) and *Me, Myself an Eye* (Atlantic SD 8805), both recorded January 1978.

261. Sy Johnson, "Charles Mingus: April 22, 1922–January 5, 1979," *Jazz Magazine*, Spring 1979, 46.

262. S. Mingus, *Tonight at Noon*, 134.

263. Collette, *Jazz Generations*, 38.

264. Joni Mitchell, *Mingus* (Asylum CD 505), recorded spring 1979.

265. David Yaffe, conversation with the author, September 28, 2013.

266. Annie Ross's first recording of "Twisted" is on *King Pleasure Sings/ Annie Ross Sings* (Prestige OJC CD217–2), recorded October 1952. "Centerpiece" and a later version of "Twisted" are on Lambert, Hendricks, and Ross, *The Hottest New Group in Jazz* (Columbia/Legacy C2K 64933), recorded August 1959.

267. Yaffe conversation.

268. Ibid.

269. "Eclipse," recorded October 28, 1953, is on Charles Mingus, *The Complete Debut Recordings* (Debut 12-CD-4402–2).

270. Santoro, *Myself When I am Real*, 376.

271. Yaffe conversation.

272. http://en.wikipedia.org/wiki/Mingus_(Joni_Mitchell_album).

273. www.rollingstone.com/music/news/joni-mitchell-defends-herself-19790726.

274. www.cbc.ca/archives/categories/arts-entertainment/music/joni-mitchell-all-sides-now/jonis-jazz.html.

275. http://jonimitchell.com/library/video.cfm?id=382. I thank David Yaffe for these references.

276. S. Mingus, *Tonight at Noon*, 175.

277. John S. Wilson, "Carter Opens Home to Jazz as an Art," *New York Times*, June 19, 1978, C13.

278. Nan Robertson, "Duke Ellington, 70, Honored at White House," *New York Times*, April 30, 1969, 1.

279. Wein, *Myself among Others*, 418.

280. Santoro, *Myself When I Am Real*, 379.

281. S. Mingus, *Tonight at Noon*, 185.

282. Ibid., 187.

283. Ibid., 189.

284. Ibid., 205.

285. Kevin Ellington Mingus, conversation with the author, April 2, 2015.

286. Ira Gitler, liner notes for Charles Mingus, *The Complete Debut Recordings* (Debut 12-CD-4402–2), 18.

287. Collette, *Jazz Generations*, 37.

288. Ibid., 39.

289. S. Mingus, *Tonight at Noon*, 242.

290. *Mingus Sisters Speak.*

291. Brian Priestley, *Chasin' the Bird: The Life and Legacy of Charlie Parker* (New York: Oxford University Press, 2005), 126.

PART II: POET, LYRICIST, AUTOBIOGRAPHER

1. Vilde Aaslid, "The Poetic Mingus and the Politics of Genre in String Quartet No. 1," *Journal of the Society for American Music* 9.1 (2015): 1–25.

2. Saul, *Freedom Is, Freedom Ain't*, 204.

3. *Triumph of the Underdog* (1998).

4. Mingus, liner notes to *Pithecanthropus Erectus* (Atlantic SD 8809).

5. Mingus, *Beneath the Underdog*, 361.

6. Santoro, *Myself When I Am Real*, 222.

7. Amiri Baraka, *The Autobiography of LeRoi Jones* (New York: Freundlich, 1984), 121.

8. Santoro, *Myself When I Am Real*, 151.

9. Baraka, *Autobiography of LeRoi Jones*, 183.

10. Santoro, *Myself When I Am Real*, 21.

11. "Mingus on Music," radio broadcast with unidentified interviewer, n.d., MPB.

12. Kathryne V. Lindberg, "Mister Joans, to You: Readerly Surreality and Writerly Affiliation in Ted Joans, Tri-Continental Ex-Beatnik," *Discourse* 20.1–2 (1998): 198–222.

13. Ted Joans, *Black Pow-Wow: Jazz Poems* (New York: Hill & Wang, 1969).

14. James Smethurst, "'Remembering When Indians Were Red': Bob Kaufman, the Popular Front, and the Black Arts Movement," *Callaloo* 25.1 (2002): 148.

15. Ibid., 158.

16. Lyrics to all those songs can be found in Mingus, *More Than a Fake Book*, ed. Sue Mingus (New York: Jazz Workshop, 1991).

17. Priestley, *Mingus*, 36.

18. "Eclipse," vocal by Janet Thurlow, recorded October 28, 1953, can be found on Charles Mingus, *The Complete Debut Recordings* (Debut 12-CD-4402–2); vocal by Lorraine Cousins, recorded May 1960, on *Mingus Revisited* (Emarcy 826 496–2); and vocal by Honey Gordon, recorded February 1972, on *Charles Mingus and Friends in Concert* (Columbia C2K 64975).

19. Saul, *Freedom Is, Freedom Ain't*, 185.

20. Mingus, autobiography typescript, 257.

21. Mingus, *Beneath the Underdog*, 204.

22. "Freedom" is on the CD release of *Mingus Mingus Mingus Mingus Mingus* (impulse! IMPD-170).

23. Charles Mingus, "This Mule Ain't from Moscow," *Down Beat*, October 3, 1956, 4.

24. Charles Mingus, *The Complete Town Hall Concert* (Blue Note CDP 7243 8 28353 2 5), recorded October 12, 1962. "Freedom" is the first track on the CD.

25. "Duke Ellington's Sound of Love" is on *Changes Two* (Atlantic R2 71404).

26. Mingus, autobiography typescript, 421–22.

27. Charles Mingus, untitled and undated poem, MPB. I have chosen where to break the poem into stanzas.

28. Dawn Frank, conversation with the author, December 1, 2010.

29. Christopher Harlos, "Jazz Autobiography: Theory, Practice, Politics," in *Jazz among the Discourses*, ed. Krin Gabbard (Durham, N.C.: Duke University Press, 1995), 132.

30. Ibid., 144.

31. For example, Lambert, Hendricks, and Ross sing Hendricks's lyrics on "Doodlin'" on *Improvisations for the Human Voice* (El Records ACMEM 168CD), recorded October 1958. Also see www.youtube.com/results?search_query=lambert+hendricks+and+ross+doodlin+

32. Rex Stewart, *Boy Meets Horn*, ed. Claire P. Gordon (Ann Arbor: University of Michigan Press, 1991).

33. Rex Stewart, *Jazz Masters of Thirties* (New York: Macmillan, 1972).

34. Louis Armstrong, *Satchmo: My Life in New Orleans* (New York: Prentice-Hall, 1954).

35. Kevin McNeilly, "Charles Mingus Splits, or All the Things You Could Be by Now if Sigmund Freud's Wife Was Your Mother," *Canadian Review of American Studies* 27.2 (1997): 51.

36. Albert Murray, *Good Morning Blues: The Autobiography of Count Basie* (New York: Random House, 1985).

37. Albert Murray, conversation with the author, April 13, 2004.

38. Murray, *Good Morning Blues*, 17.

39. Hampton Hawes and Don Asher, *Raise Up Off Me* (New York: Coward, McCann & Geoghegan, 1974).

40. Art Pepper and Laurie Pepper, *Straight Life: The Story of Art Pepper*, updated ed. (New York: Da Capo, 1994), 478.

41. Lili Anolik, "The Tale of the Tape," *Harper's*, September 2014, 89–94.

42. Billie Holiday with William T. Dufty, *Lady Sings the Blues* (Garden City, N.Y.: Doubleday, 1956).

43. John Szwed, *Billie Holiday: The Musician and the Myth* (New York: Viking, 2015), 27–53.

44. Farah Jasmine Griffin, *If You Can't Be Free, Be a Mystery: In Search of Billie Holiday* (New York: Free Press, 2001), 46.

45. Szwed, *Billie Holiday*, 27–53.

46. Robert G. O'Meally, *Lady Day: The Many Faces of Billie Holiday* (New York: Arcade, 1991), 21.

47. Holiday, *Lady Sings the Blues*, 5.

48. Louis Armstrong, *Louis Armstrong, in His Own Words: Selected Writings*, ed. Thomas Brothers (New York: Oxford University Press, 1999).

49. Louis Armstrong, *Swing That Music* (1936; reprint, New York: Da Capo, 1993).

50. William Howland Kenney, "Negotiating the Color Line: Louis Armstrong's Autobiographies," in *Jazz in Mind: Essays on the History and Meanings of Jazz*, ed. Reginald T. Buckner and Steven Weiland (Detroit: Wayne State University Press, 1991), 38–59.

51. Armstrong, *Satchmo*, 209.

52. Kenney, "Negotiating the Color Line," 51.

53. Armstrong, *In His Own Words*, 3–36.

54. James Lincoln Collier, *Duke Ellington* (New York: Oxford University Press, 1987), 295.

55. Mercer Ellington, with Stanley Dance, *Duke Ellington in Person: An Intimate Memoir* (Boston: Houghton Mifflin, 1978), 172.

56. Duke Ellington, *Music Is my Mistress*, (Garden City, N.Y.: Doubleday, 1973),164.

57. Lawrence, *Duke Ellington and His World*, 356.

58. Ellington, *Duke Ellington in Person*, 236.

59. Ellington, *Music Is my Mistress*,135.

60. Edward Morrow, "Duke Ellington on Gershwin's 'Porgy'" (1935), in *The Duke Ellington Reader*, ed. Mark Tucker(New York: Oxford University Press, 1993), 114–17.

61. Ellington, *Music Is my Mistress,*104–6.

62. Gama Gilbert, "'Hot Damn!' Says Ellington When Ranked with Bach" (1935), in Tucker (ed.), *Duke Ellington Reader,* 113.

63. Ajay Heble, *Landing on the Wrong Note: Jazz, Dissonance, and Critical Practice* (New York: Routledge, 2000), 115; italics in the original.

64. Daniel Stein, "The Performance of Jazz Autobiography," *Genre* 37.2 (2004): 195.

65. Mingus, *Beneath the Underdog,* 229.

66. Ibid., 251.

67. Goodman, *Mingus Speaks,* 308.

68. Mingus, *Beneath the Underdog,* 140.

69. Miles Davis with Quincy Troupe, *Miles: The Autobiography* (New York: Simon & Schuster, 1989).

70. Pearl Cleage, "Mad at Miles," in *The Miles Davis Companion: Four Decades of Commentary,* ed. Gary Carner (New York: Schirmer, 1996), 214.

71. Quincy Troupe, "Miles Style," *Spin,* November 1988, 72–79.

72. Jack Chambers, *Milestones: The Music and Times of Miles Davis,* rev. ed. (New York: Da Capo, 1998). Stanley Crouch, "Play the Right Thing," *New Republic,* February 12, 1990, 30, 37.

73. Chambers, *Milestones,* xxiii.

74. Davis and Troupe, *Miles,* 9.

75. See, for example, Dan Morgenstern, "Liner notes to Miles Davis, *The Complete Prestige Recordings,*" in *The Miles Davis Companion: Four Decades of Commentary,* ed. Gary Carner (New York: Schirmer, 1996), 18.

76. Davis and Troupe, *Miles,* 202.

77. Ibid., 227.

78. Quincy Jones, "I Just Adored That Man," in *Miles Davis and American Culture,* ed. Gerald Early (St. Louis: Missouri Historical Society Press, 2001), 43.

79. Burt Korall, "Mingus on Mingus," *Saturday Review,* July 31, 1971, 42.

80. Mingus, *Beneath the Underdog,* 313.

81. Sidney Bechet, *Treat It Gentle* (1960; reprint, New York: Da Capo, 1978).

82. Jessica Teague, conversation with the author, June 26, 2013.

83. Jessica Teague, "Ears Taut to Hear: Sound Recording and Twentieth-Century American Literature," Ph.D. diss., Columbia University, 2013, 121.

84. Ibid., 125–26.

85. Bryan Wagner, "Disarmed and Dangerous: The Strange Career of Bras-Coupé," *Representations* 92 (2005): 117–51.

86. Ibid., 131.

87. Ibid., 149.

88. Bechet, *Treat It Gentle,* 8.

89. Lyle Saxon, Edward Dreyer, and Robert Tallant, *Gumbo Ya-ya* (Boston: Houghton Mifflin, 1945.)

90. Teague, "Ears Taut to Hear," 125.

91. John Chilton, *Sidney Bechet: The Wizard of Jazz* (New York: Oxford University Press, 1987), 291.

92. Ibid., 292.

93. Wagner, "Disarmed and Dangerous," 138.

94. Nel King, letter to Regina Ryan, June 14, 1971, HRC.

95. Balliett, "Mingus at Peace," 44.

96. "Mingus on Mingus," MPB.

97. Regina Ryan, conversation with the author, August 16, 2013.

98. Nel King, "Preston Sturges," *Monthly Film Bulletin* 28 (Summer/ Autumn 1958): 185.

99. Nel King, application for grant from the Louis M. Rabinowitz Foundation, Inc., April 26, 1969, HRC.

100. Gary Giddins, *Natural Selection: Gary Giddins on Comedy, Film, Music, and Books* (New York: Oxford University Press, 2006), xiii.

101. Dan Lacy, letter to Charles Mingus, May 6, 1969, HRC.

102. Bob Hunter, "What Is Charlie Mingus Seeking?" *Chicago Daily Defender*, August 30, 1962, 19.

103. "Bassist Mingus Heads for Venice, May Quit U.S," *Jet*, August 30, 1962, 12.

104. Coleman and Young, *Mingus/Mingus*, 8.

105. Goodman, *Mingus Speaks*, 248.

106. Regina Ryan, e-mail message to the author, September 6, 2014.

107. Goodman, *Mingus Speaks*, 305–6.

108. Mingus, letter to Nel King, September 1, 1969, HRC.

109. Regina Ryan, contract to publish *Beneath the Underdog*, November 2, 1969, HRC.

110. Mingus, letter to Regina Ryan, September 27, 1970, HRC.

111. Nel King, letter to Charles Mingus, September 6, 1970, HRC.

112. King, letter to Mingus, September 6, 1970, HRC.

113. King, letter to Regina Ryan, July 25, 1970, 42, HRC.

114. Ibid., 33.

115. King, letter to Ryan, June 14, 1971, HRC.

116. Ibid.

117. King, letter to Ryan, October 12, 1970, HRC.

118. "Obituaries: Nel King," *Variety*, Dec 23, 1977, 21.

119. Ryan conversation.

120. King, "Preston Sturges."

121. "Knopf Editorial Fact Sheet" on *Beneath the Underdog*, n.d., HRC.

122. Ryan, e-mail message.

123. Janet Coleman, conversation with the author, April 5, 2009.

124. Goodman, *Mingus Speaks*, 309.

125. Mingus, interview on WKCR, 1971.

126. *Mingus Sisters Speak*.

127. Ibid.

128. Ryan conversation.

129. Mingus, *Beneath the Underdog*, no page number.

130. E. Porter, "Passions of a Man," 113.

131. Mingus, *Beneath the Underdog*, 3.

132. "Self-Portrait in Three Colors" is on Charles Mingus, *The Complete 1959 Columbia Recordings* (Columbia C3K 65145).

133. Laura Marcus, *Auto/biographical Discourses: Theory, Criticism, Practice* (Manchester, UK: Manchester University Press, 1994).

134. Farah Griffin's *If You Can't Be Free, Be a Mystery* is an excellent example of a writer framing her understanding of her subject within her own experience. I have tried to follow Griffin's example in the book you are now reading.

135. Marcus, *Auto/biographical Discourses*, 275, writing about André Gorz, *The Traitor* (New York: Verso, 1989).

136. Marcus, *Auto/biographical Discourses* 276.

137. W.E.B. Du Bois, *The Souls of Black Folk* (1903; reprint, New York: Knopf, 1993), 9.

138. Thomas Carmichael, "Beneath the Underdog: Charles Mingus, Representation, and Jazz Autobiography," *Canadian Review of American Studies* 25.3 (1995): 40.

139. Mingus, *Beneath the Underdog*, 328.

140. Mingus, autobiography typescript, 10.

141. Pollack, liner notes to *Black Saint and Sinner Lady*.

142. Harlos, "Jazz Autobiogrphy," 141.

143. Mingus, interview by Sy Johnson, Jazz Oral History Project, Institute of Jazz Studies, Rutgers University, Newark, N.J., 1977.

144. David Yaffe, *Fascinating Rhythm: Reading Jazz in American Writing* (Princeton, N.J.: Princeton University Press, 2006), 167.

145. Philip Roth, *Portnoy's Complaint* (New York: Random House, 1969), 285.

146. Mingus, *Beneath the Underdog*, 228.

147. McNeilly, "Charles Mingus Splits," 62.

148. "Celia" is on *Mingus Mingus Mingus Mingus Mingus* (impulse! IMPD-170); "Diane" on *The Complete 1959 Columbia Recordings* (Columbia C3K 65145); "Peggy's Blue Skylight" on *Tonight at Noon* (Atlantic SD 1416); "Sue's Changes" on *Changes One* (Atlantic R2 71403).

149. Mingus, *Beneath the Underdog*, 354.

150. Ibid., 296.

151. Ibid., 201.

152. Ibid., 84.

153. Rustin, "Cante Hondo," 322.

154. Mingus, autobiography typescript, 205.

155. Ibid., 214.

156. Mingus, *Beneath the Underdog*, 142.

157. E. Porter, "Passions of a Man," 143.

158. Gordon, *Live at the Village Vanguard*, 107–8.

159. Mingus, *Beneath the Underdog*, 141.

160. Ibid., 211–12.

161. Ibid., 212.

162. Mingus, autobiography typescript 279–87; *Beneath the Underdog,* 212–17.

163. E. Porter, "Passions of a Man," 141.

164. Mingus, *Beneath the Underdog,* 267.

165. "My Jelly Roll Soul" is on *Blues and Roots* (Atlantic SD 1305) and *The Complete Atlantic Recordings, 1956–1961* (Atlantic 72871); "Jelly Roll" on *The Complete 1959 Columbia Recordings* (Columbia C3K 65145).

166. Jelly Roll Morton, *The Complete Library of Congress Recordings by Alan Lomax* (Rounder Records CD 11661–1888–2), recorded May–June 1938; Gunther Schuller, *Early Jazz: Its Roots and Musical Development* (New York: Oxford University Press, 1968), 134

167. Mingus, *Beneath the Underdog,* 267–77.

168. Goodman, *Mingus Speaks,* 312.

169. Mingus, *Beneath the Underdog,* 141.

170. *Let My Children Hear Music* (Columbia CK 48910).

PART III: THIRD STREAM MUSIC AND
THE REST OF JAZZ HISTORY

1. Mingus, *Beneath the Underdog,* 4–5.

2. Priestley, *Mingus,* 162.

3. Nel King, letter to Regina Ryan, June 14, 1971, HRC

4. Priestley, *Mingus,* 141.

5. Mingus, *Beneath the Underdog,* 353.

6. Jack Walrath, conversation with the author, June 27, 2013.

7. Ralph Gleason, "Charlie Mingus: A Thinking Musician," *Down Beat,* June 1, 1951, 7.

8. Geoff Dyer, *But Beautiful: A Book about Jazz* (New York: North Point Press, 1996), 107.

9. David Stowe, *Swing Changes: Big Band Jazz in New Deal America* (Cambridge, Mass.: Harvard University Press, 1994), 130.

10. Barney Bigard, *With Louis and the Duke: The Autobiography of a Jazz Clarinetist* (New York: Oxford University Press, 1988).

11. Ibid., 82.

12. Ibid.

13. Gabbard, *Jammin' at the Margins,* 78–80.

14. Davis and Troupe, *Miles,* 45.

15. Mingus, interview with Ertegun.

16. Scott DeVeaux, *The Birth of Bebop: A Social and Musical History* (Berkeley: University of California Press, 1997).

17. "It's the Talk of the Town," recorded September 1933, is on *Classic Coleman Hawkins Session, 1922–1947* (Mosaic MD8–251).

18. Coleman Hawkins, *Body and Soul* (RCA 5717–2-RB).

19. Priestley, *Chasin' the Bird,* 53.

20. "Lover Man," recorded July 1946, is on Charlie Parker, *The Complete Savoy and Dial Studio Recordings, 1944–1948* (Savoy 92911–2).

21. "Relaxing on Camarillo," recorded February 1947, is also on *The Complete Savoy and Dial Studio Recordings.*

22. Mingus plays with Hawkins on *The Complete Jazz at the Philharmonic on Verve* (Verve 314 523 893–2), 1944–49; and with McGhee on *Modern Trumpet Leaders* (IAJRC 25) (LP).

23. Most of the music that Mingus arranged for Washington is on Dinah Washington, *Mellow Mama* (Delmark DD-451), recorded December 1945.

24. All of Hampton's small-group recordings from the late 1930s are on the five-CD set *The Complete Lionel Hampton Victor Sessions, 1937–1942* (Mosaic MD5–238).

25. "Flying Home" is on Lionel Hampton, *Hamp—The Legendary Decca Recordings of Lionel Hampton* (Decca GRD-2–652).

26. Hampton's recording of "Mingus Fingers" is on *Charles "Baron" Mingus, West Coast, 1945–49* (Uptown UPCD 27.48). Recordings of Hampton from the same period are on Lionel Hampton, *Sweatin' with Hamp* (MCA 1331), recorded 1947–1950.

27. *Mingus Sisters Speak.*

28. Norvo's bop band can be heard on Charlie Parker, *The Complete Savoy and Dial Studio Recordings, 1944–1948* (Savoy, 92911–2).

29. See, for example, Burt Korall's liner notes for the Red Norvo Trio with Tal Farlow and Charles Mingus, *The Savoy Sessions* (Savoy SV-0267).

30. Gary Giddins, conversation with the author, August 8, 2012.

31. "Crewcut Contest's $," *Down Beat*, November 4, 1949, 1.

32. Gennari, *Blowin' Hot and Cool*, 207.

33. The studio as well as the live recordings of the group are collected on Miles Davis, *The Complete Birth of the Cool* (Capitol CDP 594550), recorded 1948–1950.

34. Red Norvo, *The Red Norvo/Charles Mingus/Tal Farlow Trio* (Vintage Jazz Classics VJC 1008–2), recorded 1949–1950.

35. *The Greatest Jazz Concert Ever* (Original Jazz Classics OJCCD 044–2), recorded May 1953.

36. *From Barrelhouse To Bop: A History Of Jazz Piano—Narrated and Played by John Mehegan with Charles Mingus, Bassist* (Perspective PR 1) (LP), recorded late 1952.

37. Priestley, *Mingus*, 48.

38. Mingus, *Beneath the Underdog*, 323.

39. David Hajdu, *Lush Life: A Biography of Billy Strayhorn* (New York: Farrar, Straus & Giroux, 1996), 50.

40. Vincente Prudente, conversation with the author, October 12, 1995. The members of the Ellington orchestra usually referred to Duke as The Maestro.

41. "Make Believe" is on *Charles "Baron" Mingus, West Coast, 1945–49* (Uptown UPCD 27.48).

42. Charles Mingus, *A Modern Jazz Symposium of Music and Poetry* (Bethlehem BCP 6026), recorded October 1957.

43. Charles Mingus, *The Complete 1959 Columbia Recordings* (Columbia C3K 65145).

44. Charles Mingus, *Mingus Mingus Mingus Mingus Mingus* (impulse! IMPD-170).

45. Charles Mingus, *Mingus Revisited* (Emarcy 826 496–2), recorded May 1960.

46. Henry Louis Gates, Jr., *The Signifyin(g) Monkey: A Theory of Afro-American Literary Criticism* (New York: Oxford University Press, 1988).

47. Charles Mingus, *The Clown* (Atlantic LP 1260), recorded February–March 1957. Also on *The Complete Atlantic Recordings, 1956–1961* (Atlantic 72871).

48. Mingus, liner notes to *The Black Saint and the Sinner Lady* (impulse! IMPD-174).

49. Priestley, *Mingus*, 145.

50. Art Tatum, *The Complete Pablo Solo Masterpieces* (Pablo 7PACD-4404–2), recorded December 1953–August 1956; Art Tatum, *The Complete Pablo Tatum Group Masterpieces* (Pablo 6PACD-4401–2), recorded June 1954–September, 1956.

51. "The Arts of Tatum and Freddie Webster" is on Charles Mingus, *Music Written for Monterey 1965, Not Heard . . . Played in Its Entirety at UCLA* (Sue Mingus Music SSC 3041), recorded December 1965.

52. You can hear Mingus working out this reference to Tatum in his solo piano recording of "Body and Soul," in which he also quotes from "Humoresque" at an unusually slow tempo. On *Mingus Plays Piano* (impulse! IMPD-217), recorded July 1963. The two quotations are also close by on a track on the posthumous *Epitaph* recording, "The Soul" (Columbia C2K 45428), recorded June 1989.

53. Mingus, interview with Johnson.

54. John McDonough, "Macphail on the Mysteries of Charles Mingus," *Chamber Music* 27.6 (November/December 2010): 10.

55. Szwed, *So What*, 176.

56. Stanley Crouch, *Considering Genius* (New York: Basic Civitas Books, 2006), 105.

57. Mingus, interview with Ertegun.

58. *Jelly Roll Morton Centennial: His Complete Victor Recordings* (Bluebird 2361–2-RB).

59. Mingus, interview with Johnson.

60. E. Porter, "Passions of a Man," 117.

61. Santoro, *Myself When I Am Real*, 212.

62. Mingus, "Open Letter to the Avant-Garde," 119.

63. S. Mingus, *Tonight at Noon*, 27.

64. Martin Williams, *The Jazz Tradition* (New York: Oxford University Press, 1970); Martin Williams, ed., *The Smithsonian Collection of Classic Jazz* (Music CDs), 1973; *Jazz: A Film by Ken Burns* (DVDs), 2001.

65. Francis Davis, *Jazz and Its Discontents: A Francis Davis Reader* (New York: Da Capo, 2004), 18.

66. The band left no recordings, but its existence is clearly established in a photograph by William Claxton.

67. Balliett, "Mingus at Peace," 49.

68. Leonard Feather, "Another View of Coleman," *Down Beat*, May 26, 1960, 21.

69. Giddins, *Visions of Jazz*, 445.

70. Cuscuna, liner notes for *The Complete Candid Recordings of Charles Mingus* (Mosaic MD3–111).

71. Ibid.

72. E. Porter, "Passions of a Man," 137.

73. "Haitian Fight Song" is on Mingus, *The Clown* (Atlantic LP 1260) and *The Complete Atlantic Recordings, 1956–1961* (Atlantic 72871); "Better Git It in Your Soul" on Mingus, *The Complete 1959 Columbia Recordings* (Columbia C3K 65145); "Wednesday Night Prayer Meeting" on Mingus, *Blues and Roots* (Atlantic SD 1305) and *The Complete Atlantic Recordings*.

74. This version of "Celia" is on the LP *Mingus Quintet Meets Cat Anderson* (Unique Jazz J20), recorded November 1972, and available online at www.youtube.com/watch?v=yOrNRxx_UIE

75. Mingus, *Changes One* (Atlantic R2 71403) and *Changes Two* (Atlantic R2 71404). The band can be seen performing in the DVD *Charles Mingus, Live at Montreux 1975* (Eagle Vision EREVDV449).

76. Scott DeVeaux, "Struggling with *Jazz*," *Current Musicology*, nos. 71–73 (Spring 2001–Spring 2002): 361.

77. On *Music Written for Monterey 1965*.

78. DeVeaux, "Struggling with *Jazz*," 370.

79. Gunther Schuller, *Gunther Schuller: A Life in Pursuit of Music and Beauty* (Rochester, N.Y.: University of Rochester Press: 2011), 286.

80. Mingus, interview on WKCR, 1971.

81. "God's Portrait" on *Charles "Baron" Mingus, West Coast, 1945–49* (Uptown UPCD 27.48); "Extrasensory Perception" on *The Complete Debut Recordings* (Debut 12-CD-4402–2).

82. Schuller, *A Life*, 188.

83. Miles Davis, *The Complete Birth of the Cool* (Capitol CDP 594550).

84. Schuller, *A Life*, 440.

85. Gunther Schuller, conversation with the author, July 13, 2012.

86. Schuller, *A Life*, 447.

87. Modern Jazz Quartet, *Concorde* (Prestige OJC 002), recorded July 1955.

88. All of this music has been collected on *The Birth of Third Stream* (Columbia CK 64929).

89. Joshua Berrett, "Louis Armstrong and Opera," *Musical Quarterly* 76.2 (1992): 216–41.

90. "Black and Tan Fantasy," recorded November 1927, is on Duke Ellington, *The Okeh Ellington* (Columbia C2K 46177).

91. Both suites are on Duke Ellington, *Three Suites* (Columbia CK 46825), recorded June 1960.

92. Stan Kenton, "Chorale for Brass, Piano, and Bongo," on *Complete Capitol Studio Recordings* (Mosaic MD7–163), recorded September 1947.

93. John Kirby, *The Biggest Little Band in the Land* (Columbia 472184–2).

94. Darius Milhaud, *La création du monde* (Naxos MEJ2).

95. Boyd Raeburn, "Boyd Meets Stravinsky," on *Boyd Raeburn* (Echo Jazz [E]EJCD-13), recorded December 1945; Woody Herman, "Ebony Concerto," on *Woody Herman, Live At Carnegie Hall, 1946* (Verve 731455983326), recorded March 1946.

96. Szwed, *So What*, 17.

97. Ibid., 33.

98. Ellison, *Invisible Man*, 8.

99. Most of the music for the Brandeis Festival, including Mingus's *Revelations*, has been collected on a CD attributed to pianist Bill Evans, who plays on all the tracks: Bill Evans and His Orchestra, *Brandeis Jazz Festival* (Gambit 69214).

100. Dizzy Gillespie, *Complete RCA Victor Recordings* (RCA Bluebird 66528–2).

101. Buddy DeFranco, *1949–1952* (Classics 1445).

102. George Russell, *The Lydian Chromatic Concept of Tonal Organization* (New York: Concept, 1961).

103. Woody Herman, *The Complete Recordings of Woody Herman and His Orchestra and Woodchoppers (1945–1947)* (Mosaic MD7–223).

104. Howard Pollack, *Aaron Copland: The Life and Work of an Uncommon Man* (New York: Henry Holt, 1999), 118.

105. Various Artists, *Outstanding Jazz Compositions of the Twentieth Century* (Columbia C2S31). When I bought this set as a teenager, I was extremely intrigued. I was not aware that the music was designed to fuse jazz and classical, but it was like nothing I had ever heard before. My high school band director must have thought so too. He never returned the LPs after I loaned them to him.

106. Gennari, *Blowin' Hot and Cool*, 210.

107. George Avakian, conversation with the author, May 12, 2010; Gunther Schuller, conversation with the author, July 13, 2012.

108. Gleason, "Charlie Mingus," 7.

109. Ibid.

110. Nathaniel Mackey, *Bedouin Hornbook* (Los Angeles: Sun & Moon, 1993), 83.

111. Ira Gitler, "Mingus Speaks ... and Bluntly," *Down Beat*, July 21, 1960, 30.

112. "T.T.T.," recorded in November 1970, is on Bill Evans, *Piano Player* (Columbia CK 65361); "T.T.T.," recorded in January 1973, is on *The Bill Evans Fantasy Sessions* (Fantasy 9FCD1012–2).

113. Schuller, *A Life*, 462.

114. Whitney Balliett, *Collected Works: A Journal of Jazz, 1954–2000* (New York: St. Martin's Press, 2000), 64.

115. Gleason, "Charlie Mingus," 7.

116. Mingus, *Beneath the Underdog*, 354.

117. Jennifer Griffith, e-mail message to the author, August 27, 2014.

118. S. Mingus, *Tonight at Noon*, 197.

119. Max Harrison, *A Jazz Retrospect* (Boston: Crescendo, 1976), 183.

120. Saul, *Freedom Is, Freedom Ain't*, 147.

121. Gunther Schuller, liner notes for *Bill Evans and His Orchestra: Brandeis Jazz Festival* (Gambit Records 69124).

122. Griffith, e-mail message.

123. Miles Davis, *Porgy and Bess* (Columbia 65141), recorded August 1958.

124. Miles Davis, *Sketches of Spain* (Columbia 460604), recorded March 1960.

125. Dizzy Gillespie, *Perceptions* (Verve MGV8411), recorded May 1961.

126. Stan Getz, *Focus* (Verve 40337), recorded July 1961.

127. Aaslid, "The Poetic Mingus," 2.

128. Wynton Marsalis, "What Jazz Is—and Isn't" (1988), in *Keeping Time: Readings in Jazz History,* ed. Robert Walser (New York: Oxford University Press, 1999), 335.

129. http://en.wikipedia.org/wiki/George_Lewis_(trombonist).

130. Mingus, liner notes for *Let My Children Hear Music* (Columbia 48910).

PART IV: ON AND OFF THE BANDSTAND
WITH RICHMOND, DOLPHY, AND KNEPPER

1. Jimmy Heath, *I Walked with Giants: The Autobiography of Jimmy Heath* (Philadelphia: Temple University Press, 2010), 164.

2. Charles Mingus, *Pithecanthropus Erectus* (Atlantic SD 8809), recorded January 1956. Also on *The Complete Atlantic Recordings, 1956–1961* (Atlantic 72871).

3. Derek Ansell, *Sugar Free Saxophone: The Life and Music of Jackie McLean* (London: Northway, 2012), 28.

4. Ibid., 43.

5. Both LPs were recorded in the early 1960s and are available on Johnny Hodges/Wild Bill Davis, *Con-Soul & Jazz/Wild Bill Is the Boss!* (Lonehill LHJ10283).

6. Duke Ellington, *New Orleans Suite* (Atlantic 1580–2), recorded May 1970.

7. Gary Giddins, conversation with the author, August 8, 2012.

8. Santoro, *Myself When I Am Real*, 127.

9. Priestley, *Mingus*, 75.

10. Mercer Ellington, *Continuum* (Fantasy FCD-2476), recorded 1975.

11. Jeff Potter and Barry Kernfeld, "Dannie Richmond," in *The New Grove Dictionary of Jazz*, 2d ed. (New York: Macmillan, 2002), 3:411.

12. Charles Mingus, interview by unidentified announcer, Copenhagen, Denmark, August 16, 1976.

13. Priestley, *Mingus,* 75.

14. Goodman, *Mingus Speaks,* 139.

15. Primack, "Gospel according to Mingus," 40.

16. Priestley, *Mingus,* 76.

17. Mingus, liner notes for *Tijuana Moods* (RCA Victor Gold Series 74321749992).

18. David Margolick, "The Day Louis Armstrong Made Noise," *New York Times,* September 23, 2007, "Week in Review," 13.

19. Gary Giddins, *Satchmo: The Genius of Louis Armstrong* (New York: Da Capo, 2001), 127.

20. Priestley, *Mingus,* 87.

21. The wordless version of "Fables of Faubus" is on *The Complete 1959 Columbia Recordings* (Columbia C3K 65145).

22. "Original Fables of Faubus," recorded October 1960, is on *Charles Mingus Presents Charles Mingus* (Candid CCD 79005) and *The Complete Candid Recordings of Charles Mingus* (Mosaic MD3–111).

23. Howard Johnson, conversation with the author, February 14, 2015.

24. James Gavin, *Deep in a Dream: The Long Night of Chet Baker* (New York: Knopf, 2002), 297.

25. Santoro, *Myself When I Am Real,* 143.

26. www.youtube.com/watch?v=Y1RNDmegqXw.

27. Nat Hentoff, liner notes for Charles Mingus, *East Coasting* (Bethlehem BCP 6019).

28. Paul Jarrico, letter to Michael Relph et al., June 1, 1961, in the Paul Jarrico Archive, Rare Book and Manuscript Library, Columbia University, New York.

29. Priestley, *Mingus,* 200.

30. Primack, "Gospel according to Mingus," 42.

31. Dannie Richmond, *Dannie Richmond Plays Charles Mingus* (Timeless SJP148), recorded August 1980.

32. Gordon, *Live at the Village Vanguard,* 107.

33. Ibid.

34. John Szwed, "Life on the Institution's Barricades: Jazz's Permanent Avant-garde," paper delivered at the Newport Jazz Festival, August 2000.

35. John Litweiler, *The Freedom Principle: Jazz after 1958* (New York: Morrow, 1984), 60.

36. Ted Gioia, *West Coast Jazz: Modern Jazz in California, 1945–1960* (New York: Oxford University Press, 1992), 344.

37. David Keller, "Eric Dolphy—The Los Angeles Years," *Jazz Times,* November 1981, 31.

38. Three tracks by Roy Porter's band with solos by Dolphy are included on Various Artists, *Central Avenue Sounds: Jazz in Los Angeles (1921–1956)* (Rhino R2 75872).

39. Litweiler, *Freedom Principle*, 62.

40. Dolphy's *Outward Bound* (recorded April 1960), *Out There* (August 1960), and *Far Cry* (December 1960) are collected on Eric Dolphy, *The Complete Prestige Recordings* (Prestige 9PRCD-4418–2). *Out to Lunch* (Blue Note 7 465242) was recorded February 1964.

41. See, for example, the Dolphy entry in Wikipedia: https://en.wikipedia .org/wiki/Eric_Dolphy.

42. Primack, "Gospel according to Mingus," 41.

43. Vladimir Simosko and Barry Tepperman, *Eric Dolphy: A Musical Biography and Discography*, rev. ed. (New York: Da Capo, 1996), 2.

44. Ben Ratliff, *Coltrane: The Story of a Sound* (New York: Farrar, Straus & Giroux, 2007), 68.

45. Nat Hentoff, "Second Chorus: Eric Dolphy," *Down Beat*, August 27, 1964, 40.

46. John Tynan, "Take 5," *Down Beat*, November 23, 1961, 60.

47. Don DeMichael, "John Coltrane and Eric Dolphy Answer the Jazz Critics," *Down Beat*, April 12, 1962.

48. Ratliff, *Coltrane*, 143.

49. John Coltrane, *Ballads* (impulse! AS-32), recorded November 1962; *A Love Supreme* (impulse! AS-77), recorded December 1964; *Crescent* (impulse! AS-66), recorded April 1964; *John Coltrane and Johnny Hartman* (impulse! AS-40), recorded March 1963.

50. Oliver Nelson, *Blues and the Abstract Truth* (impulse! IMPD-154), recorded February 1961; Gil Evans, *The Individualism of Gil Evans* (Verve 833 804–2), recorded September 1963; Freddie Hubbard, *The Body and Soul of Freddie Hubbard* (impulse! IMPD-183), recorded March and May 1963.

51. *Charles Mingus Presents Charles Mingus* (Candid CCD 79005), recorded October 1960.

52. Ornette Coleman, *Free Jazz* (Atlantic SD1364), recorded December 1960.

53. Nat Hentoff, liner notes to *Charles Mingus Presents Charles Mingus* (Candid CCD 79005).

54. Ted Curson, interview by Gary Giddins and Bob Rusch, *Cadence* 1.8 (July 1976): 4.

55. Andrew Hill, *Point of Departure* (Blue Note CDP 7 84167 2), recorded March 1964.

56. *Charles Mingus Sextet with Eric Dolphy, Cornell 1964* (Blue Note 0946 3 92210), recorded April 1964.

57. Robert Simon, *Percy Grainger: The Pictorial Biography* (Albany, N.Y.: Whitston, 1983), 7.

58. Krin Gabbard, "The Quoter and His Culture," in *Jazz in Mind: Essays on the History and Meanings of Jazz*, ed. Reginald T. Buckner and Steven Weiland (Detroit: Wayne State University Press, 1991, 92–111).

59. Simosko and Tepperman, *Eric Dolphy*, 14.

60. Dolphy plays "In a Sentimental Mood" on *The Complete Pacific Jazz Recordings of the Chico Hamilton Quintet* (Mosaic MD6–175).

61. Simosko and Tepperman, *Eric Dolphy*, 15.

62. Charles Mingus, *Live in '64*, Jazz Icons (Naxos DVD 2–1190006).

63. Simosko and Teperman, *Eric Dolphy*, 34.

64. Frederick J. Spencer, *Jazz and Death: Medical Profiles of Jazz Greats* (Jackson: University Press of Mississippi, 2002), 37.

65. Zan Stewart, liner notes to Eric Dolphy, *The Complete Prestige Recordings* (Prestige 9PRCD 4418), 19.

66. *Eric Dolphy: Last Date* (1991), directed by Hans Hylkema and Thierry Bruneau (Rhapsody Films).

67. Simosko and Tepperman, *Eric Dolphy*, 4.

68. "In Tribute: Eric Dolphy 1928–1964," *Down Beat*, August 27, 1964, 10.

69. Dunkel, *Aesthetics of Resistance*, 56.

70. Mingus, *The Clown* (Atlantic LP 1260) and *The Complete Atlantic Recordings, 1956–1961* (Atlantic 72871).

71. Bob Porter, liner notes for *The Complete Dean Benedetti Recordings of Charlie Parker* (Mosaic MD7–129), 5.

72. Sam Burtis, conversation with the author, August 20, 2012.

73. The 1988 footage of Knepper is at www.youtube.com/watch?v= Ro3wiJgShGI. For Dickenson, see the 1957 *Sound of Jazz* broadcast in which he solos with Billie Holiday on "Fine and Mellow": www.youtube .com/watch?v=sJQiqTZfakQ. For Teagarden, see the Snader transcription of "Basin Street Blues": www.youtube.com/watch?v=hUpEU1irzYQ

74. Loren Schoenberg, conversation with the author, March 19, 2013.

75. Burtis conversation; Schoenberg conversation.

76. The LP, Jimmy Knepper, *New Faces*, is on Mingus, *The Complete Debut Recordings* (Debut 12-CD-4402–2).

77. *Miles Davis at Carnegie Hall* (Columbia CDCBS 85554), recorded May 1961.

78. Santoro, *Myself When I Am Real*, 187.

79. Collette, *Jazz Generations*, 27.

80. Santoro, *Myself When I Am Real*, 189.

81. Priestley, *Mingus*, 87.

82. Bill Crow, conversation with the author, March 19, 2013.

83. Hajdu, *Lush Life*.

84. Whitney Balliett, "A Trombone Mouth," *New Yorker*, May 20, 1991, 57.

85. Mingus, autobiography typescript, 218.

86. Santoro, *Myself When I Am Real*, 212.

87. Balliett, "Trombone Mouth," 57.

88. Santoro, *Myself When I Am Real*, 280.

89. Ibid., 355.

90. *Big Band Charles Mingus, Vol. 1* (Soul Note 121 192–2), recorded June 1988.

91. Jay D. Smith and Leonard F. Guttridge, *Jack Teagarden: The Story of a Jazz Maverick* (New York: Da Capo, 1976), 45.

92. www.youtube.com/watch?v=eOxx1-LIAWA

93. Steven Feld, "Notes on Tromboning Whiteness" (unpublished manuscript, 2012), 8.

94. Archie Shepp, "An Artist Speaks Bluntly," *Down Beat,* December 16, 1965, 11.

95. Roswell Rudd, interview by David Dupont, *Cadence* 18.11 (November 1992): 13.

96. Ibid., 13–14.

97. Feld, "Notes on Tromboning Whiteness," 18.

98. Balliett, "Trombone Mouth," 55.

99. On *Music Written for Monterey 1965, Not Heard . . .* A 1971 studio recording of "Don't Be Afraid, the Clown's Afraid Too" is on *Let My Children Hear Music.*

100. Frank O'Hara, "The Clown," in *The Collected Poems of Frank O'Hara* (New York: Knopf, 1971), 26. For a copy of this poem as well as a thorough discussion of Mingus's string quartet, see Aaslid, "The Poetic Mingus," 1–25.

101. Trevor Herbert, *The Trombone* (New Haven, Conn.: Yale University Press, 2006), 248.

102. Santoro, *Myself When I Am Real,* 127.

103. Krin Gabbard, *Black Magic: White Hollywood and African American Culture* (New Brunswick, N.J.: Rutgers University Press, 2004), 19–47.

104. Brent Hayes Edwards, "Louis Armstrong and the Syntax of Scat," *Critical Inquiry* 28.3 (2002): 648.

105. "Eat That Chicken," recorded November 1961, is on Mingus, *Mingus Oh Yeah* (Atlantic SD 1377) and *The Complete Atlantic Recordings, 1956–1961* (Atlantic 72871).

106. Griffith, "Mingus in the Act," 365.

107. Ibid., 366.

108. Mingus, liner notes to *The Clown* (Atlantic LP 1260).

109. Franz Kafka, "The Hunger Artist," in *Metamorphosis and Other Stories,* trans. Michael Hofman (New York: Penguin, 2008), 252–63.

110. Stephen Feld, e-mail message to the author, August 31, 2013.

111. Schoenberg conversation.

112. Burtis conversation.

113. Jeffrey Nussbaum, conversation with the author, July 12, 2012.

114. Gabbard, *Black Magic.*

115. Every jazz nerd in the audience, most notably me, gasped at this moment. The Davis/Coltrane performance in Stockholm was recorded in 1960, *not* 1963. If the filmmakers want to make fun of a jazz nerd, they should at least give us one who knows his discography!

116. Chris Willman, "He Shoots, He Scores: Making the *Jerry Maguire* Soundtrack," *Entertainment Weekly,* January 17, 1997.

117. "Haitian Fight Song" is on Mingus, *The Clown* (Atlantic LP 1260) and *The Complete Atlantic Recordings, 1956–1961* (Atlantic 72871).

118. David Yaffe, "'What *Is* This Music?': Mingus, Melville, and the Sounds of Covert Revolution," *Literary Imagination* 13.2 (2011): 167–71; Herman

Melville, "Benito Cereno," in *The Piazza Tales and Other Prose Pieces, 1839–1860* (Evanston, Ill.: Northwestern University Press, 1987), 47–117.
    119. Yaffe, "'What *Is* This Music?'" 168.
    120. Ibid., 171.

EPILOGUE: MINGUS IN THE MOVIES

    1. Mingus himself would record with Ivie Anderson a few years after she left Ellington: *Ivie Anderson And Her All Stars* (Storyville SLP 804), recorded January 1946.
    2. Mingus, *Beneath the Underdog*, 108.
    3. Raymond Carney, *Shadows*, BFI Film Classics (London: British Film Institute, 2001).
    4. Raymond Carney, *Cassevetes on Cassavetes* (London: Faber & Faber, 2001), 77.
    5. Mingus, *The Complete Debut Recordings* (Debut 12-CD-4402–2).
    6. Priestley, *Mingus*, 90–91.
    7. Ross Lipman, "Mingus, Cassavetes, and the Birth of Jazz Cinema," *Journal of Film Music* 2.2–4 (Winter 2009): 154.
    8. Thomas Cartelli, *Repositioning Shakespeare: National Formations, Postcolonial Appropriations* (London: Routledge, 1999), 123.
    9. Paul Jarrico, letter to Nel King, July 24, 1961, in Paul Jarrico Archive, Rare Book and Manuscript Library, Columbia University, New York (hereafter cited as PJA).
    10. Nel King, letter to Paul Jarrico, July 28, 1961, PJA.
    11. Paul Jarrico, letter to Nel King and Sylvia Jarrico, July 10, 1961, PJA.
    12. "Peggy's Blue Skylight," recorded November 1961, is on *Tonight at Noon* (Atlantic SD 1416) and Mingus, *The Complete Atlantic Recordings, 1956–1961* (Atlantic 72871).
    13. Nel King, letter to Bob Roberts, June 26, 1961, PJA.
    14. The film is scheduled to be released on DVD late in 2015 by Oscilliscope Laboratories.
    15. Ivor Miller, *Aerosol Kingdom: Subway Painters of New York City* (Jackson: University Press of Mississippi, 2002).
    16. George L. Kelling and Catherine M. Coles, *Fixing Broken Windows: Restoring Order and Reducing Crime in Our Communities* (New York: Martin Kessler, 1996).
    17. Adam Gopnik, "The Caging of America," *New Yorker*, January 30, 2012, www.newyorker.com/magazine/2012/01/30/the-caging-of-america.
    18. www.subchat.com/read.asp?Id=1316482.
    19. See, for example, Eric Felisbret and Luke Felisbret, *Graffiti New York* (New York: Abrams, 2009), as well as Miller, *Aerosol Kingdom*.
    20. Manfred Kirchheimer, conversation with the author, November 2, 2014.
    21. Ibid.

22. "Ecclusiastics" can be heard on *Mingus Oh Yeah* (Atlantic SD 1377) and Mingus, *The Complete Atlantic Recordings, 1956–1961* (Atlantic 72871).

23. Peter Lehman, "Insights, Images, and Integrity: An Interview with Manny Kirchheimer," *Wide Angle* 6.1 (1984): 42–49.

24. Kirchheimer, conversation.

Bibliography

Aaslid, Vilde. "The Poetic Mingus and the Politics of Genre in String Quartet No. 1." *Journal of the Society for American Music* 9.1 (2015): 1–25.

Adams, Pepper. Interview by Gary Carner. *Cadence* 12.2 (February 1986): 5–12, 21, 29.

Amram, David. *Vibrations: A Memoir.* New York: Thunder's Mouth, 2001.

Anolik, Lili. "The Tale of the Tape." *Harper's,* September 2014, 89–94.

Ansell, Derek. *Sugar Free Saxophone: The Life and Music of Jackie McLean.* London: Northway, 2012.

Armstrong, Louis. *Louis Armstrong, in His Own Words: Selected Writings.* Edited by Thomas Brothers. New York: Oxford University Press, 1999.

———. *Satchmo: My Life in New Orleans.* New York: Prentice-Hall, 1954.

———. *Swing That Music.* 1936; reprint, New York: Da Capo, 1993.

Balliett, Whitney. *Collected Works: A Journal of Jazz, 1954–2000.* New York: St. Martin's Press, 2000.

———. "Mingus at Peace." *New Yorker,* May 29, 1971, 42–52.

———. "A Trombone Mouth." *New Yorker,* May 20, 1991, 52–58.

Baraka, Amiri. *The Autobiography of LeRoi Jones.* New York: Freundlich, 1984.

Basie, Count. *Good Morning Blues: The Autobiography of Count Basie as Told to Albert Murray.* New York: Random House, 1985.

"Bassist Mingus Heads for Venice, May Quit U.S." *Jet,* August 30, 1962.

Bechet, Sidney. *Treat It Gentle.* 1960; reprint, New York: Da Capo, 1978.

Berger, Edward. *Bassically Speaking: An Oral History of George Duvivier.* Metuchen, N.J.: Scarecrow Press, 1993.

Berrett, Joshua. "Louis Armstrong and Opera." *Musical Quarterly* 76.2 (1992): 216–41.

Bigard, Barney. *With Louis and the Duke: The Autobiography of a Jazz Clarinetist.* New York: Oxford University Press, 1988.

Bilancioni, Guglielmo. "Everybody Knows This Is Nowhere: Structure and Performance in Rodia's Watts Towers." In *Sabato Rodia's Towers in Watts:*

Art, Migrations, Development, edited by Luisa Del Giudice, 69–78. New York: Fordham University Press, 2014.

Bishop, Jim. [Column, no title.] *New York Journal–American.* January 2, 1958, 17.

Brothers, Thomas. *Louis Armstrong's New Orleans.* New York: Norton, 2006.

Carmichael, Thomas. "Beneath the Underdog: Charles Mingus, Representation, and Jazz Autobiography." *Canadian Review of American Studies* 25.3 (1995): 29–41.

Carney, Raymond. *Cassavetes on Cassavetes.* London: Faber and Faber, 2001.

———. *Shadows.* BFI Film Classics. London: British Film Institute, 2001.

Cartelli, Thomas. *Repositioning Shakespeare: National Formations, Postcolonial Appropriations.* London: Routledge, 1999.

Catalano, Nick. *Clifford Brown: The Life and Art of the Legendary Jazz Trumpeter.* New York: Oxford University Press, 2000.

Chambers, Jack. *Milestones: The Music and Times of Miles Davis.* Rev. ed. New York: Da Capo, 1998.

Chilton, John. *Sidney Bechet: The Wizard of Jazz.* New York: Oxford University Press, 1987.

Clark, Philip. "Black Saints and Jive Ass Slippers." *Jazz Review* 28 (January 2002): 22–24.

Cleage, Pearl. "Mad at Miles." In *The Miles Davis Companion: Four Decades of Commentary,* edited by Gary Carner, 210–16. New York: Schirmer, 1996.

Coleman, Janet, and Al Young. *Mingus/Mingus: Two Memoirs.* Berkeley, Calif.: Creative Arts, 1989.

Collette, Buddy. *Jazz Generations: A Life in American Music and Society.* London: Continuum, 2000.

Collier, James Lincoln. *Duke Ellington.* New York: Oxford University Press, 1987.

"Crewcut Contest's $." *Down Beat,* November 4, 1949, 1.

Crouch, Stanley. *Considering Genius.* New York: Basic Civitas Books, 2006.

———. "Play the Right Thing." *New Republic,* February 12, 1990, 30–37.

Crow, Bill. *Jazz Anecdotes.* New York: Oxford University Press, 1990.

Curson, Ted. Interview by Gary Giddins and Bob Rusch. *Cadence* 1.8 (July 1976): 3–4, 7.

Cuscuna, Michael. Liner notes. *The Complete Candid Recordings of Charles Mingus.* Mosaic MD3-111.

Danson, Peter. "Jimmy Knepper: An Interview." *Coda,* no. 179 (June 1981): 8–13.

Davis, Francis. *Jazz and Its Discontents: A Francis Davis Reader.* New York: Da Capo, 2004.

Davis, Miles, with Quincy Troupe. *Miles: The Autobiography.* New York: Simon & Schuster, 1989.

Del Giudice, Luisa. "Sabata Rodia's Towers in Watts: Art, Migration, and Italian Imaginaries." In *Sabato Rodia's Towers in Watts: Art, Migrations, Development,* edited by Luisa Del Giudice, 155–82. New York: Fordham University Press, 2014.

DeLillo, Don. *Underworld*. New York: Scribner, 1997.

DeMichael, Don. "John Coltrane and Eric Dolphy Answer the Jazz Critics." *Down Beat*, April 12, 1962. Available at www.downbeat.com/default .asp?sect=stories&subsect=story_detail&sid=354.

———. "Shavina Philosophy." *Down Beat*, January 30, 1964, 16.

DeVeaux, Scott. *The Birth of Bebop: A Social and Musical History*. Berkeley: University of California Press, 1997.

———. "Struggling with Jazz." *Current Musicology*, nos. 71–73 (Spring 2001– Spring 2002): 353–74.

Donelian, Armen. Interview by Bob Rusch. *Cadence* 11.10 (October 1985): 24–33.

Dorr-Dorynek, Diane. "Mingus." In *The Jazz Word*, edited by Dom Cerulli, Burt Korall, and Mort L. Nasatir, 14–18. New York: Da Capo, 1987.

Du Bois, W. E. B. *The Souls of Black Folk*. 1903; reprint, New York: Knopf, 1993.

Dunkel, Mario. *Aesthetics of Resistance: Charles Mingus and the Civil Rights Movement*. Zurich: Lit Verlag, 2012.

Durham, Philip, and Everett L. Jones. *The Negro Cowboys*. New York: Dodd, Mead, 1965.

Dyer, Geoff. *But Beautiful: A Book about Jazz*. New York: North Point Press, 1996.

Edwards, Brent Hayes. "Louis Armstrong and the Syntax of Scat." *Critical Inquiry* 28.3 (2002): 618–49.

Ellington, Duke. *Music Is My Mistress*. Garden City, N.Y.: Doubleday, 1973.

Ellington, Mercer, with Stanley Dance. *Duke Ellington in Person: An Intimate Memoir*. Boston: Houghton Mifflin, 1978.

Ellison, Ralph. *The Collected Essays of Ralph Ellison*. Edited by John F. Callahan. New York: Modern Library, 1995.

———. "Going to the Territory" (1979). In *Collected Essays*, 591–612.

———. "The Golden Age, Time Past" (1959). In *Collected Essays*, 237–49.

———. *Invisible Man*. New York: Vintage, 1972.

———. *Living with Music: Ralph Ellison's Jazz Writings*. Edited by Robert G. O'Meally. New York: Modern Library, 2001.

Farrington, Holly. "Narrating the Jazz Life: Three Approaches to Jazz Autobiography." *Popular Music and Society* 29.3 (2006): 375–86.

Feather, Leonard. "Another View of Coleman." *Down Beat*, May 26, 1960, 21.

———. "Blindfold Test: Charles Mingus." *Down Beat*, April 28, 1960, 49.

Feld, Steven. "Notes on Tromboning Whiteness." Unpublished manuscript, 2012.

Felisbret, Eric and Luke Felisbret. *Graffiti New York*. New York: Abrams, 2009.

Fitzgerald, F. Scott. *Tales of the Jazz Age*. New York: Scribner, 1922.

Gabbard, Krin. *Black Magic: White Hollywood and African American Culture*. New Brunswick, N.J.: Rutgers University Press, 2004.

———. *Jammin' at the Margins: Jazz and the American Cinema*. Chicago: University of Chicago Press, 1996.

————. "The Quoter and His Culture." In *Jazz in Mind: Essays on the History and Meanings of Jazz*, edited by Reginald T. Buckner and Steven Weiland, 92–111. Detroit: Wayne State University Press, 1991.

Gans, Charles J. "Ted Curson: Memories of Mingus." *Jazz Forum* 57 (1979): 28–30, 42.

Gates, Henry Louis, Jr. *The Signifyin(g) Monkey: A Theory of Afro-American Literary Criticism*. New York: Oxford University Press, 1988.

Gavin, James. *Deep in a Dream: The Long Night of Chet Baker*. New York: Knopf, 2002.

Gennari, John. *Blowin' Hot and Cool: Jazz and Its Critics*. Chicago: University of Chicago Press, 2006.

Giddins, Gary. *Natural Selection: Gary Giddins on Comedy, Film, Music, and Books*. New York: Oxford University Press, 2006.

————. *Satchmo: The Genius of Louis Armstrong*. New York: Da Capo, 2001.

————. *Visions of Jazz: The First Century*. New York: Oxford University Press, 1998.

Gillespie, Dizzy, with Al Fraser. *To Be or Not to Bop*. New York: Doubleday, 1979.

Gioia, Ted. *West Coast Jazz: Modern Jazz in California, 1945–1960*. New York: Oxford University Press, 1992.

Gitler, Ira. "Charlie Mingus—'Mingus Dynasty.'" *Down Beat*, July 19, 1960, 26, 28.

————. *Jazz Masters of the Forties*. New York: Collier, 1966.

————. Liner notes. *Charles Mingus: The Complete Debut Recordings*. Debut 12-CD-4402 2.

————. "Mingus Speaks . . . and Bluntly." *Down Beat*, July 21, 1960, 29–31.

Gleason, Ralph J. "Charlie Mingus: A Thinking Musician." *Down Beat*, June 1, 1951, 7. Available at www.downbeat.com/default.asp?sect=stories&subsect= story_detail&sid=959.

Goodman, John F. *Mingus Speaks*. Berkeley: University of California Press, 2013.

Gopnik, Adam. "The Caging of America." *New Yorker*, January 30, 2012. Available at www.newyorker.com/magazine/2012/01/30/the-caging-of-america.

Gordon, Max. *Live at the Village Vanguard*. New York: Da Capo, 1980.

Gorz, André. *The Traitor*. New York: Verso, 1989.

Griffin, Farah Jasmine. *If You Can't Be Free, Be a Mystery: In Search of Billie Holiday*. New York: Free Press, 2001.

Griffith, Jennifer. "Mingus in the Act: Confronting the Legacies of Vaudeville and Minstrelsy." *Jazz Perspectives* 4.3 (Winter 2010): 337–68.

Hajdu, David. *Lush Life: A Biography of Billy Strayhorn*. New York: Farrar, Straus & Giroux, 1996.

Harlos, Christopher. "Jazz Autobiography: Theory, Practice, Politics." In *Jazz among the Discourses*, edited by Krin Gabbard, 131–66. Durham, N.C.: Duke University Press, 1995.

Harrison, Max. *A Jazz Retrospect.* Boston: Crescendo, 1976.

Harrison, Thomas. "Without Precedent: The Watts Towers." In *Sabato Rodia's Towers in Watts: Art, Migrations, Development,* edited by Luisa Del Giudice, 91–101. New York: Fordham University Press, 2014.

Hawes, Hampton, and Don Asher. *Raise Up Off Me.* New York: Coward, McCann & Geoghegan, 1974 .

Haydon, Geoffrey. *Quintet of the Year.* London: Aurum, 2002.

Heath, Jimmy. *I Walked with Giants: The Autobiography of Jimmy Heath.* Philadelphia: Temple University Press, 2010.

Heble, Ajay. *Landing on the Wrong Note: Jazz, Dissonance, and Critical Practice.* New York: Routledge, 2000.

Hennessey, Mike. "Charles Mingus. Changed Man?" *Down Beat,* May 13, 1971, 14, 31.

Hentoff, Nat. *The Jazz Life.* New York: Dial, 1961.

———. Liner notes. *Charles Mingus Presents Charles Mingus.* Candid CCD 79005.

———. Liner notes. *East Coasting by Charles Mingus.* Bethlehem BCP 6019.

———. Liner notes. Milt Jackson, *Plenty, Plenty Soul.* Atlantic SD1269.

———. "Mingus: 'I Thought I Was Finished.'" *New York Times,* January 30, 1972, D17.

———. "Mingus Dynasties." *Village Voice,* March 5/12, 1979, 34.

———. "Second Chorus: Eric Dolphy." *Down Beat,* August 27, 1964, 40.

Herbert, Trevor. *The Trombone.* Yale Musical Instrument Series. New Haven, Conn.: Yale University Press, 2006.

Holiday, Billie, with William T. Dufty. *Lady Sings the Blues.* Garden City, N.Y.: Doubleday, 1956.

Homzy, Andrew. Liner notes. *Charles "Baron" Mingus, West Coast 1945–49.* Uptown UPCD 27 48.

Hunter, Bob. "What Is Charlie Mingus Seeking?" *Chicago Daily Defender,* August 30, 1962, 17, 19.

I Build the Tower (DVD). Directed by Edward Landler and Brad Byer. 2006.

"In Tribute: Eric Dolphy 1928–1964." *Down Beat,* August 27, 1964, 10.

Jackson, Kevin. *Constellation of Genius 1922: Modernism Year One.* New York: Farrar, Straus & Giroux, 2012.

Joans, Ted. *Black Pow-Wow: Jazz Poems.* New York: Hill & Wang, 1969.

Johnson, Howard. Interview by Bill Donaldson. *Cadence* 30.7 (July 2004): 5–17.

Johnson, James Weldon. *God's Trombones: Some Negro Sermons in Verse.* London: Allen & Unwin, 1929.

Johnson, Sy. "Charles Mingus: April 22, 1922–January 5, 1979." *Jazz Magazine,* Spring 1979, 37–47.

Jones, Quincy. "I Just Adored That Man." In *Miles Davis and American Culture,* edited by Gerald Early, 41–43. St. Louis: Missouri Historical Society Press, 2001.

Kafka, Franz. "The Hunger Artist." In *Metamorphosis and Other Stories,* translated by Michael Hofman, 252–63. New York: Penguin, 2008.

Keepnews, Peter. "Caught: Charles Mingus and Old Friends, Carnegie Hall, New York City." *Down Beat,* March 28, 1974, 33–34.

Keller, David. "Eric Dolphy—The Los Angeles Years." *Jazz Times,* November 1981, 31.

Kelley, Robin D.G. *Thelonious Monk: The Life and Times of an American Original.* New York: Free Press, 2009.

Kelling, George L., and Catherine M. Coles. *Fixing Broken Windows: Restoring Order and Reducing Crime in Our Communities.* New York: Martin Kessler, 1996.

Kenney, William Howland. "Negotiating the Color Line: Louis Armstrong's Autobiographies." In *Jazz in Mind: Essays on the History and Meanings of Jazz,* edited by Reginald T. Buckner and Steven Weiland, 38–59. Detroit: Wayne State University Press, 1991.

King, Nel. "Preston Sturges." *Monthly Film Bulletin* 28 (Summer/Autumn 1958): 185.

Korall, Burt. Liner notes. The Red Norvo Trio with Tal Farlow and Charles Mingus, *The Savoy Sessions.* Savoy SV-0267

———. "Mingus on Mingus." *Saturday Review,* July 31, 1971, 42.

Kruth, John. *Bright Moments: The Life and Legacy of Rahsaan Roland Kirk.* New York: Welcome Rain, 2000.

LaPorta, John. *Playing It by Ear.* Redwood, N.Y.: Cadence, 2001.

Lawrence, A.H. *Duke Ellington and His World.* New York: Routledge, 2001.

Lees, Gene. *Meet Me at Jim and Andy's: Jazz Musicians and Their World.* New York: Oxford University Press, 1988.

Lehman, Peter. "Insights, Images, and Integrity: An Interview with Manny Kirchheimer." *Wide Angle* 6.1 (1984): 42–49.

Lind, Jack. "Ted Curson's Story: Life with Mingus." *Village Voice,* Jazz Supplement, June 10, 1997, 14.

Lindberg, Kathryne V. "Mister Joans, to You: Readerly Surreality and Writerly Affiliation in Ted Joans, Tri-Continental Ex-Beatnik." *Discourse* 20.1–2 (1998): 198–222.

Lipman, Ross. "Mingus, Cassavetes, and the Birth of Jazz Cinema." *Journal of Film Music* 2.2–4 (Winter 2009): 145–64.

Lipsitz, George. "Songs of the Unsung: The Darby Hicks History of Jazz." In *Uptown Conversation: The New Jazz Studies,* edited by Robert G. O'Meally, Brent Hayes Edwards, and Farah Jasmine Griffin, 9–26. New York: Columbia University Press, 2004.

Litweiler, John. *The Freedom Principle: Jazz after 1958.* New York: Morrow, 1984.

———. "There's a Mingus among Us." *Down Beat,* February 27, 1975, 12–13, 32.

Mackey, Nathaniel. *Bedouin Hornbook.* Los Angeles: Sun & Moon, 1993.

Marcus, Laura. *Auto/biographical Discourses: Theory, Criticism, Practice.* Manchester, UK: Manchester University Press, 1994.

Margolick, David. "The Day Louis Armstrong Made Noise." *New York Times,* September 23, 2007, "Week in Review," 13

Marsalis, Wynton. "What Jazz Is—and Isn't" (1988). In *Keeping Time: Readings in Jazz History*, edited by Robert Walser, 334–39. New York: Oxford University Press, 1999.

Matthews, William. "Mingus in Diaspora." In *Search Party: Collected Poems*, 243. New York: Houghton Mifflin Harcourt, 2005.

McDonough, John. "Macphail on the Mysteries of Charles Mingus." *Chamber Music* 27.6 (November/December 2010): 10–12.

McNeilly, Kevin. "Charles Mingus Splits, or All the Things You Could Be by Now if Sigmund Freud's Wife Was Your Mother." *Canadian Review of American Studies* 27.2 (1997): 45–70.

Miller, Ivor. *Aerosol Kingdom: Subway Painters of New York City.* Jackson: University Press of Mississippi, 2002.

Miller, Mark. *Cool Blues: Charlie Parker in Canada 1953.* London: Nightwood, 1989.

Mingus, Charles. "And so they come. . . . " Untitled poem. N.d. Mingus Collection, Motion Picture, Broadcasting, and Recorded Sound Division, Library of Congress.

———. Autobiography. Charles Mingus Collection, 1939–1979, Library of Congress. Typescript, n.d.

———. *Beneath the Underdog: His World as Composed by Mingus.* New York: Knopf, 1971.

———. Interview by unidentified announcers, WKCR. 1971. Mingus Collection, Motion Picture, Broadcasting, and Recorded Sound Division, Library of Congress.

———. Interview by Nesuhi Ertegun, 1962. Available at www.youtube.com /watch?v=c0uv9Gshve0.

———. Interview by Sy Johnson. Jazz Oral History Project. 1977. Institute of Jazz Studies, Rutgers University, Newark.

———. Liner notes. *East Coasting.* Bethlehem BCP 6019.

———. Liner notes. *Let My Children Hear Music.* Columbia Legacy CK48910.

———. Liner notes. *Mingus at Monterey.* JWS 001 and 002.

———. Liner notes. *Pithecanthropus Erectus.* Atlantic SD 8809.

———. Liner notes. *Tijuana Moods.* RCA Victor LPM 2533.

———. *More Than a Fake Book.* Edited by Sue Mingus. New York: Jazz Workshop, 1991.

———. "An Open Letter to the Avant-Garde." In *More Than a Fake Book*, edited by Sue Mingus, 119. New York: Jazz Workshop, 1991.

———. "An Open Letter to Miles Davis." *Down Beat*, November 30, 1955, 12–13.

———. "This Mule Ain't From Moscow." *Down Beat*, October 3, 1956, 4.

Mingus, Sue Graham. *Tonight at Noon: A Love Story.* New York: Pantheon, 2002.

"Mingus on Mingus." Radio interview by Greg Gallagher (tape recording). 1974. Mingus Collection, Motion Picture, Broadcasting, and Recorded Sound Division, Library of Congress.

"Mingus on Music." Radio broadcast with unidentified interviewer (tape recording). N.d. Mingus Collection, Motion Picture, Broadcasting, and Recorded Sound Division, Library of Congress.

The Mingus Sisters Speak. 4 audio CDs. Interviewer: Shelby Johnson. Lacecap Records. 2001.

Morgenstern, Dan. "Liner notes to Miles Davis, *The Complete Prestige Recordings*." In *The Miles Davis Companion: Four Decades of Commentary,* edited by Gary Carner, 3–20. New York: Schirmer, 1996.

Murray, Albert, and John F. Callahan, eds. *Trading Twees: The Selected Letters of Ralph Ellison and Albert Murray.* New York: Modern Library, 2000.

"Obituaries: Nel King." *Variety,* December 23, 1977, 21.

O'Hara, Frank. *Collected Poems of Frank O'Hara.* New York: Knopf, 1971.

O'Meally, Robert G. *Lady Day: The Many Faces of Billie Holiday.* New York: Arcade, 1991.

Otis, Johnny. *Upside Your Head: Rhythm and Blues on Central Avenue.* Hanover, N.H.: University Press of New England, 1993.

Pepper, Art, and Laurie Pepper. *Straight Life: The Story of Art Pepper.* Updated ed. New York: Da Capo, 1994.

Pollack, Howard. *Aaron Copland: The Life and Work of an Uncommon Man.* New York: Henry Holt, 1999.

Pollock [*sic*], Edmund. Liner notes. *The Black Saint and the Sinner Lady.* impulse! Records A35.

Porter, Bob. Liner notes. *The Complete Dean Benedetti Recordings of Charlie Parker.* Mosaic MD7-129.

Porter, Eric. "Passions of a Man: The Poetics and Politics of Charles Mingus." In *What Is This Thing Called Jazz? African American Musicians as Artists, Critics, and Activists,* 101–48. Berkeley: University of California Press, 2002.

Posen, I. Sheldon, and Daniel Franklin Ward. "Watts Towers and the *Giglio* Tradition." In *Folklife Annual: 1985,* edited by Alan Jabbour and James Hardin, 143–57. Washington, D.C.: Library of Congress, 1985.

Potter, Jeff, and Barry Kernfeld. "Dannie Richmond." In *The New Grove Dictionary of Jazz,* 2d ed., 3:411–12. New York: Macmillan, 2002.

Priestley, Brian. *Chasin' the Bird: The Life and Legacy of Charlie Parker.* New York: Oxford University Press, 2005.

———. Liner notes. *Charles Mingus: The Complete Town Hall Concert.* Blue Note CDP 7243 8 28353 2 5.

———. *Mingus: A Critical Biography.* London: Quartet, 1982.

Primack, Bret. "The Gospel according to Mingus: Disciples Carry the Tune." *Down Beat,* December 7, 1978, 12–13, 39–42.

Ramsey, Guthrie P., Jr. *The Amazing Bud Powell: Black Genius, Jazz History, and the Challenge of Bebop.* Berkeley: University of California Press, 2013.

Ratliff, Ben. *Coltrane: The Story of a Sound.* New York: Farrar, Straus & Giroux, 2007.

Roach, Max. Interview by Bob Rusch. *Cadence* 5.6 (June 1979): 3–8, 24.

Robertson, Nan. "Duke Ellington, 70, Honored at White House." *New York Times,* April 30, 1969, 1.

Roth, Philip. *Portnoy's Complaint.* New York: Random House, 1969.

Rudd, Roswell. Interview by David Dupont. *Cadence* 18.11 (November 1992): 13.

Ruff, Willie. *A Call to Assembly: The Autobiography of a Musical Storyteller.* New York: Viking, 1991.

Russell, George. *The Lydian Chromatic Concept of Tonal Organization.* New York: Concept, 1961.

Rustin, Nichole T. "Cante Hondo: Charles Mingus, Nat Hentoff, and Jazz Racism." *Critical Sociology* 32.2–3 (2006): 307–31.

Ryan, Regina. Contract to publish *Beneath the Underdog.* November 2, 1969. Knopf Archive, Harry Ransom Center, University of Texas at Austin.

Santoro, Gene. *Myself When I Am Real: The Life and Music of Charles Mingus.* New York: Oxford University Press, 2000.

Saxon, Lyle, Edward Dreyer, and Robert Tallant. *Gumbo Ya-ya.* Boston: Houghton Mifflin, 1945.

Saul, Scott. *Freedom Is, Freedom Ain't: Jazz and the Making of the Sixties.* Cambridge, Mass.: Harvard University Press, 2003.

Scambray, Kenneth. "The Literary and Immigrant Contexts of Simon Rodia's Watts Towers." In *Sabato Rodia's Towers in Watts: Art, Migrations, Development,* edited by Luisa Del Giudice, 145–54. New York: Fordham University Press, 2014.

Schuller, Gunther. *Early Jazz: Its Roots and Musical Development.* New York: Oxford University Press, 1968.

———. *Gunther Schuller: A Life in Pursuit of Music and Beauty.* Rochester, N.Y.: University of Rochester Press: 2011.

———. Liner notes. *Bill Evans and His Orchestra, Brandeis Jazz Festival.* Gambit Records 69124.

Shepp, Archie. "An Artist Speaks Bluntly." *Down Beat,* December 16, 1965, 11.

Simon, Robert. *Percy Grainger: The Pictorial Biography.* Albany, N.Y.: Whitston, 1983.

Simosko, Vladimir, and Barry Tepperman. *Eric Dolphy: A Musical Biography and Discography.* Rev. ed. New York: Da Capo, 1996.

Smethurst, James. "'Remembering When Indians Were Red': Bob Kaufman, the Popular Front, and the Black Arts Movement." *Callaloo* 25.1 (2002): 146–64.

Smith, Arnold Jay. "Charles Mingus. Developmental Changes." *Down Beat,* January 12, 1978, 22, 48, 51.

Smith, Jay D., and Leonard F. Guttridge. *Jack Teagarden: The Story of a Jazz Maverick.* New York: Da Capo, 1976.

Spencer, Frederick J. *Jazz and Death: Medical Profiles of Jazz Greats.* Jackson: University Press of Mississippi, 2002.

Stein, Daniel. *Music Is My Life: Louis Armstrong, Autobiography, and American Jazz.* Ann Arbor: University of Michigan Press, 2012.

———. "The Performance of Jazz Autobiography." *Genre* 37.2 (2004): 173–99.

Stewart, Rex. *Boy Meets Horn*. Edited by Claire P. Gordon. Ann Arbor: University of Michigan Press, 1991.

———. *Jazz Masters of the Thirties*. New York: Macmillan, 1972.

Stewart, Zan. Liner notes. *Eric Dolphy: The Complete Prestige Recordings*. Prestige 9PRCD-4418.

Stowe, David. *Swing Changes: Big Band Jazz in New Deal America*. Cambridge, Mass.: Harvard University Press, 1994.

Stratemann, Klaus. *Duke Ellington Day by Day and Film by Film*. Copenhagen: Jazz Media, 1992.

Szwed, John. *Billie Holiday: The Musician and the Myth*. New York: Viking, 2015.

———. *So What: The Life of Miles Davis*. New York: Simon & Schuster, 2002.

———. *Space Is the Place: The Life and Times of Sun Ra*. New York: Pantheon, 1997.

Taruskin, Richard. "Defending Classical Music against Its Devotees." *New Republic*, October 22, 2007. Available at www.newrepublic.com/article /books-and-arts/books-the-musical-mystique.

Teague, Jessica. "Ears Taut to Hear: Sound Recording and Twentieth-Century American Literature." Ph.D. diss., Columbia University, 2013.

Terry, Clark. *The Autobiography of Clark Terry*. Berkeley: University of California Press, 2011.

Thiele, Bob. "Mingus Ho-Hum." *Jazz* 3.6 (October 1964): 20–21.

Thiele, Bob, and Bob Golden. *What a Wonderful World: A Lifetime of Recordings*. New York: Oxford University Press, 1995.

Troupe, Quincy. "Miles Style." *Spin* (November 1988): 72–79.

Tucker, Mark, ed. *The Duke Ellington Reader*. New York: Oxford University Press, 1993.

Tynan, John. "Take 5." *Down Beat*, November 23, 1961, 60.

Wagner, Bryan. "Disarmed and Dangerous: The Strange Career of Bras-Coupé." *Representations* 92 (2005): 117–51.

Wein, George. *Myself among Others*. New York: Da Capo, 2003.

Whitworth, Bill. "The Rich Full Life of Charlie Mingus." *New York Herald-Tribune*. November 1, 1964, 13ff.

Whyton, Tony. *Beyond a Love Supreme: John Coltrane and the Legacy of an Album*. New York: Oxford University Press, 2013.

Widener, Daniel. *Black Arts West: Culture and Struggle in Postwar Los Angeles*. Durham, N.C.: Duke University Press, 2010.

Williams, Martin. *The Jazz Tradition*. New York: Oxford University Press, 1970.

Willman, Chris. "He Shoots, He Scores: Making the *Jerry Maguire* Soundtrack." *Entertainment Weekly*, January 17, 1997, 25.

Wills, Geoffrey. "Forty Lives in the Bebop Business: Mental Health in a Group of Eminent Jazz Musicians." *British Journal of Psychiatry* 183.3 (August 2003). Available at http://bjp.rcpsych.org/content/183/3/255.

Wilson, John S. "Carter Opens Home to Jazz as an Art." *New York Times,* June 19, 1978, C13.

Yaffe, David. *Fascinating Rhythm: Reading Jazz in American Writing.* Princeton, N.J.: Princeton University Press, 2006.

———. "'What *Is* This Music?': Mingus, Melville, and the Sounds of Covert Revolution." *Literary Imagination* 13.2 (2011): 167–71.

Zabor, Rafi. "Mingus in Europe, Vols. I & II." *Musician* 42 (1982): 71.

CONVERSATIONS WITH THE AUTHOR

George Avakian. May 12, 2010.
Sam Burtis. August 20, 2012.
Bill Crow. March 19, 2013.
Dawn Frank. December 1, 2010.
Gary Giddins. August 8, 2012.
Nat Hentoff. September 5, 2011.
Howard Johnson. February 14, 2015.
Manfred Kirchheimer. November 2, 2014.
Kevin Ellington Mingus. April 2, 2015.
Sue Graham Mingus. September 14, 2009.
Albert Murray. April 13, 2004.
Jeff Nussbaum. July 12, 2012.
Vincent Prudente. April 12, 1996.
Regina Ryan. August 16, 2013.
Loren Schoenberg. March 19, 2013.
Gunther Schuller. July 13, 2012.
John Szwed. June 3, 2004.
Jessica Teague. June 26, 2013.
Jack Walrath. June 27, 2013.
David Yaffe. September 28, 2013.

FILM AND VIDEO

Films with Appearances by Mingus

All Night Long (1962). Directed by Basil Dearden.
A Great Day in Harlem (1994). Directed by Jean Bach.
Charles Mingus, Live in '64. Jazz Icons. Naxos DVD 2–119006.
Charles Mingus: Orange Was the Color of Her Dress. Salt Peanuts 44613.
Charles Mingus: Triumph of the Underdog (1998). Directed by Don McGlynn.
Mingus (1968). Directed by Thomas Reichman.

Films with Music by Mingus

Absolute Beginners (1986). Directed by Julien Temple.
Jerry Maguire (1996). Directed by Cameron Crowe.
Shadows (1959). Directed by John Cassavetes.

Stations of the Elevated (1980). Directed by Manfred Kirchheimer.
Texas Carnival (1951). Directed by Charles Waters.
Top Five (2014). Directed by Chris Rock.
U Turn (1997). Directed by Oliver Stone.
The Whole Nine Yards (2000). Directed by Jonathan Lynn.

Other Films Discussed in This Book

Citizen Kane (1941). Directed by Orson Welles.
I Build the Tower (2006). Directed by Edward landler and Brad Byer.
Imagine the Sound (1981). Directed by Ron Mann.
Jailhouse Rock (1957). Directed by Richard Thorpe.
2 Days in New York (2012). Directed by Julie Delpy.

Index